sustainable residential interiors

sustainable residential interiors

Kari Foster
Annette Stelmack, ASID
Debbie Hindman

ASSOCIATES III
Interior Design

BICENTENNIAL
1807
WILEY
2007
BICENTENNIAL

John Wiley & Sons, Inc.

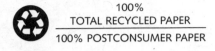

100%
TOTAL RECYCLED PAPER
100% POSTCONSUMER PAPER

This book is printed on acid-free paper. ∞

Published by John Wiley & Sons, Inc., Hoboken, New Jersey
Published simultaneously in Canada

For general information about our other products and services, please contact our Customer Care Department within the United States at (800) 762-2974, outside the United States at (317) 572-3993 or fax (317) 572-4002.

Wiley also publishes its books in a variety of electronic formats. Some content that appears in print may not be available in electronic books. For more information about Wiley products, visit our web site at www.wiley.com.

Library of Congress Cataloging-in-Publication Data:

Foster, Kari.
  Sustainable residential interiors / Kari Foster, Annette Stelmack, Debbie Hindman.
      p. cm.
  Includes bibliographical references and index.
  ISBN-13: 978-0-471-75607-1 (cloth)
  ISBN-10: 0-471-75607-5 (cloth)

  1. Ecological houses--Design and construction. 2. Sustainable engineering--United States. 3. Interior architecture--United States.   I. Stelmack, Annette. II. Hindman, Debbie. III. Title.
   TH4860.F67 2007
   728.047--dc22

                                                    2006026648

Printed in the United States of America

10 9 8 7 6 5 4 3 2 1

Everybody needs beauty as well as bread, places to play in and pray in, where nature may heal and give strength to body and soul.

—JOHN MUIR

CONTENTS

ADOPTING A NEW VISION

ACKNOWLEDGMENTS

To our collaborators one and all . . .

Like most first-time authors, we owe sincere thanks to many and would like to acknowledge the generous collaboration of everyone within the Associates III team, our supportive and loving families, and all who eagerly contributed to the creation of this dream: our first ecobook.

Our environmental passions were ignited and nurtured by trailblazers from all walks of life: Buckminster Fuller, Daniel Quinn, David Suzuki, Julia Butterfly Hill, Judith Helfand, Michael Braungart, Paul Hawken, Sarah Susanka, and Sym Van der Ryn are among them. We are thrilled that many have contributed to our book: Bert Gregory, Hunter Lovins, Janine Benyus, Paula Baker-Laporte, Ray Anderson, Steve Badanes, Trudy Dujardin, and William McDonough. Thank you for your unwavering commitment to creating a better world. You inspire us daily to do our part in creating healthy and nurturing environments.

To pioneering green interior design educator Julie Pollack of Rocky Mountain College of Art 1 Design, Nadav Malin of Environmental Building News, Jerry Yudelson of Interface Engineering, and John Fraser, dedicated wordsmith, thank you for reviewing the text.

To the interior designers and architects who submitted their green residential projects. We received innumerable submittals—a testimony that this philosophy is changing the face of residential interiors. We appreciate your enthusiasm and the wealth of creativity you shared with us, reinforcing that green principles can be beautiful as well as ecologically sound.

Thank you to Misty McNally who corralled our knowledge and concern for the future of our planet in the materials chapters. Her expertise as a responsible and professional writer allowed us to communicate the information in a meaningful and accessible voice.

We are blessed to be part of a team that personifies excellence in all that we do. Their accumulated knowledge and assistance were invaluable through research and fact checking, as readers and editors, providing drawings, cataloging images, critiquing, and lending support. Special thanks to team members Laura Cronin, Wendy Kisicki, Donna Barta-Winfield, Beth Scott, and Maggie Tandysh and to interns Kelly Webb, Alison Martinez, and Maggie Davis.

Finally, we thank and honor each other—for the trust, integrity, and mutual respect that energize our work and that have overflowed easily into this book, reflected in the long-standing friendships we have with one another. Understanding that knowledge empowers change, we dared to dream that a book such as this could support the process of changing how we all design and build.

INTRODUCTION

WHEN WE HEAL THE EARTH, WE HEAL OURSELVES.
—DAVID ORR

In everything we do as residential interior designers we create "home" for our clients. Our responsibility is to serve them in one of the most personal expressions of their world: where they live. We are privileged to engage with them on such a level, listening to their needs and their dreams for "home," where they welcome us into their living rooms, their dining rooms, their kitchens, their bedrooms, their bathrooms, and their closets.

In recent years, residential interior designers have gained a greater consciousness and appreciation for green design issues. The primary environmental focus has been to strive for comprehensive and reliable information on how to apply sustainable design principles and practices on projects. We celebrate your interest in integrating environmentally responsible design into your practice, and it is an honor to offer this book to the design community. Our intention in *Sustainable Residential Interiors* is to support your inquiry of the status quo, to ignite your spirit as a catalyst for change, to present you with information and processes, and to encourage you to ask well-informed questions as you set off on the path to creating sustaining, meaningful, nurturing residences that positively impact our world.

Consumers, too, are becoming more aware of the environmental issues affecting their homes and lifestyles, and they increasingly ask designers, architects, and builders to incorporate sustainability into their projects. To help meet this increased demand, this book will provide design professionals—primarily residential interior designers—with a comprehensive, easy-to-understand sustainable resource guide. It will:

- Answer why we must become catalysts for change.
- Share inspiring stories about today's environmental champions.
- Give visual examples of sustainable projects and applications.
- Encourage critical thinking about environmental issues within homes.
- Present strategies for incorporating sustainable design into work and projects.
- Provide a practical hands-on approach to sustainable design.
- Offer guidelines for clients and project teams.
- Provide helpful checklists for greening projects and specifications.

- Give in-depth information to promote understanding and assist in specifying interior finishes and furnishings.
- Raise questions for manufacturers and vendors.
- Share effective methods of marketing sustainable design services.

Years ago, our eyes, minds, and hearts were opened to the inspirational world of sustainable design. Since then we have been on a quest, searching for ways to exemplify integrity in our work, as articulated through the details of a project—asking how long finishes will last and which adhesives to specify; addressing indoor air quality; ensuring that woods are from certified sources; finding-low impact materials; conserving energy and water; supporting construction teams in reducing waste; providing information regarding healthy cleaning methods, while exceeding the client's expectations.

We know that paying attention to eco-friendly details on a project might not be what our clients notice initially, but we believe they are the things they will come to appreciate in the long run. And it is for the long run that we do this: for the improved health of the Earth and its inhabitants, for future generations, indeed, for the future of our planet. We have found that when something is right, there is always consensus; and we have agreed that this is the right way to practice the business of interior design.

Our goal for *Sustainable Residential Interiors* is to create a reference tool for residential interior designers as they begin to embrace green design strategies. What is green building? Simply, green building takes steps to create homes that are sustaining for families, communities, and the environment. That means, whether renovating an existing residence or designing a new home for your clients, keep in mind these three fundamental green building goals:

- Be mindful about using limited resources, such as wood and water, to limit waste, pollution, and environmental damage.
- Build and remodel with energy efficiency in mind, to save money, create a more responsible home, and reduce air pollution and global warming.
- Choose healthy materials and construction methods to prevent indoor air pollution from formaldehyde, mold, and other contaminants.

The residential design industry is rapidly moving in the direction of sustainable building for many vital reasons, among them:

- *Higher quality.* Most green building products and materials were developed to perform better than their conventional counterparts.
- *Greater durability and less maintenance.* Green building encourages the use of longer-lasting products that don't require an inordinate amount of time or the use of harsh chemicals to maintain. Products that don't need to be frequently replaced put less of a burden on natural resources and landfills.

- *Greater comfort and lower utility bills*. Energy-efficient upgrades can reduce energy bills while providing comfort and convenience.
- *Healthier products and practices*. Green building promotes the use of products and construction practices that avoid introducing harmful chemicals and other pollutants into the home.
- *Natural resource conservation*. Protecting the environment is yet another compelling reason for committing to "build green."

This book, a dream come true for us, presents a sequential process for creating sustainable residential interiors that meet the goals of the homeowner as well as the aforementioned goals of green design. Step by step, it will take you through an integrated design process, exemplifying how sustainable principles, strategies, and practices can be applied at each level of the interior design. These principles and practices can be utilized on any residential project to create a home that is functional, comfortable, sustainable, and beautiful.

Imagine if:

- We learned how to be eco friendly from our parents and grandparents, our grade schools, middle schools, high schools, and colleges?
- Clients came to us asking for homes and products that were earth and family friendly . . . One day they will; some already do.
- We as residential interior designers ascribed to the medical profession's charge, "First, do no harm," and recommended and specified only earth-healthy materials?
- We were able to provide net zero energy homes that were truly restorative for our clients and for the planet?
- Residential contractors and architects embraced green concepts and researched and promoted green products and practices?
- Government mandated environmentally sustainable construction for residences?
- The core principle of all manufacturers of residential products included "environmental and social responsibility"?
- All materials were safe—with "all-clear, all-healthy" contents?
- There was a practical, positive book to assist residential interior designers in converting their practice into one that is socially and environmentally responsible . . . well, *here it is!*

Our challenge is to learn how we can leave a lighter footprint on the planet and have a positive impact on our clients, and at the same time make every effort possible to create a sustaining future for generations to come. As residential interior designers, we can actively promote change and progress in the residential building industry—change that also supports our clients' vision and respects the environment, fully integrating environmentally responsible design. On each project we are motivated to create designs that are appropriate to the client and that meet traditional goals—the homeowner's needs, budget, and aesthetics—as well as to give back more than we take from the surrounding environment.

Thank you for taking time to read this book. We hope that you will find it informative and helpful and that it will inspire you to action. We look forward to engaging in conversations with you about green residential design, and with that in mind we welcome your feedback, your insight, and your questions.

why be sustainable?

Photo courtesy
of Mithun Architects.
Architect: Mithun

There is no greater potential for personal expression than building one's own shelter. For this reason alone, every effort should be made to enable new home construction to be sustainable for generations to come. Today, we realize that to be truly sustainable, it is not enough to imagine methods of minimizing damage to the environment; instead the results must have a net positive impact on it.
—DENNIS WEDLICK, AIA

The answer to the question why, as residential designers, we should be sustainable is simple: There is only one planet Earth that sustains all life, and if we destroy its ability to do so, we will no longer have life on our planet. Numerous speeches have been made and publications written by credible sources who, over the past decades, have been leading the market transformation in the building industry. This book will share knowledge and provide motivation from a different perspective, specifically that of the residential interior design community.

Through our experiences and the information that we have gathered and organized, we will demonstrate to residential design professionals that it is absolutely possible to build a home that is beautiful, pleasing, functional, healthy, affordable, *and* life-sustaining. The time is now to become a catalyst for change within the residential design community and to accelerate the integrated practice of sustainable residential design.

Interior designers are resourceful beings; they are information-gathering, solution-seeking, innovative creatures—ideal characteristics for promoting the change to sustainability. Our profession as a whole is a natural for revolutionizing the industry by transforming environments. It is, after all, what we do daily. By focusing our creative energy and adopting sustainable design, we become positive instruments of change. If we have clear intentions, coupled with the belief that each positive action makes a difference, our contribution to a healthy planet will be assured.

Before us lies a remarkable opportunity to connect with where we are and where we have been and to be mindful about where we're going. Creating healthy, life-enhancing design is an invigorating prospect. Is it challenging? Absolutely! But it is the right thing to do.

As we set out to meet this challenge, it is instructive to ask why everything that is considered good for us is termed an "alternative"—alternative health care, alternative medicine, alternative food. Sustainable design should no longer be considered an alternative; it is, simply, the responsible way to conduct good business. It benefits us all to work together toward better solutions that "respect all of the children of all of the species, for all times," to quote renowned architect William McDonough, principal and founder of William McDonough + Partners and MBDC.

Sustainability is transforming the building industry, and expertise in sustainable design is becoming highly regarded and regularly sought after on projects. Clients, architects, and contractors value the knowledge and skills that we bring to the table as part of the professional services team. As designers, we can offer the team numerous possibilities for creating eco-friendly homes. The finishes in a home can exemplify environmental responsibility, as well as reflect the inherent beauty of design. By combining materials in a unique and environmentally responsible way, we have a rich opportunity to make a difference on projects.

As interior designers and architects we have the power to create, a gift and a unique responsibility for sustaining life on the planet. The methods that we employ, often beyond the realm of other professions, compel us to practice sustainable design. By doing so, we are, as defined by the Brundtland Commission in 1987, "meeting the needs of the present without compromising the ability of future generations to meet their own needs."

Designers have much to teach the world. Of all people, designers understand that there is never only one right way to design anything. Searching for new solutions, creatively adapting what we know into what we need and solving problems are what designers do. Perhaps, then, we as designers need to expand our vision to include sustainability and start showing ordinary people how to look at the world from a green design point of view.
—Daniel Quinn, *Ishmael*

Countless options are available that enable us, as design professionals, and those we work with to make a significant difference. Green building practices, coupled with emerging technologies, are changing our industry, hence the buildings that we live and work in. By making conscious decisions to utilize principles and practices that sustain our natural resources, we can actively support the continuation of a healthier life on our planet for those who follow.

As we all were taught, for every action there is an equal reaction, and for every choice we make there is a consequence. As designers, we can play a major role in accelerating change in our industry by gathering information, learning new strategies, attending conferences, questioning the status quo, sharing information, and aligning with like-minded individuals, project teams, and clients.

Market transformation begins with individuals who integrate sustainability into the core of their interior design process, one step at a time, one material at a time, one project at a time, and one question at a time. We can and do make a difference. (See the sidebar on Ray Anderson, page 7).

What Are "Green Buildings"?

The American Society for Testing and Materials (ASTM) describes green buildings as structures that are designed, constructed, renovated, operated, and reused in an environmentally and energy-efficient manner. Green buildings, including green residences, exhibit a high level of environmental, economic, and engineering performance including:

- Energy efficiency and conservation
- Indoor environmental quality
- Resource and materials efficiency
- Occupant health and productivity
- Transportation efficiency
- Improved environmental quality including air, water, land, limited resources, and ecosystems

The U.S. Green Building Council states that the built environment is growing globally at a rate that is three times faster than the growth rate of the population. Buildings have a major impact on the environment as a whole, in that they:

- Consume between 30 to 40 percent of *all* energy used.
- Add 30 to 40 percent of *all* emissions into the atmosphere.
- Use up to 30 percent of *all* raw materials.

In addition, statistics show that the United States, though it comprises less than 6 percent of the world's population, consumes 25 percent of the world's energy, and its citizens own 32 percent of the world's automobiles. Our ecological footprint is enormous compared to that of other countries. If everyone in the world were to have access to the standard of living that we enjoy in this country, we would need four Earths to support us!

Buildings account for nearly half of the global output of the greenhouse gas carbon dioxide, as well as half of the output of sulfur dioxide and nitrogen oxide, both agents of acid rain. We must, therefore, recognize that the building industry shares the responsibility for environmental disasters related to energy production, such as oil spills, nuclear waste, the destruction of rivers by hydroelectric dams, the runoff from coal mining, the mercury emissions from burning coal—the list goes on and on.

This is motivation enough to rethink the way that we practice design. By designing and adapting the places where we live in an ecologically responsive style, we can contribute to the well-being of our planet and its limited natural resources. To encourage, inform, and assist you in navigating through it all, we have assembled some of the most compelling reasons to be sustainable in the key areas where residential interior designers can actively improve the current state of the industry and the planet—before it is too late and the damage to the planet and its ecosystems become permanent.

- Environmental stewardship and the improved environmental quality of the planet, including air, water, and land, protecting limited resources and ecosystems
- Personal responsibility to do good business equals a successful business
- Good design, supported by the Council for Interior Design Accreditation and the American Institute of Architects (AIA)
- Natural resource and materials conservation, minimizing the use of nonrenewable natural resources and building with low-impact materials
- Improved indoor air and environmental quality
- Energy efficiency, lower energy consumption, and promotion of renewable energy sources
- Water efficiency and conservation
- Waste reduction and management
- Optimized operational and maintenance practices
- A healthy planet for future generations

ENVIRONMENTAL STEWARDSHIP

For the children and the flowers are my sisters and my brothers, come and stand beside me, we can find a better way.

—JOHN DENVER, CO-FOUNDER, WINDSTAR

Nature is the precious source of life. As such, living in and engaging with nature should be treated as a privilege. All Earth's citizens must develop a broader perspective and become stewards of our planet. If we do not, the results promise to be disastrous. The evidence is mounting, for example, that we are headed toward the dire consequences of global warming. We would be foolish to wait for a calamity, such as disappearing coastlines, to take action.

How Did the Ecology Movement Begin?

Over 100 years ago, John Muir wrote to the editor of *Century Magazine*, "Let us do something to make the mountains glad." So they founded the Sierra Club, the first major organization in the world dedicated to using and "preserving" wild nature. It is from this act that the modern ecology movement was born.

Throughout his life, Muir was concerned with the protection of nature both for the spiritual advancement of humans and, as he said so often, for nature itself. This dual vision still informs the ecology movement and inspires millions to reform their thoughts and minds and to orient themselves as part of nature. Though the arguments in favor of ecological thinking are often couched in scientific terms, the basic impetus remains as Muir stated it: "When we try to pick out anything by itself, we find it hitched to everything in the universe" (www.ecotopia.org/ehof/muir/index.html).

How Did the Environmental Movement Begin?

When, in 1962, Rachael Carson wrote the book *Silent Spring,* the public at large became aware that nature was vulnerable to human intervention. In it, she made a radical proposal: that, at times, technological progress is so fundamentally at odds with natural processes that it must be curtailed. Prior to the book's publication, conservation had never before raised much broad public interest, for until then few people had worried about the disappearing wilderness. But the threats Carson outlined—the contamination of the food chain, cancer, genetic damage, extinction of entire species—were too frightening to ignore. For the first time, the need to regulate industry in order to protect the environment became widely accepted, and environmentalism was born.

Carson was well aware of the larger implications of her work. Appearing on a CBS documentary about *Silent Spring* shortly before her death from breast cancer in 1964, she remarked, "Man's attitude toward nature is today critically important simply because we have now acquired a fateful power to alter and destroy nature. But man is a part of nature, and his war against nature is inevitably a war against himself . . . [We are] challenged as mankind has never been challenged before to prove our maturity and our mastery, not of nature, but of ourselves."

The message of *Silent Spring,* one of the landmark books of the twentieth century, continues to resonate loudly today, more than four decades after its publication. Equally inspiring is the example of Rachel Carson herself. Against overwhelming difficulties and adversity, and motivated by her unabashed love of nature, she rose like a gladiator to its defense. (Reprinted with permission from the Natural Resources Defense Council)

What Is Environmental Stewardship?

How does it relate to sustainable design? Sustainability is a concept with many definitions that vary across national borders and over time, but most agree that at its center is the advancement of societies in a way that balances the social, economic, and environmental needs of current and future generations. Here are two examples:

- The Office of the Federal Environmental Executive (www.ofee.gov/sustain/sustainability.htm#sustain) definition of sustainable environmental stewardship

The more clearly we can focus our attention on the wonders and realities of the universe about us, the less taste we shall have for destruction.
—RACHEL CARSON (© 1954 REPRINTED WITH PERMISSION FROM THE NATURAL RESOURCES DEFENSE COUNCIL, WWW.NRDC.ORG/HEALTH/PESTICIDES/HCARSON.ASP)

includes those concepts, strategies, tools, practices, and approaches that lead to environmental improvement in a manner that is sustainable over time; that considers the long-term effects as well as the shorter-term, more immediate effects; and that contributes positively, even if indirectly, to the social and economic condition.

■ The Energy Alternative (www.theenergyalternative.com/glossary.html) defines environmental stewardship as the "wisest use of both finite and reusable energy resources to produce the most work guided by a principle of causing the least known harm to the environment and driven by a desire to aid in the restoration of a healthier environment."

PERSONAL RESPONSIBILITY

Never doubt that a small group of thoughtful committed people can change the world: indeed it's the only thing that ever has!

—MARGARET MEAD

As interior designers, we must make a personal commitment to become environmental champions. The most important factor for achieving success is the human element, and a person who makes things happen and gets things done can make a significant difference in the world.

Change occurs by the actions we take and the choices we make. We can be change agents who set an example by demonstrating environmental responsibility through our work and business practices. We, collectively, have the power to drive change within our industry. By specifying interior finishes that include recycled content, selecting woods that are responsibly harvested, and ensuring that the materials that we specify do not contribute to out-gassing and exacerbate human health problems, we can re-shape our industry's traditions at the same time we accelerate acceptance and implementation of environmental principles and practices. As environmental champions, we can accept the challenge to be innovative risk takers, and push the boundaries of the status quo. We may experience an occasional setback, but if we continue to challenge the industry we can help to raise it to the next level of environmental performance.

By seeking reliable information and surrounding ourselves with like-minded people, we nurture our environmental aspirations. But first we need to recognize how directly our actions as residential interior designers affect the environment, either positively or negatively. Then we must acquire the skills we will need to move forward, one step at a time, to further develop our expertise as well as our personal commitment to improving the environment.

On a personal level, identify what inspires you to "take on" environmental issues and to make change happen. Then, with proactive leadership, and in respectful cooperation and with enthusiastic energy, be tenacious in your personal pursuit to sustain the environment. Influence others through your involvement with professional organizations such as the American Society of Interior Designers (ASID), the International Interior Design Association (IIDA), the American Institute of Architects (AIA), the AIA Committee on the Environment (AIA COTE), Architects, Designers, and Planners for Social Responsibility (ADPSR), and the U.S. Green Building Council (USGBC). As part of the whole, always greater than the sum of its parts, you will serve to integrate environ-

Environmental Champion: Ray Anderson

One of the greatest examples of an environmental champion in the interior design industry is Ray Anderson, who made a strong personal commitment and, as a result, made great strides in changing the floor-covering industry. In 1994, as CEO of Interface, the world's largest commercial floor-coverings producer, Anderson was invited to give a keynote address to Interface's newly formed environmental task force. He was reluctant to accept because he didn't have an environmental vision beyond obeying the law. Then he happened to receive a book, Paul Hawkens' *The Ecology of Commerce* (1994). Anderson recalled, "I read it, and it changed my life. It hit me right between the eyes. It was an epiphany. I wasn't halfway through it before I had the vision I was looking for . . . and a powerful sense of urgency to do something." After this chance introduction to environmental issues, Anderson embarked on a mission to make Interface a sustainable corporation by leading a worldwide war on waste and by pioneering the processes of sustainable development within his company and beyond.

mental consciousness at all levels, both personally and professionally. Make a very personal decision to take moral responsibility for what you do as a designer of the built environment, and then put that commitment into action on all projects.

GOOD DESIGN

Good design and sustainable design are one and the same, synonymous with each other. Integrating sustainable design principles and practices is creative and rewarding, opening doors to vast possibilities for personal expression and personal growth for the designer, the client, and the project team.
—ADAPTED FROM DENNIS WEDLICK, AIA, DENNIS WEDLICK ARCHITECT, LLC

As conscientious creatures, by habit and training, we accept responsibility for creative design solutions in each interior circumstance. Along with this, our professional organizations provide codes of ethics that specify our responsibilities as designers with regard to function, safety, codes, and aesthetics. We are required to find solutions to design questions and to prepare drawings and specifications that illustrate how we intend to implement these solutions. But until recently, the subject of sustainability had not yet been fully addressed within the field of interior design. This is now changing.

Effective January 1, 2006, the board of directors for the Council for Interior Design Accreditation (formerly FIDER) adopted revisions to its professional standards. All interior design programs undergoing its accreditation process in 2006 and in the future will be reviewed under these revised standards. This will have immediate and far-reaching effects for interior design education and professional practice.

These revisions focus primarily on strengthened expectations for student learning in sustainability and communication. The new standards maintain that every student who graduates from a Council for Interior Design Accreditation school must demonstrate his or her understanding of the principles and theories of sustainability.

These standards are supported by the AIA. In December 2005, the AIA board of directors adopted position statements to promote sustainable design and resource conservation. To achieve, by the year 2010, a minimum reduction of 50 percent of the current consumption level of fossil fuels used to construct and operate buildings, and to reduce that amount an additional 10 percent in each of the following five years, which would result in a 70 percent reduction from current levels by 2015. To accomplish this goal, the AIA will collaborate with other national and international organizations, the scientific research community, and the public health community. As part of this initia-

Council for Interior Design Accreditation Standards Pertaining to Sustainability

Standard 2: Professional Values

The program leads students to develop the attitudes, traits, and the values of professional responsibility, accountability, and effectiveness.

The program *must* provide learning experiences that address:

- *Environmental ethics* and the role of *sustainability* in the practice of interior design . . .
- A *global perspective* and approach to thinking and problem solving (viewing design with awareness and respect for cultural and social differences of people; understanding issues that affect the *sustainability* of the planet; understanding the implications of conducting the practice of design within a world market).

Standard 3: Design Fundamentals

Students have a foundation in the fundamentals of art and design; theories of design, *green design,* and human behavior; and discipline-related history.

- Students work *must* demonstrate understanding of principles and theories of *sustainability.*

Standard 6: Building Systems and Interior Materials

Students design within the context of building systems. Students use appropriate materials and products.

- Students *must* demonstrate understanding of the concept of *sustainable building* methods and materials.

Standard 7: Regulations

Students apply the laws, codes, regulations, standards, and practices that protect the health, safety, and welfare of the public.

- Students *must* demonstrate understanding of the impact on health and welfare of . . . *indoor air quality* . . . noise . . . lighting.

These educational standards will substantially raise the bar of knowledge, credibility, and responsibility regarding protection of the environment within the interior design community.

tive, the AIA will also develop and promote the integration of sustainability into the curriculum for the education of architects and architecture students, so that this core principle becomes a guide for current and future architects (www.aia.org).

The AIA recognizes a growing body of evidence that demonstrates current planning, design, construction, and real estate practices contribute to patterns of resource consumption that seriously jeopardize the future of the Earth's population. Architects will now accept responsibility for their role in creating the built environment and, consequently, alter the actions of the profession. By encouraging our clients and the design and construction industries to join with us, we can change the course of the planet's future. This is great news for the entire built community!

The AIA's goals, itemized in the table on page 8, are to alter the current practices of design and construction to achieve significant reductions in the use of natural resources, nonrenewable energy sources, and waste production, and promote regeneration of natural resources. The association acknowledges that this will require a multiple-year effort, one that must be undertaken in conjunction with clients, industry partners (that's us), and other concerned organizations.

Through ingenuity, drive, and commitment, we can make sustainability and design ideal partners. Coupled with the undivided support of the higher educational system, the accelerated adoption and implementation of sustainable interior design are absolutely certain. (See table, "High-Performance Building Position Statements," page 11)

LOW-IMPACT BUILDING MATERIALS

Mountain men left no physical trace of their lives upon the western landscape— they moved so lightly upon the world that only the land and the river remain a witness to those shining times.

—1838 RENDEZVOUS ASSOCIATION

The AIA is now requiring the reduced use of nonrenewable natural resources through the reuse of existing structures and materials, reductions in construction waste, promotion of recycled content materials, and use of materials independently certified as from sustainable sources. This strong stance will change how every building is created from this moment forward and, because we work so closely with architects, it will likewise change the approach we take to projects.

Conventional building practices consume large quantities of wood, stone, metal, and other natural resources that unnecessarily lead to their depletion. Wood, for example, one of the most frequently used building materials, is often inefficiently utilized on projects. Reports indicate that we have already harvested 95 percent of this nation's old-growth forests. Plainly, this practice cannot go on.

According to the Worldwatch Institute and the USGBC, buildings have a significant measurable impact on the environment.

- As much as 10 percent of the global economy is dedicated to buildings, their construction, operation, and the equipping of these homes and offices.
- Buildings account for 40 percent of the materials entering the global economy each year. Three billion tons of raw materials are turned into foundations, walls, pipes, and building finishes.

- Buildings consume enormous resources: one-sixth of the world's freshwater withdrawals, one-quarter of the world's wood harvest, and two-fifths of the world's material and energy flows.
- Residential construction represents roughly half of all construction activity in the building industry, as measured in dollars spent.
- There are nearly 2 million new housing units built each year, approximately 80 percent of which are single-family homes.
- It takes 1-1/4 acres of forest to construct the average U.S. home.

Products specified for the design and construction of homes consume resources and energy, and produce air and water pollution and solid waste during manufacturing. The availability of some raw materials, such as granite and marble, is declining and, therefore, prices for some of these products are rising faster than inflation. Following installation, these products also require maintenance and periodic replacement; and when the building is demolished, these products and materials are usually disposed of in landfills.

The point is that resource efficiency must now become common practice. Building materials that minimize the use of natural resources and that are durable or reusable contribute to sustainable building practices. Consider the following overarching criteria when selecting and specifying materials.

Reduced Resource Quantity

A fundamental strategy for resource-efficient building is to build less square footage and use smaller quantities of materials in the construction process. The most cost-effective conservation strategy is to buy fewer products, and use the products more efficiently.

Reused Materials

Many durable products such as doors, cabinets, and other easily removed millwork, and some architectural metals and glass, can be readily salvaged and reused. This practice has typically been limited to restoration work, but deconstruction is becoming more common in building and renovation projects. Salvaging does require extra time and effort, but the quality of materials—such as old-growth hardwood flooring—and the cost savings can be considerable. The additional labor cost is often entirely or partially offset by savings on new materials, transportation, and landfill-tipping fees.

Recycled Content

Using recycled content products keeps materials out of the waste stream. Although many building products are now available with a high content of recycled materials, there is confusion about the definition of the term. There are at least three types of recycled content materials:

- *Postconsumer material,* generated by commercial, industrial, and institutional facilities or households, which can no longer be used for its intended purpose, such as paper.

High-Performance Building Position Statements

Sustainable Architectural Practice Explanation

The AIA recognizes a growing body of evidence that demonstrates current planning, design, construction, and real estate practices contribute to patterns of resource consumption that seriously jeopardize the future of the Earth's population. Architects need to accept responsibility for their role in creating the built environment and, consequently, believe we must alter our profession's actions and encourage our clients and the entire design and construction industry to join with us to change the course of the planet's future. Altering current practices of design and construction to realize significant reductions in the use of natural resources, nonrenewable energy sources, and waste production, and promote regeneration of natural resources will require a multiple-year effort in conjunction with clients, industry partners, and concerned organizations. To achieve these changes, the AIA will act through all its Board Committees, Knowledge Communities, Task Forces, Working Groups, and related activities to:

1. Promote sustainable design, including resource conservation to achieve a minimum 50 percent reduction from the current level of consumption of fossil fuels used to construct and operate new and renovated buildings by the year 2010, and promote further reductions of remaining fossil fuel consumption by 10 percent or more in each of the following five years;

2. Collaborate with other national and international organizations, the scientific research community, public health community, and industry leaders engaged in issues related to sustainable/restorative design to facilitate the dialogue, share knowledge, and accelerate the rate of change for all those seeking to improve the industry's current practices and utilize integrated approaches to achieve a sustainable future;

3. Develop and promote the integration of sustainability into the curricula for education of architects and architectural students to enhance their design skills;

4. Develop standards for the architectural profession that incorporate greater sustainability into design, education, management, and licensure standards, and provide resources to assist integrating these standards into the daily practices of all architects;

5. Promote documentation of the measurable contributions resulting from implemented sustainable design and construction approaches to the health of humankind and the planet to promote the value and achievements of increased use of sustainable design;

6. Promote research by industry, scientific, and governmental entities to provide the design and construction industry with full life-cycle assessment data for all products and assemblies used in the construction of the built environment at every scale in order to facilitate decision making and communicate benefits to all;

7. Promote the AIA's building performance design targets to local, state, and national governments;

8. Communicate possible beneficial economics of environmentally responsible design to both public and private sector clients; and

9. Assume a global role as advocates for sustainable design, freely sharing knowledge and actively promoting sustainable practice throughout the world.

Source: American Institute of Architects, Washington, DC; www.aia.org.

- *Recovered industrial process waste* that cannot be reused in the same process, such as slag from metal and mineral smelting.
- *Materials that are internally recycled* within a manufacturing plant, such as scraps from trimming and rejected or substandard product.

Renewability and Use of Sustainable Management Practices

Renewable materials include wood, plant fibers, wool, and other resources that are potentially replaceable within a limited time period (a few decades or less) after harvesting. Information on wood harvested through sustainable management practices is becoming more readily available, including certification programs and standards such as the Forest Stewardship Council (FSC).

Life-Cycle Cost

Over the useful life of a building, which could be 100 years or more, most materials will require maintenance and replacement more than once. When the full range of costs is considered, materials that are more costly upon initial purchase may be justified in terms of "avoided future costs." The higher initial cost may be justified if the product compares favorably with others over their entire life cycle.

Regionally Appropriate Materials

Some types of construction and materials are more appropriate in one region than another, due to climatic differences. It is well known, for example, that utilizing thermal mass in building design has important energy and comfort benefits in the Southwest, where daily temperature swings can be extreme. In a hot, humid climate, like that of the Southeast, lightweight construction and high ceilings may be more beneficial.

Local Content

Specifying products made with local materials and labor can contribute to lower embodied energy consumption, eliminating or reducing transportation costs.

Resource Recovery and Recycling

Once a material has completed its initial service in a home, it potentially has additional use as a resource that can later be recovered and recycled. The potential recyclability of metal, plastic, glass, wood, and masonry are as follows:

- Metals are recyclable if they can be separated by type. Steel and aluminum building elements, particularly, have a high recycling value. Approximately 50 to 70 percent of the energy and pollution from steel production can be avoided by current recycling technology. Up to 85 percent of the energy and pollution from aluminum manufacturing can be avoided by remelting.
- Most plastics are recyclable, but the current rates of recycling are not high because the wide variety of plastics in use makes them difficult to separate. Some plastics, such as pure polyvinyl chloride (PVC), would be recycled from buildings

more often if they were designed for easy removal. Additives, coatings, and colorants make recycling difficult.

- Glass products are recyclable if separated and uncontaminated; however, little recycling of glass building products now occurs. Recycled glass products are made with consumer container glass salvaged from the waste stream. Although remelting glass offers only marginal energy and pollution reduction, it saves on virgin materials.

- Heavy timber is recyclable by salvaging and resawing. Engineered structural wood products, wood panels, and millwork are candidates for salvage and reuse, particularly if they are fastened in such a way that they can be more easily removed.

- Concrete, clay, ceramics, and other masonry products are examples of materials that are usually difficult to salvage and reuse. Some recycling of these products occurs by crushing them for use as granular fill in road and sidewalk bases.

- Furniture, area rugs, and artwork fall into the category of resource recovery and recycling. Most quality casework pieces, although a substantial up-front investment, become collectibles as decades pass.

Ecologically minded design requires that we consider the environmental impact of a product. By conserving natural resources, we will begin the rebuilding and restoration of our natural capital—the natural resources and ecological systems that provide vital life-support services to our planet.

INDOOR AIR QUALITY

A nation that destroys its soils destroys itself. Forests are the lungs of our land, purifying the air and giving fresh strength to our people.
—FRANKLIN ROOSEVELT

Healthy interiors are organic by nature. They feel good, live well, look great, and are sustaining for all. We are all part of the integrated system called "nature," and more than any other species, what we do affects the health and longevity of life on the planet.

According to the American Lung Association, August 1999, air pollution contributes to lung disease, including respiratory tract infections, asthma, and lung cancer. Poor indoor air quality can cause or contribute to the development of chronic respiratory diseases, as well as cause headaches, dry eyes, nasal congestion, nausea, and fatigue. Some of the most common indoor air pollutants in our homes are asbestos, biological contaminants, chemicals, combustion, formaldehyde, lead, ozone, particulates, pesticides, radon, tobacco smoke, and volatile organic compounds (VOCs).
(*Source:* Minnesota Indoor Air Quality Consortium, University of Minnesota www.dehs.umn.edu)

In our efforts to build energy-efficient homes that are tightly constructed, we have inadvertently created indoor air problems due to poor ventilation and the use of toxic materials and finishes. Exacerbating the situation, statistics indicate that we now spend 90 percent or more of our time indoors, further heightening our concern over indoor air quality. The consequence of polluted indoor environments is an overall deterioration in health and well-being. The United States Environmental Protection Agency (EPA) reports that the air in new homes can be 10 times more polluted than outdoor air; and the World Health Organization (WHO) reports that as many as 30 percent of our buildings exhibit signs of what is referred to as sick building syndrome (SBS). According to the New England Journal of Medicine, 40 percent of children will develop respiratory disease, in part due to the chemicals in their homes. Poor indoor air quality (IAQ) is caused by the off-gassing of chemicals found in many building materials, as well as mold and mildew that build up in poorly designed and maintained heating and cooling systems.

In light of these facts, there can be no question that the choices we make in designing homes and materials we use have a long-term effect on the indoor environment. Interior designers can, simply, contribute positively to making a safer, healthier environment. Good indoor air quality, then, must be an important environmental consideration throughout the design process. As designers, we have the responsibility to improve the air quality of the homes we design.

Fortunately, good IAQ is a top priority for clients, once they understand that a home that provides a healthy environment for their family is an attainable goal. Delivering an indoor environment that will not cause headaches, watery eyes, or raspy throats, and that ensures children with allergies and asthma can breathe a little easier, is paramount to good design. By paying close attention to the products that we specify, we can produce a healthy environment that supports good air quality.

In addition to IAQ, we must also consider indoor environmental quality (IEQ), which also has a significant impact on the health, comfort, and productivity of a home's

Common Factors That Affect IAQ

- People (exhalation, body odors, diseases)
- Human activities (work such as cleaning; using correction fluids, carbonless paper, pest control products; and personal activities such as wearing fragrances and smoking)
- Technology (photocopiers and laser printers)
- Furnishings (furniture, draperies, floor coverings)
- Finishes (paint, varnish, vinyl wall coverings)
- Building materials (caulking compounds, adhesives, wood laminates)
- Outdoor air quality
- Inadequate or contaminated air-handling units
- Inadequate cleaning practices

(*Source:* Carpet & Rug Institute, www.carpet-rug.org)

inhabitants. Among the attributes of IEQ, a sustainable building should maximize day-lighting; provide appropriate ventilation and moisture control to minimize the opportunity for microbial growth; avoid the use of materials with high-VOC emissions; and provide adequate fresh air supply.

One of the most common indoor pollutants is formaldehyde, a common VOC and a probable human carcinogen (per WHO). When combined with urea, an organic compound, it becomes a toxic emitter of VOCs at room temperature. Common culprits include kitchen cabinets, countertops, shelving, and furniture, all typically constructed from particleboard held together by formaldehyde-based adhesives. The formaldehyde continues to be released into the home for years after these products have been installed, and it is known that these emissions have a damaging effect on human health. These emissions are also easily absorbed by soft materials, including carpets and fabrics, reemitting toxic VOCs at a later time, thereby prolonging their exposure.

Paints, finishes, solvents, and adhesives also contain unhealthy VOCs. What is commonly called a "new house smell" is caused by the off-gassing of these volatile compounds, and a good indication that harmful chemicals are present in the indoor environment. Children are at a greater risk than adults, as their bodies and minds are still developing, hence more susceptible to damage from these chemicals.

Potentially harmful substances come from every room in the home, including, but not limited to, finishes and furnishings, household cleaning agents, personal toiletries, paints, solvents, pesticides, and herbicides, all products that we use every day.

Fortunately, the building products industry is rising to the challenge of improving indoor air pollution by developing alternative adhesives, paints, and finishes. One alternative to traditional particleboard (made with urea formaldehyde resin) is a medium-density fiberboard (MDF) that uses a formaldehyde-free resin. MDF is typically made with wood sawdust or with straw, recyclables now finding a niche market.

As an overall course of action, we designers must practice "cautious prevention" when dealing with chemicals in building materials. It is known that many of these chemicals range from extremely to somewhat unhealthy and, when combined, can create a veritable "chemical soup." From an economical point of view, it is far easier—and less costly—to prevent indoor contamination from the outset. This means including strategies for good IAQ within the design and construction process, which will also serve to reduce the need for mitigation (cleanup), and lower the risk of potential liability issues. (See table, "Understanding IAQ," pages 16–18)

By designing responsibly—following a set of guidelines for good indoor air quality and using low-emission materials and pollutant source control—we can deliver healthy, clean, nontoxic homes.

CONSERVATION OF ENERGY AND WATER

Energy

I believe that the average guy in the street will give up a great deal, if he really understands the cost of not giving it up. In fact, we may find that, while we're drastically cutting our energy consumption, we're actually raising our standard of living.
—DAVID R. BROWER

Understanding IAQ

Indoor Air Quality Sources

The quality of indoor air results from the interaction of many complex factors, each contributing different effects. With potentially hundreds of different contaminants present in indoor air, identifying indoor air quality (IAQ) problems and developing solutions is difficult. The ways in which these factors contribute to IAQ are summarized as follows:

Construction Materials, Furnishings, and Equipment

These items may emit odor, particles, and volatile organic compounds (VOCs), and absorb and desorb VOCs. Individual VOCs from a specific material may combine with VOCs from other materials to form new chemicals. VOCs and particulates can cause health problems for occupants upon inhalation or exposure. In the presence of adequate heat and moisture, some materials provide nutrients that support the growth of molds and bacteria, which produce microbial volatile organic compounds (MVOCs).

These organisms can affect occupants adversely if fungal spores containing mycotoxins and allergens or the MVOCs are inhaled. A great deal of research remains to be done to identify individual metabolic gases, their odors, the microbes that produce them, and the human response to molds and fungi.

Building Envelope

The envelope controls the infiltration of outside air and moisture, and may include operable or inoperable windows.

Ventilation Systems

Acoustical materials in heating, ventilating, and air conditioning (HVAC) systems may contribute to indoor air pollution in the same way as construction materials, mentioned above. Ventilation systems also control the distribution, quantity, temperature, and humidity of air.

Maintenance

Lack of maintenance allows dirt, dust, mold, odors, and particles to increase. The use of high-VOC cleaning agents pollutes air.

Occupants

The number of occupants and the amount of equipment contribute to indoor air pollution. People and pets are major sources of microorganisms and airborne allergens in indoor environments. Occupant activities also can pollute the air.

Electric and Magnetic Fields (EMF)

The possible health effects of electric and magnetic fields generated by power lines and electric appliances are not well understood at this time. There is considerable debate regarding possible health effects of these sources. More research is required.

Understanding IAQ *(Continued)*

Health and Indoor Air Quality Issues
Poor indoor air quality can cause human illness. Health problems that can result from poor indoor air quality may be short term to long term, and range from minor irritations to life-threatening illnesses. They are classified as follows.

Sick Building Syndrome (SBS)

SBS describes a collection of symptoms experienced by building occupants that are generally short term and may disappear after the individuals leave the building. The most common symptoms are sore throat, fatigue, lethargy, dizziness, lack of concentration, respiratory irritation, headaches, eye irritation, sinus congestion, dryness of the skin (face or hands), and other cold, influenza, and allergy-type symptoms.

Building-Related Illnesses (BRI)

BRIs are more serious than SBS conditions and are clinically verifiable diseases that can be attributed to a specific source or pollutant within a building. Examples include cancer and Legionnaires' disease.

Multiple Chemical Sensitivities (MCS)

More research is needed to fully understand these complex illnesses. The initial symptoms of MCS are generally acquired during an identifiable exposure to specific VOCs. While these symptoms may be observed to affect more than one body organ system, they can recur and disappear in response to exposure to the stimuli (VOCs). Exposure to low levels of chemicals of diverse structural classes can produce symptoms. However, no standard test of the organ system function explaining the symptoms is currently available.

Typical Indoor Air Pollutants
Poor indoor air quality is caused by outdoor and indoor sources of gaseous and particulate air pollutants that exceed the capacity of the building's ventilation and filtration equipment to dilute or remove them to an acceptable level. Although many pollutants originate outdoors or from occupant activities, equipment, and processes, other pollutants are generated from materials.

The various types of indoor air pollutants are:

- Volatile organic compounds (VOCs) emitted by interior materials and their components
- VOCs emitted by cleaning and maintenance products periodically used with those materials
- Fiber shed from textiles, insulation, and panel products
- Soil, biological materials (e.g., fungi and bacteria), and gases released by biological activity
- Dust and other particulates from spraying, sanding, or finishing

These material-based pollutants may affect the health and productivity of building occupants, maintenance personnel, and construction tradespeople.

Understanding IAQ *(Continued)*

Emission Levels

Review emission levels from building products at the following stages:

- *Installation.* Exposure among tradespeople and building occupants during construction or renovation. Information on potential hazards during the installation period is documented in manufacturers' material safety data sheets (MSDSes). These sheets are a requirement by law for any material that may have health risks; however, they typically do not disclose a full list of contents. Additional information is available from the Occupational Safety and Health Administration (OSHA).

- *Building occupancy.* To prevent exposure of building occupants to emissions from materials during building use. Information on risks of occupant exposures (typically those risks extending more than a few weeks after construction) is difficult to determine, because emissions data are difficult to obtain or unavailable from manufacturers. This information will become more available in the next few years as standards are developed for accurately measuring and interpreting such data.

- *Maintenance and removal.* To prevent exposure of building occupants and tradespeople during maintenance procedures and removal or demolition. Maintenance and removal risks are reasonably well known for many conventional materials.

Consider these additional materials issues and effects:

- *Sink effect.* Rough and porous materials may contain microscopic planes and cavities that can absorb airborne molecules. These molecules, which may be pollutants, can be released ("desorbed") from the material after several hours or days. This "sink" effect of materials can be quite significant when pollutant molecules are absorbed. Hard, smooth, and nonporous surfaces typically have a low sink effect.

- *Moisture and temperature.* Moisture and heat in materials increase their deterioration and increase emissions of pollutants. Moisture also supports microbial growth.

- *Soiling and cleaning.* Improper cleaning practices may disturb soil and introduce exposure to chemicals in cleaning products. Soft floor coverings such as carpet are susceptible to this improper practice. Nonporous flooring with minimal seams and low-maintenance coatings are less prone to this occurrence.

- *Natural materials.* There is a common perception that "natural materials" are better environmental choices and less of a health risk than man-made "synthetic materials." Toxicity and emissions testing of products should help clarify which is the better choice with regard to health risk; however, predicting all potential health effects is not always possible.

Source: U.S. Environmental Protection Agency, www.epa.gov.

The United States, home to only 6 percent of the world's population, consumes 25 percent of the world's energy and generates 25 percent of global warming pollution—six times that of the automobile. In 1990, American households consumed $110 billion worth of energy alone. The United States is also the largest contributor to CO_2 emissions and, therefore, to global warming.

As members of the construction and design industry, we residential interior designers also have a serious responsibility to promote change in the key areas of high-efficiency appliances and lighting.

AIA: Press Release: January 2006

"Buildings account for 48 percent of U.S. energy consumption and generate far more greenhouse gas emissions than any other sector," said R. K. Stewart, FAIA, facilitator of the AIA Sustainability Summit Task Force. "As architects, we must accept responsibility for our role in creating the built environment. We feel it is incumbent upon the architecture profession to alter our actions and encourage both our clients and the entire design and construction industry to join us in plotting a course of measurable changes that will improve the quality of life for everyone." (Go to www.aia.org for more information.)

The goal of reducing fossil fuel use by 50 percent was inspired, in part, by recent work by Santa Fe, New Mexico, architect Ed Mazria, AIA, who modified some standard assumptions made in analyzing U.S. energy use by (economic) sector. Including the energy embodied in building materials and some other adjustments, Mazria found that the share of energy use attributable to buildings grows dramatically, from 27 percent to nearly 50 percent. Mazria argues that, to avoid a global catastrophe, it is necessary to cut global fossil fuel use immediately by 50 percent, and to reduce emissions much further by 2030. Other actions on the list include collaborating with other organizations to integrate sustainability into architecture curricula, documenting the contributions to humankind and the planet from sustainable design practices, and advocating globally for sustainable design. (Go to www.architecture2030.org for more information.)

Energy efficiency is one of the cornerstones of any green building project and, for residential designers, high-efficiency appliances and lighting are primary areas to focus on. Generation and use of energy are major contributors to air pollution and global climate change. With the world's supply of fossil fuel dwindling, concerns for energy security increasing, and the impact of greenhouse gases on world climate rising, it is essential to find ways to reduce loads, increase efficiency, and utilize renewable energy.

We can begin by targeting energy savings when specifying appliances for clients. Many manufacturers have made tremendous strides in increasing the energy efficiency of their appliances, aided by the U.S. Department of Energy (DOE) minimum efficiency standards, the federal ENERGY STAR program, and efforts of the Consortium for Energy Efficiency (CEE). These energy-efficient choices can save families approximately a third on their energy bills, while reducing greenhouse gas emissions by a third, as well. Most importantly, we must always meet or exceed ENERGY STAR requirements when specifying appliances; and when selecting appliances, look for products that are high energy- and water-conserving, durable and easy to maintain, designed for disassembly, and that carry long-term warranties.

When addressing the lighting program within a project, we must specify lamps and lighting controls that will make a difference in the energy loads and operating budget. There are basically three options that meet the needs of residential lighting: incandescent, fluorescent, and halogen. Ideally, we should work to replace incandescent bulbs with compact fluorescents (CFLs). This will initially cost more, but these lamps will last 8 to 10 times longer and save up to 50 to 80 percent in energy costs.

It's also important to engage with and challenge the client and project team in a discussion regarding alternative energy sources. Consider wind power, geothermal and photovoltaic, with a goal of zero-energy usage. This will be a valuable contribution to the project's discussions and goal. That said, there are different definitions of zero energy. The Net-Zero-Energy Home Coalition, a multistakeholder group in Canada, comprising corporations and nonprofit organizations, defines a zero-energy home as follows:

> A net-zero-energy home at a minimum supplies to the grid an annual output of electricity that is equal to the amount of power purchased from the grid. In many cases the entire energy consumption (heating, cooling, and electrical) of a net-zero-energy home can be provided by renewable energy sources.

Water

For many of us, water simply flows from a faucet, and we think little about it beyond this point of contact. We have lost a sense of respect for the wild river, for the complex workings of a wetland, for the intricate web of life that water supports.
—SANDRA POSTEL, *LAST OASIS: FACING WATER SCARCITY* (2003)

In many parts of this country and around the globe, freshwater has become a limited resource. Current studies indicate that the building industry consumes one-sixth of the world's freshwater supply, per the USGBC and Worldwatch Institute. A sustainable building aims to reduce, to control, or to treat site runoff; use water efficiently; and reuse or recycle water for on-site use whenever feasible.

How much water is used in a typical home? Per the New York City Department of Environmental Protection:

- National average indoor residential water use per day per person is 60 to 70 gallons.
- Fifty to 75 percent of all residential water use occurs in the bathroom.
- The average faucet uses 0.5 to 5 gallons per minute.
- Faucet aerators reduce flow by 1 gallon per minute.
- Standard showerheads use 4 to 7 gallons per minute.
- Low-flow showerheads use 2.5 gallons per minute (or less).
- A dishwasher uses 5 to 15 gallons per load.

To protect and conserve water, designers can begin by recommending the following:

- Low-flow or flow reducers on faucets and showerheads
- Ultra-low or dual flush toilets
- ENERGY STAR laundry appliances and dishwashers
- Chlorine filters on showerheads
- Water filtration units on faucets
- Hot water on-demand systems

The convenience of plumbing fixtures has led to the largest use of water in a typical family home. Therefore, specifying water-conserving plumbing fixtures and fittings is our responsibility. In addition, retrofitting most devices in older buildings is cost-effective and supports water efficiency by reducing water usage and wastewater; these devices will pay for themselves within one to three years from date of installation.

In homes, bathrooms offer the greatest opportunity for water savings. There is no disputing the fact that toilets are the biggest water guzzlers within a household. Per a report from *Environmental Building News* (EBN), January 2004, nearly all flushed water in North America starts as clean, drinkable water. The American Water Works Association (AWWA) Research Foundation examined water use in approximately 1,200 homes in 14 North American cities and found that an average household uses approximately 146,000 gallons of water annually, 42 percent indoors and 58 percent outdoors. In households where water-conserving plumbing fixtures have not been installed, toilets use an average of 20.1 gallons of water per day, or 26.7 percent of total indoor water use. In homes with water-conserving fixtures, toilets use an average of 9.6 gallons per day, or 19.3 percent of the total—though plumbing leaks account for another 10 to 14 percent of water use, and much of that is due to toilets.

Another water-saving device from the world of plumbing is the hot water on-demand system. Running cold water down the drain while waiting for hot water to reach the faucet wastes more than 10,000 gallons each year in an average American household. These hot water on-demand systems rapidly distribute hot water to the faucet while cold water is pumped back to the water heater. A pump attaches easily under the sink, and its heat sensor shuts off the unit when the water is hot.

It is paramount to protect and preserve water. Fortunately, this is now easy to do, as new products are regularly coming onto the market with continued quality improvement. By reducing the gallons per flush (GPF) and gallons per minute (GPM), we can help to achieve dramatic reductions in water use, meaning that less of our clean, clear water will be going down the drain in vain.

WASTE REDUCTION AND MANAGEMENT

The packaging for a microwavable "microwave" dinner is programmed for a shelf life of maybe six months, a cook time of two minutes, and a landfill dead-time of centuries.

—David Wann, *Buzzworm*, November 1990

A green building includes waste reduction and management from the inception of a project through its completion. The best waste reduction strategy embraces the three Rs: reduce, reuse, and recycle. This is accomplished by incorporating a comprehensive green building approach that includes resource conservation, material reuse, construction and demolition debris recovery, as well as the use of recycled content materials. This strategy is vital to reducing pressure on landfills; saves money by reducing landfill-tipping fees; provides raw materials for future building products; helps the environment; and enhances the economic bottom line.

Those in the building industry need to be strongly challenged to incorporate waste reduction and recycling specification language into their projects. To drive the point home, consider these facts: In the United States alone, 32 truckloads of waste are created for every truckload of goods produced. And 90 percent of *everything* made in this country ends up in a landfill within one year. Relative to our industry, nationwide, approximately 4 billion pounds of carpet are sent to the landfill each year. More than 136 million tons of construction and demolition debris, per the EPA, are generated each year. We are in a runaway, throwaway society that is leaving its mark on the Earth for future generations, who will have to clean up after their predecessors.

At a minimum, we must address these materials in the project waste management plan. A measurable goal can be tracked by identifying the types and quantities of materials estimated to be generated at the job site: target recycling of at least 50 percent of the construction and/or demolition debris, and contact local recycling facilities and haulers to identify terms and conditions required for recycling these materials.

Many cities have adopted regulations supporting construction waste management. A stellar example is the City of Chicago, which has adopted new regulations aimed at reducing the amount of construction and demolition (C&D) waste sent to landfills. All contractors are required to recycle at least 25 percent, by weight, of all C&D waste in the city in 2006, according to Chicago's Department of Streets and Sanitation. In 2007, the required recycling rate will double to 50 percent. Look into your projects' local ordinances to see what is available and/or required for construction and waste demolition.

Additionally, we can donate unused materials from the job site. Salvaged materials, such as leftover wood, windows, doors, and other uninstalled items, are ideal for posting on Web sites, donating to organizations such as Habitat for Humanity, local art programs, and design or architecture schools.

C&D debris occupies a large percentage of our landfill space. The continued steady growth of building activities has been cited as a major reason why landfill volumes have been increasing, despite expanding recycling efforts. One example of this is in Alameda County, California, where citizens recycle a high percentage of their waste, yet more than 355,000 tons of construction and demolition materials are still unnecessarily disposed of in county landfills annually.

Landfills are expensive to build and no one wants one "in their backyard." The more we reduce waste, the less need we have for building new landfills. Knowing that waste reduction on the job site ultimately helps the bottom line, a business that practices source reduction and reuse and/or recycling can help reduce expenses. By working with the contractor to develop a waste management plan and developing resources to assist in the diversion of C&D materials, we support environmental stewardship.

> *Instead of defining success as getting the most materials, we need to move to a new standard: getting the most from them. Recycling 60 percent of U.S. solid waste would save the energy equivalent to 315 million barrels of oil each year.*
> —WORLDWATCH INSTITUTE, SEPTEMBER 1994

OPERATION AND MAINTENANCE

The practice of sustainable design does not end when construction is complete and the homeowners move in. Once the owner occupies the home, it is crucial to ensure that it operates according to design intent. Prior planning, recommended cleaning products, and long-term system maintenance guidelines all determine how well a home will perform over its useful life. Incorporating operating and maintenance considerations into the design of a home greatly contributes to healthy and safe living environments, quality of life, and reduced use of energy and other resources.

To that end, specify materials and systems that are cost-effective and require less maintenance—less water, energy, toxic chemicals, and cleaners to maintain. Providing guidelines that address all aspects of maintaining a home over the course of its useful life will help maintain a well-designed building.

A Pilot Study by Yale and Columbia Universities Ranks the United States 28th in Environmental Performance

The 2006 Environmental Performance Index ranked countries based on 16 indicators related to environmental health, air quality, water resources, productive natural resources, biodiversity, habitat, and sustainable energy. New Zealand scored first among all countries, earning 88 out of 100 possible points. Sweden, Finland, the Czech Republic, the United Kingdom, and Austria also scored 85 points or higher. The United States scored 78.5 points, coming in behind most of Western Europe, Canada, Malaysia, Japan, Costa Rica, Colombia, Australia, Taiwan, and Chile. (The full report is available online at www.yale.edu/epi.)

FOR FUTURE GENERATIONS

We do not inherit the earth from our ancestors; we borrow it from our children.
—NAVAJO PROVERB

I do not believe that the process of human life on this globe has degenerated to a point of no return. I do believe, however, that we are fast approaching that point and we must redirect and correct our course in life to ensure health and a good life for the seventh generation coming. This legacy is passed down not to ensure the present, but to guarantee the future. Thinking of future generations is an enormous responsibility that requires vision.
—CHIEF OREN LYONS, AUGUST 1997

Protecting the environment and preserving the planet for future generations is, without doubt, one of the primary benefits of aligning ourselves with the key areas of sustainability. Many definitions exist concerning sustainability and what we will pass on to our children's children:

- The ability to provide for the needs of the world's current population without damaging the ability of future generations to provide for themselves. When a process is sustainable, it can be carried out over and over without negative environmental effects or impossibly high costs to anyone involved (www. sustainabletable.org).

- To keep in existence, maintain; meeting the needs of future generations. . . . The ability to provide a healthy, satisfying and just life for all people on earth, now and for generations to come while enhancing the health of ecosystems and the ability of other species to survive in their natural environments (www. earthethics.com).

- Seven-generation sustainability is the tenet that all decisions should be made with consideration for the effect they will have on the next seven generations to follow us (http://en.wikipedia.org).

There are common threads to these definitions. Sustainability requires meeting environmental, economic, and community needs simultaneously. All three are essential to ensure that quality of life continues for living systems and future generations.

What if we, as residential interior designers, embraced the message from Catherine Ryan Hyde in her book *Pay It Forward* (1999)? It is an idea and an action plan within a work of fiction. But does it have to be fiction?

In the book, Reuben St. Clair, the teacher-protagonist, starts a movement with this voluntary, extra-credit assignment: Think of an idea for world change, and put it into action.

Trevor, the 12-year-old hero, thinks of quite an idea. He describes it to his mother and teacher this way: "You see, I do something real good for three people. And then when they ask how they can pay it back, I say they have to Pay It Forward. To three more people. Each. So nine people get helped. Then those people have to do twenty-seven." He turned on the calculator, punched in a few numbers. "Then it sort of spreads out, see. To eighty-one. Then two hundred forty-three. Then seven hundred twenty-nine. Then two thousand, one hundred eighty-seven. See how big it gets?"

This idea, this concept, could create enormous momentum in healing the planet and creating a change in the market. If each of us designers implemented three great things for the environment on each of our projects and then asked project team members to "Pay it forward," the exponential growth would truly be extraordinary!

Conclusion

As we take sustainability seriously to heart, we can be inspired over and over by William McDonough's design challenge:

> We need a new design assignment and we need a new design. In order to do this we need to ask new questions. "How do we love all the children, of all species, for all time?" Please notice that I am not just saying our children; I am saying all of the children. And notice I am not just saying our species, I am saying all species. And notice I am not just saying now, I am saying for all time. When we integrate this question into our designs, wonderful and beautiful things begin to happen.

RESOURCES

"It's the Architecture, Stupid!" Edward Mazria, AIA, www.architecture2030.org, June 2003
"Shades of Green," Anita Baltimore, FASID, *Interiors & Sources Magazine,* April 2005
"What Makes a Product Green," *Environmental Building News,* January 2000, Volume 9, Number 1 (updated February 2006)
"Why Green Design Matters," Penny Bonda, ASID, *Icon Magazine,* May 2003

CHAPTER 2

inspiring stories

I nspiration typically comes through personal experiences, touching our hearts and opening our minds to new ways of thinking. In acknowledgment of the power of such experiences in our own lives, we invited some of our mentors and associates to share their stories of inspiration. To hear these pioneers speak encourages us to think beyond ourselves, and the flame of environmental stewardship reignites.

William McDonough: Designing the Future

William McDonough is a world-renowned architect and designer and winner of three U.S. presidential awards: the Presidential Award for Sustainable Development (1996), the National Design Award (2004), and the Presidential Green Chemistry Challenge Award (2003). Time magazine recognized him as a "Hero for the Planet" in 1999.

Founding principal of William McDonough + Partners, Architecture and Community Design, Charlottesville, VA, an internationally recognized design firm practicing ecologically, socially, and economically intelligent architecture and planning in the United States and abroad, William is also the cofounder and principal, with German chemist Michael Braungart, of McDonough Braungart Design Chemistry (MBDC), which employs a comprehensive cradle-to-cradle design protocol to chemical benchmarking, supply-chain integration, energy and materials assessment, clean-production qualification, and sustainability issue management and optimization.

Photo courtesy of William McDonough.

"MY LIFE IN DESIGN HAS BEEN INFLUENCED STRONGLY BY EXPERIENCES I HAD ABROAD—first in Japan, where I spent my early childhood. I recall land and resources being scarce, but also the beauty of traditional Japanese homes, with their paper walls and dripping gardens, their warm futons and steaming baths. I also remember quilted winter garments, and farmhouses with thick walls of clay and straw that kept the interior warm in winter and cool in summer.

Later, in college, I accompanied a professor of urban design to Jordan to develop housing for the Bedouin who were settling in the Jordan River Valley. There, I was struck again by how simple and elegant good design can be, and how suited to locale. The tents of woven goat hair the Bedouin had used as nomads drew hot air up and out, creating not only shade but a refreshing interior breeze. When it rained, the fiber swelled, and the structure became tight as a drum. This ingenious design, locally relevant and culturally rich, contrasted sharply with modern home design, which applied universal solutions to local circumstances and sharply separated indoors and out. The Bedouin tent, on the other hand, was in constant, intelligent dialogue with place; only a permeable membrane separated the landscape from the interior. Imagine if American homes and interiors were designed to make equally good use of the particular gifts of particular locales—the varieties of sunlight, wind, terrain, and vegetation that show what works in each place and make shelter a living, breathing presence in the landscape.

After graduate school, I apprenticed with a New York firm esteemed for its socially responsible urban housing, and founded my own architectural firm in 1981. Three years later we were commissioned to design the offices of the Environmental Defense Fund, which became the first "green" office in New York. I worked on indoor air quality, a subject almost no one had studied in depth. Of particular concern to us were volatile organic compounds, carcinogenic materials, and anything else in paints, wall coverings, carpeting, flooring, and fixtures that might cause indoor air problems or multiple chemical sensitivity. With little or no research available, we turned to manufacturers, who often told us the information was proprietary and gave us nothing beyond vague safeguards in the material data safety sheets mandated by law. We did the best we could at the time. We used water-based paints. We tacked down carpet instead of gluing it. We provided 30 cubic feet per minute of fresh air per person instead of 5. We had granite checked for radon. We used wood that was sustainably harvested. We did our best, but I hoped for more. I wanted to design buildings and materials that were completely positive and beneficial for people and nature. I wanted to make things that celebrated human creativity and the abundance of the natural world.

A meeting with Michael Braungart, the world-renowned German chemist, launched the design protocol that made this possible. Both Michael and I wanted to challenge the entrenched idea that industry and commerce inevitably damage the natural world. We saw pollution, toxicity, and waste as signals of design failure, which could be positively addressed by design. Michael was highly skilled at analyzing the chemistry of materials and identifying the human and ecological health effects of plasticizers, PVC, heavy metals, and many other harmful substances. My practice and my design sensibility complemented Michael's scientific knowledge, and we were soon helping some of the world's most successful companies make products that were both environmentally safe and highly profitable. Moreover, those products were conceived so that, after their useful lives, they provided nourishment for something new—either *biological nutrients* for the soil, or t*echnical nutrients* for industry. We called our approach Cradle-to-Cradle design. One of the companies I designed products with was DesignTex, which worked with the Rohner textile mill in Germany to make Climatex Lifecycle, an upholstery fabric that blends pesticide-residue-free wool and organically grown ramie, dyed and processed entirely with nontoxic chemicals. The fabric is so safe the trimmings from the mill become mulch for local gardens, returning the material's biological nutrients to the soil. And instead of producing dangerous effluents, the fabric solved the mill's hazardous waste problem: when the mill made Climatex Lifecycle, the processing water flowing out of the mill was as clean as the water flowing in. Meanwhile, companies taking up Cradle-to-Cradle design began to make technical nutrients for interiors: perpetually recyclable synthetic fabrics, carpet yarns, carpet tiles, and other household materials that can be recovered and used in generation after generation of high-quality products—not simply used in a product of lesser value, as in conventional recycling.

The things I make, and the way we make things, are a part of my story because they are the product of my influences and my hope for the future. They are part of this particular story because good design is transforming the materials we use in our homes. Interior designers still have to work hard to find materials that will be safe and beneficial for their clients, but thankfully they are easier to find today than they were when I designed the Environmental Defense Fund offices more than 20 years ago. Since then, our collective knowledge has grown, numerous high-quality, environmentally safe products have entered the marketplace, and the demand for them has expanded immensely. As young designers well schooled in the principles of ecological design enter the profession, demand and expertise will continue to grow. The future looks bright indeed.

But only if we create the future with intention. We can all be innovators and market catalysts today. We can imagine what a world of prosperity and health will look like and begin designing it right now. We can make things and places so intelligent and safe they leave an ecological footprint to delight in rather than lament. This will not be easy, of course. Creating a sustaining world is going to take us all, and it's going to take forever. But then, that's the point."

Used with permission and adapted especially for this book from Cradle to Cradle: Remaking the Way We Make Things *(New York: North Point Press, 2002).*

Photo courtesy of Hunter Lovins.

Hunter Lovins: Thinker of Sustainability

President of Natural Capitalism Solutions, Eldorado Springs, CO, Hunter Lovins is a founding professor of Business at Presidio School of Management. Hunter has helped create a variety of for-profit and nonprofit companies, including Tree People in California, Rocky Mountain Institute, and E Source in Colorado. Through Natural Capitalism, Hunter and her team implement the ideas of greater sustainability in companies and governments around the world and build the new intellectual capital we need to advance these ideas. She is also working with educational institutions here and abroad to inject the ideas of sustainability into all of the disciplines.

"IN SOME WAYS, I AM NOT SURE THAT I HAD MUCH CHOICE IN MY CAREER. MY PARENTS were both activists. My mother organized in the coalfields of West Virginia with John L. Lewis. My father helped to mentor Martin King and Cesar Chavez. I was carried as a baby to my first demonstration, in support of the Quakers who were sailing the boat *The Golden Rule* into the South Pacific to try to stop the atmospheric testing of nuclear bombs. They taught me to leave the world a better place than I found it, to believe that I could make a difference and that I had a responsibility to do so. Growing up on a small farm gave me a connection with natural and growing things, and I am still more comfortable outdoors. My parents gave me the blessing of knowing that there were things worth protecting, and a belief in the importance of being involved. They never put limits on me, but gave me the sense that anything was attainable if I wanted it bad enough. This made me a bit rebellious against the stupider parts of the 'system' at an early age but also developed the recognition that I was devoting my life to causes that were larger than my passing desires.

My own activism started in about 1963, working in such movements as fair housing and Civil Rights; then moved into organizing anti-Vietnam War protests, human rights work, and environmental protection. I resigned from the Sierra Club in protest at the first firing of Dave Brower, and went with him to Friends of the Earth. In 1970, I planted a tree on the first Earth Day.

Lots of things inspire me. It's been an enormous honor to be able to travel to many beautiful places, from my own beloved Colorado mountains to the Hindu Kush range of Afghanistan, from the jungles of Jamaica to the veldt of Africa. Many people inspire me, from my friends and mentors, Dave Brower and Dana Meadows, the two greatest environmental luminaries of our age, to such current colleagues as Lester Brown, Gwen Hallsmith, Paul Hawken, Denis Hayes, and Janine Benyus.

Rather than spend all my time with like-minded people, [I find] it is good to be exposed to different thinking. People tend to think in ways that are comfortable, and so we get into ruts. I try to spend as much time as I can with young people who don't know what is impossible, who have not had limits set on their ability to be creative and freethinking. Alan Savory, founder of Holistic Management, advises us to assume we are wrong and to always question our assumptions. The great activist, Saul Alinsky, and Andy Lipkis, founder of Tree People, both taught me to engage in conversations with people from their perspective, not from my own. So I have a history of working with people from varying backgrounds, from the military and corporate leaders to community activists, academicians, and politicians. Each brings a perspective that we need if we are to craft solutions that can tackle the sorts of challenges now facing us.

This is especially important when seeking to convey the idea that green design can work. Understanding what it is that people care about, and speaking to that, can enable advocates to show people how green design can enhance their quality of life. Visuals are also very important and communicate these ideas in a compelling way. My presentations use lots of pictures and relatively few words. In the design and environmental field we tend to focus more on the precise technical information, but this is much harder to learn from. We took great care when building RMI to create a structure that was beautiful and comfortable, as well as efficient. It was a technically fascinating house, the first to integrate passive solar and superefficient construction. But what sold the concept was that people could walk in from a snowstorm in February and see luscious tomatoes being grown. They could come in out of the dry Colorado clime and feel the humidity. The beauty of hand-painted Mexican tile and rubbed oak did a better job than we did of selling efficient passive and active solar architecture within a superinsulated environment.

It is important to get the numbers right, but it is equally important to demonstrate a higher quality of life. A sustainable future can solve such challenges as climate change, but people are more likely to adopt it if they realize that our unsustainable society of material wealth has brought with it an inner poverty that no amount of Wal-Marts selling cheaper products can fill. This was brought home to me most strongly during my work in Afghanistan, where despite crushing poverty, the people have a greater closeness in their families and friendships, and an oral tradition that values conversation and listening, which our commercial media cannot match, and a dignity and happiness that does not derive from how much stuff they possess. Simple things—they love to fly kites—bring great enjoyment. When was the last time that you flew a kite with the entire neighborhood? There is much that we can do to bring sustainable ways to meet basic human needs for energy, water, housing, sanitation, and so on. But the Afghans have given me far more, in lessons in how to be truly happy.

My friend, the folk singer Kate Wolf, said: 'Find what you really care about and live a life that shows it.' It is a great honor to have been given the opportunity to do this. Will you join me?"

Paula Baker-Laporte: Designer of EcoNests

Hailed by Natural Home Magazine *in 2005 as one of the top 10 green architects in the United States, Paula leads the EcoNest design team, in Santa Fe, NM. She is the primary author of* Prescriptions for a Healthy House: A Practical Guide for Architects, Builders & Homeowners *(New Society Publishers, British Columbia, Canada, 2001), is coauthor, with Robert Laporte of* EcoNest, Creating Sustainable Sanctuaries of Clay, Straw and Timber *(Gibbs Smith, 2005) and is a contributing author to* A People's Ecology *(Santa Fe, NM: Clear Light Book, 1999). Paula graduated from the University of Toronto School of Architecture in 1978 and moved to Santa Fe in 1981, where she currently lives with her husband, Robert Laporte, and daughter, Sarah. Paula has been designing fine custom homes in Santa Fe since 1986. She is an architect, a certified Bau-biologist (building biologist), and a cofounder of the Healthy Housing Coalition.*

Photo courtesy of Paula Baker-Laporte.

"I AM A RESIDENTIAL ARCHITECT WHO HAS ALWAYS CARED DEEPLY ABOUT THE NEEDS OF MY clients. However, I never understood how much I could influence their health and well-being until I realized that my own inexplicable chronic illness was caused by a home I had once lived in. I had multiple chemical sensitivities, or environmental illness. That was 15 years ago. Until that time, designing for health and environmental considerations had been of only peripheral concern to me. I, like many architects, considered myself to be an artist, not a technician! Once faced with the daunting task of creating a chemical-free sanctuary, in which I could regain my own health, I had the opportunity for much soul-searching. I began to realize that the standard building practices on which I had built my career were often destructive, not only to the health of the occupants but to the environment as well. Together with my physician, Dr. Erica Elliott, and John Banta, a dedicated building scientist, I wrote my first book, *Prescriptions for a Healthy House,* in the hopes of influencing other architects, builders, and homeowners to build healthier homes. I wanted to make the process accessible and easier than it had been for me.

It was during the time of my recovery that I became a student of Bau-biologie (the philosophy of building for human and planetary health, which originated in Germany, is widely practiced in Northern Europe, but is, as yet, little known in the United States). I was discouraged by the lack of opportunities for actually designing in this way in this country, until one day I read about the work of natural homebuilder, Robert Laporte. He had developed a building system that embodied the concepts of Bau-biologie. His buildings were made of natural unprocessed materials . . . 'breathable,' low in embodied energy, energy-efficient, and free of toxins and harmful waste products. The clay/straw timber frame wall systems that he had perfected were not only ecological, they were finely crafted. I found the timber frame to be a powerful and challenging design element.

I attended one of his hands-on workshops in 1992 and came away with the distinct feeling that our futures would be intertwined. I felt a calling to work with him, although I must admit he was, at first, pretty oblivious to this possibility. (Men!) Before any real clients materialized we collaborated on a series of conceptual plans, and one home at a time our collaboration began to bear fruit. Our work evolved into a body of homes that we dubbed 'EcoNests.'

In March of 1999, Robert and I were married in our own newly completed 'nest.' Previously, my knowledge about the benefits of a natural home had been intellectual. From that day on it became visceral as well. Just as motherhood has made me a better person, with its lessons in patience, nurturing, compassion, and deep love, living in a natural and healthy home has embraced me and sheltered me so profoundly that I have become a more avid environmentalist, crusader, lecturer, hostess, tour guide, writer, and teacher, in an effort to share this deeply satisfying experience with as many people as I can reach.

Together, Robert and I work to create humble dwellings 'for the rest of us,' which serve as a demonstration of:

- Design for human health and comfort
- Design for energy efficiency
- Design for sustainability of the environment and natural resources

In September 2005, we had the great privilege of publishing the fruits of our collaboration to date in a book called *EcoNests: Creating Sustainable Sanctuaries of Clay, Straw, and Timber.*"

Janine Benyus: Biologist at the Design Table

Janine Benyus is the author of several remarkable books, including Biomimicry: Innovation Inspired by Nature *(New York, NY: Harper Perennial, 2002), and is cofounder of the Biomimicry Guild. The Biomimicry Guild helps communities and companies consult nature to create products, processes, and policies that are well adapted to life on Earth over the long haul. These "biologists at the design table" offer research services, workshops, and really cool talks about the genius that surrounds us.*

"WHEN I WAS NINE OR TEN, I HAD AN EARLY GRIEF EXPERIENCE THAT SHAPED my life. WE lived in New Jersey. As development and building expanded, my parents would move us further and further out to the edge of the suburbs, so that we could be surrounded by nature. Each time this occurred, my dad would need to commute further and further to get to work, but it was important to him that my sister and I have a forest in which to wander.

Photo courtesy of Janine Benyus.

In the mixed hardwood forest behind our home, in a ravine too steep to build on, I discovered a secret, almost miraculous world of vines and nests and box turtles. There, I read books, pored over field guides, pressed plants, and tried to learn the names of all the critters in my world. I observed animals through all of the seasons over several years. I got to know when nestlings would hatch and where bats would roost. Magnifying glass in one hand, test tubes in the other, I was (as the desk sign from my dad read), 'Janine Benyus, Microscopist,' the naturalist sleuth! I brought home owl pellets and pond water and insect wings to share with my equally curious and indulgent parents.

It was my *Watership Down, a Wind in the Willows* experience, if there ever was one. My most magical experiences were in the outdoors, and this was my initial inspiration to do what I have been doing all my life.

One day, while picking wild strawberries in the open meadow next to my ravine, I came across some orange flags on wooden stakes. Following their trail led me into a summer of watching as bulldozers rolled up the sod, scraped the land bare, and replaced the thrumming meadow with a housing subdivision. I watched day by day and, slowly, the grief from what was happening settled in my cells. I was convinced that the casual destruction was simply a lack of understanding. If these men on the machinery only knew what I knew about this meadow, I thought, if only I could have shown them the life of this place, they would have turned the bulldozers off.

I knew that my affection for the natural world—the breath-held-in wonder I felt when I walked outside—was something that I wanted to share with others. By giving people that chance, I thought I could engender a wider appreciation, and that's how I could be useful. I love to write; I've written six books to date and have another in the wings. The story I try to tell is how incredible our world is and how we can learn so much from it. I feel as though I'm holding something precious in my hand, like a robin's egg, and uncurling my fingers to share it with others.

I had no design knowledge before writing *Biomimicry*. I realized that I had been asking questions about the adaptive genius in the natural world years before in my books, commenting that maybe doctors could use this strategy, or architects could learn from that design. I wrote a lot about the elegant functionality in nature. As I learned more about our materials science, energy systems, medicine, business, and sustainable agriculture, I began to see how nature's designs could inform our own. Biomimicry—the idea of going to nature for advice—is an idea that acquires people; and like any good meme, it's been spreading rapidly. That's because looking to nature is a powerful method of innovation. Life has been adapting to this earth for 3.8 billion years. By adopting nature's design principles, by asking, How would nature do it?, we find not only solutions that work, but also problems worth solving. Problems that are important to the survival of all life.

Jane Jacobs is an essayist whose writing I'd admired for years. In 1997, she recognized that Biomimicry was relevant to, of all things, urban design. She, among others, helped me to recognize that I am in the middle of an idea whose time is come. I had an opportunity; and when she asked, What do you want to do with your moment?, I decided that this was what I needed to do, this was important to me.

Then Paul Hawken began holding up my book at conferences and saying that it might be interesting to check it out; that *Biomimicry* talks about ideas that matter. My life began to shift. I wasn't prepared for the changes that it would bring to my world. I was comfortable as I was, content to work hard and write books in my private place in

Montana. Now I can see the value of speaking and brainstorming in person with designers, engineers, and architects. When businesses ask Biomimicry Guild biologists to come to the design table, something very new is happening. We're exploring what's possible for us as a species by looking at what other species have already learned.

Designers are some of my favorite people. I love good design. I didn't know what it was, but I knew I loved things that work well. I always have. And that's what I look for in the natural world—things that work well over the long haul, for both the organism and the ecosystem. This new career, called "Biologist at the Design Table," gives biologists a chance to share the best practices of those communities. Every week more people are calling, asking if they can get involved in bioinspired design. I tell them, 'This is not mine; it is ours.' Collaboration is a key.

So we're doing a lot of teaching these days. Dayna Baumeister, my partner in the Biomimicry Guild, conducts workshops where innovators get to practice bioinspired design in places like Costa Rica and Montana. Millions of great ideas right outside the door! The people who come to these workshops in turn inspire me everyday.

Writing *Biomimicry* changed my path, and my story is still unfolding and evolving. So is the story of our species. If we really start to see nature as a teacher, a wise mentor, it will change our relationship with the natural world. As apprentices, we'll come to admire and respect the organisms that teach us. I believe the words of Bab Dioum, a Senegalese conservationist, 'In the end we will conserve only what we love. We will love only what we understand. We will understand only what we are taught.'"

Trudy Dujardin: What Brought Me Here?

Trudy Dujardin, ASID, president of Dujardin Design Associates in Greenwich, Connecticut, and Nantucket, Massachusetts, is an award-winning designer and national expert on nontoxic building materials and sustainable design.

"THIS IS VERY MUCH MY PERSONAL STORY, MY OWN QUEST FOR HEALTH, meaning, and the inner peace that comes from 'doing the right thing,' whatever that might mean to you.

As a child, I lived on a farm in South Carolina and was continually exposed to pesticides and crop dusting. I was the first and long-awaited grandchild and very treasured. At night, my grandparents would give me the best place to sleep, on a cot by a bank of windows to get the cool evening breeze. To protect me from the mosquitoes, they would spray the window screens with a Flitgun, filled with a DDT solution. Even as a child, I knew something was terribly wrong with this. Since I could barely stand

Photo courtesy of Trudy Dujardin.

the smell, I would try to hold my breath and keep my hands over my nose and mouth all night. So, unknowingly, my quest for health began.

As an adult, I spent more than 20 years on construction sites, where I saw little or no attention paid to the toxicity of materials used, or concern for the health of the tradesmen. So in 1987, when I purchased land on the harbor of Nantucket Island, overlooking the town itself, I made a solemn vow to do this project 'right.' Right meant that since this was such a delicate site within a very fragile ecosystem, it was critical that anything done on it had to be 'mindful' and with intention—that is, non-toxic. I was determined not to add to the pollution in any way with runoff from my construction process.

So, my passion for green design came out of a desire for harmony in myself and with the environment of this beautiful island. Nantucket Island is a world unto itself. It made sense to me to have as little impact as possible. It also made sense that the building to be constructed should be healthy for the occupants and the construction workers alike. I wanted my walk and talk to match.

I began to plan my dream house, my forever house. My first mentor was Paul Bierman-Lytle. He led me in the right direction for low-toxic building materials. My education was just beginning. I began a five-year research project to achieve my healthy home.

What I didn't realize was that, at the same time, I was developing a condition known as multiple chemical sensitivity, or environmental illness. I was diagnosed in the mid-'90s. With the help of Dr. Phillip J. Cohen and Dr. Adrienne Buffaloe (American Academy of Environmental Medicine, Prairie Village, KS), we began the task of uncovering causes and starting detox. The pesticide exposures of my early years, my studio classes as an art major using oil-based products, and the toxic products on many construction sites were all suspect.

Many days it was difficult for me to work, to concentrate, to go to the office—even to get out of bed. I could no longer go on construction sites or be around clients who were wearing perfume or had tobacco odors on their clothing. I was having allergic reactions to almost everything, and was being tested for everything from lupus to rheumatoid arthritis. Even though all of the tests were negative, it was hard to feel any relief because my world was shrinking more and more everyday.

This story does have a happy ending. After almost two years of living in my healthy house full-time, I became well. The healing process was a learning journey as well and one I now want to share. I'm active and happy again and free to move about in the world. My firm is thriving; we handle calls everyday from people with chemical sensitivities. I'm on several boards, both national and international, and feel that I'm truly giving back to the world.

A reminder: this is an ongoing journey. We will never reach a point where we can stop and rest. Saving the planet, saving the health of every person, requires constant vigilance and effort. We must continue to question the role of coal-burning factories and mercury toxicity; our dependence on oil; the consequences of air pollution, acid rain, and pesticide use; and manufacturers producing products harmful to their workers and the public. We must question the impact this is all having on our health and the future of the planet."

Bert Gregory: Greening Architectural Interiors

As President and CEO of Mithun, Seattle, Washington, Bert Gregory has led the 200-person firm to national recognition for concept-based, environmentally intelligent design. He is renowned as an expert in the development of resource-efficient structures and communities and serves as a national leader, speaker, and advocate for sustainable building and urbanism. His perspective reaches beyond traditional architecture to merge science and design—an interdisciplinary approach for the future that creates lasting urban places for people. Bert currently serves on the USGBC's LEED, the Neighborhood Development Core Committee, Downtown Seattle Association Waterfront Task Force, and City of Seattle Mayor's Urban Sustainability Advisory Panel.

Photo courtesy of Bert Gregory.

"GROWING UP IN A RAILROAD FAMILY IN DENVER, COLORADO, I GOT TO SEE MUCH OF THE United States as a youngster. Trains took me to see exciting cities and big, cool buildings. I have vivid memories of elegant, beautiful, dramatically huge spaces. You know your home one way and then come back to see it another. All that influenced my interest in the physical built world. My dad and I put together train sets, and I would build the buildings. When I was in the seventh grade, two architects moved onto our street, and that was an awakening for me. I realized, 'Hey, grown-ups do this kind of stuff.'

At the same time, the wilderness of Colorado, Utah, and Wyoming was just as much a part of my world. My family spent lots of time skiing and backpacking in the mountains, getting close to nature. Through high school and college, I continued to explore outdoors. This combination of buildings and cities and nature got me into architecture with a green focus.

My studies began at the University of Colorado. During the late '60s and early '70s, an awareness of the natural world was just beginning. My professors included Richard Whittaker, who was part of the team that designed Sea Ranch, a milestone project for harmonizing with the environment. Core curricula included the study of the thought leader, Ian McHarg, who wrote the seminal book, *Design with Nature* (New York: John Wiley & Sons, 1995), which discussed how to place buildings in the landscape; and a semester studying Buckminster Fuller, who came to Colorado for a few days and shared lots of wonderful ideas, creative thinking, about 'Spaceship Earth,' a metaphor for our planet where we must work together as a crew if we are to survive. I was further influenced by another professor, who had worked with Louis Kahn; he shared his thoughts on the integration of design with nature, buildings having great meaning, and terms such as silence and light.

After three years of college, I spent five years as a ski bum while working in a ski shop, completely immersing myself in the mountains, until the need for creativity drew me to Montana State University to complete my degree. As if predicting my career, Bozeman merged the best of both worlds: rigorous design in a beautiful place. It was there that I won a competition sponsored by Reynolds Aluminum for sustainable design. Applying careful analysis to an available resource, I designed a solar energy collector out of beer cans that gathered heat during the day and released it at night, using paraffin as a phase-change medium for energy storage. The concept is inexpensive and works in many different climates.

Seattle was a logical next destination. I liked the idea of living where you could power a boat with wind instead of an engine. In 1985, I joined Mithun, which already had a legacy for innovative technology, respect for the land, and the design of buildings that feel like the outdoors. The firm continues to follow a progressive philosophy, a pioneering attitude that translates lessons learned from previous projects into new successes with current projects.

Environmental stewardship is increasingly important as the changes occurring on our planet become clearer. Scientific research has revealed our world as a global system, and it drives me to find ways to merge science and design. Design provides the intuitive aspect of what makes great buildings, while understanding the cause-and-effect relationship of our actions, and gives us better options for making intelligent choices. For example, architects, civil engineers, biologists, and landscape designers must work together not only to create but also to restore habitats. I have a four-year old daughter. When she's approaching my age, the world's population will be 50 percent larger. We must do everything we can to deliver a healthy environment for future generations.

We're at a similar point in time around the world in terms of an awareness of environmental issues. Curitiba, Brazil, is a wonderful example of a major city incorporating innovative sustainable principles into its daily routines, developing incentives for cooperation that match the needs and culture of its citizens. Jamie Lerner, Curitiba's mayor and chief architect of the city's master plan, says, 'You teach the parents by teaching the children.' Mithun has pioneered the design of outdoor learning centers for children, such as IslandWood and Zoomazium in Seattle. The most important thing we can do is to help our kids to become environmental stewards themselves.

Leadership by example is the key to an individual's ability to import excitement regarding cool, great, thoughtful green design. As design leaders, we can offer infinite choices to clients. With the first line we draw, the first materials we specify, or the first type of energy or lightbulb we recommend, we can influence the future of the planet. Each one of us has the responsibility and the power to create positive change. On a personal level, we should start by calculating our individual carbon footprints and offset them, and then figure out a strategy to reduce them. (This can be done at www.climatetrust.org.)

I have moments of tremendous optimism, as well as moments of feeling overwhelmed by the magnitude of the challenges we're confronting. Buckminster Fuller trusted the ingenuity of humankind to overcome problems, and I see a lot of encouragement for a positive future. But we have to make it happen faster. It will take each of us as individual leaders to help power that rapid change."

Steve Badanes: Jersey Devil

As a practicing architect, Steve Badanes' commissions have included private homes, artist's studios, and the winning entry, "The Fremont Troll," in the Hall of Giants 1990 Competition in Seattle, Washington. For 25 years the members of Jersey Devil have been constructing their own designs while living on-site, in tents or Airstream trailers, and making adjustments to their structures in response to problems encountered during the building process.

Jersey Devil is a name that has been attached to work by Steve Badanes, John Ringel, Jim Adamson, or any combination of the above, plus other people who have participated in their diverse projects. This loose-knit group of designer-builders has created projects that eschew conventional practice, both the process of making architecture and the accepted definitions of architecture itself. Jersey Devil's architecture shows a concern for craft and detail, an attention to the expressiveness of the construction materials, and a strong environmental consciousness.

Photo courtesy of Steve Badanes.

"I'VE BEEN INSPIRED BY A LOT OF PEOPLE I'VE MET, ESPECIALLY TWO ELDERS OUTSIDE OF THE architectural community who have greatly inspired me. First, Toshiko Takaezu, a ceramic artist in New Jersey. She makes world-class art and beautiful food and grows amazing flowers—an integration of process that I love and admire.

The other is Meng Huang—an artist from Red China who worked in Hong Kong illegally building movie sets. On a trip back to China to see his family, he was caught, almost killed, his passport seized, and he spent 20 years in Red China where artists couldn't work. When I met up with him in Seattle where one of his children had helped to bring him, he was 70 and had filled his Section 8 apartment with incredible masks and creatures which he made out of cast offs & recycled garbage from American culture. Meng traveled with us on Jersey Devil jobs—to Hawaii, Palm Springs, Florida, and Mexico and built amazing work from construction scraps and taught school kids to make recycled art. The life he had lived in China could have destroyed many, but it made him stronger. He was always in a good mood and had a great sense of humor.

People are at the heart of what we do, not the architecture. Most architects and designers typically work at the top of the food chain. As architects, we are given a gift but we usually squander that gift on the top 2 percent of the population who can afford to hire an architect. That gift we have comes with social, political, and environmental responsibilities. Architecture has the potential to make all our lives better and should benefit everyone equally.

We're at a crisis point. We're now seeing that buildings are responsible for half of global warming. In the next 10 to 15 years, cars will become more efficient and we'll be manufacturing in more productive ways. However, buildings last 40 to 50 years, and we can't just replace them with bigger more inefficient versions. We've peaked in the production of oil and gas, and the only thing we have left is lots of coal, and of course, burning coal will accelerate global warming.

Architecture has the potential to harness environmental forces and give them form and to provide solutions to social problems. We need to meet the challenge and do it with sustainability and with social justice, to be the heroes who provide hope rather than the villains who exacerbate the problem.

There are those who have been good at pointing out a path—either the wrong one when we are screwing up, or the right one—Wendell Barry in Kentucky, and Malcolm Wells, father of underground buildings, and Margery Stoneman Douglas in the Florida Everglades.

I was born in New York and grew up in New Jersey. My dad was a builder, which influenced me early on. I realized I was good at art and mathematics and drew well, naturally gravitating to architecture—which can hopefully synthesize art and building. And although CAD is prevalent today, it's an abstraction of a hand drawing (which is already an abstraction of a building) and has less depth. Everyone's drawing looks the same when you press that print button. A hand-drawn sketch can be more individual and tap into emotions—the hand and the heart are connected and that bar of soap we push around often short circuits the connection.

I was in school in the late 60's, when the ecology movement was taking shape. Three of us created Jersey Devil right after graduation. We had no money, so we set up a shop at the university construction shop, which was a separate building on a remote part of campus. It was an intense time—the Bobby Kennedy and Martin Luther King Jr. assassinations, the Vietnam War, the civil rights movement, feminism, revolutionary music and lifestyles, polarization between the old and the young. We tried to take the political energy of the sixties—all our community-based design, environmental activism, and desire for social justice—and turn it into something useful for the environment.

I enjoy my work tremendously. Giving lectures about it is a great way to influence a lot of people in a positive way. In speaking—we take 30 years of work and pack it into an hour and half and can sugarcoat the message with humor rather than taking a strident "gloom and doom" approach to the environment.

I've found that engaging students in the real world design/build studios stimulates them at a deeper level and can change the course of their careers. In the Neighborhood Design Build Studio at the University of Washington, students design and build community facilities for nonprofit groups in Seattle. We built a library for Laotian refugees who had escaped their villages that had been burned and bombed after the Vietnam War, and had relocated to Seattle. We have also taken teams of students to work in impoverished international communities in Mexico, Cuba, Ghana, and India. These projects provide empathy and understanding for other cultures, and gives students a positive experience of teamwork and hands on skills; however, the skilled workers in these countries often earn only a few dollars a day. In the United States, where laborers can earn $25 an hour or more and skilled workers far more, student labor can make a huge difference on outreach projects here, without the embodied energy of shipping them half way around the world. The old saying "think globally, act locally" is a great guidepost.

There is a need to make people both laugh and think, for us to become heroes and provide hope. Do I feel that I inspire others? I've heard that I do. I'll hear from former students, *"I just completed a great project, your class gave me the courage to do something different."* That inspires me, keeps me going, makes me feel good when an awful lot of things seem to be going wrong.

I'd like to be remembered as someone who stuck to my guns and didn't sell out. That's not particularly the only thing I'd like to be known for, but even now it is gratifying to look back and know that, 25 years later, we were on the right path. I'd tell you to have a positive attitude, have a sense of humor, don't take yourself too seriously. And that being involved in the design profession is a gift, with social and environmental obligations. Have fun doing it; if you can't laugh about it, it's not worth doing.

Without art or nature—there isn't much anyway. Thanks!"

Ray C. Anderson: Midcourse Correction

Ray C. Anderson is chairman and CEO of Atlanta-based Interface, Inc. and the author of Mid-Course Correction: The Interface Model *(Atlanta: Peregrinzilla Press, 1999).*

Since the days following his graduation from Georgia Institute of Technology as an industrial engineer, Ray Anderson has quietly gone about fostering an entrepreneurial spirit that has resulted in his building one of the world's largest commercial interior furnishings companies. After founding Interface in 1973, Ray and his company have revolutionized the carpet and floor-covering industry. Now, Ray has embarked on a mission to make Interface a sustainable corporation by leading a worldwide war on waste and pioneering the processes of sustainable development.

Photo courtesy of Ray C. Anderson.

"WHEN I WAS 60 YEARS OLD, AND MY COMPANY, INTERFACE, BASED IN ATLANTA, GEORGIA, was 21 years old, we started hearing rumblings from our customers, 'When it comes to the environment, Interface just doesn't get it.' As I look back now at how I responded to that assertion, I am amused that I asked, 'Interface doesn't get what?'

More than 10 years and a sea of change later, that same company, the world's largest manufacturer of commercial carpet and other interior finishes, is a leader in industrial ecology: It is a company on a different course, developing new technologies and rethinking everything we do, from the way we source raw materials and manufacture our products, to how we sample, transport, install, maintain and—importantly— reclaim them.

Back in 1994, I wasn't all that different from most industrialists. What put me on a different path was reading a book, Paul Hawken's *The Ecology of Commerce* (1994).

His thesis, that the Earth and all natural systems are in decline, and that business and industry are the biggest culprits, and also the only forces pervasive and powerful enough to reverse the decline, was at once crystal clear and completely compelling. I have described it as a 'spear in the chest,' a painful, powerful awakening.

As I read Hawken's book, I was dumbfounded by how much I did not know about the environment and the impacts of the industrial system on the environment—the industrial system of which I and my 'successful' company were an integral part. A new definition of success began to creep into my consciousness, and a latent sense of legacy asserted itself. I got it. I was a plunderer of Earth, and that is not the legacy one wants to leave behind.

Today, I remember clearly the visceral nature of my own awakening, and I have come to believe that the transformation of society into a sustainable society for the indefinite future depends totally and absolutely on a vast mind-shift, a shift that will happen one mind at a time, one organization at a time, one technology, one building, one company, one university curriculum, one community, one region, one industry at a time, until the entire system coexists in ethical balance with Earth's natural systems.

The fundamental realization behind this transformation is that industrialism—of which we are each a part—developed in a different world from the one we live in today: fewer people, more plentiful natural resources, simpler lifestyles. The resultant take-make-waste system, so common today, simply cannot go on and on and on in a finite world with increasing population and diminishing resources.

At Interface, our journey began when our customers asked us a question. Now I ask you: When will your journey begin?"

CHAPTER 3

inspiring projects

A dhering to sustainable guidelines, these inspiring homes exemplify the fact that eco-friendly designs can also be cost-effective, functional, and beautiful. In the hands of creative designers, earth-friendly materials provide a richness of experience and delight, as they echo the natural world. Enjoy.

Arkin Tilt Architects, Berkeley, CA

© 2004 Edward Caldwell.
Architect: Arkin Tilt
Architects.

See color insert

THE OWNERS SPENT A YEAR EXPLORING AND FALLING IN LOVE WITH THEIR LAND—A 20-ACRE parcel that rises steeply on the east face of the Lovall Valley in northern California—before retaining the services of Arkin Tilt. They wanted a house that was both glamorous and ecological, a place for both contemplation and celebration. Most importantly, they wanted a "villa" that took advantage of the spectacular site without negating it. With a limited budget, each decision was scrutinized for value.

Hidden from view from the valley floor, the residence nestles above a saddle in the land, tucked behind a small tree-crowned knoll. The program is split between four individual structures to take advantage of the views and to reinforce connection with the site: vistas are framed by the classic oak and grass landscape and the spectacular views both west toward Sonoma and south toward San Francisco. Organized along the contour of the hill, the rooms create places of privacy while defining outdoor spaces that focus outward. Each space balances view and solar gain with careful window placement and shading devices; even the tower is located to create afternoon shade at the pool terrace.

On a north-south axis, to fit into the hillside, and opening up to the western view, the great room presented a passive solar challenge. The doors to the west are shaded by a deep loggia, the roof of which bounces light through the high windows to illuminate the ceiling. By holding down the roof of the kitchen, a high south-facing window allows daylight and low winter sun deep into the space. A dormer in the kitchen both adds daylight and relief from the lower ceiling.

The main spaces are of sprayed earth construction (a.k.a. PISE). Taking advantage of diurnal temperature fluctuations, the 18-inch-thick earthen walls provide both thermal moderation as well as a rich, patina finish. The sprayed earth forms site retaining walls as the structure cuts into the hill. For drama, a more labor-intensive rammed earth is used at the fireplace and loggia columns. A modern version of an ancient building system, the earthen walls give the structure a timeless quality. These thick walls are topped with a roof structure of recycled fir trusses and cypress ceiling decking salvaged from pickle barrels.

Drawn from the agrarian California vernacular, wood-framed secondary spaces are clad in plywood and batten and—in a few key locations—slatted salvaged cedar "cribbing." While serving as a counterpoint to the earthen spaces, these "add-ons" also have the practical advantage of keeping the plumbing out of the sprayed earth walls and keeping the overall cost of the project down. The carport and propane enclosure are also cribbed. The spaced boards allow for plenty of ventilation while providing a visual screen.

Stained concrete floors and the natural walls are balanced by a rich collection of salvaged materials—such as a recycled glass countertop and a piece of a bowling alley lane—chosen for their durability as well for their sustainability.

One recent guest wrote: "The irony for me was [that by] getting away from cell phones, beepers, e-mail and voice mail, I was able to find connection—to [my partner], to nature, and myself.

This is a sacred place that allows and encourages the spirit to come forth and be present in so many ways—in quiet solitude (not loneliness), in intimacy, and in good fellowship. Unlike other retreats, it offers focus rather than distraction. It gets you to look beyond the struggles—not just to avoid them for awhile—and know that there are wonderful places and ways to be in this world in spite of the struggles."

Eric Logan, Carney Architects, Jackson Hole, WY

See color insert

Photo by Paul Warchol. Architect: Eric Logan, Carney Architects.

THE PROJECT PARAMETERS FOR THIS NEW RESIDENCE, NESTLED INTO AN ASPEN GROVE AT THE base of the Teton mountain range, included a desire for a building that offered a better connection to its pristine site, one less literally derived from the traditional western vernacular of the previous log structure and one that could be built on a very tight budget (a major challenge to meet in rapidly growing Jackson Hole, Wyoming).

The first floor contains two guest rooms, a full bath, laundry room, and storage for sports gear. The front door, off of the cedar-screened porch, opens to an entry, flanked on the left by a closet for coats and shoes. Ahead, a dramatic staircase, constructed of Parallam stringers and treads, leads to the main floor above. On the south face, two-story glazing, composed of standard windows in varying sizes, floods the staircase hall with natural daylight.

Upstairs, the open-plan living, dining, and kitchen areas are in the west wing. A floor-to-ceiling glass corner opens to the deck above the entrance porch. The remainder of the second level is given over to a master bedroom and bath. The Breueresque bay window, which the architect added to enliven the exterior, has, unexpectedly, helped to modulate the interior space as well.

Eco-materials in the residence include concrete floors embedded with radiant heating and finished with linseed oil sealer, low-emissivity (low-e) insulated glazing throughout, walls and ceilings of recycled-content medium-density fiberboard (MDF), and recyclable aluminum countertops.

Eric Logan, Carney Architects, Jackson Hole, WY

Photo by Greg Hursley. Architect: Eric Logan, Carney Architects.

See color insert

THIS PROJECT FULFILLED THE ARCHITECT'S LONGSTANDING WISH TO DESIGN AND BUILD A home for his family. The site, on a sagebrush plain just north of Jackson, Wyoming, commanded 260-degree views of the Teton and Gros Ventre mountain ranges, which define Jackson Hole. As architect, client, and general contractor for Logan Pavilion, his hope was to design an appropriate and eloquent house for the site, and to build it on the incredibly tight budget of $75/square foot and with a very aggressive construction schedule. This budget would be difficult to meet in the inflated economy of the Jackson Hole resort community.

The goal was to create a home that belonged in the western landscape but whose design would not be mediated by conventional rustic notions. Of necessity, the building's structure would be simple. By choice, that structure would be clearly and explicitly expressed. It would borrow its form from the simplest of vernacular structures: the hay shed, whose plain gable, held aloft on tall columns, has always been seen as a symbol for shelter.

Manufactured and recycled materials, carefully chosen and deliberately detailed, would give the interior a modern look. The oiled masonite wall paneling, raw MDF cabinetry, and oiled concrete floor were interior finish solutions that allowed inexpensive materials, commonly disguised or consigned to the back room, to hold their own.

Much thought was given to connections and connectors. By choosing them carefully and exposing them to view, the clarity of the structure would be enhanced and a design element would be added to simple surfaces. Elsewhere, as in the hanging, slide-aside garage doors, solutions were found that were more direct and obvious than the usual.

David Bergman, New York, NY

© 2006 David Bergman.
Architect: David Bergman.

See color insert

THE RENOVATION OF THE LIVING AREA OF THIS UPPER EAST SIDE MANHATTAN APARTMENT was prompted by the clients' desire to break open the apartment's typical New York City enclosed kitchen by opening to a combined living, dining, and home office space, creating a "miniloft" experience within a standard postwar high-rise unit. The clients' other primary request was for an environment rich in color, expressing their collections of colorful glass objects and other accessories. Environmental issues were not on their radar until the architect showed them the diverse and exciting material possibilities that could match their aesthetic.

The design concept revolves around creating a unified space while simultaneously making a home office zone within the open area that is also perceived independently from the kitchen. This is accomplished by having the cabinetry transition gradually, rather than break abruptly, with overlapping areas, from kitchen cabinets to shelving and desks. By extending the kitchen uppers partway into the office area, adding a custom pocket-swing door of brightly colored eco-resin and hiding a file storage cabinet behind, a sense of division is implied. The resin door is echoed by a sliding panel of the same material, which hides the broom closet at the opposite side of the kitchen. Further enhancing the flexibility of the space, the island cabinet is built on casters.

Eco-materials are, from the bottom up, a new cork floor with random maroon stained tiles dotting a field of natural dark cork. Cabinetry was built of wheatboard cores and non-VOC finishes (including the color stain on the desk surround). Countertops (aside from the natural stone on the island) are a composite of green recycled glass and cement. Kitchen backsplash tiles are of recycled glass. The desktops are a deep blue linoleum. The blue panels forming the closet and the file area doors are constructed of eco-resin. Paints are water soluble and low VOC.

Doug Graybeal, Graybeal Architects, Carbondale, CO

LOCATED OUTSIDE OF CARBONDALE, COLORADO, THIS RECENTLY COMPLETED RESIDENCE was designed by an architect for himself and his wife, both self-employed, work-at-home professionals. The project goal was to be as energy-efficient and environmentally friendly as possible within a reasonable budget. At an altitude of 7,000 feet, in a dry mountain environment, the architecture is both responsive to the climate and reflective of the local mountain vernacular. Building forms and materials were selected to work and blend with the natural surroundings. The environmental impact of each building component, including delivery distance, was reviewed.

The structure is heated by passive solar energy and designed to maximize the outstanding southern views of the Elk Mountain range. Concrete floors provide thermal mass and incorporate radiant heat tubes for the backup conventional heating system (as required by mortgage companies). A 2-foot-thick cast earth wall provides additional thermal mass for heating and cool tempering of the structure. This wall also divides living spaces from secondary uses. During the design process, computer modeling showed a 3°F to 5°F temperature swing in the home year-round, without the

Photo by Doug Graybeal.
Architect: Doug Graybeal.

See color insert

use of conventional heating or cooling systems. The calculated temperature swing has proven to be correct. The temperature in the house during the cold winter construction, with outdoor temperatures below zero, ranged from a low of 35°F to an average daytime high of 50°F-plus. Minimal supplemental heat was used during two extremely cold weeks in January. The house is maintaining 73°F to 76°F temperatures during warm—90°F—summer days. Photovoltaic panels should provide approximately 50 percent of the electrical needs and are running the utility meter backward during daytime energy gains.

An attached solar greenhouse provides year-round vegetables. Water tubes and circulation of hot air from the top of the greenhouse through rock beds under the planting soils keeps the greenhouse comfortable for plant growth year-round.

Green design, or environmentally friendly, features of the house include: cast earth interior walls; straw-bale exterior walls; concrete floors with radiant heat; energy-efficient lighting, including daylighting; formaldehyde-free cabinetry; water-saving plumbing fixtures; and ENERGY STAR-rated appliances.

A majority of the project goals were achieved, and only time will tell how the house performs. So far, so good. The house is a wonderful space to live in, and the use of the natural materials has made it a warm, cozy, and comfortable home.

Baker Laporte & Associates, Tesuque, NM

Photo by Laurie E. Dickson.
Architect: Baker Laporte &
Associates.

See color insert

THIS NEW MEXICAN GUEST HOUSE WAS DESIGNED AS AN EXAMPLE OF SUSTAINABLE construction. As such, the goals in creating it were threefold: to promote good health and comfort for the occupants; to use construction materials and techniques with low environmental impact; and to design in harmony with nature by making use of sun, wind, vegetation, and water to reduce energy consumption and pollution in the completed home.

The structure, a Japanese style timber frame with dowelled joinery, is made from lumber that has been sustainably harvested in northern New Mexico. The timber frame is used to define the individual spaces while keeping them open to one another, facilitating a spacious feeling in a small space.

A 12-inch-thick exterior wall system of a rammed straw and clay mixture (known as light straw-clay construction) surround the structure, creating an energy-efficient envelope with an approximate R-value of 24. Weighing approximately 50 pounds per cubic foot, the wall provides both mass and insulation for year-round comfort. The walls are plastered with earth-based plasters both inside and out.

A 4-foot roof overhang and stone plinth protects the mud plasters and natural wall system from the elements. The sun bump projects out toward the edge of the overhang, providing winter solar gain while remaining shaded during the summer. Very little additional heating is required in the winter. Ample cross ventilation, extra roof insulation, and shading roof overhangs keep the home comfortably cool in the heat of summer without the need for air conditioning. A roof gutter system directs runoff into a 3,000-gallon cistern; this runoff is used to water the gardens.

Nontoxic and natural building materials, finishes, furnishings, and cleaning products have been used in the construction and maintenance of the home. Materials include formaldehyde-free cabinetry, natural slate flooring at the entry, sun bump and bathrooms, and natural wax finishes on the maple flooring. Furnishings are solid wood pieces from Chas Moser and custom site-built built-ins of solid wood. Banco seating and pillows were locally made using organic cotton batting and hemp covers. All interior plasters are clay-based, with colors derived from natural pigments mixed on-site.

Two aspects of ecologically sound architecture are building small and building to last. As the ancient European and Japanese predecessors exemplify, a timber frame home is built to last for centuries. When its useful life comes to an end, the straw/clay walls and earthen plasters, if demolished, will decompose into nontoxic organic matter, and the timber frame structure can be disassembled and reused.

Hagman Architects, Basalt, CO

See color insert

Used by permission of My House Magazine.
Photo by Mikel Covey.
Architect: Hagman Architects.

THIS HOUSE IN THE ROARING FORK VALLEY OF COLORADO SITS ON A SAGE- AND scrub-oak-covered knoll with 360-degree views of snowcapped peaks, rolling meadows, and red rock ridges. The first home that was designed for the lot was double the size and consisted of three separate buildings. The more the clients learned about environmentally sensitive construction, however, the more it made sense for them to build a sustainable house that fit into the land. They decided to scale down the size and look at ways to incorporate energy-efficient techniques and materials, such as straw bales, without sacrificing the design.

The new set of plans was for a modern trilevel home that tiered into the land, featured straw bale walls, and called for poured concrete and renewable bamboo flooring and hand-troweled stucco siding. The new design was much smaller, simpler, and more straightforward than the original, with a curved roof reminiscent of local historic Victorian barns. The home was oriented to the south to capture sunlight and solar potential, and the living room and master bedroom levels were set high to take advantage of the views.

Eco-materials include bamboo stairs, softly rounded straw bale walls with truth window, 19-foot birch ply ceilings, poured concrete floors and countertops, and hand-hewn cabinets by Neil Kelly, in Portland, Oregon. The fact that the home coexists within the environment so well makes it an even better fit.

Lydia Corser, Eco Interiors, Santa Cruz, CA

Photo by Emily Hagopian,
www.essentialimages.us.
Designer: Lydia Corser.

See color insert

THE INTERIOR DESIGNER HAD LONG DREAMED OF WORKING ON AN ECO-FRIENDLY KITCHEN project. It would be an elegant example of earth- and health-friendly design, where the elements that made it so weren't necessarily what impressed people. Finally, in Santa Cruz, California, there came an opportunity for her to work with those materials that were lesser known, possibly controversial, newer on the market, and always, always green.

Originally a tiny 7-by-10-foot galley space, the kitchen was expanded to what seemed a luxurious 10 by 12 feet. Transom windows were added along the south side, along with an opening into the dining room, bringing light throughout that formerly dark space. The kitchen became a pass-through area on the way into the house from the garage, and a window facing out to a beautifully landscaped backyard slid over to better access that view from the sink.

Eco-materials include cabinetry from Neil Kelly, in Portland, Oregon. The cabinet boxes were fabricated from wheatboard, a nonformaldehyde content particleboard of agricultural waste. The doors were crafted of certified, sustainably harvested cherry. Some of the old cabinets were donated to a nonprofit organization working with elderly housing. Others were reused in the garage-laundry room. None went to the landfill.

Some of the recessed panels at the base cabinets, as well as the bottom panel of the refrigerator, incorporated agriboard made from recycled sunflower seed hulls. The floor is natural linoleum; backsplash tiles are 100 percent recycled glass; and the sink and baking area countertop are manufactured from compressed, recycled paper and resin. Reclaimed California walnut was remilled and used as trim above, below, and between stacked wall cabinets and at the raised countertop behind the cooktop. All lumber was Forest Stewardship Council (FSC) certified, and the insulation in the walls and under the floor was made from denim scraps from the clothing manufacturing industry. Appliances are ENERGY STAR-rated wherever possible. The walls and ceiling were hand-plastered with integral colored plaster, and then sealed with a natural oil product, as were the walnut details and window moldings.

donnalynn Design and Interiors, El Granada, CA

THE CHALLENGES OF THIS SOUTHERN CALIFORNIA RENOVATION PROJECT WERE APPARENT. HOW to improve usability? How to progress from utilitarian to functional? How to create space without physically creating space? And to do this by utilizing as many green products and principles of green design as possible, while making a statement of beauty.

The project began in the dark, constricted entry area, which had limited access and functionality. It was separated from the similarly uninviting and semi-functional, galley-type kitchen by a non-structural wall. This wall was removed to create additional space and allow daylighting to enhance both areas.

A distracting bank of upper cabinets, including an obtrusive overhang, were removed and reused at the entry wall, creating a functional and pleasing artifact. The new, open, user-friendly kitchen area was embellished by sustainable bamboo cabinetry, paper and resin countertops, and linoleum flooring. Natural paints, with eucalyptus and

*Photo by swaffordimaging.com.
Designer: donnalynn Design and
Interiors.*

See color insert

rosemary pigments, highlight all the way through from the kitchen to the great room on this level.

Bathrooms were dated, cramped, and visually unappealing. The master bath, traditional but contemporary, is now more open and easily incorporates an additional sink and multiple storage spaces. Low-voltage lighting accentuates unencumbered shelf space, drawers, under the table sinks, bamboo cabinetry and tumbled river rock flooring with ceramic inserts. "Green" additions on the upstairs level include (FSC) white tiger-wood stairs and flooring, wool carpet with eco-friendly padding, and (Homasote) sound barrier underlayment made from 100% recycled wood fiber material.

Annette Stelnack, Associates III, Denver, CO

The challenge on this renovation project was to unify the floor plan of a home that had been victim to years of add-ons and enlargements, rendering it dysfunctional and stylistically confused within. The owners envisioned a contemporary family home reflecting the natural, organic beauty of their rural Colorado surroundings. Encouraged by the design team, they embraced the opportunity to create a healthy, environmentally friendly home using an eco-sensitive approach.

The clients wanted all products and materials that were removed from the original residence to find new homes, so that nothing went to the landfill. The original doors, cabinetry, plumbing fixtures, and fittings were conscientiously removed and donated

See color insert

Photo by David O. Marlow.
Designer: Associates III.

to ReSource, a local recycling center in the community, for reuse. The older furnishings were given to Habitat for Humanity, and other pieces were passed along to friends. Throughout the construction process, waste was saved, sorted, and recycled.

Care was taken at every level to incorporate environmentally sound practices and products. Special attention was paid to indoor air quality (IAQ) issues. An efficient hot water radiant heating system was chosen over a more typical forced-air HVAC system. It operates using a high-efficiency boiler, a well-insulated storage tank, and a recirculation loop to save water. ENERGY STAR appliances and thermostats, programmed by region, save energy throughout the home.

The interiors reflect the understated, earthy quality of the high desert plains location, incorporating organically inspired tones and textures. To complement the contemporary theme, natural integral colored plaster walls and ceilings throughout, a palette of low-VOC paints, and locally manufactured art glass panels establish a warm setting.

Interior finishes include European white beech millwork, locally manufactured sycamore and myrtle cabinetry with water-based finishes, readily renewable bamboo floors flanked by durable limestone and glazed concrete floors, and wool, jute-backed area rugs. The bathrooms incorporate low-flow dual-flush toilets, efficient bath fittings, and cradle-to-cradle glass tile and countertops, all applied with low-VOC adhesives and grout.

From the site and landscaping to the exterior and interior materials, each element added to the home was carefully considered, with an eye toward sustainability.

The success of the project is a direct reflection of the collaboration among all of the design disciplines and, most importantly, the team's commitment to a renovation that incorporates a strong environmental focus.

greening projects

Photo by Cesar Rubio.
Architect: John Cary.

Earth provides enough to satisfy every man's need, but not every man's greed.
—MOHANDAS K. GANDHI, QUOTED IN E. F. SCHUMACHER, *SMALL IS BEAUTIFUL*

Getting Started on a Green Project

The world of design is about making statements. What if we designers regarded each project as a platform, from which we could not only serve client needs and enhance design expertise but also achieve the greater objective of saving the environment?

Within the interior design industry, the choices we make on each project have far-reaching consequences for the near and distant future. By making sustainable choices, we can, without a doubt, help to ensure that we *have* a future. In this way, we can make our planet's continued existence the fundamental component in the design process, along with raising awareness that building environmentally is critical to sustaining our natural resources, air and water quality, and energy sources. Therein lies the principle value for doing good: sustainable design is sustaining life.

More and more evidence demonstrates the many benefits possible from designing and building using sustainable principles and practices:

- Lower dependency on foreign energy sources.
- Improved indoor air quality.
- Improved materials and products.
- Higher-quality, longer-life materials.
- Increased fresh air filtration in buildings.
- Improved operations and maintenance in buildings.
- Prevention of pollution and waste generation.
- Increased recycling of building materials.
- Materials from sustainable resources.
- Reduced landfill disposal, waste incineration, and associated pollution.
- Increased energy efficiency.
- Resource conservation and management.
- Conservation of precious water.
- Improved lighting quality.
- Lower operating costs.
- Higher comfort level.
- Healthier indoor environment.
- Reduced life-cycle costs.
- Stewardship for future generations.
- Increased property value.

Once you have made a personal and professional commitment to embrace sustainable design principles, it is time to apply this decision to your practice. But for that, you need education—knowledge.

EDUCATING YOURSELF

Educating yourself, gaining the knowledge available in the field of sustainable interior design, is crucial to moving forward. Your education can take many forms. For example, invite environmental consultants in for brown bag lunches, attend conferences, research products, surf the Internet, align with like-minded individuals, read books and publications that address sustainable strategies in the realm of interior design, and investigate local groups offering programs on sustainable design.

Once you have a firm grasp on the underlying principles of green design, as a natural next step, you can begin to integrate them so they become an intuitive part of the process. Consider, as starting points, incorporating the following principles in the overall design of your projects:

- Minimize the size of a residence.
- Integrate design aspects for diverse function, adaptive reuse, and/or disassembly.
- Design for climate and region.
- Design for durability and longevity.
- Specify materials that use resources most efficiently.
- Use local and regional resources.
- Use products with recycled or salvaged content.
- Specify the least toxic materials and manufacturing processes available.
- Integrate energy conservation and direct solar energy collection or passive solar, such as daylighting.
- Consider alternative energy sources such as wind power.
- Specify alternative, environmentally friendly materials made from renewable content.
- Design for optimal indoor air quality and human health.
- Specify woods from sustainable forestry.
- Research and specify products that are recyclable.
- Adopt the seven Rs: reduce, reuse, recycle, recover, repair, remove, and respect.
- Integrate water conservation strategies.

Next, begin to research the attributes of the products you are considering for inclusion in your specifications. To that end, seek out those products that emit low or no VOCs. Information is readily available through manufacturers. Learn to interpret the material safety data sheet (MSDS) for each product and to understand its components. (Chapter 5, "Greening Specifications," has more information about MSDS.)

With greater awareness and comprehension of these products you will reach a heightened comfort level in specifying and working with them. Step by step, your experience will transform into knowledge, and vice versa. The voice, your voice, of sustainable design will emerge.

When a new project is pending, get involved as early as possible; introduce the subject of sustainability at the outset—ideally, during the schematic design phase of the architectural planning. Address sustainability with the entire team—client, architect, and contractor—to encourage the early adoption of an environmental focus on the project. From that point on, you can proceed as an integrated team to establish the mission, vision, and goals for the project.

ESTABLISHING THE PROJECT MISSION, VISION, AND GOALS

A successful team generates synergy. Set the tone and gain commitment from all members of the project team by holding a kickoff meeting, where the team, together, develops the project mission, vision, and goals.

The mission, reflecting foresight and vision, provides the overarching incentive that charges the design and construction team to move forward. To establish the mission, the team should brainstorm and agree upon the organizing principles of the project, as these will ultimately lead to the creation of goals.

Goals establishment, the next stage in the process, will help to determine the sustainable design parameters of the project. They should be stated to ensure that everyone rallies to support and achieve them. To that end, when planning the project goals, combine the client's programming and functional requirements and design vernacular with an emphasis on the environmental and health impacts to the family, community, and ecological systems. Initiate brainstorming sessions to determine how you plan to develop the green principles outlined previously and how to effectively incorporate these strategies into the project. Examples of straightforward goal statements are:

- Establish budget parameters.
- Adopt an integrated design approach.
- Assign an environmental champion.
- Quantify measurements of sustainable success.
- Design for energy conservation.
- Integrate renewable resources.
- Plan for construction waste management.

Interior designers can make a significant impact on a project by volunteering to be the environmental champions. By taking on this role, we are charged to question how we, as a team, are practicing environmental responsibility throughout the project. Doing so steps up the implementation of environmental principles and practices and is an effective way to test the status quo by raising the bar of environmental performance.

Integrated Design Approach and Criteria

There has been a lot of talk recently about "integrated design." This is an interconnected approach that centers on how to engage all disciplines in doing the work as a committed, coordinated, and collaborative team.

To successfully create a high-performance residence, an interactive approach to the design process is essential. The central philosophy behind integrated design is to require all individuals responsible for the design and construction of the home to interact closely with each other throughout the process, from the inception of design to construction through completion. This differs from a traditional tack where the client, architects, engineers, designers, contractors, and consultants talk to each other only periodically or occasionally attend the same meetings. Under an integrated approach, each individual involved in the design, construction, operation, and its use, spends time together to ensure that everyone fully comprehends the issues and concerns of all other parties.

Integrated design, also sometimes called "whole systems thinking," creates a platform for taking a holistic approach to the design of a project. According to Merriam-Webster's dictionary, "holistic" relates to or is concerned with wholes or with complete systems, rather than with the analysis of, treatment of, or dissection into parts. For example, holistic medicine attempts to treat the mind as well as the body, and holistic ecology views humans and the environment as a single system. The AIA defines whole systems thinking, or integrated design, as promoting the development and application of innovative designs and collaborative processes intended to improve environmental performance.

The primary challenge of a holistic design approach is to ensure that everyone involved in a project understands that all building systems are interdependent. By interconnecting the materials, the systems and products of a building overlap; the result is a successful whole buildings design whose result is greater than the sum of its parts.

This design approach asks all members of the team to look at the materials, systems, and assemblies from different perspectives. The design is evaluated at all levels, including, but not limited to, quality-of-life and health, future flexibility, efficiencies, costs, environmental impacts, creativity, and indoor air quality. A review of interdependencies in this way produces a more effective, healthier, and more cost-efficient house. For example, the mechanical system might impact the indoor air quality, the ease of maintenance, global climate change, operating costs, whether the windows are operable and, in turn, what type of window coverings to use. Similarly, the size of the mechanical system would take into account how the space should be organized, the type of lighting system to use, the availability of natural daylight, the finishes and materials to specify, and the local climate.

THE CHARRETTE

Invite everyone who is significant to the success of the project to the first all-inclusive design meeting, or *charrette*. At minimum, the client, architect, mechanical engineer, interior designer, lighting consultant, and contractor should be part of this first meeting.

Typically, a charrette is a collaborative and interactive brainstorming session that establishes an open forum for exchanging ideas and information, thereby allowing integrated solutions to be considered and to take shape. Each team member is given the floor, in turn, for the purpose of exchanging ideas and discussing problems within and beyond his or her field of expertise. This interactive approach establishes a team culture early on and engenders respect for all participants.

Ideally, several charrettes will be held throughout the key phases of the design process to ensure that the group efforts are on track and meeting or exceeding goals.

As part of the process, participants have the opportunity to become further educated about the issues, to better enable them to "buy in" to the schematic solutions. This, then, becomes a collective wisdom, which expedites the design development, because issues can be identified more quickly and problems solved more readily.

Another benefit of the charrette process is that all attendees connect with one another, as well as the project mission; they begin to inspire each other to meet the agreed-upon environmental goals: to integrate sustainable designs into the work and collaborate with the entire team. This leads to two other projectwide benefits: lower costs and, most importantly, high-performance, healthy buildings. Ultimately, this enables professionals, working together, to transform the industry one building at a time through harmonious, holistic designs.

Compare these outcomes to those that result from thinking and working on an insular level, which isolates professionals from each other and the bigger picture. When we aim to create integrated, holistic designs, which take into account all players and disciplines on a project, the process becomes thoughtful and filled with intention, with project goals clearly in mind at all times. This is a worthy journey, one that leads to success.

CHALLENGES OF INTEGRATION

Working on a project where the team collaborates as described above is a greatly rewarding experience. But there will also be challenges that arise, and these, too, must be recognized from the outset so that they do not delay or derail the project.

In particular, occasionally, individual team members will be resistant to change from the traditional approach. When this happens, first remind the team of the mission and goals of the project. Solicit the help of the environmental champion, or call upon a team member who has had experience in the area of contention to share how he or she has previously addressed the issue. For example, perhaps a contractor or subcontractor is hesitant to use a water-based finish that has been specified. Here are some possible approaches:

- Provide the contractor/subcontractor with a quart of the alternative material to test (and abuse) in the field prior to applying it to the entire project.

- Ask a supplier to substantiate, to stand behind, the product, to ease concerns about the product's performance.

- Bring in an expert to work with the contractor/subcontractor, to demonstrate how new methods can be used successfully in lieu of traditional and often unhealthy ways.

- If there is a language barrier, provide specifications and instructions in the contractor's/subcontractor's native language. This not only demonstrates respect but will also serve to facilitate an open exchange of ideas and solutions.

- If relevant, explain the personal health benefits of using the product in question. Note that by specifying products that are less toxic and healthier to live with, this also shows concern for the health of the workers in the field, who are applying and installing these products.

Interior Designer's Role

Conviction, passion, and creativity are integral to the character of interior designers who are committed to sustainable design, enabling them to craft environments and products that look good, last long, function well, enrich lives, and support client needs. Traditional practice, which thoughtlessly takes from the earth to make products and buildings for a single purpose, produces an inordinate amount of waste. Sustainable design shifts the perspective to one that respects and works in tandem with nature, supports abundance, and is economically viable. This groundbreaking trend, which represents a transformation to a new business model of environmental effectiveness, has been eloquently described by William McDonough and Michael Braungart from McDonough Braungart Design Chemistry. They point us in this new direction by first taking into account the outcome from the Industrial Revolution:

> Consider looking at the Industrial Revolution of the nineteenth century and its aftermath as a kind of retroactive design assignment, focusing on some of its unintended, questionable effects. The assignment might sound like this.
>
>   Design a system of production that:
>
> - Puts billions of pounds of toxic material into the air, water, and soil every year.
> - Produces some materials so dangerous they will require constant vigilance by future generations.
> - Results in gigantic amounts of waste.
> - Puts valuable materials in holes all over the planet, where they can never be retrieved.
> - Requires thousands of complex regulations to keep people and natural systems from being poisoned too quickly.
> - Measures productivity by how few people are working.
> - Creates prosperity by digging up or cutting down natural resources and then burying or burning them.
> - Erodes the diversity of species and cultural practices.
>
> Does this seem like a good design assignment?
>
>   Even though none of these things happened intentionally, we find this "design assignment" to be a limited and depressing one for industries to perpetuate—and it is obviously resulting in a much less enjoyable world.
>
>   We are proposing a new design assignment where people and industries set out to create the following:
>
> - Buildings that, like trees, are net energy exporters, produce more energy than they consume, accrue and store solar energy, and purify their own waste water and release slowly in a purer form.
> - Factory-effluent water that is cleaner than the influent.
> - Products that, when their useful life is over, do not become useless waste, but can be tossed onto the ground to decompose and become food for plants and animals, rebuilding soil; or, alternately, return to industrial cycles to supply high-quality raw materials for new products.
> - Billions, even trillions of dollars worth of materials accrued for human and natural purposes each year.
> - A world of abundance, not one of limits, pollution, and waste.
>
> Welcome to the next industrial revolution.

McDonough and Braungart's words are inspiring! Where do you begin? One place might be to look at what you are already doing that makes an environmental difference, and reach first for the "low-hanging fruit." This translates to taking the simple, easier steps until your comfort level begins to rise. Then, on your next project, perhaps research and specify low-VOC paints and natural carpet. As you become more confident, continue to build on your experiences and successes. Consider using nontoxic adhesives and water-based finishes. Next jump into the world of renewable materials and explore the variety of options that can be offered to the client. Use your designer's creativity to continue to push the envelope.

On project teams, embody the role of collaborator and environmental champion with the client, consultants, contractor, and architect. Become the ecological cheerleader, rallying the team as they gain knowledge and experience. Learn together; invite experts in the field to coach all the players through process stages where knowledge or experience is lacking, or where adversity, in the form of the aforementioned challenges, presents itself.

Volunteer to examine the goals and guidelines on a monthly basis to ensure that the project is on track and progressing. As you become well informed and comfortable with the principles and practices of green design, educating clients and collaborators will further increase your abilities and establish you as a credible resource within the arena of sustainable design.

The quality of life for future generations lies in the palms of our hands. Contributing to the well-being of all contributes to our own. On a daily basis we can support the continuation and improve the quality of life on this planet. And while on this course of action, we will become more fulfilled as human beings. We invite you to choose to make a difference through your work in interior design.

Job-Site Procedures

A true green building must include a waste-reduction plan, one that has to be managed from the inception of the project design through its completion. A comprehensive approach addresses more than construction and demolition debris management—that is, recycling on the project site. It challenges us to look at conserving resources *during* design, making use of recycled content products and salvaging valuable materials removed during demolition.

To help in this regard, it's a good idea to encourage the involvement of environmental consultants. Bring them to the job site so that carpenters and other tradespeople can learn new, improved, and healthier techniques and applications. Schedule brown bag lunches with the construction team to share ideas; and never stop asking whether there are better, more sustaining or healthier ways to fabricate residences.

It is also important to work with the contractor to develop waste management strategies and resources to assist in the diversion of construction and demolition (C&D) materials from landfills. Compile a list of materials for which recycling programs are relatively easy to find, such as cardboard, clean dimensional wood, beverage containers, land-clearing debris, concrete, bricks, concrete masonry units (CMU), asphalt, and metals from various sources.

From the outset of the major phases of construction, brainstorm with the construction team to decide on strategies and agree on solutions. Request signage designating job-site policies; make sure these are translated into all languages used on the job site. Set up discussions to solicit best practices, and encourage tradespeople to talk to their counterparts who have had success with new products and better installation methods.

Incorporate the storage and collection of recyclables, not only on the job site but also in the completed home. Setting up a recycling center can be as simple as designating collection bins for commonly recycled materials such as paper, glass, plastic, metals, and corrugated cardboard. If you make it convenient, and educate people about its use, positive results will be assured.

Construction Waste Management Strategies

- Ensure that the infrastructure for recycling of construction and demolition materials is in place and operating from the outset of the project; identify in advance where different materials should be taken for recycling.
- Establish a recycling plan that sets goals to recycle or salvage a minimum of 50 percent (by weight or volume) of construction, demolition, and land-clearing waste. Then aim for 75 percent on your next project!
- Set up an on-site system to collect and sort waste for recycling or reuse, and monitor the system throughout all phases of construction.
- Consistently track the amount of waste production during construction, and measure it against preexisting goals and guidelines.
- Mark bins clearly for various types of usable wood scraps, for example: kindling, sawdust for compost, and materials for art projects.
- Purchase materials in sizes needed, rather than cutting to size.
- Minimize packaging waste; ask suppliers to avoid excessive packaging, or leave packaging at the point of purchase.
- Centralize cutting operations to reduce waste and simplify sorting.
- Educate the work crew regarding recycling procedures; emphasize that this is an environmentally friendly effort.
- Donate salvaged materials to charity and cultural groups, such as low-income housing projects, and Habitat for Humanity.

Client's Role and Responsibilities

The major ingredient in any successful green project is the role of the client. If a client is motivated as an environmental steward from the outset, team integration of environmental priorities will fall naturally into place, in support of the client's vision. Put

Helpful Home Maintenance Measures for Clients

- Develop a plan for regular maintenance of vents, filters, plumbing, and combustion equipment (gas heater, stove, dryer).
- Institute a no-smoking policy for the home, especially during construction. Cigarette smoke is a major indoor air pollutant, containing formaldehyde, carbon monoxide, and other carcinogens. Once introduced, cigarette odors are difficult to remove.
- Recommend the use of low-toxic or citrus-based cleaning products and the elimination of all solvent-based products. Ideally, choose products that are biodegradable and ammonia- and chlorine-free. For light cleaning, use vinegar, baking soda, and borax. The best options to consider are products labeled: nontoxic, nonpetroleum-based, water-based; free of ammonia, phosphates, dye, or perfume; readily biodegradable; and using recyclable containers. Avoid products with the words: "warning," "caution," "danger," "flammable," "poison," "reactive," unless there are compelling reasons for their use.
- Use pump sprays rather than aerosol cans that contain chemical propellants.
- Use high-efficiency particulate arrestance (HEPA) filtered vacuum cleaners. Eliminate excessively wet carpet cleaning to help reduce particulate and mold buildup.
- Purchase products with less packaging by ordering supplies in bulk or in concentrated form.
- Utilize a properly vented separate storage area for cleaning supplies, paints, and other toxic materials. Locate storage areas away from air intakes and windows, and thoroughly seal and isolate them from living spaces. Follow safe handling, disposal, and storage practices.
- Eliminate pesticide and herbicide use on and around the home, as they can be harmful to plants, animals, and local waterways.
- Create a well-designed in-house recycling center, or recycle items that can be diverted from landfills.
- Compost fruit, yard, and vegetable clippings. This produces excellent yard mulch and reduces material sent down the drain or to the landfill.
- Encourage clients to check their electricity, natural gas, water, and waste billing records to determine operating efficiency.
- Encourage clients to discuss and evaluate their energy use, water consumption, and waste generation with their family members.

another way, the client's position sets the tone for the project and creates energy leading to the successful integration of green design. In this ideal project scenario, the entire team works effectively together to serve the client's programming requests.

Each step taken in the direction of "greening a project" is an important endeavor. The first step is to consider how the home will ultimately be utilized and cared for once the client moves in. With this heightened level of consciousness, throughout the progression of design and construction, think about the operation and maintenance methods that can be implemented to support the environmental design priorities. Through prior planning, green designs will markedly improve the living environment and quality of life for the client, supporting health and safety and reducing energy and resource costs. Specify materials and systems that simplify and lower maintenance requirements. Designs and techniques that conserve water and energy, that use nontoxic chemicals and cleaners to maintain, and that are cost-effective, reduce costs over the lifetime of the home.

Prior to occupation, assist the client in establishing care and maintenance procedures, to ensure that the home performs optimally. Take into account cleaning products and techniques, long-term system maintenance, and owner awareness to determine how well the home will perform according to design intent throughout the life of the home.

Green Builder Programs

We've said it before, but it bears repeating: buildings consume vast amounts of our resources and threaten the ecological systems that support life as we know it, from dissipating the ozone layer to depleting the world's forests. Shifting and changing building practices is necessary for the reasons previously outlined, and renewed commitment to using resources wisely is paramount to our future.

In recognition of that fact, throughout the country, municipalities are rapidly adopting green building programs, codes, and regulations. From Alameda County, California, to Boulder, Colorado, and New York City, there are guidelines and regulations advising, and even requiring, the practice of green design. Currently, there are more than 50 local green homebuilding programs across the United States, among them: Austin's Green Builder Program, Built Green Colorado, Vermont Builds Green, Atlanta's EarthCraft House, and the EPA's ENERGY STAR homes. They take into consideration regional issues such as weather and precipitation zones; the local recycling infrastructure; energy and water conservation options; renewable, biodegradable, and locally produced materials; and waste and pollution prevention methods. The intent of these municipal programs is to strive to raise the bar in the green building movement, on an ongoing basis.

PROGRAM PARAMETERS

The mission of many of these programs is to increase the effectiveness of the local building industry, to share knowledge and provide information to the building trades in order to preserve our natural resources. Most programs allow for flexibility in design criteria to accommodate a wide range of alternatives to create better buildings. Generally, they promote the reduction of construction waste, the use of renewable resources, energy efficiency, improved indoor air quality, use of renewable energy, water conservation, and more efficient building techniques. As the cost of using our natural resources continues to increase, resource efficiency will become more cost-effective. This fact alone drives our industry toward more rapid market transformation.

Most environmental or efficient building programs are point-based, and the number of points required to achieve a green building rating relates to the size and type of the project. Points are awarded for incorporating efficient use of materials, water and energy, climate-appropriate landscaping and siting, and other issues relative to producing a high-performance building. Typically, green building source books or resource guides are available for use in conjunction with these municipal programs. These publications provide information relevant to the area, such as climate and regulatory issues; some assist in finding local green vendors, and supply other information to support the success of the project. Some programs are voluntary, offering savings to homeowners when applying for permits; others are mandatory, meaning penalties are imposed if they are not followed.

These programs target environmental benefits that reduce impact and waste in the building industry. They also encourage design innovation that exemplifies environmental stewardship.

GREEN BUILDING RATING SYSTEMS

The following are examples of national green building rating systems that all interior designers should become familiar with:

- *Leadership in Energy and Environmental Design (LEED) for Homes.* A new green building rating system from the U.S. Green Building Council (USGBC) that is in its pilot program phase. At the time of this writing, LEED for Homes is expected to launch in early 2007. It is designed to assist homebuyers in identifying newly constructed residences that are environmentally friendly as well as affordable. A LEED-certified home is third-party verified, which gives it greater credibility than voluntary programs. The benefits include healthier indoor air, a minimum of 30 percent greater energy and water efficiency, improved durability, the use of environmentally friendly building materials, climate-appropriate landscaping, a minimum of 30 percent less stormwater runoff, and higher market value.

- *EPA ENERGY STAR.* New homes qualified by this program achieve their energy savings through a variety of reliable and established technologies and building practices. Because ENERGY STAR-qualified new homes offer significant utility bill savings each month, special financing opportunities are available to new owners, such as energy-efficient mortgages. These special mortgages make it easier for borrowers to qualify to purchase homes with specific energy-efficiency improvements. The bottom line is that by installing energy-efficient features in a home, such as a high seasonal energy efficiency ratio (SEER) heating and cooling unit, low-emissivity (low-e) windows, and improved insulation, clients save money on monthly utility bills and live in a more comfortable space, thus helping reduce energy demands.

■ *American Lung Association Health House Builder Guidelines.* This is the oldest voluntary health organization in the United States. Originally founded to fight tuberculosis, today it fights lung disease in all forms, with special emphasis on asthma, tobacco control, and environmental health. Developed and reviewed annually by some of the leading indoor air quality experts in the United States, the American Lung Association Health House Builder Guidelines are among the most stringent in the nation for building a healthier, more energy- and resource-efficient home. Typical components of a Health House address foundation waterproofing and moisture control; advanced framing techniques; air sealing and advanced insulation techniques; energy-efficient, high-performance windows; energy-efficient and sealed combustion appliances; high-efficiency air filtration; whole-house ventilation and humidity control; careful selection and review of interior finishes.

The environmental initiatives offered by these programs help to shift thinking and, thus, encourage the building industry to develop better, healthier, more economical options for the homeowner, thereby accelerating market transformation.

Green Building Cost Considerations

The initial reaction to green building strategies is that they are good in theory but cost more in practice. It is true that costs may be slightly higher for energy-efficient HVAC and appliances, energy- and water-conserving construction, and nontoxic and environmentally friendly building materials. These up-front costs typically balance out over the lifetime of the residence, often saving costs in the long run.

Costs and Financial Benefits of Green Buildings

Financial Benefits of Green Buildings Summary of Findings (per sf^2)*	
Category	20-Year-Net Present Value
Energy Savings	$5.80
Emissions Savings	$1.20
Water Savings	$0.50
Operations and Maintenance	$8.50
Productivity and Health Benefits	$36.90 to 55.30
Subtotal	$52.90 to 71.30
Average Extra Cost of Green Building	<$-3.00 to -5.00>
Total 20-Year Net Benefit	$50.00 to 65.00

Source: U.S. Green Building Council, October 2003.
*The entire study was published by the U.S. Green Building Council and can be found at www.usgbc.org/Docs/News/News477.pdf.

In a recent study of 40 green buildings, selected because of the solid cost data that was available, the results clearly showed that despite an average $4 per square foot green cost premium, the total financial benefit was more than 10 times the average initial investment. Tracking sustainable attributes and strategies on projects provides vital feedback the industry can utilize to effectively sell and promote green designs to clients.

From California to New York, more states are offering significant tax rebates and credits for "going green." These incentives encourage development and construction of smarter, more sustainable homes and communities; help conserve undeveloped land, reduce air and water pollution, improve public health, reduce traffic congestion, ensure more efficient water usage, and reduce energy bills and transportation costs.

Green building and environmental benefits add value to the client's home in the form of energy efficiency, improved indoor air quality, a healthier home for the family, and durability. In short, green design does not necessarily need to cost more than conventional methods. So when it comes to addressing cost issues, rather than focusing on the up-front costs (materials and installation) involved in incorporating green features into a home, focus on the benefits. Rather than questioning how much more a green building will cost, ask what is most important to the client and the project: quality of life, sustaining the environment, a healthy home, flourishing eco-systems, saving the Earth?

A tangible starting position is to focus your client on energy savings. Sharing cost studies will confirm the need for a sustainable design approach and for solutions connecting back to the values that motivate. The Sustainable Building Task Force, a group of more than 40 California state government agencies, issued a report in October 2003 entitled "The Costs and Financial Benefits of Green Buildings." The report indicated that green buildings use an average of 30 percent less purchased energy than conventional buildings. The Department of Energy has estimated that homeowners can cut their utility costs by as much as 50 percent. These are just two examples that can assist in rousing your client's interest.

The aim of designing green buildings is to achieve a higher level of performance and quality. This is based on the choices we make in the design process, how we use materials, and the construction process we follow. Coupled with the creativeness and knowledge of the entire team, including the owner, determine the quality standards for the home, striving for something different, better, greener. Green building improves overall performance of the home, creating a long-life building, and increased owner satisfaction. These are all quantifiable attributes that typically save money, time, and environmental resources through reduced maintenance, replacement, and energy costs. We have the opportunity here to do something truly meaningful: create residences that we can leave to our children without trepidation, without guilt. Let's take it.

RESOURCES

Green by Design: Creating a Home for Sustainable Living, Angela M. Dean, AIA, LEED AP, (Gibbs Smith, 2003)

"Turning Green through LEED," Penny Bonda, *Interior Design Magazine,* May 2005

"The Whole Building Design Approach," Don Prowler, FAIA, *Whole Building Design Guide* (WBDG), April 2006

greening specifications

Photo courtesy of BDAL,
Architect.
Architect: BDAL, Architect.

To waste, to destroy our natural resources, to skin and exhaust the land instead of using it so as to increase its usefulness, will result in undermining in the days of our children the very prosperity which we ought by right to hand down to them amplified and developed.
—THEODORE ROOSEVELT, SEVENTH ANNUAL MESSAGE, DECEMBER 3, 1907

In addition to meeting the client's needs, budget, and design vision, ecologically minded design requires that we carefully consider the environmental impacts of the items that we specify. That is the purpose of this chapter—the nitty-gritty of applying sustainability to the interior of a home, by highlighting the how-to aspects of making a project green.

Key questions to ask before designing, specifying, buying or using a product (Aveda, http://aveda.com/protect/you/actions.asp):

1. Do we need it? Can we do without it?
2. Can we borrow, rent, or get it gently used?
3. Is the project designed to minimize waste? Can it be smaller, lighter, or made from fewer materials?
4. Is it designed to be durable or multifunctional?
5. Is it available in a less toxic form? Can it be made with less toxic materials, no VOCs, or certified organic?
6. Does it use renewable resources?
7. Is reuse practical and encouraged?
8. Is the product and/or packaging refillable, recyclable, or repairable?
9. Is it made with postconsumer recycled or reclaimed materials? How much?
10. Is it available from a socially and environmentally responsible company?
11. Is it made locally?
12. Again, do we need it? Can we live without it?

The primary criteria to consider in materials selection and specifications—whether specifying fixed interior finishes, designing furniture, or selecting fabrics—and applicable to all, are the following:

- Certification standards
- Reduced material content
- Recycled material content
- Renewable material content
- Sustainable manufacturing practices
- Reduced toxic emissions
- Low-impact materials
- Locally manufactured
- Durable and long-lasting

- Adaptable and reusable
- Biodegradable
- Indoor air quality performance
- Reduced packaging
- Shipping and handling

Green Product Criteria

Locating and identifying green materials can be challenging. Becoming familiar with the language, definitions, and consequences of using materials and products may seem daunting at first but, after applying the preceding principles a few times, it becomes second nature. Rather than replacing or providing an alternative structure to your design process, this environmental overlay enhances your creative and problem-solving capabilities, and earth-friendly design becomes a natural, logical extension of your work. Soon, you won't know how to design in any other manner.

This section outlines, in turn, each of the key overarching principles listed above in qualifying green products. Meeting the criteria for a product is not a black-and-white process; it is more like balancing a scale, evaluating the pros and cons and selecting the appropriate solution for the given situation. An understanding of these environmental concepts is the first step on the path to greening project specifications.

CERTIFICATION

Certification that a material or product meets certain standards takes the headache out of deciding which product may come from a greener source. There are three levels of certification:

- *First-party, or self-certification,* is often offered by manufacturers for their own products or operations, but this information is not confirmed or validated by others.

- The next tier of certification is often called *second-party certification,* where an industry trade association sets a level of standards for a certain group of manufacturers or suppliers (e.g., RugMark certifies area rugs and carpets). In this process, manufacturers regularly supply documentation and evidence that certain levels are being adhered to and maintained.

- *Third-party certification* is a comprehensive, usually more technical process by which a product, process, or service is reviewed by a reputable, independent, and unbiased third party and meets an established set of criteria, claims, and standards.

Of these, third-party certification is the most helpful to professionals, as it reduces the time and expense needed for identifying, selecting, and purchasing products. The process typically is quite stringent, involving submission of manufacturer data, supporting documents and usually a thorough on-site assessment. It assists with environmental, health, and safety comparisons. In addition, it can verify a single attribute of a product or service, or take on a more comprehensive approach, addressing multiple elements.

Third-party certification and consensus standardization help eliminate the need for government to create bureaucratic laws and regulations that may restrict market access and delay the introduction of new technologies. Third-party certifications have been successfully used for decades. Underwriters Laboratory (UL)-listed light fixtures, stovetops, and safety equipment are examples of products that are third-party certified. Other examples are the Forest Stewardship Council (FSC), Green Seal, GreenGuard, ENERGY STAR, and Cradle to Cradle.

Another third-party certifier is Scientific Certifications Systems (SCS). SCS offers a certification program for Environmentally Preferable Products (EPP), which addresses the growing demand for products and services that have the least impact on the environment. The EPP programs development follows Executive Order 13101, which directs federal agencies and their contractors to identify and purchase products designated as "environmentally preferable."

SCS uses a combination of criteria to guide the development of its specifications; currently, standards are available for: carpet face fiber, carpet (broadloom and tile), and flooring management systems. EPP standards now under development include: adhesives and sealants, cabinetry and casework, interior and exterior doors, flooring (nonwoven), paints (architectural and anticorrosive) and wall coverings. This structured development process addresses all stages of the product/services life cycle, incorporates key environmental and human health issues relevant to the category, and undergoes outside stakeholder review.

REDUCED MATERIAL CONTENT

The objective of this criterion is to encourage specification of furniture that is made simply and processed minimally. Most furniture and case pieces are assembled with screws, nuts, bolts, or other fasteners that loosen with age. A sustainable alternative is to utilize the inherent strength of wood with a system of self-locking joinery to hold furniture together. With dovetailed connection, components slide and lock into each other, allowing for the seasonal movement of wood with minimal warping or loosening of the structure. Using simple methods of construction and minimal processing also allows for ease of maintenance and repair.

Choosing a stronger material for one component may result in a reduced need for materials for the assembly as a whole. An engineered assembly presents a stronger and less material-intensive option than using individual components for a particular application. A wise use of resources might be to utilize the attributes of a material for more than one purpose, thereby resulting in a reduced use of materials. Concrete, for example, can be used as both the structure and finish of flooring.

RECYCLED MATERIAL CONTENT

Recycling is the process of collecting, processing, marketing, and ultimately reusing materials that were formerly discarded. Antiques and collectible furniture exemplify the beauty of recycling and refurbishing.

Products made with recycled materials offer countless benefits, among them:

- Reduces the volume of waste sent to landfills and incinerators.
- Decreases the demand for virgin or raw materials, which consequently lessens the environmental impacts associated with the extraction and harvesting of materials.
- Results in business expansion and additional jobs as new product technologies emerge.

These benefits associated with recycling cannot be achieved, however, unless a market exists for recycled content products. We must, therefore, purchase products with recycled material content to ensure that the recycling process continues. When enough demand for recycled content products is generated, entire markets can and will shift.

To make proper use of recycled content products, it's essential to know the terminology: pre- and postconsumer recycled content, postindustrial recycled content, closed-loop recycling, and downcycling. All have positives and negatives, depending on the project goals. The more often a material can be utilized/reutilized without losing integrity, the better. The longer a material can be recycled and kept out of the landfill, the better. (Refer to the glossary for helpful definitions as you make decisions about the products you select for your projects.)

RENEWABLE MATERIAL CONTENT

Renewable materials hold environmental appeal in that they are able to replenish themselves readily, as needed. Bamboo is an example of a material that is self-sustaining and can be harvested every 5 to 10 years. Other examples include wheatboard, wool, cotton, coir and jute fabrics, linoleum, and cork.

Simply defined, a renewable material is distinguished by its shorter harvest rotation, typically less than 10 years. The environmental impact associated with a building can be reduced with the use of materials that are readily renewable. Often agricultural-based materials, these consume less energy in their preparation and are less problematic to dispose of at the end of their useful life. They are often biodegradable and, typically, have low VOC emissions.

When it comes to deciding whether to use a renewable material, first ask how quickly the resource is renewed. Then confirm that the material lasts longer in application than it takes to replace the amount used. Also, research the environmental impacts associated with the cultivation, collection, and harvest of the renewable material.

SUSTAINABLE MANUFACTURING PRACTICES

To meet this criterion requires searching for manufacturers and companies that are on the journey toward sustainability, those committed to understanding and reducing their impact on the natural environment. Environmental policies will vary from company to company, of course, so the goal should be to support suppliers that are adopting sustainability as a corporate priority, who "walk their talk"—embracing the use of environmentally friendly materials and practices themselves, from the front door to the back door. How can you determine this? Ask:

- Do they incorporate waste reduction, energy reduction, recyclable packaging, and other environmental initiatives into their plan?
- How do they evaluate their products, and at what stage of design do they begin the evaluation?
- What is the material chemistry, ease of disassembly, and recyclability of their products?

Believe it or not, another good indicator of a manufacturer's commitment is to take a look at the employee bathrooms. This will give you an insight to the company's culture; specifically, how they value the safety, health, and quality of life of their team members and visitors. Do you find eco-friendly supplies and cleaning products under the sink?

Similarly, the design of the building may directly reflect a company's commitment to environmental values. Likewise the approach they take to the working relationships with their customers, vendors, and peers. In all areas, does the company seek to raise the environmental consciousness and standards of the industry?

The best single guideline is to seek out vendors that push the envelope with their operations and policies, manufacturing products without reducing the capacity of the environment to provide for future generations. One that actively tracks and publishes their improving results is most likely a company on an environmentally responsible path.

REDUCED TOXIC EMISSIONS

Reductions of smog-causing pollutants and particulate matter are important because of the health and environmental problems they can cause. The amended Clean Air Act of 1990 established standards issued by the EPA to control emissions and toxic pollutants. These standards strive to reduce the emissions of more than 100 different air toxins. When fully implemented, all of these standards reduce toxic emissions by about 1.5 million tons per year—almost 15 times the reductions achieved prior to 1990.

Because some air toxins are also smog-causing VOCs (e.g., toluene) or particulate matter (e.g., chromium), some of these air toxin regulations have the added benefit of reducing ground-level ozone (urban smog) and particulate matter. In addition, some of the technologies and practices designed to control air toxins also reduce VOCs or types of particulate matter that are not currently among the 188 listed air toxics.

As an example, by changing their metal finishes from solvent-based wet-spray materials to completely reusable, nonsolvent powder coatings, some companies are eliminating VOC emissions and reducing their use of hazardous materials. As another example, some manufacturing facilities have replaced toxic stains and topcoats with waterborne stains and topcoats.

Another furniture manufacturer prefers to use a traditional approach, also avoiding toxic finishes. It uses an oil and wax finish, which allows air and sunlight to naturally color the wood with a subtlety unmatched by anything from a can. The heated linseed oil penetrates the surface of the wood, adding greater visible depth to the wood and revealing the grain pattern. Linseed oil and wax finishes are easy to maintain and age gracefully as the wood's natural patina emerges.

LOW-IMPACT MATERIALS

Low-impact materials or products are often derived from natural sources such as wood, agricultural or nonagricultural plant products, and mineral products such as natural stone and slate shingles. They are subject to minimal processing, are most often selected for their inherent strength and beauty, and use less energy to manufacture into a usable product. Because of their source, they are less likely to out-gas chemicals or VOCs during manufacture or when eventually disposed of.

LOCALLY MANUFACTURED

Specifying and purchasing regional products reduces the significant environmental impacts of the energy needed to transport materials long distances. This practice also encourages a building style vernacular which, typically, makes use of regionally available materials, supports the local economy, and connects users directly with the impact of their choices.

DURABLE AND LONG-LASTING

Durable products are environmentally friendly, in that they need replacement less frequently. Low-maintenance products are environmentally friendly simply because their maintenance routine is low-impact. This varies, however, depending on the standard and quality of the product and its application. Tile, stone, and concrete are examples of products that, once manufactured and installed, last indefinitely.

When you specify durable, high-quality goods, it translates to a longer product life outside of the landfill. Durable goods may cost a little more up front, but they typically will save money in the long run. Note that durable alone may not mean, however, that a material is green or a better environmental choice.

ADAPTABLE AND REUSABLE

Designing for future reuse and adaptability is a fun and an interesting challenge from an interior designer's perspective. To that end:

- Consider designing a piece of furniture that can be adapted for multiple uses; for example, a coffee table that also serves as an ottoman, and/or a storage piece.
- Choose materials and components for products that can be reused or recycled after their useful life.
- Think about repairing, selling, or donating items to reduce waste.

Reuse means that a product can be used more than once. Furniture and area rugs are examples of products that have a long life and can be reused over and over again.

BIODEGRADABLE

Merriam-Webster's dictionary defines biodegradable as being capable of decomposing by biological agents or capable of being broken down, especially into harmless products, by the action of living things, such as microorganisms.

One carpet mill produces wall-to-wall carpeting and area rugs from 100 percent biodegradable, all-natural materials, including wool, hemp, jute, and natural rubber. Its wool carpeting is nonwoven and uses a 100 percent biodegradable adhesive to bond the wool to a hemp-cotton primary backing and then to a secondary backing of jute fibers. No chemical treatments are used, and color variation is achieved through the selection of naturally pigmented wool. An item that decomposes into the earth without leaching toxins or polluting the area fits the definition of biodegradable.

INDOOR AIR QUALITY (IAQ) PERFORMANCE

It is often perceived that outdoor air is polluted but indoor air is of acceptable quality. Scientific studies indicate this perception is false. Indoor air is, in fact, often a greater health hazard than the corresponding outdoor setting, especially given that statistics show we spend an average of 90 percent of our time indoors.

The IAQ of any building is measured according to guidelines set by the government and is used as a measuring stick for the efficiency of air purification and filtration systems. IAQ assessment covers: microbial contaminants (mold, bacteria), chemicals (carbon monoxide, radon), allergens, fibers (asbestos), or any mass or energy stressor that can affect the heath of people or animals.

Techniques for analyzing IAQ include collection of air samples, collection of samples on building surfaces, and computer modeling of the airflow inside buildings. The resulting samples are analyzed for mold, bacteria, chemicals, and other stressors. These investigations can lead to an understanding of the sources of the contaminants and, ultimately, to strategies for removing the unwanted elements from the air.

To meet this criterion for sustainable design, search out low-emitting products such as zero-VOC paints or water-based adhesives and finishes that avoid the release of significant pollutants into interior spaces.

REDUCED PACKAGING

In most regions of the developed world, packaging waste represents as much as one-third of the nonindustrial solid wastestream. As living standards are raised, more countries in the developing world are also seeing significant growth in their packaging waste. At least 28 countries currently have laws designed to encourage the reduced use of packaging and greater recycling of packaging discards. Many of these countries require manufacturers to take back packaging discards or to pay for their recycling.

By using products and materials with reduced packaging, and encouraging manufacturers to reuse or recycle their original packaging materials, materials are diverted from disposal at the landfill, and the use of raw materials is reduced. The associated reduction in waste and disposal cost also results in cost savings to the contractor and owner.

At this time, there are no U.S. federal mandates enforcing manufacturers to take back their packaging discard or to pay for their recycling. New types of containers continue to emerge that further complicate recycling efforts and there is growing concern at the state and local government levels regarding packaging waste. More recently, government reductions in recycling subsidies and a growing demand for materials from abroad have increased pressure on domestic recyclers, especially plastics recyclers, who are competing fiercely for limited materials. New methods of increasing the recovery of materials from the landfill, including packaging and plastics in particular, are clearly needed.

Packaging can be made more sustainable by applying the principles of product stewardship, including: eliminating toxic components, using less material, making packaging more reusable, including more recycled content, and making packaging more readily recyclable.

Blue Angel Mark

The Blue Angel Mark is an environmental label system promoted by the German government for numerous products, including furniture and finishes. This mark is attached to an item to enable purchasers to recognize that it meets standards.

Economical use of raw materials, production, usage, service life, and disposal—all these factors are assigned a high degree of importance. Products awarded the label bear the logo of the Blue Angel directly on the product, and service companies include it on sales materials used to offer their services.

A superb element of this program is that the manufacturer is responsible for the entire life cycle of the product forever. The manufacturer maintains a program for recycling the product, in concert with the guiding principles of the Blue Angel program (www.blauer-engel.de).

Sustainable design practice in this regard requires asking manufacturers to package their products in an environmentally responsible way. Specifically, request:

- Minimal packaging
- Use of only recycled content materials
- Biodegradable peanuts and bubble wrap made from 100 percent recycled plastic that is in turn 100 percent recyclable
- Packing and boxing materials that are 90 percent postconsumer waste material and are themselves 100 percent recyclable
- Packaging materials that can be returned for their reuse

SHIPPING AND HANDLING

We transport more than 9 billion tons of goods across the United States each year, consuming 35 billion gallons of diesel and producing high levels of carbon dioxide and nitrogen oxides along the way.

The EPA's Smartway Transport Partnership (www.EPA.gov/smartway) challenges freight-shipping companies to improve their environmental performance. By 2012, through various methods—such as promoting the use of trains, which are more efficient, and improving the aerodynamics of trucks—the program aims to eliminate as much as 66 million tons of carbon dioxide emissions and as much as 220 thousand tons of nitrogen oxide emissions per year from the atmosphere.

The ability to move air product by ground, and ground product by rail, produces significant reductions in energy use, fuel consumption, and emissions. Environmentally efficient modes of transport will eventually lessen the impact on global warming trends.

Utilize shipping companies that commit to reducing greenhouse gas emissions and improving the fuel efficiency of ground freight transportation. Look for companies that strive for the highest operational efficiencies, thus minimizing the impact on the environment. Responsibility for the environment ranges from the construction, maintenance, and operation of facilities to the maintenance and operation of vehicles and aircraft to the conservation of resources. Ask companies for their sustainability statements or policies; confirm they work towards a balanced economic, social, and environmental objectives.

Samples

From fabrics to finishes, the world of design creates a surplus of samples. It is projected that it takes approximately 1 quart of oil and 2 gallons of water to produce the nylon fiber in a typical carpet sample. Ultimately, after the short-term use of these resources, most of the samples produced end up in the landfill.

Throughout the design process, consider how to be resource-efficient within the sampling process to reduce waste and inefficiency, which tends to be standard practice. Here's how:

- Encourage manufacturers to sample initially through a digital process via Internet or email distribution during the schematic design process.
- Insist that showrooms take back all samples and catalogs for reuse.
- Donate excess samples to design and architectural schools.

Sustainable Products Research

As residential designers, we delight in researching the latest and greatest sources and products available in our field; we thrive when seeking innovative solutions. Our creative juices flow as we begin to develop cutting-edge original designs. Our newly acquired knowledge of sustainable solutions, green product criteria and design concepts opens up a whole new world of options, giving us a fresh and exciting arena in which to explore the many possibilities in creating environmentally conscientious designs.

As we set out on this exciting venture, William McDonough and Michael Braungart, of MBDC, challenge us to ask two very basic questions about any product:

- Where does it come from?
- Where does it go?

Beginning our research with these two simple, straightforward questions takes our thinking to the next level of inquiry. Consider the following general issues as you move into researching products and alternative design solutions:

- Will this product make the home more energy-efficient and/or comfortable?
- Will this product save water?
- Will this product out-gas harmful chemicals?
- Is this product safe for the client and his or her family during and after installation?
- Is this product durable, so that it won't need to be frequently repaired or replaced?
- Is this product made from recycled materials?
- Is this product manufactured in an environmentally friendly way?
- Is this product made locally?
- What is *not* sustainable about this product?

Understanding the properties of materials—their sources and composition, whether dangerous or toxic—enlightens the search for better materials and products, thus benefiting quality of life.

Materials Safety Data Sheets

A materials safety data sheet (MSDS) is a fact sheet developed by the product manufacturer to provide safety information, primarily intended for its workers. It is required by the Occupational Health and Safety Administration (OSHA) for all hazardous materials. Each MSDS contains the general composition of the product, as well as a wide variety of data such as the known health effects, proper handling, and recommended storage of the material.

As a standard aspect of your sustainable interior design practice, request the MSDS for products that you will use in the residential design process. Manufacturers and

Top 20 Hazardous Substances List

The Comprehensive Environmental Response, Compensation, and Liability Act (CERCLA) section 104 (i), as amended by the Superfund Amendments and Reauthorization Act (SARA), requires ATSDR and the EPA to prepare a list, in order of priority, of substances that are most commonly found at facilities on the National Priorities List and that are determined to pose the most significant potential threat to human health due to their known or suspected toxicity and potential for human exposure at these NPL sites. (Note: This is not a list of "most toxic" substances, rather a prioritization of substances based on a combination of their frequency, toxicity, and potential for human exposure at NPL sites.)

Substance	Examples of some common products
1. Arsenic	Wood preservatives
2. Lead	Batteries, metal products
3. Mercury	Light bulbs
4. Vinyl chloride (PVC)	PVC piping, PVC siding, packaging
5. Polychlorinated biphenyls (PCB)	Coolants, insulation for electrical equipment
6. Benzene	Dyes, rubber, detergents
7. Polycyclic aromatic hydrocarbons (PAH)	Dyes, plastics, roofing tar
8. Cadmium	Batteries, pigments, plastics, metal coatings
9. Benzo(a)pyrene (PAH)	Incomplete combustion from coal, oil and wood-burning
10. Benzo(b)fluoranthene (PAH)	stoves and furnaces
11. Chloroform	Swimming pools, plant growth chemicals
12. DDT, p,p'-	Pesticides
13. Aroclor 1254	Rubber and synthetic resin plasticizers, adhesives, sealants, caulks,
14. Aroclor 1260	PCB waste materials and products in landfills
15. Dibenzo(a,h)anthracene (DbahA)	Product of incomplete combustion
16. Trichloroethylene (TCE)	Adhesives, paints, paint removers
17. Dieldrin	Insecticide
18. Chromium, hexavalent	Leather tanning, wood preserving, dyes, pigment
19. Phosphorus, white	Pesticides, fireworks
20. DDE, p,p'-	Pesticides

(*Source*: Agency for Toxic Substances and Disease Registry (ATSDR) www.atsdr.cdc.gov/cxcx3.html)

distributors should have on hand copies of an MSDS for every product that they sell that may contain hazardous materials. Retailers often have an MSDS file or database, as well. Almost all are available online on the manufacturers' Web sites. It is a good idea to compile a notebook containing the MSDS for all products used, to keep on-site for easy reference concerning proper storage, handling, and safety precautions.

The MSDS assists designers and clients in making product choices based on their safety or potential for ecological and human harm. Although it may be highly technical, and sometimes difficult to decipher (there are many thousands of chemicals in existence and it's unrealistic for anyone to know them all), the MSDS can be used as a compass to point toward relative safety or danger. A product with an MSDS devoid of listed hazards and known health effects is likely to be much safer, for example, than one that requires a respirator for application and has cancer-causing agents.

That said, there are shortcomings to relying solely upon the MSDS as an indicator. Proprietary information is usually excluded from the MSDS, therefore leaving out important information about trade-secret ingredients. Inert components, which often comprise the bulk of the product, are also exempt from inclusion—and the fact that they are inert does not mean they are safe for humans or the environment. Third, the safe levels of exposure to chemicals, as listed on the MSDS, are determined through limited testing to one substance at a time—not a real-world scenario. Last, the MSDS is primarily intended to educate workers as to the risks while the product is being used or applied; it does not adequately address the long-term risks that might occur after the curing, drying, or deterioration of the product.

The best course of action is to know what information the MSDS offers and to use it as a guideline for specifications or purchases, not as a mandate. Steer toward those products with the least amount of risk and away from those with serious safety, human health, or environmental limitations.

One final note: Even though the content of an MSDS is dictated by OSHA, the format can vary. However, the MSDS will contain pertinent information about the following, whichever the format, when required by OSHA:

- Product name(s), manufacturer contact info, emergency phone number.
- Hazardous ingredients that make up more than 1 percent of the substance. This will include all known carcinogens. In general, the smaller the amount of recommended exposure, the more dangerous the chemical; anything expressed in parts per million (ppm) is highly suspect. The hazards may be expressed in several different ways, including but not limited to the following:
  - Formally regulated OSHA permissible exposure limit, or PEL
  - Recommended limits, from the National Institute for Occupational Safety and Health (NIOSH), recommended exposure limit (REL), or the American Conference of Governmental Industrial Hygienists (ACGIH) threshold limit value (TLV)
  - Parts per million (ppm) of dust or vapor per cubic meter of air (mg/m^3)
  - Time-weighted average (TWA), a concentration averaged over an eight-hour day
  - Short-term exposure limit (STEL), a 15-minute TWA that should not be exceeded
  - Ceiling limit (c), which should not be exceeded at any time.
- Physical characteristics of the material, such as whether or not it can vaporize (vapor pressure), what it might smell or look like, its boiling or melting point, flammability, and out-gassing potential (expressed as "volatile organic content").

- Health hazards through normal exposure or overexposure. Most determinations of health risks are determined through testing on animals, which is a cruel and unnecessary practice, and the hazards may be expressed through these results. "Acute" exposure is over the short term, while "chronic" is long term or sustained.

- Emergency and first-aid measures for eye contact, skin contact, inhalation, ingestion, and so on.

- Recommendations for safe handling, storage, accidental release (leaks or spills), and fires.

- Exposure controls and personal protection, such as recommendations to wear gloves, a respirator, dust mask, or other protective item.

- Chemical and physical properties of the chemical, as well as stability and reactivity, to help determine which chemicals should not be used together or in close proximity.

- Toxicological information and ecological information, to provide more information about the substance's potential for harming humans, plants, animals, and the environment.

- Disposal considerations, to help determine appropriate or allowable disposal methods.

- Transport information and regulatory information, both detailing additional regulations.

While very technical, the content of the MSDS will become more familiar with use, and you'll come to find them invaluable in your quest to specify safe and healthy materials.

Questions for Manufacturers and Suppliers

Over the years, we have, as a firm, developed numerous questionnaires regarding the qualification of environmental products. The first was a very extensive questionnaire we sent to our vendors quizzing them on materials, manufacturing processes, energy use, air quality, packaging, transportation, installation methods, and waste disposal. Understandably, due to the overwhelming nature of our questions, we received fewer than a handful of replies.

Eventually, we simplified the list of questions to the vital few, getting to the heart of the matter when discussing green issues with manufacturers and suppliers. We have organized the questions, as well as the subsequent chapters of this book, using the Construction Specifications Institute (CSI) MasterFormat, the most widely used standard for organizing specifications and other written information for commercial and institutional building projects in the United States and Canada. We utilize this format in preparing our specifications in order to best serve the architectural and construction teams and the clients with whom we are working.

The CSI MasterFormat provides a master list of divisions, with section numbers and titles within each division, as a means of consistently organizing information and specifications regarding a building's construction requirements and associated activities. We have found that standardizing the presentation of project specifications in this same manner significantly improves communication among all parties involved in residential construction projects. This approach also assists the project team in delivering a standardized, organized structure to owners, tailored to meet their requirements, timelines, and budgets.

Because so many participants interact on a building project, its details must be carefully documented and communicated. The process begins with identifying the owner's needs, to which the architect gives shape. The architect, in turn, engages specifiers and other consultants to develop the project's particulars.

Specifications are the detailed written data about a structure's materials, products, and systems, ranging from the details of the HVAC system to the kind of window glass to the type of doorknobs. A building's specifications are contained in its project manual, developed by architects, interior designers, specifiers, and engineers. Contractors use the project manual to bid on the project, and the winning bidder uses the manual to construct the building.

This format enhances communications among everyone involved in delivering construction projects.

The table on pages 87–104 offer a glimpse at the CSI divisions that are relevant to the practice of residential interior design, accompanied by key questions to ask of manufacturers and suppliers. Use these lists—these are ours—as a starting point, a guide, then build on them. They will assist you in finding answers to the key questions regarding a product: "Where does it come from?" and "Where does it go?"

FIXED RESIDENTIAL INTERIOR FINISHES

Interior finishes, reflected in the CSI outline, are the finishes applied in the field, to the floors, walls, and ceilings of the home. They are the predominant and most tangible aspects of a residential project where we, as interior designers, are able to offer sustainable solutions as we interface with the other design disciplines: Low-emitting stains and finishes on FSC millwork and cabinetry; long lasting and colorful recycled glass tiles in baths and kitchens; natural earth plasters on walls throughout the home. This is also the area where designers can energize the team about the creation of an eco-friendly home. Here we have the opportunity to model and share important information with other project team members—architects, contractors, and subcontractors—regarding sustaining practices and materials. This information demonstrates the added value that we, as interior designers, bring to the project.

Through the design details, the edges, the unique use of materials, and their layouts, we can use sustainable materials, combining them in unique and creative applications. By being conscientious specifiers, we become change agents in our industry.

Questions for Manufacturers

CSI Division 3   CONCRETE
✓ Where is it fabricated?
✓ Is fly ash used, and if so, what percentage is used?
✓ How is it colored, stained, or sealed?
✓ Can you recommend or use adhesives, grout, mortar, or sealants without solvents, additives, or formaldehyde?
✓ How does the manufacturing process use water and energy efficiently?
✓ Where does the waste go?
✓ How is the waste safely disposed of or reused?
✓ Does the product or its waste emit toxins into the land at disposal?
✓ What recycling programs are in place to assist in the recycling of this product?

CSI Division 4   MASONRY

Stone

✓ Where is it quarried?
✓ How rare is it?
✓ What is the process used for quarrying?
✓ What percent of it, if any, is reclaimed?
✓ How does the quarry give back to the land, town, community?
✓ Where is it fabricated and finished?
✓ How is it packaged and transported?
✓ Can it be dry-stacked?
✓ Can you recommend or use adhesives, grout, mortar, or sealants without solvents, additives, formaldehyde?
✓ How does the manufacturing process use water and energy efficiently?
✓ What sustainable manufacturing processes do you use?
✓ How is it packaged and shipped?
✓ How can packaging be returned for reuse?
✓ Where does the waste go?
✓ How is the waste safely disposed of or reused?
✓ What programs are in place that assist in the reuse of this product?

Brick

✓ What are the materials used?
✓ Where is it fabricated?
✓ What portion of it, if any, is reclaimed?
✓ Do you have salvaged brick?
✓ Can it be dry-stacked?

Questions for Manufacturers *(Continued)*

✓ Can you recommend or use adhesives, grout, mortar, or sealants without solvents, additives, formaldehyde?

✓ How does the manufacturing process use water and energy efficiently?

✓ What sustainable manufacturing processes do you use?

✓ How is it packaged and shipped?

✓ Can packaging be returned for reuse?

✓ Where does the waste go?

✓ How is the waste safely disposed of or reused?

✓ Are there programs in place that assist in the reuse of this product?

CSI Division 5	METALS

✓ Where does the metal originate?

✓ What percentage of this product is from recycled content?

✓ How is waste handled?

✓ How is it finished and sealed?

✓ How does the manufacturing process use water and energy efficiently?

✓ What sustainable manufacturing processes do you use?

✓ How is it packaged and shipped?

✓ Can packaging be returned for reuse?

✓ Where does the waste go?

✓ How is the waste safely disposed of or reused?

✓ Does the product or its waste emit toxins into the land at disposal?

✓ Are there recycling programs in place that assist in the recycling of this product?

CSI Division 6	WOOD AND COMPOSITES

Wood

✓ Where does the wood come from?

✓ If a hardwood, is the wood third-party-certified?

✓ If not, how is it farmed/logged?

✓ If you use MDF or particleboard, is it formaldehyde-free?

✓ Is it treated with chemicals (e.g., copper chromated arsenate)?

✓ Does the company participate in reforestation?

✓ If reclaimed, where is it from? Barn? Railroad? Other?

   ■ Is it free of lead, nails, tar, creosote, and so on?

✓ How does the manufacturing process use water and energy efficiently?

✓ What sustainable manufacturing processes do you use?

✓ Does the product off-gas or emit toxins to installers or end users?

✓ How is it packaged and shipped?

✓ Can packaging be returned for reuse?

Questions for Manufacturers *(Continued)*

✓ Where does the waste go?

✓ How is the waste safely disposed of or reused?

✓ Are there recycling programs in place that assist in the recycling of this product?

Composites

✓ Where do the components of the material or product come from? What are they?

✓ Where does the product itself come from?

✓ Does it include any binders or adhesives? What are they made from?

✓ Is it formaldehyde-free?

✓ Is it treated with chemicals or preservatives?

✓ Where is it fabricated?

✓ How does the manufacturing process use water and energy efficiently?

✓ Does the product off-gas or emit toxins to installers or end users?

✓ Is it, or would you consider, getting it Greenguard-certified?

✓ What sustainable manufacturing processes do you use?

✓ How is it packaged and shipped?

✓ Can packaging be returned for reuse?

✓ Where does the waste go?

✓ How is the waste safely disposed of or reused?

✓ Does the product or its waste emit toxins into the land at disposal?

✓ Are there recycling programs in place that assist in the recycling of this product?

CSI DIVISION 8	OPENINGS (Doors and Windows)

✓ If new wood, is it third-party-certified?

  ■ Is it formaldehyde-free?

  ■ Is solid or engineered wood used?

✓ If reclaimed wood, where is it from? Barn? Railroad? Other?

  ■ Is it free of lead, nails, tar, creosote, and so on?

✓ What are the components in composite-made frames?

  ■ Are they formaldehyde free?

✓ What are the glues, dyes, glazes, paints, or other ingredients used?

  ■ Are they water-based or low-VOC?

✓ What is the R-value of the door or window?

✓ What is the R-value of the glazing?

  ■ Is the window or door NFRC-rated?

  ■ Is it ENERGY STAR rated?

✓ Do you take back old frames for reuse or remanufacture?

✓ How does the manufacturing process use water and energy efficiently?

✓ Does the product off-gas or emit toxins to installers or end users?

✓ What sustainable manufacturing processes do you use?

Questions for Manufacturers *(Continued)*

- ✓ How is it packaged and shipped?
- ✓ Can packaging be returned for reuse?
- ✓ Where does the waste go?
- ✓ How is the waste safely disposed of or reused?
- ✓ Does the product or its waste emit toxins into the land at disposal?
- ✓ Are there recycling programs in place that assist in the recycling of this product?

CSI Division 9   FINISHES

Plaster and Gypsum Board

- ✓ Where is it made?
- ✓ What are the material(s) contents?
- ✓ What happens to any by-products of manufacturing?
- ✓ How does the manufacturing process use water and energy efficiently?
- ✓ Does the product off-gas or emit toxins to installers or end users?
- ✓ What sustainable manufacturing processes do you use?
- ✓ How is it packaged and shipped?
- ✓ Can packaging be returned for reuse?
- ✓ Where does the waste go?
- ✓ How is the waste safely disposed of or reused?
- ✓ Does the product or its waste emit toxins into the land at disposal?
- ✓ Are there recycling programs in place that assist in the recycling of this product?

Tile

- ✓ Where is it made?
- ✓ What are the material(s) contents?
- ✓ What happens to any by-products of manufacturing?
- ✓ What dyes or paints are used?
- ✓ Is there recycled content?
- ✓ Can the tile be recycled?
- ✓ How does the manufacturing process use water and energy efficiently?
- ✓ Does the product off-gas or emit toxins to installers or end users?
- ✓ What sustainable manufacturing processes do you use?
- ✓ How is it packaged and shipped?
- ✓ Can packaging be returned for reuse?
- ✓ Where does the waste go?
- ✓ How is the waste safely disposed of or reused?
- ✓ Does the product or its waste emit toxins into the land at disposal?
- ✓ Are there recycling programs in place that assist in the recycling of this product?

Questions for Manufacturers *(Continued)*

Flooring

Stone Tile or Flooring

✓ Where is it quarried?

✓ How rare is it?

✓ What is the process used for quarrying?

✓ What percent of it, if any, is reclaimed?

✓ How does the quarry give back to the land, town, community?

✓ Where is it fabricated and finished?

✓ Can you recommend or use adhesives, grout, mortar, or sealants without solvents, additives, formaldehyde?

✓ How does the manufacturing process use water and energy efficiently?

✓ Does the product off-gas or emit toxins to installers or end users?

✓ What sustainable manufacturing processes do you use?

✓ How is it packaged and shipped?

✓ Can packaging be returned for reuse?

✓ Where does the waste go?

✓ How is the waste safely disposed of or reused?

✓ Does the product or its waste emit toxins into the land at disposal?

✓ Are there recycling programs in place that assist in the recycling of this product?

Terrazzo

✓ Where does the material or product come from?

✓ Does it include any binders or adhesives? If so, what are they made from?

✓ Is it formaldehyde-free?

✓ Is it treated with chemicals or preservatives?

✓ How does the manufacturing process use water and energy efficiently?

✓ Does the product off-gas or emit toxins to installers or end users?

✓ What sustainable manufacturing processes do you use?

✓ How is it packaged and shipped?

✓ Can packaging be returned for reuse?

✓ Where does the waste go?

✓ How is the waste safely disposed of or reused?

✓ Does the product or its waste emit toxins into the land at disposal?

✓ Are there recycling programs in place that assist in the recycling of this product?

Bamboo

✓ Where does the bamboo come from?

✓ Is it made using sustainable manufacturing practices?

✓ What other components or materials are added to the product?

Questions for Manufacturers *(Continued)*

✓ Does this product impact indoor air quality?

✓ What finishes and/or dyes are used?

✓ Can you recommend or use adhesives or sealants without solvents, additives, formaldehyde?

✓ How does the manufacturing process use water and energy efficiently?

✓ Does the product off-gas or emit toxins to installers or end users?

✓ Is it, or would you consider getting it, Greenguard-certified?

✓ What sustainable manufacturing processes do you use?

✓ How is it packaged and shipped?

✓ Can packaging be returned for reuse?

✓ Where does the waste go?

✓ How is the waste safely disposed of or reused?

✓ Does the product or its waste emit toxins into the land at disposal?

✓ Are there recycling programs in place that assist in the recycling of this product?

Leather

✓ Where do the hides for your leather products come from?

✓ Do these hides come from humanely and organically raised animals?

✓ What sustainable manufacturing processes do you use?

✓ How is your leather tanned? Do you use chromium in your tanning process? Do you use vegetable-based tanning agents?

✓ What types of dyes do you use on your leathers? Do your dyes contain any toxic substances? Do you use any natural vegetable and mineral dyes?

✓ Are your leathers treated with any surface treatments (stain repellents, etc.)?

✓ How does the manufacturing process use water and energy efficiently?

✓ Does the product off-gas or emit toxins to installers or end users?

✓ How is it packaged and shipped?

✓ Can packaging be returned for reuse?

✓ Where does the waste go?

  ■ How do you handle the chemical and protein-based waste products that result from the manufacturing of your leather?

  ■ How is the waste safely disposed of or reused?

✓ Does the product or its waste emit toxins into the land at disposal?

✓ Are there recycling programs in place that assist in the recycling of this product?

Cork

✓ Where does this product come from?

✓ How is this product harvested?

✓ What sustainable harvesting practices are used in acquiring the cork?

Questions for Manufacturers *(Continued)*

✓ How is the cork cleaned and processed once it has been harvested?

 ▪ Are any toxic substances used to clean or process the cork?

✓ Is a binder added to the cork? If so, what is the binder made of?

✓ Is a backing used on the cork? If so, what is the backing made of?

✓ Is the surface of the cork product finished or unfinished?

 ▪ If it has been finished, what kind of finish has been used?

✓ How does the manufacturing process use water and energy efficiently?

✓ Does the product off-gas or emit toxins to installers or end users?

✓ Is it, or would you consider getting it, Greenguard-certified?

✓ What sustainable manufacturing processes do you use?

✓ How is it packaged and shipped?

✓ Can packaging be returned for reuse?

✓ Where does the waste go?

✓ How is the waste safely disposed of or reused?

✓ Does the product or its waste emit toxins into the land at disposal?

✓ Are there recycling programs in place that assist in the recycling of this product?

Wood

✓ Where does the wood come from?

✓ If a hardwood, is the wood third-party-certified?

✓ If not, how is it farmed/logged?

✓ If you use MDF or particleboard, is it formaldehyde-free?

✓ Is it treated with chemicals (e.g., copper chromated arsenate)?

✓ Does the company participate in reforestation?

✓ If reclaimed, where is it from? Barn? Railroad? Other?

 ▪ Is it free of lead, nails, tar, creosote, and so on?

✓ How does the manufacturing process use water and energy efficiently?

✓ What sustainable manufacturing processes do you use?

✓ Does the product off-gas or emit toxins to installers or end users?

✓ How is it packaged and shipped?

✓ Can packaging be returned for reuse?

✓ Where does the waste go?

✓ How is the waste safely disposed of or reused?

✓ Are there recycling programs in place that assist in the recycling of this product?

Linoleum

✓ Where does this product come from?

✓ What is this product made of? Does this product contain PVC-vinyl?

✓ Has a surface finish been applied to this product? If so, what kind?

Questions for Manufacturers *(Continued)*

✓ How is this product maintained?

✓ How does the manufacturing process use water and energy efficiently?

✓ Does the product off-gas or emit toxins to installers or end users?

✓ What sustainable manufacturing processes do you use?

✓ How is it packaged and shipped?

✓ Can packaging be returned for reuse?

✓ Where does the waste go?

✓ How is the waste safely disposed of or reused?

✓ Does the product or its waste emit toxins into the land at disposal?

✓ Are there recycling programs in place that assist in the recycling of this product?

Carpet

✓ Does the product meet or exceed the Carpet & Rug Institute (CRI) Green Plus standards?

✓ Where is this product manufactured?

✓ What is the backing made from?

✓ What are the adhesives used?

✓ Does this product have a high recycled material content?

✓ Does this product have low or no VOC content?

✓ What is this product's total life-cycle cost, including durability and embodied energy?

✓ Does this product have a high cleanability rating?

✓ Does this product have a high durability rating?

✓ How does the manufacturing process use water and energy efficiently?

✓ Does the product off-gas or emit toxins to installers or end users?

✓ Is it, or would you consider getting it, Greenguard-certified?

✓ What sustainable manufacturing processes do you use?

✓ How is it packaged and shipped?

✓ Can packaging be returned for reuse?

✓ Where does the waste go?

✓ How is the waste safely disposed of or reused?

✓ Does the product or its waste emit toxins into the land at disposal?

✓ Are there recycling programs in place that assist in the recycling of this product?

Wallcoverings

✓ Where is this product manufactured?

✓ What is it made of (vinyl, paper, etc.)?

✓ Does it contain recycled material content?

✓ Does it contain renewable material content (e.g., wood pulp from managed forests)?

✓ Is this product compostable or biodegradable?

✓ What types of dyes are used in the making of this product?

Questions for Manufacturers *(Continued)*

✓ Are any toxins emitted in the manufacturing of this product?

✓ Can you recommend or use adhesives without solvents, additives, or formaldehyde?

✓ How is this product maintained—that is, what type of cleansing agents must be used?

✓ How durable is this product?

✓ How does the manufacturing process use water and energy efficiently?

✓ Does the product off-gas or emit toxins to installers or end users?

✓ Is it, or would you consider getting it, Greenguard-certified?

✓ What sustainable manufacturing processes do you use?

✓ How is it packaged and shipped?

✓ Can packaging be returned for reuse?

✓ Where does the waste go?

✓ How is the waste safely disposed of or reused?

✓ Does the product or its waste emit toxins into the land at disposal?

✓ Are there recycling programs in place that assist in the recycling of this product?

Paints, Finishes, Coatings, and Adhesives

✓ Does this product exceed EPA standards?

✓ Is this product water-based or biodegradable?

✓ Is it silicone-based?

✓ Is it considered low- or no-VOC?

✓ How does the manufacturing process use water and energy efficiently?

✓ Does the product off-gas or emit toxins to installers or end users?

✓ What sustainable manufacturing processes do you use?

✓ How is it packaged and shipped?

✓ Can packaging be returned for reuse?

✓ Where does the waste go?

✓ How is the waste safely disposed of or reused?

✓ Does the product or its waste emit toxins into the land at disposal?

✓ Are there recycling programs in place that assist in the recycling of this product?

CSI DIVISION 10   SPECIALTIES

Fireplaces

✓ Where is this product manufactured?

✓ What are the primary materials used in the manufacturing of this product?

✓ Does this product contain any recycled materials (steel, for example)?

✓ What type of fuel is used in this product?

✓ Does this product rely on a secondary energy source to ignite?

✓ How energy-efficient is this product?

Questions for Manufacturers *(Continued)*

✓ If a masonry stove:
- ▦ Does this product come equipped with a catalytic converter?
- ▦ What is the hourly smoke emission rate?

✓ How does the manufacturing process use water and energy efficiently?

✓ Does the product off-gas or emit toxins to installers or end users?

✓ What sustainable manufacturing processes do you use?

✓ How is it packaged and shipped?

✓ Can packaging be returned for reuse?

✓ Where does the waste go?

✓ How is the waste safely disposed of or reused?

✓ Does the product or its waste emit toxins into the land at disposal?

✓ Are there recycling programs in place that assist in the recycling of this product?

CSI DIVISION 11	EQUIPMENT (Appliances and Equipment)

✓ Where is the appliance manufactured?

✓ What are the main components of the appliance made of?

✓ Are any toxins emitted in the manufacturing or end-use of this product?

✓ Is the appliance ENERGY STAR-rated? How much energy is used?

✓ If the appliance uses water:
- ▦ Is it a water-conserving appliance?
- ▦ How much water is used?

✓ How durable is this appliance? What is its average life span?

✓ How much of the appliance can be disassembled and recycled?

✓ What type of materials or products are used or needed in the maintenance of this appliance?

✓ How does the manufacturing process use water and energy efficiently?

✓ Is it, or would you consider getting it, Greenguard-certified?

✓ What sustainable manufacturing processes do you use?

✓ How is it packaged and shipped?

✓ Can packaging be returned for reuse?

✓ Where does the waste go?

✓ How is the waste safely disposed of or reused?

✓ Does the product or its waste emit toxins into the land at disposal?

✓ Are there recycling programs in place that assist in the recycling of this product?

CSI DIVISION 12	FURNISHINGS

Cabinetry

✓ If a hardwood, is the wood third-party-certified? If not, how is it farmed/logged?

Questions for Manufacturers (Continued)

✓ If you use MDF or particleboard, is it formaldehyde-free?

✓ Where does the wood come from?

✓ Is it treated with chemicals (e.g., copper chromated arsenate)?

✓ Does the company participate in reforestation?

✓ If reclaimed, where is it from? Barn? Railroad? Other?

  ■ Is it free of lead, nails, tar, creosote, and so on?

✓ What are the elements (drawer fronts, box, etc) made from?

✓ Are the adhesives or finishes toxic?

✓ How does the manufacturing process use water and energy efficiently?

✓ Does the product off-gas or emit toxins to installers or end users?

✓ Is it, or would you consider getting it, Greenguard-certified?

✓ What sustainable manufacturing processes do you use?

✓ How is it packaged and shipped?

✓ Can packaging be returned for reuse?

✓ Where does the waste go?

✓ How is the waste safely disposed of or reused?

✓ Does the product or its waste emit toxins into the land at disposal?

✓ Are there recycling programs in place that assist in the recycling of this product?

Textiles/Fabrics

✓ What is the fabric made of? Where does it come from?

✓ Where is the fabric manufactured?

✓ If it is a natural fabric or fiber:

  ■ Were any chemicals used in the growing process of this fiber?

  ■ How was the natural fiber cleaned and processed?

✓ If it is a synthetic fabric:

  ■ Is it made from recycled content?

  ■ Is it recyclable?

  ■ Is it made from renewable content—that is, bio-based fibers?

  ■ Is it biodegradable/compostable in any way?

✓ What types of dyes were used in the fabric?

✓ Do you use flame retardants or other chemical finishes on the fabrics?

✓ How is the fabric maintained or laundered?

✓ How durable is the fabric?

✓ How does the manufacturing process use water and energy efficiently?

✓ Does the product off-gas or emit toxins to installers or end users?

✓ What sustainable manufacturing processes do you use?

✓ How is it packaged and shipped?

Questions for Manufacturers *(Continued)*

✓ Can packaging be returned for reuse?

✓ Where does the waste go?

✓ How is the waste safely disposed of or reused?

✓ Does the product or its waste emit toxins into the land at disposal?

✓ Are there recycling programs in place that assist in the recycling of this product?

Leather

✓ Where do the hides for your leather products come from?

✓ Do these hides come from humanely and organically raised animals?

✓ What sustainable manufacturing processes do you use?

✓ Are your leathers treated with any surface treatments (stain repellants, etc.)?

✓ How is your leather tanned? Do you use chromium in your tanning process? Do you use vegetable-based tanning agents?

✓ What types of dyes do you use on your leathers? Do your dyes contain any toxic substances? Do you use any natural vegetable and mineral dyes?

✓ How does the manufacturing process use water and energy efficiently?

✓ Does the product off-gas or emit toxins to installers or end users?

✓ How is it packaged and shipped?

✓ Can packaging be returned for reuse?

✓ Where does the waste go?

  ■ How do you handle the chemical and protein-based waste products that result from the manufacturing of your leather?

  ■ How is the waste safely disposed of or reused?

✓ Does the product or its waste emit toxins into the land at disposal?

✓ Are there recycling programs in place that assist in the recycling of this product?

Case Pieces

✓ If a hardwood, is the wood FSC- or third-party-certified? If not, how is it farmed/logged?

✓ If you use MDF or particleboard, is it formaldehyde-free?

✓ Where does it come from?

✓ What are the glues, paints, or finishes used?

  ■ Are they water-based or low-VOC?

✓ Are any recycled or reclaimed materials used?

✓ What happens to by-products of manufacturing?

✓ How does the manufacturing process use water and energy efficiently?

✓ Does the product off-gas or emit toxins to installers or end users?

✓ Is it, or would you consider getting it, Greenguard-certified?

✓ What sustainable manufacturing processes do you use?

✓ How is it packaged and shipped?

Questions for Manufacturers *(Continued)*

✓ Can packaging be returned for reuse?

✓ Where does the waste go?

✓ How is the waste safely disposed of or reused?

✓ Does the product or its waste emit toxins into the land at disposal?

✓ Are there recycling programs in place that assist in the recycling of this product?

Upholstery

✓ Are woods used for the frames FSC- or third-party-certified?

✓ What are the main components and what are they made of?

✓ Are components formaldehyde-free?

✓ What are the glues, paints or finishes?

■ Are they water-based or low-VOC?

✓ How does the manufacturing process use water and energy efficiently?

✓ Does the product off-gas or emit toxins to installers or end users?

✓ Is it, or would you consider getting it, Greenguard-certified?

✓ What sustainable manufacturing processes do you use?

✓ How is it packaged and shipped?

✓ Can packaging be returned for reuse?

✓ Where does the waste go?

✓ How is the waste safely disposed of or reused?

✓ Does the product or its waste emit toxins into the land at disposal?

✓ Are there recycling programs in place that assist in the recycling of this product?

Bath/Bedroom Linens

✓ What is the fabric made of? Where does it come from?

✓ Where is the fabric manufactured?

✓ If it is a natural fabric or fiber:

■ Were any chemicals used in the growing process of this fiber?

■ How was the natural fiber cleaned and processed?

✓ If it is a synthetic fabric:

■ Is it made from recycled content?

■ Is it recyclable?

■ Is it made from renewable content—that is, bio-based fibers?

■ Is it biodegradable/compostable in any way?

✓ What types of dyes were used?

✓ Do you use flame retardants or other chemical finishes?

✓ How is the fabric maintained or laundered?

✓ How durable is it?

Questions for Manufacturers *(Continued)*

✓ How does the manufacturing process use water and energy efficiently?

✓ Does the product off-gas or emit toxins to installers or end users?

✓ What sustainable manufacturing processes do you use?

✓ How is it packaged and shipped?

✓ Can packaging be returned for reuse?

✓ Where does the waste go?

✓ How is the waste safely disposed of or reused?

✓ Does the product or its waste emit toxins into the land at disposal?

✓ Are there recycling programs in place that assist in the recycling of this product?

Area Rugs

✓ Is the product Rugmark-certified?

✓ Where is the rug made or manufactured?

✓ If the rug is made of a natural fiber:

- Were any chemicals used in the growing process of this fiber?
- How was the natural fiber cleaned and processed?
- What types of fabric treatments/or enhancements has the fabric been treated with?

✓ If the rug is made of synthetic fibers:

- Are they made from recycled content?
- Are they recyclable?
- Are they made from renewable content—that is, bio-based fibers?
- Are they biodegradable or compostable in any way?

✓ What types of dyes were used?

✓ What is the backing made of?

✓ What, if any, adhesives are used?

✓ How is the rug maintained or cleaned?

✓ How does the manufacturing process use water and energy efficiently?

✓ Does the product off-gas or emit toxins to installers or end users?

✓ Is it, or would you consider getting it, Greenguard-certified?

✓ What sustainable manufacturing processes do you use?

✓ How is it packaged and shipped?

✓ Can packaging be returned for reuse?

✓ Where does the waste go?

✓ How is the waste safely disposed of or reused?

✓ Does the product or its waste emit toxins into the land at disposal?

✓ Are there recycling programs in place that assist in the recycling of this product?

Window Treatments

✓ Where is the product made?

Questions for Manufacturers *(Continued)*

✓ Is it made from a natural or renewable source?

✓ What is the process used in manufacturing it?

✓ Does the product contain low- or no-VOC contents?

✓ Does the product contain formaldehyde?

✓ What are the energy savings to be gained by using this product, or its R-value?

✓ How is the material maintained or laundered?

✓ How does the manufacturing process use water and energy efficiently?

✓ Does the product off-gas or emit toxins to installers or end users?

✓ Is it, or would you consider getting it, Greenguard-certified?

✓ What sustainable manufacturing processes do you use?

✓ How is it packaged and shipped?

✓ Can packaging be returned for reuse?

✓ Where does the waste go?

✓ How is the waste safely disposed of or reused?

✓ Does the product or its waste emit toxins into the land at disposal?

✓ Are there recycling programs in place that assist in the recycling of this product?

Art and Framing

✓ Are woods used FSC-certified, third-party-certified and/or formaldehyde-free?

✓ What are the components in composite-made frames?

✓ What are the glues, dyes, glazes, paints, or other ingredients used?

■ Are they water-based or low-VOC?

✓ Do you take back old frames for reuse or remanufacture?

✓ How does the manufacturing process use water and energy efficiently?

✓ Does the product off-gas or emit toxins to installers or end users?

✓ What sustainable manufacturing processes do you use?

✓ How is it packaged and shipped?

✓ Can packaging be returned for reuse?

✓ Where does the waste go?

✓ How is the waste safely disposed of or reused?

✓ Does the product or its waste emit toxins into the land at disposal?

✓ Are there recycling programs in place that assist in the recycling of this product (frames)?

Accessories

✓ Where is the product manufactured?

✓ What is the product made of? (Depending on materials used—wood, glass, metal, fabric, etc., see other manufacturer questions.)

✓ Is any part of this product made from recycled content?

Questions for Manufacturers *(Continued)*

✓ Is any part of this product made from renewable content?

✓ Is this product biodegradable?

✓ Is this product recyclable?

✓ Can this product be disassembled and reused in any other way after end-of-life?

✓ Does this product contain any toxic materials?

✓ How does the manufacturing process use water and energy efficiently?

✓ Does the product off-gas or emit toxins to installers or end users?

✓ What sustainable manufacturing processes do you use?

✓ How is it packaged and shipped?

✓ Can packaging be returned for reuse?

✓ Where does the waste go?

✓ How is the waste safely disposed of or reused?

✓ Does the product or its waste emit toxins into the land at disposal?

✓ Are there recycling programs in place that assist in the recycling of this product?

CSI DIVISION 22	MECHANICAL (Plumbing)

✓ Where is the product made?

✓ What happens to any by-products or waste from manufacturing?

✓ How is the waste safely disposed of or reused?

✓ Are any of the ingredients toxic?

✓ How is the product finished and sealed?

✓ Is there recycled content in the fixture?

✓ Can the fixture be recycled?

✓ How does the manufacturing process use water and energy efficiently?

✓ Does the product off-gas or emit toxins to installers or end users?

✓ What sustainable manufacturing processes do you use?

✓ How is it packaged and shipped?

✓ Can packaging be returned for reuse?

✓ Does the product or its waste emit toxins into the land at disposal?

✓ Are there recycling programs in place that assist in the recycling of this product?

CSI DIVISION 26	ELECTRICAL (Lighting/Light Fixtures)

✓ Where is the product made?

✓ What happens to any by-products of manufacturing?

✓ Are the dyes, glazes, paints, and ingredients toxic?

✓ If wood:

   ■ If a hardwood, is the wood FSC- or third-party-certified?

Questions for Manufacturers *(Continued)*

> - ■ If not, how is it farmed/logged?
> - ■ If you use MDF or particleboard, is it formaldehyde-free?
> ✓ If metal
> - ■ Is any recycled content used?
> - ■ How do you handle waste?
> - ■ How is it finished and sealed?
> ✓ Is there recycled content in the fixture?
> ✓ Does it have an ENERGY STAR rating?
> ✓ What kinds of lamps (bulbs) are recommended?
> - ■ Are they energy-efficient, or can the fixture be retrofitted to use energy-efficient lamps?
> ✓ How does the manufacturing process use water and energy efficiently?
> ✓ Does the product off-gas or emit toxins to installers or end users?
> ✓ Is it, or would you consider getting it, Greenguard-certified?
> ✓ Is it UL-listed?
> ✓ What sustainable manufacturing processes do you use?
> ✓ How is it packaged and shipped?
> ✓ Can packaging be returned for reuse?
> ✓ Where does the waste go?
> ✓ How is the waste safely disposed of or reused?
> ✓ Does the product or its waste emit toxins into the land at disposal?
> ✓ Are there recycling programs in place that assist in the recycling of this product?

Fixed Project Checklist

Once knowledgeable about which sustainable qualities and characteristics to look for when researching products and solutions, we are ready to tackle the arena of fixed interior finishes, specifically. We have found that utilizing a checklist helps direct the process and deliver a green home to the client. Over time, we have assembled an easy-to-use listing that applies to the most commonly used sustainable fixed architectural interior elements in a home, and could be added to on a project-by-project basis.

For the checklist to be an effective tool, it is vital that the team first agree to the sustainability goals. Engage all project team members—both internal and external teams. Begin at the outset of design, as concepts are taking shape and brains are storming. Utilize the checklist during the research, design, and approvals from the client. Prior to finalizing and submitting the design documents for construction, go through the checklist again, to ensure that the materials selections and specifications meet the criteria.

Equally important is rigorous and continual follow-up with the contractor throughout construction, to assure that the sustainability goals that were set at the beginning of the project are accomplished. Once construction is complete, request that the contractor submit in writing, with an MSDS and/or product spec sheets, that green products were purchased and installed.

FIXED Project Checklist

FIXED—Energy Efficiency
Energy-Efficient Appliances and Equipment
✓ ENERGY STAR-qualified equipment and appliances; dishwasher, washer, refrigerator, freezer, ice maker, microwave
✓ Gas clothes dryer
✓ Gas cooktop with electric ignition
Energy-Efficient Lighting and Light Controls
✓ ENERGY STAR-qualified lighting package, which includes the following:
■ Fluorescent light fixtures or compact fluorescent lightbulbs installed in place of standard incandescent bulbs for all fixtures (fixed and furniture).
■ Unified automation of light controls; efficient lighting controls, including occupancy/motion sensors, dimming controls, and automatic daylight dimming controls. Installed at specific locations or as a whole house system .
■ No recessed can lights in an exterior insulated ceiling.
✓ Window shade light sensors
FIXED—Resource Efficiency
Surfaces
✓ All particleboard (PB) and urea-formaldehyde-based medium-density fiberboard (MDF) inside envelope of house eliminated, or
✓ All exposed edges of particleboard (PB) and medium-density fiberboard (MDF) to be sealed with three coats of nontoxic, low volatile organic compounds (VOCs), low-permeability paint or sealer prior to installation
Adhesives, Finishes, Sealants, and Stains
✓ Low-toxic, solvent-free, water-based for all interior applications; that is:
■ Installation of subfloor, wood trim, flooring, countertops, wallcoverings, paneling and tub/shower enclosures, woodwork, cabinetry
■ Less than 150 grams per liter of VOCs
Interior Doors
✓ Recycled and/or salvaged doors
✓ Domestic wood from reclaimed sources
✓ Third-party-certified sustainably harvested wood
✓ Rapidly renewable materials and products made from plants that are typically harvested within a 10-year or shorter cycle
✓ Materials and products extracted, harvested, or recovered, and manufactured regionally within 500 miles of the project

FIXED Project Checklist *(Continued)*

Interior Floor Finishes

Carpet

✓ Natural fiber carpet made with natural latex rather than styrene butadiene rubber (SBR) latex backing

✓ Natural or recycled-content carpet pad made from textile, carpet, carpet cushion, or tire waste (including rebond)

✓ Carpet to be tacked not glued

✓ Cork or 100 percent recycled content product for underlayment

✓ Fifty to 100 percent recycled content carpet

Wood

✓ Domestic wood from reclaimed sources

✓ Third-party-certified sustainably harvested wood

✓ Rapidly renewable materials and products made from plants that are typically harvested within a 10-year or shorter cycle

✓ Materials and products extracted, harvested, or recovered, and manufactured regionally within 500 miles of the project

✓ Cork or 100 percent recycled content product for underlayment

Linoleum, Bamboo, and Cork

✓ Bamboo or cork flooring or another rapidly renewable material

✓ Natural linoleum with low-toxic backing

Tile

✓ Ceramic tile with 50 percent or more recycled content

✓ Ceramic tile installed with plasticizer-free grout

✓ Cork or 100 percent recycled content product for underlayment

Interior Wall Finishes

✓ Plaster veneer with natural color pigments and natural sealers

✓ Biodegradable wallcoverings with recycled content

✓ Ceramic tile with 50 percent or more recycled content

✓ Ceramic tile installed with plasticizer-free grout

✓ Paint with low or no VOCs (less than 250 grams per liter of VOCs)

✓ Paints with recycled content

Cabinetry and Shelving

✓ Domestic wood from reclaimed sources

✓ Formaldehyde-free medium-density fiberboard (MDF)

✓ Third-party-certified sustainably harvested wood

✓ Agricultural-based particleboard (PB) or 100 percent recycled wood content PB

FIXED Project Checklist *(Continued)*

✓ Rapidly renewable materials and products made from plants that are harvested within a 10-year or shorter cycle

✓ Materials and products extracted, harvested, or recovered, and manufactured regionally within 500 miles of the project

Countertops

✓ Domestic wood from reclaimed sources

✓ Formaldehyde-free medium-density fiberboard (MDF)

✓ Third-party-certified sustainably harvested wood

✓ Agricultural-based particleboard (PB) products

✓ Rapidly renewable materials and products made from plants that are typically harvested within a 10-year or shorter cycle

✓ Materials and products extracted, harvested, or recovered, and manufactured regionally within 500 miles of the project

✓ Ceramic tile with 50 percent or more recycled content

✓ Ceramic tile installed with plasticizer-free grout

✓ Natural linoleum with low-toxic backing

✓ Reclaimed stone (local or regional preferred)

✓ Recycled content materials (e.g., Richlite, Icestone, Paperstone, Terrazzo)

Trim and Millwork

✓ Domestic wood from reclaimed sources

✓ Formaldehyde-free medium-density fiberboard (MDF)

✓ Third-party-certified sustainably harvested wood

✓ Rapidly renewable materials and products made from plants that are typically harvested within a 10-year or shorter cycle

✓ Materials and products extracted, harvested, or recovered, and manufactured regionally within 500 miles of the project

Storage and Collection of Recyclables

✓ Built-in recycling center with two or more bins

Water Efficiency

✓ ENERGY STAR washing machine and dishwasher

✓ Bathroom and kitchen faucets fitted with flow-restricting aerators

✓ Dual-flush toilets in all bathrooms

✓ Low-flow showerheads fitted with flow-restricting aerators

The Fixed Project Checklist encompasses specific areas where we, as interior designers, can quickly and easily create healthier IAQ, conserve resources and materials, and become better environmental stewards on a project. More general issues have been added, one by one, as we have come to understand their relevance and importance to projects. These areas are not always under our scope of services or in our control, but they are equally important. We recommend that you familiarize yourself with these concepts and how they interface with the areas for which we do have responsibility, for understanding the impact of these and other key issues on a project will expand your knowledge and add value to the project team.

FIXED INTERIOR SPECIFICATIONS GUIDELINES

As the schematic design and research phases begin, continue to explore green product options. Utilizing the preceding questions for manufacturers and suppliers, we have developed guidelines for the types of products to specify, or not specify.

Armed with knowledge about the various finishes and fixed components (see Chapters 6 to 16) begin questioning your suppliers about their products (see this chapter, starting on page 88). Our recommendations are provided to assist in the selection of green products. They derive from lessons learned in practice; they are not intended to be comprehensive or necessarily the most critical factors. The point is, we encourage you to add to these checklists and questionnaires and to share with others, and with us, what you learn through your own practice.

We recommend employing a simple format when writing specifications for finishes. Sustainable requirements can be added under notes or within the body of the form, whichever you prefer. As always, work directly with your suppliers to create close working relationships, benefiting all of your projects.

FURNITURE SPECIFICATIONS GUIDELINES

When it comes to furniture and fabrics, it has been challenging to find sustainable product lines that are appropriate for our residential projects. Push the envelope by continually asking for products with sustainable attributes. Increased market demand will result in a steady growth of options. If you also practice commercial design, you know that available options have been growing exponentially since the inception of USGBC's LEED rating systems.

The information here can be applied to furnishings as easily as to fixed interior finishes. By following the same sustainability guidelines, you can create specifications for fabrics and furnishings. Begin by asking questions of the manufacturers or suppliers long before you begin writing the specification or purchase order. Question their methodology as well as the ingredients in their products. The more you know, the easier it will be for you to suggest alternatives for manufacturers to consider in making their pieces more environmentally friendly and healthy. You may have better luck, at the outset, with smaller custom manufacturers who are traditional builders and already have some of these practices in place.

As with fixed interior finishes, focus on the type of long-life, durable furnishings that will work best for your project. Ask:

- Are there recycled, reclaimed, or salvaged products or materials that you can use?
- Are there materials with a lower embodied energy, that are durable, that you can use?

And consider when you use antiques and collectibles, you are recycling—eliminating a manufacturing process. Finally, furnishings that are regionally produced require less energy and resources to transport to project sites.

In Summary

The effort and challenge required in qualifying green products will result in sustainable and responsible project specifications. True, often, it may feel as though the evaluation process is similar to comparing cantaloupe to kiwis. Comparisons range from the resource-extraction impacts of one product with the manufacturing impacts of another, and the indoor-air-quality impacts of a third. All have varying degrees of environmental impact.

Even in the greenest of projects it is likely that products will be used that are not themselves green. They may, however, be used in a manner that helps reduce the overall environmental impacts of the building. Again, creating a green home is a balancing act, matching the products and materials to the specific design to minimize the overall environmental impact. In a well-thought-out design, substituting green products for conventional products can make the difference between a good building and a great one.

For success, commit time to begin learning the options that are available to you as an interior designer. Seek out training and set applications into motion on your next project. Through practical applications and by gaining knowledge, your confidence level and credibility will grow. This is a wonderful cycle of moving forward with sustainable solutions; do this in as many areas as you possibly can. The payoffs are infinite. Penny Bonda, in *Green Design Matters* (2005), written for ASID, said it well:

> As interior designers you know, instinctively, how influential you are in the marketplace.
>
> Now you must accept responsibility for that influence and use your colossal purchasing power to create safer, better furnishing materials. It's time for each designer to think about himself or herself as an active participant in reshaping the old industrial marketplace into a cleaner postindustrial system. Here's how you do that, each one of you, separately, and collectively as a group:
>
> Remember that big order for ergonomic chairs you signed recently? Did you ask your supplier if the chairs were designed for disassembly, if they had recycled content, if the factories that made the parts were known for polluting the water and air, if the parts were made by semislave labor, if the chairs were shipped long distances and used up a great deal of energy to reach their destination? These are questions that consumers—especially large-volume consumers like interior designers—are beginning to ask today. Your questions will

be welcomed by many manufacturers who are looking to please you, their valued clients. And you will understand how powerful you can be as an agent of change in a marketplace looking to fit into the twenty-first century.

If interior designers insist on making environmentally informed material choices, the profession will have a crucial role in society. To achieve this noble goal, you need to become true collaborators with manufacturers—many of whom still think of you as part of their sales teams—and use your understanding of people to create better, more relevant products. You also need to see yourselves as experts trained to safeguard the health and welfare of people in the kind of life-supporting environments you so ably plan and design. This way of thinking is the way of leaders. You are poised to take on the mantle of that important design leadership. But if you ignore the deep and wide social need for safer materials, among other people-oriented issues, your profession will surely go the way of kings and queens.

RESOURCES

"Evaluating Green," *ED+C Magazine,* Mark Ryan, January 2004

"Navigating the Maze of Environmentally Preferable Products," Nadav Malin, *Environmental Building News,* November 2003

"A Simple Formula for Change," Michael Washburn and Christina Koch, *Eco-Structure Magazine,* September/October 2004

"What Makes a Product Green," Alex Wilson, *Environmental Building News,* January 2000

concrete

Drawing: Donna Barta-Winfield.
Design: Annette Stelmack,
www.associates3.com.
Photo: David O. Marlow.

Concrete, in its simplest form, has been around since ancient civilizations first incorporated lime, chalk, oyster shells, and gypsum to make a substance that hardened and formed a permanent bond. The Romans developed a type of concrete made from ground volcanic rock, lime, and aggregates called *pozzolana;* the Greek Parthenon, one of many structures built with that material, still stands today. The use of portland cement in this country came about in the 1800s (see the sidebar, "Cement or Concrete?"). Modern-day concrete is the most common building material in the United States. It's estimated that, worldwide, more than 6 billion tons of it are produced annually—one ton for every person alive, every year (University of Texas at Austin College of Engineering, "Concrete Composed of Waste Materials Promises Environmentally Friendly Impact," December 14, 2004; www.engr.utexas.edu).

Concrete's superior longevity and indestructibility give it an eco-advantage over shorter-lifespan treatments for walls, floors, fireplaces, and countertops. It's also thrifty: new homes already feature a concrete slab floor, so by using the concrete structure as the visible finish, the need for carpet, wood, or linoleum on top of a subfloor is eliminated. The client will never need to replace the floor covering (since there is none), further improving its ecological value.

Even though concrete is manufactured, the material has rocklike properties: It doesn't outgas, rust, mold, rot, or otherwise wear out. It has inherent thermal mass; light-colored concrete is naturally cool and perfect for hot climates, and darker colors collect passive solar or radiant heat well in cold-weather locations. A home with a high structural concrete content may actually allow for lesser-capacity heating and cooling equipment. Concrete may be poured and molded to fit almost any specification. It can be recycled indefinitely into more concrete by crushing it into aggregate.

Basic concrete is nondescript, although mineral pigments, stains, texture treatments, and polishing make it shine. Concrete is also an excellent matrix for aggregates

Cement or Concrete?

Although the two words are often used interchangeably in common language, technically, cement and concrete are not the same substance. Joseph Aspdin invented portland cement in 1824 when he ground up a mixture of limestone and clay, then cooked it on his stove. Cement is just one ingredient in concrete. Concrete, on the other hand, is made up of four basic elements: sand, gravel, cement, and water.

And cement's connection to Portland? It's neither Maine nor Oregon. Rather, Aspdin named his creation for its resemblance, when set, to limestone found on the tiny isle of Portland in the English Channel. Portland is now the most common type of cement, and there are many others made of widely varying mineral and synthetic components.

like recycled glass, forming a beautiful, terrazzolike finish for floors and countertops. By incorporating a high percentage of recycled materials, concrete's environmental value increases. And when postindustrial waste replaces some of the aggregate or cement in concrete, the result is increased product strength and conservation of raw materials (see the sidebar, "Recipe: Recycled, page 114").

Although it has many positive environmental attributes, concrete is made primarily of nonrenewable resources. Aggregates such as sand and gravel make up 60 to 80 percent of the mixture. Portland cement, a mix of calcium (lime) and silicon (silica), along with aluminum, iron, and gypsum, comprise 10 to 15 percent of the mixture and is the complex key ingredient that holds concrete all together. To obtain the minerals to make portland cement, a variety of sources are mined or collected, including limestone, chalk, seashells, marl (loose, earthy deposits), shale, clay, slate, or silica sand. The collective minerals and by-products are then ground and fired at extremely high temperatures, so the resulting embodied energy is very high.

Other ingredients, especially postindustrial waste, may figure prominently in the mix. While many postindustrial compounds are quite safe, there has been concern about the risk of contaminants from heavy metals, hydrocarbons, sulfur, or other toxins. Little testing has been done, but the general consensus is that the toxins from postindustrial additives are minuscule, bound up in the concrete, and unlikely to leach or outgas once the concrete is hardened. The verdict about relative safety is still out, but using fly ash and other recycled materials in concrete greatly reduces both the amount of waste going to landfills as well as the need for energy-intensive cement (see the sidebar, "Recipe: Recycled"). Admixtures—chemical "enhancements" that may slow the dry time or improve the flow, bond, finish, or look—are also common in concrete mixes. They are more important when building or designing outdoor applications, where the elements are harsher and greatly affect proper curing and the life span of concrete. For interiors, admixtures are rarely needed if optimal temperatures and conditions for pouring and curing are specified.

Cement production takes a heavy toll on the environment. High CO_2 emissions—3 to 4 percent of the U.S. total—are generated at these plants. Concrete production also requires large amounts of water, and the wastewater from the process is highly alkaline, posing a serious problem for disposal or neutralization. Cement dust exposure puts workers at a high risk for silicosis. Add these factors to the embodied energy in concrete from the mining, transport to factory, firing, transport to retailer, then transport again to the site, and the strikes against concrete become numerous.

Concrete, however, pays off some of its environmental debts by virtue of its amazing durability, longevity, and low need for maintenance. It will outlast some interior finishes by two or three times or even more. And if the client has chemical sensitivities, concrete (without questionable aggregates or admixtures) offers an inert, easy-to-keep-clean surface that will not become a sink for allergens and irritants.

Concrete is a relatively permanent interior design element, although a concrete floor or countertop may be easily covered with another finish. Weigh pros and cons carefully with the client. All in all, concrete offers longevity that is hard to beat—albeit at an environmental price.

Recipe: Recycled

Scientists and manufacturers have found that a variety of by-products otherwise headed for the landfill may be incorporated into concrete. The practice reduces waste, and the addition of some recycled content actually enhances the strength, plasticity, or imperviousness of concrete. Also, the percentage of cement needed in the concrete may be reduced significantly if fly ash, silica fume, blast furnace slag, or rice husk slag is added. The following are common postindustrial ingredients used in concrete.

- *Blast furnace slag* is the residual left over from the manufacturing of pig iron or other metal ores.
- *Cement kiln dust (CKD)* is collected from cement firing, then reused as raw material.
- *Fly ash* is a by-product of coal-fired power plants. It is used as a substitute for cement in concrete, increasing concrete strength and decreasing permeability so that less water is needed for production.
- *Foundry sand* is a by-product from metal casting.
- *Lime sludge* is generated when recycling paper.
- *Rice hull ash* is left over from rice milling. Rice husks are used to fuel the parboiling process, and the resulting ash is roughly 85 to 90 percent amorphous silica.
- *Silica fume* is postindustrial waste from the production of silicon alloys. It was discharged into the atmosphere prior to the 1970s, but air quality controls necessitated its capture.

Where Does It Come From?

- Concrete is a mixture of sand, gravel, water, and cement.
- Cement is manufactured mostly from limestone and a combination of minerals (calcium, silicon, aluminum, iron), which are fired at high temperatures, then ground and combined with gypsum.
- Concrete may use postindustrial waste as a substitute for part of the cement or some of the aggregate.
- Aggregates may also include decorative recycled glass, stones, or other manufactured or natural materials.

- A variety of chemical admixtures may be present, although it is possible to make concrete without them.
- Natural or synthetic pigments may be added to wet concrete.
- Concrete may be left unfinished, or it may be finished with epoxy, polyurethane, or other chemical sealants.
- Linseed oil and beeswax can be used as a finish.
- Concrete may be acid-stained with water-based, acidic liquids that contain metallic salts.

Installation

This is an example of how concrete floors are good for capturing solar mass. The space also features zero-VOC paints, formaldehyde-free trim, insulated window blinds, and wheatboard cabinets, and takes advantage of south-facing windows and over-hangs. Photo by Michael Mathers.
Architect: Robertson, Merryman, Barnes Architects, Inc.

CONCRETE SUBSTRATE FINISHING

If the client's desire is to have the concrete substrate become the finished floor or surface, there are many factors to consider. While it is certainly possible to remove a finish such as carpet or wood to reveal the concrete underneath, decorative or protective finishes may not take to the previously covered substrate. Prior use of adhesives, oils, or finishes prevents a good bond of new finishes, and the end product may be unsatisfactory. Solvent-based cleaners or acid strippers are not recommended; the outgassing, VOCs, and harsh chemicals are not eco-friendly. Power washing may be adequate to remove light soil.

PRECAST CONCRETE

Some concrete applications, such as countertops and sinks, may be precast off-site. The installation process for these is simpler, usually requiring nothing more than placement, fastening, and/or adhesives. Precast pieces are excellent options for clients with chemical sensitivities, as they may also be finished by the supplier before installation and allowed to outgas, if needed. (Outgassing will still affect the environment and air quality overall, but if done outdoors, it is easier on a chemically sensitive client.)

CAST-ON-SITE CONCRETE

If new concrete is to be poured, specify that the content of the cement and/or concrete be completely safe for use in residential interiors. Rarely, the aggregate or cement will emit radon gas (present in natural stone). Specify radon testing before purchase or installation, if it is a concern.

For maximum strength and durability in cast floors, walls, fireplace surrounds, countertops, and similar applications, concrete must be properly cured (hardened), meaning it must achieve maximum hydration at optimum temperature (not lower than 50°F/10°C). This will take anywhere from five days to a month, depending on the project and material specifications.

Specify that potable water be used for curing so as not to introduce any contaminants. Highly alkaline wastewater from the work site should not be allowed to drain onto landscaping.

If the pouring won't be completed in one day, consider specifying (in advance) the use of safe sucrose-based retardants so that the unused wet concrete may be kept for use later and not wasted. Alert contractors and workers to the fact that the concrete design element will not be covered with another finish such as wood flooring or a composite countertop. The slab must be protected at all times from dust, chemicals, nails, and other construction debris with a tarp or similar covering, and all tradespeople should take precautions to avoid marring it. Even the tiniest amount of dust and debris will adversely affect the final outcome of a finished concrete surface.

When casting concrete on-site, there are numerous treatments available to add color, shine, and durability. Some products are negative contributions to ecological values or human health. Mineral pigments are generally benign. Rely on companies that sell low-VOC, low-solvent, water-based materials and finishes, and on products that meet stricter air quality standards. Consult the MSDS to learn of worker safety precautions, residual odors, and potential outgassing.

ADMIXTURES

Although most admixtures are negative contributions from an environmental stand-point, those that slow the drying time, called retarders, may be marginally environ-mentally beneficial because they reduce waste. Normally, wet concrete must be used immediately, but with retarders (mostly sucrose-based, and innocuous), the remaining material may be saved and used the following day.

Superplasticizers usually contain hazardous formaldehyde. There are a host of other chemicals that might be added to supposedly "improve" concrete, but many outgas or pose a known health risk. Ideally, specify no admixtures; or, if they must be used, spec-ify low-VOC, water-based, reduced-solvent types, and finish the concrete with a water-based sealer to prevent outgassing.

PIGMENTS, STAINS, AND PAINTS

For subtle color, pigment may be added directly to wet concrete mix. Specify inorganic, mineral-based pigments that become inert when dry, and the effect will be long-lasting and eco-friendly.

Stains and paints (see Acid Staining or Etching, below) that are specifically de-signed for concrete and masonry may also introduce permanent color to the sur-face. Although some are water-based, they still rely on petroleum-based polymers and chemical colorants; therefore, specify that dyes do not contain aniline, chromium, or other heavy metals.

Concrete can be colored and sealed using natural by-products of corn, sunflowers, or soybeans coupled with water-based acrylic technology that effectively penetrate and seal concrete. Most water-based acrylic stains are typically composed of acrylic resins in a water-base, which allow the stains to penetrate deeply into the concrete surface and adhere to the concrete to bring out color. They are low odor and low VOC, and require only a simple soap and water clean up.

AGGREGATES AND SEEDING

When aggregates are added for visual effect, the process is called seeding. Terrazzolike recycled glass is probably the most popular aggregate, or seed. Seashells, rocks, and pieces of hardware are also used, to name a few. The client can highly personalize the results by featuring artifacts or a special stone from the property. Computer compo-nents are showing up as aggregate seeding in some countertops and flooring, and they are not recommended as they may contain toxic heavy metals.

TEXTURAL EFFECTS

For texture, concrete may be molded, stamped with designs, scored, or sawcut into "tiles" or grids. These techniques usually require only simple power or hand tools, and so they are basically earth friendly. Specify adequate ventilation and worker protection from dust when cutting dry concrete.

Polishing

Concrete can be polished to a high sheen using progressively finer diamond stones; this technique is common for countertops and floors. Specify worker protection from dust. A nonporous finish completes the effect (see Sealants and Finishes, below).

Acid Staining or Etching

Acid staining isn't really a stain, in that there's no true pigment. The products used to color or "etch" concrete are usually corrosive, toxic liquids such as hydrochloric acid and metallic salts that together react with calcium compounds to form permanent blues, greens, and browns on the surface. Once the "staining" is finished, the concrete may continue to react subtly with water in the air or on the surface, so a waterproof sealant is recommended. The process is very unhealthy and time consuming—it may take up to a month for the chemicals to complete their reactions. Hydrochloric acid, if inhaled or if it comes in contact with the skin, is harmful to workers and residents. It is a known carcinogen.

Although the final product is beautiful, inert, and will last indefinitely with regular sealing, acid staining is controversial among those who are environmentally conscious. Disposal of acid stain is toxic to the environment. If color is desired, there are less harmful, more eco-friendly methods, such as adding pigment or recycled glass.

Paint

On walls, ceilings, fireplaces, and similar concrete applications, silicate dispersion paint forms a permanent, inert, chemical bond. It's popular in Europe for exteriors, but is effective for interiors as well. The surface becomes breathable, and is nontoxic, zero-VOC, noncombustible, and moldproof.

Sealants and Finishes

Because concrete is porous, reacts with certain compounds, and stains easily, all horizontal surfaces should be sealed or finished with polyurethane or epoxy. The best alternative, rather than leave the concrete prone to damage, is to specify water-based or water-reducible, low-VOC, formaldehyde-free sealants.

Linseed oil and beeswax are also options to easily seal concrete surfaces.

Maintenance

Concrete, once sealed, is a breeze to keep clean with a bit of mild detergent and water. Unsealed concrete should be dusted or lightly scrubbed with a nonmetallic brush and water. Advise the client to avoid the use of cleansers or detergent on either sealed or unsealed concrete.

Sealants and finishes, and eventually the concrete underneath, may be prone to scratches or abrasion from dirt, shoes, cutlery (on countertops), and so on. Resealing

This gallery has radiant-heated concrete floors with a natural color pigment added and has been sealed with linseed oil. The space also features recycled content masonite walls with integral color added, also sealed with linseed oil.
Photo by Greg Hursley.
Architect: Eric Logan, Carney Architects.

may be necessary every few years, depending on the particular sealant and the amount of wear on the concrete surface.

Where Does It Go?

Concrete's extreme durability guarantees a decades-long life span under optimum conditions. Nevertheless, concrete currently makes up more than half of all construction and demolition waste, and only a small fraction is being recycled because the market for it has not fully developed and the cost to transport it is high (AIA Colorado, *Sustainable Design Resource Guide,* www.aiacolorado.org). Concrete slabs can easily be ground up and recycled as aggregate for new projects—most road and bridge construction departments already use recycled concrete as roadbed.

Spec List

Specify:

- Concrete (and cement mix) made without admixtures
- Aggregates (or "seeding") and cement from all-natural materials or from verified-safe recycled materials
- Natural mineral pigments (if any)
- Potable water for curing
- Factory-finished slabs (for countertops and small applications)
- Low-VOC, water-based or water-reducible, low-solvent, no formaldehyde stains, sealants, and finishes
- Silicate dispersion paint

Avoid:

- Aggregates or recycled ingredients that may introduce environmental contaminants or health hazards
- Admixtures (with the possible exception of sucrose-based retardants)
- Chemical pigments or paints with chromium, aniline, or heavy metals
- Acid stains
- Seeding with manufactured, possibly hazardous materials such as computer chips

RESOURCES

ConcreteNetwork.com
Portland Cement Association: www.cement.org
See also: Plumbing Fixtures, page 284; Concrete Countertops, page 305.

CHAPTER 7

masonry

Drawing: Donna Barta-Winfield.
Design: Maggie Tandysh, www.associates 3.com.
Photo: David O. Marlow.

The definition of masonry is broad—it's any work a mason performs. For interiors, a mason's materials might include rock and brick, stone tile and veneer. The project may be dry-stacked (no mortar), glued in place, mortared, grouted, or simply cut to fit.

Stone, the literal building block of all masonry, is formed through millions of years of volcanic eruptions (igneous rock), sifting and settling of sediment (sedimentary rock), and powerful geologic change (metamorphic rock). Masonry work is as ancient as human history, when our ancestors began to create homes by stacking stones for shelter and protection. Mortar was first made from clay. Then primitive forms of concrete were devised to grip the masonry, and bricks were made by baking or drying clay in the hot sun. Eventually, masonry became more than just structure; it developed into an art form. Ancient temples, pyramids, monuments, and other symbolic edifices were constructed from rock and clay to give them permanence and authority.

Masonry is an obvious choice for construction if the structure is to last for centuries. The Great Wall of China, possibly the most impressive structural feat of all time, stretches for more than 4,000 miles and is composed of millions of individual blocks of stone and brick. Most of the world's great government, cultural, and religious buildings, as well as most of its monuments, are made of stone and brick. And Chicago, Denver, and London, cities that were all devastated by disastrous fires in earlier centuries, rebuilt with stone and brick, then added requirements for masonry to their building codes.

For home design purposes, there are few materials that are as long-lasting as natural masonry. Stone and brick don't emit VOCs; will outlast many other materials such as wood or bamboo; and are water-resistant, fireproof, insect-proof, and moldproof. Most stone or brick applications require only simple dusting or soap-and-water cleaning, although occasional sealing may improve stain and scratch resistance. The materials can also be reused or recycled.

Both stone and brick are excellent choices where thermal qualities are critical, such as for fireplaces, flooring over radiant heat, or walls and floors that collect passive solar radiation. The masonry stores up warmth and releases it slowly. The same masonry will stay cool if kept out of direct sunlight or away from sources of heat. Well-designed placement of stone or brick actually decreases heating and cooling costs.

If stone for interior design purposes is gathered from the site or found locally, with no mining involved, it has few ecological downsides. Stone that is reclaimed from deconstruction is another superb green choice. The environmental value of new masonry goes down when the tally includes quarrying, mining, manufacturing, firing, or long-distance transportation.

Quarried stone, by definition, is that which is cut or shoveled. There is usually less waste from quarrying than from mining. Still, the United States alone produces almost a million and a half metric tons of quarried and cut stone. Each year the figure has been increasing, and most is used in construction applications. Some U.S.-quarried stone was exported, but Americans imported even more than they shipped out (USGS, http://minerals.usgs.gov).

Mining, on the other hand, acquires relatively small amounts of ore from larger beds of rock. Methods include blasting and stripping, open pits, underground mines, or the use of hydraulics or augers. Once mined, the sought-after mineral must be ex-

Fact Check

- Houses, buildings, cars, telephones, countertops, driveways, computers, even laundry detergent and salt—they all are made from minerals. Each person in the United States uses an average of 47,000 pounds of newly mined materials every year. Notably, there are more than 60 identifiable minerals in the typical computer (National Mining Association, www.nma.org).

- 13 million of the world's poorest people work in mining, and 1 million of the labor force in small scale mines and quarries are children, many unprotected by labor laws, working long hours without proper training or tools, risking their health and unable to attend school (Global March Against Child Labor, www.globalmarch.org).

- 80 percent of Nauru, a tiny, independently governed island in the South Pacific, is now uninhabitable and completely devastated after decades of phosphate mining (Microsoft Encarta Online Encyclopedia 2005, http://encarta.msn.com).

tracted from the ore. Although mined rock has far more embodied energy than quarried, both methods put permanent scars on the land and upset the ecosystems. They affect runoff and water downstream, soil composition, and the plants and animals dependent on the area. In addition, changes in slope or soil affect absorption of rain, sometimes further damaging the landscape through erosion, landslides, toppled trees, and flooding.

Human health is also tested. Both quarrying and mining workers are subjected to many risks such as dust inhalation, poor air quality, exposure to chemicals, injury, and repetitive motion disabilities, especially in developing countries where labor standards are lax.

Most stone used in residential settings is quarried, not mined. If the design application will last for generations and then be recycled or reused, or if the stone is locally acquired, it may be a wise, all-natural choice.

Brick has one distinct advantage over stone: it's made from common clay that is easily dug from local pits. Yet to become brick, the clay must be processed, pressed, and then fired at high temperatures, raising the embodied energy total.

Salvaged brick is readily available in many locations, and the use of it will conserve natural resources and raw materials. Salvaged or reclaimed stone from deconstruction is less commonly available. Research local land resources such as properties where field stones or flagstone are easily gathered. Obtaining stone from a quarry in the same region also makes sense ecologically. By relying on local sources, whenever possible, the embodied energy is greatly reduced.

Conversely, specifying a scarce stone that is shipped from abroad is more difficult to justify environmentally, especially if the main reason for its selection is aesthetic. Weigh all of the options and find the best masonry design element that is heavy on durability and light on the eco-scale.

The Risks of Radon

Some types of stone may emit radon gas, which is tasteless, odorless, and colorless, and is believed to cause more lung cancer than anything else except smoking. Radon can enter a home environment through well water and through lower air pressure in the foundation that pulls the gas in from the surrounding soil. It's less common, although still dangerous, to find radon emitted from concrete or stone (usually granite) used in construction or design applications.

Fortunately, radon exposure in the home can be prevented because the gas is detectable. To lower the risks of radon exposure, the whole house should be tested for it, or individual building materials should be checked before use. If a very small surface is the culprit, then a water-based, low-VOC sealer may help prevent gas emissions. If there are dangerous radon levels within the home, mitigation should be pursued, which involves installation of abatement systems or, in rare cases, removal of the offending material. The requirements for mitigation licensing vary from state to state; contact the local public health department or visit this EPA website: www.epa.gov/iaq/whereyoulive.html.

Where Does It Come From?

- Stone is mined, quarried, or simply collected from various landscapes.
- Brick is made from clay that is processed, pressed, and fired.
- Some stone or brick may be reclaimed from old roads, buildings, and fences.
- Some stone (especially granite) emits radon gas, although it's rare.

Installation

Dry-stack masonry is by far the most eco-friendly masonry installation choice, where minimal mortar or adhesives are used, and stones or blocks are simply set in place. Within a home, dry-stack applications are mostly limited to décor or walls.

The nonquarried granite wall shown here illustrates an effective application of a durable product. This space also features a handmade terra-cotta floor and organic upholstered furniture.
Photo courtesy of Stefano Dorata Architetto, www.stefanodorata.com.

Specify darker colors of stone and brick and nonreflective sealants if the thermal absorption and release is to be maximized. Specify lighter colors in hot climates where cooling is the main concern.

Some masonry dust, such as that from soapstone, is hazardous if inhaled. Cut stone outdoors with proper worker protection, and wet-cutting methods are preferable. Consult with the contractor or fabricator for other recommended precautions depending on the particular type of masonry.

Specify that underlayments are made from FSC-certified wood, gypsum, or agricultural by-products, and are formaldehyde-free. Specify all-natural cement (see Chapter 6, "Concrete," page 111), mortar, and grout, whenever possible. If all-natural is not available or appropriate for the particular job, go with the least-toxic, low-VOC, zero-solvent, minimal-additive material available.

Mastic or other adhesives may be necessary to secure masonry veneer or stone tiles, although they may outgas VOCs or contain hazardous materials. If an adhesive is needed for the particular application, consult the MSDS, and specify a water-based, low-VOC type that has no petroleum base, no toluene, hexane, benzene, or other solvents.

Sealants prolong the beauty and even the life span of masonry, but use with caution. Many sealants for masonry are solvent-based. Specify low-solvent, low-VOC, no-formaldehyde, and water-based. Avoid drying agents containing heavy metals. Also avoid spray-on sealants, which release molecules more readily into the air than wipe-on types, and expose occupants and workers to more VOCs and odors.

As with any natural material, plan carefully to avoid undue waste. Unused stone or brick may be saved for future use or recycled to a construction exchange or salvage operation. Inexpensive filler stone or small pieces that can't be salvaged can be crushed on-site and mixed into the topsoil or used in landscaping.

Maintenance

Masonry design elements require minimal maintenance over the years, and some masonry installations may be left without any protective finish at all. Countertops and floors may need regular reapplication of sealants to maintain stain resistance and scratch resistance or to protect the grout between tiles; consult with the supplier or installer as to how often this should be done. Advise the client to avoid spray-on sealants if future reapplications are needed.

This stone wall, made from local material taken from the client's land, was dry-stacked with minimal mortar use. The stone was laid on the interior and exterior walls, with an insulated wall between. Photo by David O. Marlow. Designer: Associates III.

Where Does It Go?

Brick and stone may be reused or salvaged into new purposes. If the masonry application has been damaged beyond use in its original purpose, it can be downcycled into roadbed, landscaping, or possibly tile or terrazzo. Eventually, all types of masonry decompose and again become part of the greater geological processes. Masonry is truly a cradle-to-cradle resource.

Natural grouts and mortars, such as those with lime or sand, will also follow the cycle of deterioration. Synthetic grout, adhesives, and mortar will not break down as easily.

Spec List

Specify:
- Reclaimed, salvaged, or recycled brick and stone
- Stone or brick from local sources
- Radon testing of materials before installation
- Natural mortars and grouts
- Low-VOC, low-solvent, water-based, formaldehyde-free sealants and adhesives
- Wipe-on or brush-on sealants

Avoid:
- Imported stone or brick
- Adhesives, grout, mortar, or sealants with solvents, additives, or formaldehyde
- Spray-on sealants

RESOURCES

Brick Industry Association (BIA): www.bia.org
"Consumer's Guide to Radon Reduction": www.epa.gov/radon/pubs/consguid.html
Environmental Protection Agency (EPA): 800-438-4318
See also: Chapter 6, "Concrete"; Tile, page 188; Countertops, page 305.

CHAPTER 8

metals

Drawing: Donna Barta-Winfield.
Design: Annette Stelmack,
www.associates3.com.
Photo: David O. Marlow.

According to the *Encyclopedia Britannica*, the term *metal* includes all of those elements and alloys that are "characterized by high electrical and thermal conductivity as well as by malleability, ductility, and high reflectivity of light" (www.britannica.com). The category includes copper, aluminum, iron, and gold, as well as many alloys such as steel and bronze. (Calcium, sodium, and potassium are metallic elements in the scientific sense, but for design purposes, this discussion will be limited to the common definition.)

Metals are so important to human civilization that historical epochs, such as the Bronze Age and Iron Age, get their names from the "discovery" and first known uses of the respective materials. Many metals and alloys are practically impervious to abuse. This characteristic, combined with their universally valued beauty, has made them the material of choice for coins around the globe.

Modern residential construction relies on various metals for their superb strength, especially in joists, supports, flashing, shields, plumbing, and essential hardware. Builders in ancient times also found metals useful. Copper piping found in the pyramid of Cheops was recently found to be in serviceable condition after 5000 years (www.eurocopper.org). Metals can be stamped, poured, hammered, and extruded. Railings, fireplace surrounds, and castings are often made from metal, as are decorative hardware, appliances, kitchen hoods, and countertops. Yet metals are more than just utilitarian; they are beautiful, possessing unique lusters and textures. They are also so versatile that they are also made into delicate powders or leaf, perfect for faux finishes and fine detailing.

From an ecological standpoint, the use of metal in the home has significant advantages. It won't outgas in its natural state (unfinished) or irritate chemical sensitivities; and depending on the particular metal, it may outlast the house itself. It's pestproof, fireproof, and moldproof. Many metals need little upkeep. Plus, metal has the potential to be recycled infinitely. Although recycled metal has yet to become a mainstay in residential design products, some factory-made hardware may already contain it, and many custom fabricators rely on it for their craft.

But before they are manufactured into usable products, metals must be mined from the earth, and the toll on nature due to this process is heavy, no matter how it's done. Mining scars the land, contaminates the water, uses vast amounts of fossil fuel for the machinery, and contributes to poor air quality. As an example, approximately 220 tons of earth are excavated for each ton of copper ("From Rio to Johannesburg: Mining Less in a Sustainable World," by Payal Sampat; Worldwatch Institute, www.worldwatch.org). The loss of habitat for plants and animals due to mining is enormous, and the ecological upset permanent.

Once removed from the earth, the actual metal, sometimes only a fraction of the total ore, must be extracted. From earth to mine to smelter to ore requires huge amounts of energy in the form of transportation, mechanization, power, and heat. And that's only the raw material: the metal must go to the fabricator, then possibly to a factory for assembly or to a retailer or dealer. It's an arduous trip, resulting in, possibly, the highest cost of embodied energy of any natural resource, ahead of wood, tile, or stone.

Some metals can be reused and recycled, over and over and over again, but once they have been removed from the earth, they can't be "put back." Unlike wood or straw, which biodegrade back into the earth rather quickly, the massive geological

Heavy or Not?

There's an important distinction to be made between those metals that are positive contributors to interiors and those that are to be feared for their toxicity—specifically, heavy metals. The term *heavy metals* technically refers to those with high specific gravity, but in everyday usage it has come to mean "metals with toxic properties." Lead, chromium, cadmium, mercury, and beryllium, along with other less common metals, are categorized as heavy.

Lead, the heavy metal that was used as the primary whitening pigment and drying agent in common house paint until it was banned in 1978, is the greatest environmental offender in residential applications. According to OSHA, lead poisoning is still the most prevalent environmental illness in children (www.osha.gov). Chromium is found in pigments, textile dyes, and chrome plating, and in wood preservation, leather tanning, and anticorrosion coatings. Cadmium shows up in some pigments and batteries. All three of these, along with others such as mercury and beryllium, are serious risks to workers who use them regularly or manufacture products that contain them.

All people are exposed to heavy metals on a daily basis through industrial emissions, fertilizers, pesticides, and even natural sources such as the food we eat and water we drink. All the more reason to avoid them at all costs when specifying materials for a healthy, green home. There is a direct relationship between a host of serious illnesses and prolonged or constant inhalation, ingestion, or contact with these metals.

For more information on heavy metals and other toxins, consult the *National Report on Human Exposure to Environmental Chemicals*, available online at www.cdc.gov/exposurereportOSHA, and "Safety and Health Topics, Toxic Metals," at www.osha.gov/SLTC/metalsheavy.

---

forces that created these metallic elements take millennia. And some metals are quite rare. Although aluminum and iron are relatively abundant in the earth's crust, other metals such as zinc, tin, nickel, and manganese are scarce. For these reasons designers must ask: Will the longevity of an application make it worth the environmental cost?

One way to minimize the heavy ecological cost of metal is to recycle. Scout architectural salvage shops and metalworks, especially when the intention is primarily for décor and not protection or structure. By reusing what's already in circulation, the only embodied energy added is that of travel, or possibly for modifications to the piece.

This stair railing was constructed with high recycled-content metal. In addition, the treads were constructed of recycled fir.
Photo by Kelly Lerner, www.one-world-design.com.
Designer: Boa Constructor.

Specify recycled metal, and the ramifications are much improved. Every ton of recycled steel utilized saves 2,500 pounds of iron ore, 1,400 pounds of coal, and 120 pounds of limestone (Steel Recycling Institute, www.recycle-steel.org), much of it through "minimills" that utilize locally collected scrap (see the sidebar, "Minimills Gone Max" on page 133). Recycled aluminum reduces the amount of energy needed by 95 percent over production from virgin bauxite ore. Look for products that contain a high percentage of recycled metal, such as steel, aluminum, and copper.

There are other considerations beyond the particular metal's origin. It's important to consider the coatings or paints used on them, either in the factory or on-site. When-

Minimills Gone Max

A minimill is a steel production facility that relies on scrap rather than iron ore. An electric arc furnace melts it down into product that is first graded then sold to manufacturers.

The minimill industry has taken off in the last few decades, fueled by the growing value of recycled materials and the availability of scrap steel for stock. In 1970, only 10 percent of U.S. steel production was at minimills; in 2001, it had grown to nearly 50 percent. There's more diversity now in the steel grades and product types, as well. The size of the mills has grown, too, so much so that "mini" has become a bit of a misnomer.

ever possible, specify a type of metal such as stainless steel that requires no finish or chemical cleaning solutions to prevent rust or oxidation or to maintain the sheen.

Sometimes an "unfinished" metal element such as a kitchen hood will be shipped with a protective coat of natural or synthetic oil that should be removed before installation (synthetic oils may be especially aggravating to chemical sensitivities). Check with the manufacturer or dealer to determine whether the coating is standard, or if a synthetic oil can be avoided, and whether simple soap and water will remove it.

If a finished or painted piece of metal is desired, it's best to leave the process to the manufacturer or fabricator, especially when client chemical sensitivities are an issue. Most paints and permanent finishes for metals are solvent-based and emit considerable VOCs, especially when wet. Manufacturers control the application conditions, and the surface will have the opportunity to outgas before arrival in the home. (Outgassing will still be harmful to the environment, but it will be better for a sensitive client if it is done outdoors.)

Avoid chromium, cadmium, brass, and nickel plating, which produce toxic emissions and by-products and put workers at significant risk for environmental illnesses. Galvanized metals have zinc coatings, and though the factories produce relatively low emissions, they use large amounts of energy. The zinc galvanizing industry may also produce discharge that is harmful to aquatic life. Zinc is also relatively scarce, although some is recovered for use from other industries. Plastic polymer or powder coatings are extremely durable, are comparable to or better than plating, and are applied through a heat-fusion process that outgasses very little after the initial drying.

Inquire about the finishes and patinas a manufacturer or artisan produces, as many are created using acidic or caustic toxic chemicals. Instead request others with more benign methods. Some metals have a predisposition to rust or discoloration when exposed to the elements or handling. Understand the natural tendency of each metal and specify a subtle and beautiful patina that is created through less toxic methods. Inquire about the waste or wastewater that is produced, as this may be an indicator as to how toxic a method is employed.

In general, when contemplating metal for decorative or structural pieces in the home, it's a good idea to ask whether there's a better, less environmentally taxing material that might be used. That said, when the design element is permanent, such as with stair treads and railings, the advantage of metal may be its superior durability. In such a case, adding recycled content improves the eco-value; and if the piece is 100 percent recycled, the raw materials haven't been wasted.

Where Does It Come From?

- Metal is mined from various locations around the globe.
- Some metal is extracted from ore through intensive manufacturing processes. Other metals such as silver and gold are found in veins, so the separation from the ore is slightly less energy-intensive.
- Metals are often combined into alloys to increase their strength, sheen, or resistance to natural oxidation.
- Various factory coatings and finishes may be applied to metal such as paint, powder coating, protective (natural or chemical) oils, metal platings, and zinc galvanizations.
- Metal can be easily recovered from recycling and fabricated into new products.

Installation

Metal pieces may create thermal bridges or be highly reflective, bringing heat or cold from another source into the location. This may be either advantageous—for example, with a metal fireplace surround—or a real problem, as with aluminum-clad windows that collect condensation or ice in a cold climate. Study the potential location of a significant metal design element before specifying it, and factor in the probable amount of solar radiation, hot or cold thermal bridging, and condensation that might occur.

Metal may affect both the length and direction of electromagnetic waves within a room or building. Any substantial piece of metal, especially that which has significant conductivity (such as copper or steel), should not be installed in the vicinity of electronic equipment, electrical wires, or appliances such as microwave ovens. Although the effect of electromagnetic radiation is a hotly debated issue, the risk from exposure within the home has not been well established. For every claim there seems to be a counter to it. Prudence is still the best measure, so consult with the electrician and the general contractor before adding a large metal design element.

Recycle all metal scrap. The recycling rate for steel is the highest of any construction and demolition material due to its high demand and good price, and steel recycling now costs less than disposal.

This kitchen features a recycled stainless steel hood. The flooring is recycled oak that was removed from another demolition project.
Photo courtesy of Rockhill and Associates.
Architect: Dan Rockhill.

Maintenance

It's important to know the client's expectations for the appearance of any metal design element. Many types of metal require special cleansers, polishing, or coatings to remain in pristine condition. Copper and silver oxidize rapidly in contact with air; iron and some types of steel will rust. Commercial polishes and cleaning solutions often contain highly toxic or outgassing chemicals such as kerosene, naphtha, perchloroethylene, chromic acid, silver nitrate, or solvents. Natural products such as vinegar, table salt, or food-grade oils, along with simple scrubbing, can be easily substituted.

A certain degree of patina, such as a naturally occurring verdigris on copper or bronze, may be desirable, so no polishing or cleaning will be necessary. Whenever possible, specify a type of metal that allows for minimal upkeep.

Fact Check

- The building construction industry is the major consumer of copper; more than 3 billion pounds are used in the United States alone (Copper Development Association, www.copper.org).
- Each year, steel recycling saves the energy equivalent to electrically power about one-fifth of the households in the United States (or approximately 18 million homes) for one year (Steel Recycling Institute, www.recycle-steel.org).
- In 2001 alone, more than 30,000 airplanes could have been built with the 750,000 tons of aluminum that was thrown away. Aluminum-can waste was up 28 percent over 1991 (Container Recycling Institute, www.container-recycling.org).

Where Does It Go?

Most metals can be continually recycled. As with all materials, however, the consumer is primarily responsible for the amount actually recycled, and much is still sent to landfills. In theory, metal debris will eventually become part of the earth's crust again through millennia of geomorphological processes.

Spec List

Specify:

- Salvaged architectural metal pieces
- One hundred percent recycled content, or the highest percentage possible
- Local fabricators to eliminate transportation
- Metal that develops a natural patina or verdigris
- Metal that needs minimal or no upkeep with cleansers and polishes
- Natural, nonoutgassing protective oil coatings or none at all
- No paint or finish
- Factory-finished powder coating, galvanization, or paint
- Silicate dispersion paint
- Recycling of all scrap

Avoid:

- Pieces made with virgin metal
- Synthetic oil coatings

- Imported fabrications
- Painting or finishing metal on-site
- Chemical polishes, treatments, or cleansers
- Unwanted thermal bridging, reflectivity, condensation, or electromagnetic field disturbances as a result of poor placement of the metal design element

RESOURCES

Copper Development Association: www.copper.org
Specialty Steel Industry of North America: www.ssina.com

wood and composites

Drawing: Donna Barta-Winfield.
Design: Kari Foster, www.associates3.com.
Photo: David O. Marlow.

From the stick-and-hide lean-tos of primitive humans to the massive timber frames of European cathedrals, and from early American log homes to modern Western houses, much of our world has been built from wood. It is one of the most fundamental construction materials, used since ancient times and still the primary building resource in many regions today. Wood has the tensile strength of mild steel and the strength-to-weight ratio of reinforced concrete. Yet wood "gives," adjusting to fluctuations in temperature and humidity, balancing static electricity, flexing slightly with exerted pressure, and absorbing sound.

Wood is also durable—a wooden monument in the Horyu-ji area of Japan, still standing tall after more than 1300 years, is listed as a World Heritage Site (www.worldheritagesite.org). It is also renewable—that is, if proper measures are taken to sustain the supply and to control demand. Sadly, as is well documented today, forests are disappearing at a rapid rate, especially the largest trees. Half of the world's forests have already been cut, and at the current rate, the last expanses of undisturbed tropical forest will vanish in the next 50 years (Environmental Defense Fund, www.edf.org). The culprits? Booming commercial and residential construction, the expansion of mining, and the need for fuel and cropland, among others.

It isn't just about clear-cutting. A single oak might take a couple of centuries to reach maturity, but a complete forest ecosystem requires thousands of years to fully develop. Fell a few trees carelessly and the complex biodiversity surrounding them is destroyed. Unquestionably, clear-cutting is disastrous in most settings, but selective logging that chooses only the biggest and best trees is also harmful. The remaining trees may be vulnerable to erosion, soil compaction, and high winds. Removal of even a small percent of the trees may damage or destroy those that remain.

As is true for damage to any ecosystem, the effects are not just local, but global as well. Trees, like all plants, are critical to earth's "breathing." Trees take in carbon dioxide as they grow and capture the carbon, then emit only oxygen (O_2). Human beings obviously need oxygen to live. Concentration of carbon dioxide in our atmosphere is also a major component of climate change, and the cumulative effect from deforestation over the decades and centuries is large.

Although it is commendable that some countries, including the United States, have planted millions of saplings to replace the cut timber—some estimates even say forest losses have stabilized—this secondary growth will not likely sustain such diverse ecosystems nor achieve the stature of its forested forebearers. Growth-augmentation agents are often added to the soil, promoting taller stands in lesser time—and of lesser quality. Tree farms can't replace or even successfully replicate nature. Sadly, only 10 percent of the original old-growth forests now remain in the United States (Environmental Defense Fund, www.edf.org).

There are other things to consider when contemplating the use of wood for interior design purposes. Once the trees have been harvested, wood can't be recycled in the same sense as metal, which can be melted down and reformed into a different product without losing the metal's integrity. Most wood is downcycled when no longer useful; it's cut up, chopped up, or ground into sawdust to make a lower-grade material. Wood posts become particleboard, board becomes paper, and paper is shredded for insulation, and so on. The good news is that the cycle may continue for decades and even centuries, and that wood and paper will ultimately biodegrade.

A lot of guilt is attached to cutting down trees, but the fact remains that few materials are better suited for many aspects of home construction and design, especially considering the all-natural assets of wood. Wood is ultimately renewable in far fewer years than many alternatives such as stone or metal. It biodegrades simply, quickly, and completely into the earth, where new soil is formed that will provide for the growth of more trees so that the cycle can continue. And when carefully protected, the life cycle of cut timber can outlast the life span of its still-standing relatives. If grown, harvested, and used sustainably, wood can truly be a green choice.

Sustainable Wood Choices

Although framing is the largest wood consumer in home construction, casework, paneling, trim, flooring, and other interior design elements make up a large portion of the total. Design teams should be judicious in selection and acutely aware of wood consumption, setting an example to both contractors and clients. Specify reclaimed wood, sustainable species, locally available sources, and certified products, then carefully calculate the dimensions to optimize efficiency and minimize waste. These simple yet wise decisions will limit the detrimental effects on our fragile forests; encourage the production and certification of sustainable wood; and provide the client with a truly renewable, beautiful, and durable material.

This handcrafted millwork was made from the trees on the site that were killed by a fire. Photo by Emily Hagopian, www.essentialimages.us. Designer: San Luis Sustainability Group.

RECLAIMED WOOD

Wood is a favorite for reclaiming (that is, salvaging and using for a second purpose, sometimes called "rediscovering"). It's easy to disassemble from warehouses, barns, homes, and orchards. Timbers are also collected from the bottoms of lakes and other bodies of water, left there from previous forestry operations or sunken along with wrecks. Submerged-wood reclamation is excellent quality, as the resins have been washed away and thus the wood density has increased. The downside is that reclaiming wood from natural environments such as lake bottoms may disturb established ecosystems for decades, making the earth friendliness debatable.

Remanufactured Wood

The term *remanufactured* may mean many things, but for wood flooring, it usually means reclaimed wood from various sources that is remilled to fit the intended purpose. Sometimes it designates recycled wood chips, planks, or even sawdust that is pressed into flooring (usually called "engineered" wood). The distinction is significant. Specify reclaimed or remilled to keep the distinction clear, and be cautious when analyzing a product labeled as remanufactured.

Reclaimed wood is the best ecological choice for many interior wood applications, especially if acquired locally. The U.S. market for reclaimed wood is expanding so rapidly that it is being shipped in from overseas to meet demand, but this imported reclaimed wood requires long-distance transportation that raises the embodied energy. By opting for local "used" wood, trees are spared from the ax, long-distance transportation is eliminated, and the used wood product is deterred from landfill demise.

Locally reclaimed wood varieties will often feature the species that grow (or once grew) in the region, making them especially well suited for the particular environment. Decades of acclimatization may prevent further warping, shrinking, or expansion in the home. The quality of reclaimed wood is typically higher. While no one advocates chopping down old-growth trees as our ancestors did, reclaimed wood may have been harvested from such trees—and thus have wider planks and tighter grain than new wood.

Reclaimed wood offers one more aesthetic advantage: there's a special joy in seeing and touching a "historic" product that will soon be custom-fit to a home.

It's sometimes difficult to track the origin of reclaimed wood, and the FSC does not certify for sustainability as it does for new wood (see Certified Wood in the following section), but the source is especially important when the application is to be indoors. Ask for details about where the wood came from. Arsenic-treated lumber or salvaged pieces with chipped paint are risky to human health. Verify the safety of wood originating from an industrial or agricultural site, as it might be tainted with chemicals.

Although it has yet to gain widespread use and acceptance, SmartWood, a program of the Rainforest Alliance, has established a certification program for Rediscovered

The cabinetry and wood trim in this kitchen were created using the trees that were cut down to build the home. Photo courtesy of © 2005 Farr Associates Architecture | Planning | Preservation, Chicago, Illinois.

Wood Operations (RWOs). Much like the FSC, for companies that voluntarily comply, the wood species, chain of custody, and operational practices are closely monitored by the program. In addition, wood with SmartWood certification is recognized by the FSC and qualifies for use in FSC-Mixed products.

Antique Wood

It's fairly common to refer to reclaimed wood as "antique," but it's a misnomer. The source may be 200 years old, or just a few. Although old wood may have its feel-good charms, from an eco-viewpoint, reusable wood of any age is better than new.

In spite of the limited availability of certified reclaimed wood, noncertified doesn't necessarily have to be avoided. Many rediscovered wood operators (RWOs) both recover and sell the wood locally, know the source well, and may have deconstructed the site themselves. They may be able to supply details about the species, origin, and safety of the product for indoor use.

CERTIFIED WOOD

One of the best methods for selecting new or recycled wood products is straightforward. The Forest Stewardship Council (FSC) was established as an independent nonprofit in the mid-1990s to "promote environmentally appropriate, socially beneficial, and economically viable management of the world's forests" (FSC, www.fsc.org). It is the world leader in third-party chain-of-custody certification, meticulously requiring verifications of the source(s) and ensuring quality and environmental controls along the way to the consumer. Fair labor and responsible tree farming are also embraced by the agency. The FSC and its logo are recognized worldwide.

In brief, choosing FSC-certified wood products ensures that the particular tree species is not endangered, that eco-friendly forestry practices have been monitored,

The FSC logo identifies products that contain wood from well-managed forests and certified in accordance with the rules of the Forest Stewardship Council.
© 1996 Forest Stewardship Council A.C.

and that the processing or manufacturing meets stringent guidelines. When specifying FSC-certified wood products, there are several options from which to choose:

- *FSC Pure.* This means 100 percent of the wood comes from "well-managed forests." The content won't have potential contaminants from recycled wood products—a key to designing a sensitivity-free home.

- *FSC Recycled.* This labeling designates that postconsumer material is used. The label may or may not indicate the exact percentage of recycled content used to make the wood product, however, depending on the manufacturer's preference on whether to reveal these details.

- *FSC Mixed.* Depending on the applicable standards, wood with this label may contain a blend of certified-forest wood, reclaimed or recycled sources, and/or "controlled" sources (those that are strictly monitored by FSC but do not meet the other criteria). The label should indicate the combination (although precise amounts or percentages don't need to be listed).

All the wood used in the product must meet the FSC guidelines in order to qualify for one of these labels. The program now provides certification for almost any product made from wood: underlayments, furniture, paneling, trim, and decking, in addition to lumber.

Suppressed wood—small undergrowth trees that are thinned and culled to aid in forest fire prevention on public lands—is not yet certified (due to technical issues). Nevertheless, this type of wood, if the source can be verified, may be another environmentally positive choice.

The FSC certification system is not flawless, but it is certainly one of the best currently available. And the agency continues to raise its standards and to represent the interests of diverse parties, from loggers and indigenous peoples to consumers and conservation groups.

There are other eco-labels that may be found on new wood products. Some are regionally based or not recognized outside of a particular country. Others are affiliated with forestry, wood, or paper industries, so they can't really be considered third-party and objective. The American Forest and Paper Association (AF&PA), for example, requires its members to comply with Sustainable Forestry Initiative (SFI) standards. The SFI does encourage self-monitoring of forestry practices and sets a positive model of "cut a tree, plant a tree." Its guidelines, however, have been criticized as limited and somewhat ineffective. Old-growth forests and tree farms are not considered separately, and the governing board members are almost exclusively industry-related. SFI efforts may be a step in the right direction, albeit not far enough. SmartWood is an example of a third-party certification program of the conservation organization Rainforest Alliance, and is accredited by the FSC, which they helped found. They evaluate forestry operations for new growth, working with all types of landowners, as well as mill and manufacturer operations that are reclaiming or using reclaimed, recycled and salvaged wood materials. (See previous section on Reclaimed Wood in this chapter.) In the coming years, probably other new standards and wood certification agencies will emerge. As with any certified product, it's vital that designers know and understand the group and the standards behind the labels (see Chapter 5 on certification, page 75).

SPECIES

When it comes to choosing wood products, knowing the best one for the job and the one least likely to be endangered are key. As designers, we do both ourselves and the environment a favor when we dispel desires for a threatened species by presenting this knowledge at the beginning of a project.

Softwood or hardwood may be the initial preference, depending on the purpose intended. Softwood is the source for 80 percent of the world's production of lumber for construction. Hardwood includes deciduous trees in nontropical regions, such as oak, maple, ebony, walnut, hickory, beech, and mahogany, among others. As the name implies, most hardwood varieties are more durable than soft woods, with finer grain that typically accepts stains more evenly—making them the frequent choice for flooring, fine furniture, exposed casework elements, and trim.

The high desirability and slow growth of many hardwoods make them especially vulnerable to deforestation. And with the focus on rain forest depletion, it's easy to specify "no tropical hardwoods." But some so-called tropical species might be acceptable choices if they are plantation-grown regionally. Moreover, some hardwoods are softer and some softwoods are harder; the casual designations are not reliably descriptive. So don't rely upon these rather arbitrary definitions for specifications; be particular about the species. It helps to have a working knowledge, or at least a chart on hand, of those species most at risk in order to avoid them in specifications (see the table at right, "Selected Endangered, Threatened, and Vulnerable Tree Species").

Knowing what to use is as important as knowing what to avoid. Responsible forestry and lumber companies have worked diligently to discover and "farm" trees that grow quickly yet provide a high strength-to-weight ratio. Lyptus, a hybrid of two eucalyptus species, is an example. Grown primarily on formerly deforested land in Brazil, the species can be harvested at 15 years rather than every 60 to 80 years for comparable mahogany. Still, there is high embodied energy in any imported wood, and questions of equity arise where trees are farmed on deforested land in socially underprivileged regions. And faster-growing hybrid trees, like intensive agriculture, deplete soil and water more quickly, take the place of naturally diverse ecosystems, and compete with nonhybrids.

Some lumber and furniture industries specialize in the use of secondary-growth species and leave old-growth trees undisturbed. Neither fast-growth species nor secondary stands is an adequate answer to deforestation, but the benefits are undeniable, as ancient forests are preserved while the supply of wood products is increased.

Environmentally Friendly Wood Alternatives

Two species that are more environmentally friendly than most tropical woods are bamboo and palmwood. Palmwood is usually culled from past-their-prime coconut "trees" that would be felled anyway, making it a new-wood option with reclaimed-wood characteristics. Bamboo is really a grass but compares favorably to wood, and it can be cut and regrown in less than a decade.

The sink in this yoga-inspired econest overlooking the Sangre de Cristo foothills is fashioned from solid rock. The solid wood countertop is finished with natural wax.

Designer: Lydia Corser.

Photo by Emily Hagopian, www.essentialimages.us.

This environmentally friendly kitchen has FSC-certified wood throughout, cherry cabinet doors, and formaldehyde-free wheatboard inserts. Rem reclaimed walnut is used on all trim. It features natural linoleum flooring, and walls are integral colored plaster with hard wax sealers. The compre paper and resin countertops are complemented by the colorful recycled glass tile backsplash. Appliances are Energy Star rated wherever possible. Transom windows add light all the way through the kitchen and into the adjacent dining room. The walls and ceiling were hand-plastered with integ colored plaster, and then sealed with OS Hardwax oil, as were the walnut details and window mouldings.

The concrete countertop in this bathroom incorporates stainless steel sinks. The mirrors are framed with reclaimed barn siding. *(Used by Permission of My House Magazine.)*

The bamboo tread stairs have a railing of mahogany and horse fence wire. Bamboo flooring complement strawbale walls with an integral colored stucco wall in the background. *(Used by Permission of My House Magazine.)*

inspiring projects: donnalynn Design and Interiors, El Granada, CA

The perception of added space and light without increasing the footprint was accomplished by the use of fluorescent lighting. Finishes include bamboo cabinets (with wheatboard core) and new compressed paper, resin countertops, and tumbled river-rock flooring.

The kitchen area of this remodel was opened up and brightened by the removal of a wall separating it from the entry area, and by the addition of strategically placed fluorescent lighting. Linoleum flooring accents the new vertical grain bamboo cabinets; a new palm wood cabinet above the refrigerator has been added. Compressed paper and resin countertops complete the picture.

Designer: Associates III.

Photo: David O. Marlow.

A locally crafted pivot door and curved wall of sustainably certified beech enhance the entry to this powder room. A local-ly crafted custom mirror with integral lighting is centered above a reclaimed mesquite slab counter with an efficient bath fitting. The durable limestone flooring was adhered with nontoxic adhesives and sealed with a water-based sealer.

inspiring projects: Annette Stelmack, Associates III, Denver, CO

This living room embraces daylighting along with fiber-optic lighting at the fireplace. The hearth is crafted from locally obtained stone slab. Furnishings include a 50 percent recycled-content bronze table, a certified wood coffee table with water-based finishes, and locally manufactured upholstery.

Ample daylighting illuminates this eco-rated kitchen and its ENERGY STAR appliances. The recycled glass tile back-splash coordinates with a locally crafted integral colored concrete countertop and sink. The glass bar counter is sourced locally and surrounded by integral colored plaster walls. Durable limestone flooring is adhered by nontoxic adhesives and sealed with a water-based sealer.

This master bathroom's environmental products include locally manufactured cabinetry, water-based cabinet finishes, a locally manufactured glass countertop with an integral glass sink, and a natural hemp rug.

This master bedroom features a certified wood headboard, a locally sourced nightstand, a glass bedside lamp, natural silk bedding, and bamboo flooring.

Designer: Associates III.

Photo: David O. Marlow.

Designer: Associates III.

Photo: David O. Marlow.

This sitting area features locally sourced reupholstery on the chair, locally crafted recycled stainless steel shelves, and low-toxic finishes on the millwork.

Sections of wood salvaged from the lanes of a bowling alley are utilized here as island and peninsula tops. Reclaimed fir is used for the custom cabinetry and for framing the storage wall in the kitchen. The countertops and backsplash tiles are custom sized, stained concrete, as is the flooring. Undercounter fluorescent fixtures supplement the abundant daylighting that fills the kitchen. Nontoxic water-based finishes are used throughout. Between the kitchen and dining area is an 18-inch sprayed earth construction wall (a.k.a. "PISE") wall.

The countertops have recycled glass content, and the bathtub is salvaged. Separating the bathroom from the master bedroom is an 18-inch pneumatically impacted stabilized earth (PISE) wall. High south-facing windows bring in light. Reclaimed fir cabinets include perforated metal panels and nontoxic finishes.

A leftover piece of fireslate from the cooking range, using the "burner" cutout, was used for the countertop on the wash basin. More fireslate was reused as a cap on the adjacent storage shelving. The cabinetry is of reclaimed fir with nontoxic water-based finishes.

inspiring projects: Eric Logan, Carney Architects, Jackson Hole, WY

Architect: Eric Logan, Carney Architects.

Photo by Paul Warchol.

The stairwell is flooded with light from the two-story, south-facing window wall constructed of varying sized low-E windows.

Architect: Eric Logan, Carney Architects.

Photo by Paul Warchol.

A high-efficiency Danish fireplace with sandblasted surface warms the open-plan living, dining, and kitchen areas.

Architect: Eric Logan, Carney Architects.

Photo by Paul Warchol.

The concrete floors in this space are embedded with radiant heating and sealed with linseed oil. The walls and ceilings are recycled, raw MDF. The window openings are low-E insulated glazing with wood frames.

In this tightly budgeted Wyoming residence, the use of relatively inexpensive materials defines the interior space and furnishings. Raw recycled content MDF cabinetry with clear sealer is used throughout.

Architect: Eric Logan, Carney Architects.

Photo by Roger Wade.

Architect: Eric Logan, Carney Architects.

Photo by Greg Hursley.

...e eco-friendly materials used in constructing this ...me reflect a contemporary vision of a Wyoming ...yshed, incorporating oiled concrete floors and ...rrugated steel ceilings.

The structure, which commands 260° views of the Teton Range, is simply expressed and held aloft with tall columns, and features raw MDF cabinetry.

inspiring projects : David Bergman, New York, NY

The floors, of natural, readily renewable cork, feature random maroon-stained cork tiles.

Eco-friendly materials were researched and selected for this kitchen. The veneered cabinetry is built of wheatboard cores with zero VOC finishes. The backsplash and cabinet pulls are of recycled glass tile, and the countertops are natural terrazzo, formed from recycled glass and cement. The paints and finishes are low-VOC-rated.

The client wanted an open kitchen, rich in color, incorporating environmental materials, so glass tile, recycled-content counters, wheatboard-based cabinetry, and natural resin panels were used.

Architect: Doug Graybeal.

Photo by Doug Graybeal.

The cast earth wall incorporates a water feature to add beauty and humidity to the dry mountain environment.

The decorative and functional glass sink in this powder room is incorporated into an indigenous Colorado buff sandstone countertop.

Architect: Doug Grayheal

The concrete tub surround melds with the cast earth walls.

The utility sink was constructed by recycling a classic old-fashioned washtub.

Cabinet doors of certified cherry and glass complement the durable stone countertop; behind the scenes are formaldehyde-free Medite II boxes. The appliances are ENERGY STAR-rated.

inspiring projects: Baker Laporte & Associates, Tesuque, NM

The rammed straw and clay walls are 12 inches thick to provide an efficient envelope. The kitchen wall surfaces are clay-based plaster with natural pigments. The formaldehyde-free cabinetry has natural wax finishes.

The lumber for this Japanese-styled timber-framed structure was sustainably harvested in northern New Mexico. The entry has natural slate flooring leading to maple floor with a wax finish. Interior plasters are clay-based with natural pigments mixed on-site. The Banco seating and pillows were locally made from organic cotton batting with hemp covers.

Selected Endangered, Threatened, and Vulnerable Tree Species Traded Internationally (March 2006)

Common Name(s)	Scientific Name	Threats and Uses	Distribution	Listings
African ash: Koto, kyereye, oporoporo	*Pterygota macrocarpa*	Major international trade.* Used in joinery, furniture.	West Africa	IUCN Red List: Vulnerable
African mahogany	*Khaya grandifoliola, Khaya senegalensis*	Major international trade.* Mature trees are over-exploited. Illegal logging.	Central and Northern Africa	IUCN Red List: Vulnerable
African teak	*Pericopsis elata*	Commercial use, clear-felling habitat.* "Endangered"—FAO. Used in joinery, furniture, boatbuilding.	Central and Western Africa	IUCN Red List: Endangered
Afzelia; Aja, doussie, odo niyan	*Afzelia bipindensis*	Major international timber trade;* heavy commercial exploitation; few remaining seed trees.	Western and Central Africa	IUCN Red List: Vulnerable
Alcerce	*Fitzroya cupressoides*	Clear-felling of habitat, increased human settlement.* Alcerce forests have been reduced to 15% of their original size, and many of the remaining populations are small fragments. Illegal logging still occurs. Traded internationally as furniture, cladding, and joinery.	Argentina, Chile	CITES, Appendix I IUCN Red List: Endangered
Almaciga (Philippines)	*Agathis philippinensis, Agathis* spp.	Clear-felling habitat; rare. Used in cabinet work, joinery, boat masts, moldings.	Philippines, Indonesia	IUCN Red List: Vulnerable
Bintangor: damanu, beach calophyllum	*Calophyllum insularum*	Major international trade, human settlement, agriculture.* Seriously endangered small population. Used for construction, flooring, and furniture.	Indonesia (Irian Jaya)	IUCN Red List: Seriously Endangered
Brazilian cherry (aka Jatoba)	*Hymenaea courbaril*	Used for cabinetry, flooring, joinery. Threatened due to growing demand and overharvesting in certain regions. Ask supplier where wood came from, as some companies provide non-endangered and FSC-certified wood. Avoid if possible.	South America, Brazil	

Selected Endangered, Threatened, and Vulnerable Tree Species Traded Internationally (March 2006) *(Continued)*

Common Name(s)	Scientific Name	Threats and Uses	Distribution	Listings
Bleedwood tree, Mukwa Kiaat	*Pterocarpus angolensis*	Commercial use, disease, local use.* Major international trade. Small populations are heavily exploited by local people. Mature individuals suffer from a fungal disease. Some large protected populations.	East and Southern Africa	IUCN Red List: Near Threatened
Honduras mahogany	*Swietenia* spp.	International trade. Seriously endangered. Possible extinction in the next 15 years. Often used as an alternative to other mahoganies but is becoming highly threatened itself.	Central and South America	IUCN Red List: Vulnerable CITES, Appendix III
Ipe (a Brazilian rainforest hardwood, also called Brazilian walnut or diamond walnut or lapacho)	*Coriniana estrellenis*	Some FSC wood is available, but best to avoid. Used for hardwood flooring,	South America	
Kauri	*Agathis borneensis, Agathis* spp.	Clear-felling habitat.	Malayasia, Philippines, Borneo, Brunei, PNG, Fiji	IUCN Red List: Vulnerable
Lauan	*Shorea* spp., *Dipterocarpus* spp.	Clear-felling habitat.* FAO— "Requires conservation action." Illegal logging.	Southeast Asia, Philippines	IUCN Red List: Critically Endangered
Meranti, Batu	*Shorea* spp., *Parshorea* spp.	Clear-felling habitat.* Major international trade for varieties of yellow, white, light and dark red meranti. Illegal logging.	Indonesia, Malaysia, India, China, Thailand, Singapore	IUCN Red List: Critically Endangered
Molave, Vitex	*Vitex parviflora*	Clear-felling.* Overexploitation. Minor international trade. Illegal logging.	Indonesia, Philippines, Malaysia	IUCN Red List: Vulnerable
New Guinea walnut, paldao, dao	*Dracontomelum dao,* spp.	Clear-felling habitat.* FAO— "Requires conservation action." Used in construction furniture, decking.	Southeast Asia	
Nyatoh	*Palaquium* spp., *Payena* spp.	Clear-felling habitat, extensive agriculture.* Minor international trade in plywood, furniture, and moldings. Illegal logging.	Indonesia, Philippines	IUCN Red List: Critically Endangered

Selected Endangered, Threatened, and Vulnerable Tree Species Traded Internationally (March 2006) *(Continued)*

Common Name(s)	Scientific Name	Threats and Uses	Distribution	Listings
Parana pine; Brazilian pine, pino blanco	*Araucaria angustifolia, Araucaria* spp.	Major international timber trade.* Logging has decreased Araucaria forests to less than 20% of their original range, and much of the remaining forest is small and fragmented. Few seed trees remain, but fruit and seeds are still collected for human consumption.	Argentina, Brazil, Peru	IUCN Red List: Vulnerable
Parlatorei, red podocarp	*Podocarpus vitiensis, Decussocarpus vitiensis*	Clear-felling habitat; commercial use. Used in joinery and furniture.	Argentina, Bolivia, Peru	Included on list of Imported Timbers Whose Use Should Be Avoided
Pencil cedar, red nato	*Palaquium* spp.	Clear-felling habitat. International trade in plywood, joinery. Illegal logging. Per USDA: Used in furniture, interior joinery, plywood. A general utility wood	Indonesia, Philippines, Africa, India, Southeast Asia	IUCN Red List: Low Risk to Critically Endangered
Ramin, Merang	*Gonystylus bancanus*	Commercial use, clear-felling habitat.* Regeneration may decline due to overharvesting. Major international trade in furniture, moldings, picture frames, joinery. Illegal logging.	Indonesia, Malaysia, Brunei	CITES, Appendix II IUCN Red List: Vulnerable
Red sandalwood, Almug, Saunderswood	*Pterocarpus santalinus*	Commercial use, local use, clear-felling habitat.* Valuable as timber, dye, medicine, cosmetics extracts. Plantations are being established.	India	CITES, Appendix II
Rosewood, tulipwood, Bahia/Brazilian/Rio rosewood	*Dalbergia nigra*	Commercial use, clear felling habitat, seed predation. USDA: Used in decorative veneers, fine furniture and cabinets, parts of musical instruments, knife and other handles, fancy turnery, piano cases, marquetry. Also used for therapeutic purposes and deodorants and many body and skin care products.	Brazil	CITES, Appendix I IUCN Red List: Vulnerable
Teak: Borneo teak, Moluccan ironwood	*Intsia bijuga*	USDA: Used in furniture components, floorings, back of plywood, boat framing, joinery.	Australia, Asia, Africa, especially Southeast Asia, Oceania	IUCN Red List: Endangered

Selected Endangered, Threatened, and Vulnerable Tree Species Traded Internationally (March 2006) *(Continued)*

Common Name(s)	Scientific Name	Threats and Uses	Distribution	Listings
Teak: Philippine teak	*Tectona philippinensis*	USDA: Used in furniture components, floorings, back of plywood, boat framing, joinery.	Philippines	IUCN Red List: Endangered
Utile, African mahogany, sipo, sapele	*Entandrophragma utile, En. cylindricum*	Overharvesting, pests. Heavy exploitation, particularly of older trees. Major international trade as paneling and furniture. Slow growth rates. Insect predation. Some populations protected. USDA: Used in furniture and cabinetwork, joinery, decorative veneers, plywood, boat construction.	Central and Western Africa	IUCN Red List: Vulnerable
Guatemalan fir	*Abies guatemalensis*	Extensive logging, timber.	Central America	CITES, Appendix I IUCN Red List: Vulnerable
Agarwood, aloewood, eaglewood, Malayan eaglewood tree	*Aquilaria malaccensis*	Type of core wood found in Aquilaria tree species. Used in the production of incense and perfume; threatened by extensive logging and growing demand.	South Asia, Southeast Asia	CITES, Appendix II IUCN Red List: Vulnerable
Ajo, garlic tree, Costus	*Caryocar costaricense*	Logged and harvested for timber, herbal, and medicinal uses.	Costa Rica, Panama, Colombia, Venezuela	CITES, Appendix II IUCN Red List: Vulnerable
King William pine, King Billy pine	*Athrotaxis selaginoides*	Vulnerable numbers due to extensive logging. Used for joinery, musical instruments, and building boats.	Australia	IUCN Red List: Vulnerable
African teak, Afrormosia, Assembla, Ayin, Egba	*Pericopsis elata*	USDA: Used for timber as an important alternative to teak. Used in boat building, joinery, flooring, furniture, decorative veneers.	West Africa	CITES, Appendix II, in the Democratic Republic of the Congo and Cameroon IUCN Red List: Endangered
West Indian satin-wood, yellow sanders, yellowhead, yellow heart	*Zanthoxylum flavum*	Highly sought for timber, cabinetry, and veneers.	Florida, West Indies	IUCN Red List: Vulnerable
African cherry, Kanda stick, red stinkwood	*Prunus africana*	Heavily exploited for medicinal uses (for prostate cancer), and cabinetry. USDA: Bark used, especially on European medicinal market.	Africa, Madagascar	CITES, Appendix II, in the Democratic Republic of the Congo and Cameroon IUCN Red List: Vulnerable

Selected Endangered, Threatened, and Vulnerable Tree Species Traded Internationally (March 2006) *(Continued)*

Common Name(s)	Scientific Name	Threats and Uses	Distribution	Listings
Cedar, Central American cedar, cedarwood, cigar-box cedar, cigar-box wood, red cedar, Spanish cedar, stinking mahogany, West Indian cedar	*Cedrela odorata*	Threatened by heavy logging and felling before trees reach maturity. Used in boat building and cabinetry. Also used as logs, sawn wood, and veneer sheets. USDA: Used in plywood and veneer. One of the world's most important timber species.	Most of Central and South America, and parts of Mexico	CITES, Appendix III, in Colombia and Peru IUCN Red List: Vulnerable
Walnut	*Juglans neotropica*, *Juglans* spp.	Decreased habitat, commercial use, food, construction. USDA: Timber used for decorative purposes.	South America	IUCN Red List: Vulnerable
Other species to avoid and the names they are marketed under: Kurupay (South American rosewood) Lapacho (diamond walnut) Yvyraro (crystal mahogany) Guatambu (ivory wood) Curuguay (South American cherry)				

Sources: Forestworld.com, 2001; WCMC. 1992 Conservation Status Listing: Trees and Timbers of the world. WCMC, Plants Program, 1999. Tree Conservation Database. WCMC, Plants Program. Forests.org 2001; FAO=United Nations Food & Agriculture Organisation; IUCN 2004, *2004 IUCN Red List of Threatened Species;* www.iucnredlist.org, accessed March 16, 2006.

WOOD-BASED SHEET GOODS

Cabinet boxes and faces, shelving, and furnishings, which do fall into the realm of interior design, are commonly made with wood-based sheet goods. Sheet goods—various forms of particleboard, engineered wood products, fiberboard, MDF, and plywood—are common components in the cores, backings, and nondecorative components of finish carpentry. These materials are usually specified by architects and/or contractors, although designers can positively influence the specifications toward eco-friendly choices.

There is at least one environmental advantage to not choosing solid wood: smaller and younger trees, along with waste products such as sawdust, wood chips, and even old pallets can be used instead. The end result is that fewer older-growth trees are needed. If engineered wood is the choice, then specify formaldehyde-free and FSC-certified wood. Look for products that have 100 percent recycled content.

The downside to these engineered boards? Typical cabinetry, shelving, millwork, and anything with cores and veneers are likely to contain urea-formaldehyde binders and solvent-based finishes that outgas considerably and are of particular risk to those with chemical sensitivities. Imperfect but improved substitutes have been developed, such as methylenediphenyl isocyanate (MDI), a common particleboard binder that does not outgas yet still poses a known risk to factory workers. Specify formaldehyde-free and low-VOC adhesives, binders, finishes, and naturally derived adhesives (the latter are not yet widely available).

In addition, the wood content varies considerably from product to product, from recycled lumber-milling chips to cheap tropical species that were clear-cut. The FSC aids in determining the content and environmental responsibility of the manufacturer, as its

This space consists of sustainably grown mahogany wall paneling, trim, and millwork.
Photo by David O. Marlow.
Architect: Poss Architecture.

certification programs have expanded to include engineered wood products. Specify FSC-certified whenever possible.

It may be possible to avoid wood altogether. Biocomposite boards made from renewable agricultural byproducts are an alternative for cabinets, doors, trim, and even floors (see Biocomposites, page 157). Biocomposites compare quite favorably with their wood counterparts and offer an earth-conscious solution.

Where Does It Come From?

- Wood products come from both domestic and exotic trees.
- Reclaimed wood is culled from residential, commercial, and agricultural floors, walls, and structures. It may also be culled from rivers, lakes, streams, orchards, or from fallen trees.
- Some wood products are made from recycled (downcycled) wood scraps or sawdust, with acrylics or resins added.
- Wood sealants are usually polyurethane; resin-oil primers are a more environmental option.
- Wood finishes or stains may contain a variety of natural oils, resins, or pigments; solvents; chemical compounds; petroleum distillates; metal drying agents; formaldehyde; and sometimes water.

Installation

Emphasize the importance of careful measurements with the contractor, and request that they eliminate all but the tiniest fraction of potential waste.

Fact Check

- Three-quarters of an acre of forest goes into the average American home, and well over a 1.6 million new homes are built every year (Natural Resources Defense Council, www.nrdc.org; National Association of Home Builders, www.nahb.org).
- The most alarming number, perhaps, reflects a profound disregard for the environment: one-sixth of the wood delivered to each construction site is thrown away (NRDC).

Request that the installer or contractor do the cutting outdoors to keep sawdust down, and specify protective masks for the workers. Sawdust from untreated or naturally treated wood may be bagged for use in mulch or compost, or may be taken to a public drop-off that accepts it for such purposes.

Dovetailed, finger-jointed, or mortise-and-tenon joints may outlast those made with glue, staples, or nails alone, and may cut down on the amount of adhesives needed.

Veneer will contain adhesives, by design; the core, if not solid wood, may also contain binders. Both core and veneer could outgas or irritate sensitivities. Solid wood may be a better choice in many situations—and the client will never have to replace the woodwork because the laminate veneer separated from the core.

The beauty of wood is that it only needs minimal protective treatments. Finishes and stains that will be applied on-site allow for greater control in their selection. Plant-based extracts offer the safest, most eco-friendly method for deepening or changing wood color. Avoid stains with heavy metals or chemical pigments—or specify no stain at all, the most ecological choice.

Look for formaldehyde-free, solvent-free, or water-based low-VOC, and nontoxic treatments. Natural resins and oils are excellent alternatives to typical petroleum-based synthetics such as polyurethane. Choose food-safe varieties whenever possible, and check with the client for sensitivity to odors or natural VOCs that may be emitted.

Earth-friendly penetrating oils are usually less offensive to both the environment and the lungs, and they come from renewable sources such as linseed, tung, and beeswax. The treatments absorb into the wood rather than cover it with a hard finish, leaving a softer surface that stands up well to moderate use and moisture.

Toxic to Insects, Mold . . . And Humans

In general, manufacturers use fewer preservatives and pesticides for interior finish carpentry wood than for framing, decking, and other construction. For applications exposed to weather or pests, toxic wood treatments have been the norm—sadly, even on children's playground sets. The list of harmful substances used on wood includes creosote, pentachlorophenol, chromated copper arsenate (CCA), and ammoniacal copper arsenate (ACA). All should be avoided. Borate and natural penetrating oils are common alternatives that are acceptable in earth-friendly applications.

For a hard finish, specify one that is water-based and low-VOC, as opposed to one with a solvent base. Although water-based finishes and stains were once inferior to solvent-based when used for wood, they now compete favorably, dry quickly, and usually outgas far less. Specify no-formaldehyde preservatives. Avoid the use of metallic hardening or drying agents; for example, zinc is frequently used in floor finishes but is toxic to aquatic life. Consider products that meet more rigid air quality standards (such as those accepted for use in California, schools, or health-care facilities). High-quality sealants are superprotective and may last for many, many years with proper care, thus eliminating the need for frequent refinishing or floor replacement due to damage.

Either way, with a water-based finish or penetrating oil, ventilate well when applying. If the client or installer suffers from chemical sensitivities or allergies, the smells and natural outgassing of all-natural or low-VOC treatments may be a problem until the surface fully dries and the air clears.

The treads and stringer of this staircase were made from pine glulams, which were assembled by gluing smaller pieces of wood together, thereby avoiding the need to cut down old-growth trees.
Photo by Ron Pollard Photography.
Designer: Brandy Lemae.

Specify factory-finished wood if the client has chemical sensitivities that might be aggravated with on-site application. If the wood has already been stained, finished, glued, or otherwise treated by the manufacturer or carpenter, air out the pieces before installation to allow for any residual VOCs to outgas. (Keep in mind, still, that the VOCs will affect the atmosphere.)

Maintenance

Wood is simple to maintain, as long as it is treated with care. The softer the species, the more prone it will be to scratches, dents, stains, and other marks. Thus, a harder finish might be in order if heavy wear is anticipated. The client may wish to establish a "no shoes" rule where there are wood floors. Advise clients to use the mildest detergents and minimal water for cleanups.

If the client wants a more weathered patina, the wood can be "preaged" before installation or on-site with sanding and intentional marks, thus minimizing the need to keep up appearances.

Where Does It Go?

The largest component of residential construction and demolition waste is usually wood, comprising more than 40 percent, according to the National Association of Home Builders.

Work with contractors closely to ensure careful estimations, precise measurements, and thoughtful reuse of scraps—it's a simple method to reduce the volume of debris. Specify that all wood large enough for practical use is taken to a construction exchange or saved for use on a future project. Smaller pieces might be donated to scouting programs, schools, or senior centers for crafts. Sawdust and very small bits, if free of contamination from hazards such as lead-based paint or chemicals (from deconstruction or demolition), may be incorporated into the soil.

Recycling Wood Makes Dollars and Sense

According to the Associated General Contractors of America (www.agca. org), wood recycling from construction pays off—literally. Regular landfill disposal rates average $70 to $84 per ton, but wood recycling costs only $40 to $60 per ton (this may vary even more by region).

There are more than 500 plants in the United States that accept wood for recycling (American Forest and Paper Association, www.afandpa.org). All of them accept clean, unpainted or untreated wood, and a growing number have the technology to deal with paint. Nails or other bits of hardware are not an issue because they are easily sorted during the processing. The recycled wood goes into many new products such as particleboard, animal bedding, mulch, and paper.

When no longer useful in the particular application, the wood may be salvaged for a similar or different use or downcycled into a wood-based product. Permanently tainted wood, such as that which has been treated with chemicals or lead paint, may not be suitable for reuse.

Spec List

Specify Wood That Is:
- Fallen on or thinned from the property
- Reclaimed
- Locally harvested, third-party-certified, nonthreatened species
- Suppressed (no certification available)
- Protected from moisture before and during the installation

Specify Finishes and Stains (either on prefinished wood or to be applied on-site) That Are:
- Water-based
- Made of natural (sometimes called food-grade) oils, resins, pigments, and waxes

- Low-VOC
- Formaldehyde-free
- Free of metallic hardening or drying agents (such as zinc)
- Solvent-free

  Avoid:
- Reclaimed wood of uncertain origin
- Chemically tainted wood (lead, arsenic, factory chemicals)
- Uncertified wood
- Rare or threatened species
- Pentachlorophenol or creosote preservatives
- Solvent-based finishes
- Formaldehyde and other preservatives in the wood product or finish
- Metal-based drying agents in the finish
- Engineered wood, unless certified

RESOURCES

Forest Stewardship Council U.S.: www.FSCUS.org
Green Seal Floor Care Products: Finishes and Strippers: www.greenseal.org/recommendations.
   htm
SmartWood (Rainforest Alliance): www.Smartwood.org

Biocomposites (Wood Alternatives)

One of the newest technologies to emerge from the green building industry is the development of various types of biocomposite board, also called wheat sheet, agricultural or ag board, crop board, straw board, or wheatboard. Pulp from crop residue is pressed with adhesive into sheets, then cut into boards, much like the manufacturing of wood-based particleboard, oriented-strand board (OSB), and medium-density fiberboard (MDF). Wheat straw is the most common fiber, but others are being used or researched for their potential: sunflower hulls; rice, barley, and oat straw; bluegrass and rye grass stubble; cornhusks and sorghum stalks; hemp; soybean plants; and bagasse (sugar cane pulp).

Designers specify these composites for shelving, flooring, paneling, furniture, and cabinetry boxes, frames, and doors. While crop-based biocomposites have yet to become widely used, the potential is great for both design and construction applications. The crops are harvested annually, making them a truly renewable resource, whereas trees need decades of growth before maturity. So instead of using almost an acre of forest, an entire home might be built with only 15 to 20 acres of wheat (HUD, 2003).

Most manufacturers of ag boards are fundamentally eco-minded in their quest for wood substitutes, so low-VOC, formaldehyde-free binders are standard. MDI is a common formaldehyde substitute that bonds well with straw and similar crop residues.

A few companies do incorporate petrochemicals that outgas, so make the specifications similar to those for the equivalent wood products. Borate is also commonly used as a low-toxic preservative and pest preventative. Unfortunately, biocomposites labeled "pesticide-free" or "non-GMO" can't yet be found, and standards for such have yet to be established. Some biocomposites are designed to take finishes, paints, stains, and hardware like their wooden counterparts, although results vary greatly from product to product. Therefore, consult the manufacturer for details and recommendations. Depending on the particular fibers incorporated, the board might have a smooth, consistent grain throughout, granite-looking speckles, or a dark-and-light, highly textural look. Crop boards may also be lighter in weight than solid wood options, yet be similar in strength. They are not recommended for places where constant moisture is present, as they lack long-term water resistance and may warp.

The wall veneers in this stairwell are made of durable fiberboard that assures longevity. The metal steps are made of 50 percent recycled content steel, and the wood ceiling joists are all reclaimed.
Photo courtesy of Robert Meier; © 2006 Robert Meier.
Architect: Locus Architecture.

It would seem that ag-based boards would be the answer to the imperiled forests worldwide, but the removal of some types of chaff or straw directly from cropland may leave topsoil precariously exposed to erosion—a negative for both the earth and the farmer. Some crop-board materials, however, such as sunflower hulls or bagasse, are not chaff but are by-products from processing and so pose few ecological drawbacks.

Where Does It Come From?

- Biocomposite boards are made from a variety of crop residues and agricultural by-products that may include: wheat, rice, barley, or oat straw; sunflower hulls; bluegrass or rye grass stubble; cornhusks and sorghum stalks; hemp; soybean plants; or bagasse (sugar cane pulp).
- Biocomposite adhesives and binders may include low-VOC glues, outgassing solvents, formaldehyde, soy-based products, and natural or synthetic resins.
- Borate may be used as a pesticide, especially in the manufacturing plant. Other residual pesticides may be present from the use of cropland.
- Finished biocomposite boards may use water- or solvent-based polyurethanes.
- Formaldehyde may or may not be present in boards, as a preservative, or in the finish.

Installation

In general, biocomposites are not as water repellent as wood and are more prone to warping. Countertops and backsplashes made of composites are not usually recommended, although a few water-resistant biocomposites have emerged on the market. Low-VOC, water-based adhesives and sealants should be specified in all applications.

Biocomposite boards, depending on the composition, take stains and finishes easily and evenly or not, much like the variations between different species of wood. The beauty of these wood substitutes is in their unusual grains and textures, which may best be highlighted with a clear finish. Test all stains and finishes on a sample before installation.

Consult with the manufacturer for the best stains, finishes, and adhesives for the particular fiberboard used, or have the contractor do a spot-test to check for suitability.

Maintenance

Because biocomposites are new to the market, their long-term suitability for particular design applications, along with specific needs for future maintenance, have not been established. Consult with the manufacturer for recommendations.

Where Does It Go?

Like wood, biocomposite boards decompose naturally, back into soil. Binders, resins, stains, and finishes used within or on the board will do so much more slowly.

Spec List

Specify:

- Boards made from 100 percent renewable crop residue or agricultural by-product (no plastics added, for example)

- Formaldehyde-free, low-VOC, water-based binders, sealants, adhesives, and stains

- Borate (if necessary) for preservative qualities or pest resistance

Avoid:

- Formaldehyde in the binder or finish

- Preservatives or pesticides (other than borate)

RESOURCES

Forest Stewardship Council (FSC): www.fsc.org
See also: Wood Flooring, page 208; Cabinetry, page 322

CHAPTER **10**

openings:
doors and windows

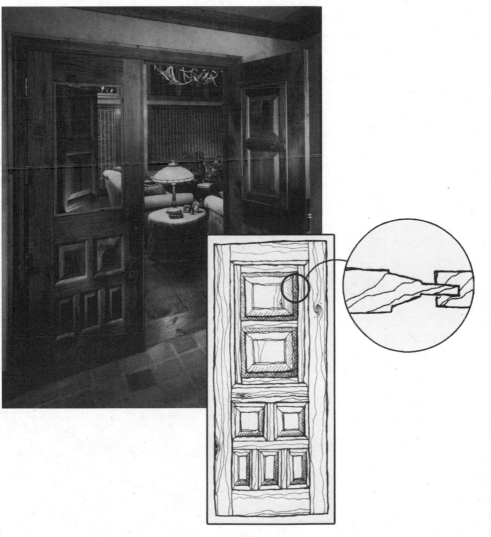

Drawing: Donna Barta-Winfield.
Design: Kari Foster,
Annette Stelmack,
www.associates3.com.
Photo: David O. Marlow

Originally, the main function of a door was to provide access to a home while maintaining protection from the elements. A door was also a barrier against unwanted intruders, both human and animal. In today's homes, exterior doors still offer security, but they also greet guests with welcoming design features. Interior doors define spaces, control noise, provide privacy, and allow or impede airflow through the home.

Windows, too, served a utilitarian purpose in the days before electricity: to allow daylight into an otherwise dark structure. Openings in the walls provided ventilation, as well, especially in hot climates. The Romans, one of the first civilizations to use glass extensively, put windows in their bathhouses, recognizing the function that glass panes played in illumination while keeping warmth and vapors in and cold temperatures out. Yet windows are more than just daylit openings. They've been elevated to the highest artistic levels, gracing the world's cathedrals and architectural wonders with awe-inspiring color and geometrics.

People living in developed countries spend the majority of their lives indoors, so natural sunlight through a window is vital to their physiological and emotional health.

A locally crafted pivot door and curved wall of sustainably certified beech enhance the entry to this powder room.
Photo by David O. Marlow.
Design: Associates III, www.associates3.com.

Windows in a home provide an essential aesthetic, permitting visual communication between occupants and nature. A well-placed and well-designed opening connects a person emotionally to the outdoors, nurturing a thoughtfulness for the environment while maintaining control of indoor climate and comfort, no matter the external forces.

Fact Check

- Glass has high emissivity. One pane of clear glass will transfer 84 percent of the infrared energy from a warm indoor room to the outside on a cold day.
- Daylighting may save 30 to 60 percent of the energy used for lighting purposes in a building.
- The windows in a home may be responsible for more than a third of the heat gain or loss within, depending on their size, location, construction, and mechanics.
- A poorly insulated window in a cooler climate may cost the equivalent of a gallon of heating oil per square foot per year.

Source: National Fenestration Rating Council, www.nfrc.org; "Windows: Looking through the Options," BuildingGreen.com, www.buildinggreen.com.

Designers most often specify interior doors, some exterior doors, and, seldom, windows. As with any element of green home design, the materials from which these are made are an important consideration. They need to be renewable or recyclable, be free of toxins, and be durable.

Exterior doors and windows in a home, much like the lighting and appliances within, affect our ecosystems in another way: they are major "consumers" of energy, directly determining residential energy use every minute of every day of every year. A cold, drafty door or a windowpane letting in the too-hot sun can shift the temperature and comfort level of a room, or even the entire house, and the heating or air conditioning systems compensate. Well-designed and well-placed windows and exterior doors, conversely, will conserve energy.

For this reason, green designers need to view interior doors distinctly from exterior doors and windows, considering them primarily for the natural resources consumed in their construction. Windows and exterior doors, on the other hand, should be viewed much like electrical appliances, for their impact on overall home energy use.

Interior Doors

Evaluating interior doors for eco-friendliness is quite different from that of exterior doors and windows. Materials are usually the most important consideration when selecting interior doors for their eco-friendly characteristics.

Reclaimed or salvaged doors are excellent choices for interior applications. Most older door styles are made from solid wood, whereas those made more recently—within the last 50 years—may vary greatly in materials content and construction. Plywood cores with a better-quality wood veneer are common, as are hollow doors made from steel, vinyl, or aluminum, with or without wood, mineral, or synthetic cores. It may be difficult to determine the content of salvaged doors. Check paint for lead, even if the door is to be refinished (see Lead-Based Paint, page 246).

Opt for locally harvested species of wood, reclaimed wood, culled deadwood, or third-party-certified wood. Specify plant- and animal-based glues, mechanical fastening, and low-VOC, low-odor, water-based, formaldehyde-free finishes.

New doors manufactured from solid wood, veneer, and/or engineered wood are eco-friendly if the forest products are FSC-certified. Avoid all imports and threatened wood species, and look for locally crafted woods. Unfinished solid wood or veneer allows the client to select an eco-friendly stain or sheen. For all on-site finishing, specify all-natural or nontoxic, formaldehyde-free, low-VOC, solvent-free stains, finishes, and oils.

If engineered wood is the preference for an interior door, specify recycled content, and avoid formaldehyde in the binder. Cellulose cores made from recycled paper are another option in wood-veneer doors.

Biocomposites are relatively new to the green scene and offer annually renewable agricultural products as alternatives to wood. Although solid doors and veneers made from biocomposites are still uncommon, wheatboard is becoming a popular core for interior doors. Specify a formaldehyde-free binder, and look for FSC-certified wood veneers. Almost all biocomposite doors are factory-finished.

Vinyl doors are not eco-friendly. PVC-vinyl is a hazard for the Earth and its inhabitants (see Wallcoverings, page 224), and should never be used in a home.

Some interior doors are made from lightweight aluminum or steel over foam cores. There are pros and cons to each of these materials. The metal, especially if recycled, has great durability and potential for more recycling, but the core may be hazardous.

Fiberglass doors are lightweight, durable, and may be painted if the surface needs refreshing or a change of color is desired. Fiberglass can't be recycled like beverage glass, but it is basically eco-friendly in that it's mostly made from simple silicon dioxide. The door's foam core material may be polystyrene, however, a material that is hazardous to humans and that is also a challenge to dispose of or recycle.

Where Does It Come From?

■ Interior doors are commonly made from wood and wood composites, vinyl, lightweight metals such as aluminum and steel (with foam cores), or fiberglass.

Installation

An interior door that's the entrance to a room usually requires an undercut (a small gap between the floor and door) to allow for air circulation in order to balance the heating and cooling systems. Tighter interior door fit is important if the purpose of the door is to separate areas to confine odors from a basement or storage area, maintain temperature in a sauna or vestibule, or protect belongings in a closet from dust or moisture. Weather stripping in these situations may be desirable as long as airflow is not an issue.

Maintenance

Interior doors require little maintenance. Usually a regular dusting or wipedown with a damp cloth is sufficient. Oil or wax finishes on wood doors require periodic reapplication.

Where Does It Go?

Interior doors are frequently salvaged and reused. Wood, biocomposites, and cellulose break down easily at the ends of their life cycles; synthetic binders or glues used may not do as well. Metal is usually recyclable, although the core material, usually polystyrene, is not. Some recycling facilities may not accept metal doors because they don't have the capability to separate the components. Fiberglass is exceedingly durable and will eventually break down like glass, but it is not (yet) easily recyclable. Vinyl has little potential for reuse, and it contaminates landfills, soil, and water.

Spec List

Specify:
- Wood doors (solid, engineered, reclaimed, veneer, custom-made or prefabricated)
- High recycled or reclaimed wood content or FSC-certified wood content
- Biocomposite doors
- Low-VOC, low-toxic, formaldehyde-free binders, stains, finishes, and glues
- Tight fit and weather stripping for closets, unheated spaces, odorous storage spaces, or wherever strict climate control is desired (such as in a sauna or vestibule)

Avoid:
- PVC-vinyl
- Synthetic foam cores

Windows and Exterior Doors

Ideally, any thermal exchange that occurs through windows and exterior doors should be intentional, not accidental. Windows and doors should allow for desirable breezes, not unwanted drafts. Solar radiation is a positive in cold weather, but protection from it is necessary where summers are hot and sunny.

These windows, offering abundant daylighting, are of anodized heavy-gauge aluminum, which never rots or needs painting. The space also features durable stone flooring, kitchen cabinets made of 10-ply solid maple and ENERGY STAR appliances.
Photo by Emily Hagopian, www.essentialimages.us.
Architect: Russell Johnson.

Whenever possible, work with the client, the architect, and the contractor to ensure optimal placement of windows and doors to take advantage of features such as the location of shade trees, the seasonal changes in sun angle, and directional breezes. Windows or doors that can be fully opened will allow for excellent ventilation. Skylights will decrease dependence for electrical lighting, but may conversely increase the need for cooling in the summer, so thoughtful placement and insulating blinds or reflective coatings are needed. South-facing windows under wide overhangs welcome low-angle winter sunlight but will be shaded from high-angle summer solar radiation.

Carefully consider window frames and exterior doors for their material compositions; this can significantly impact the insulating value, the ecological assets, and the health within a house. Reuse can be a green choice, and reclaimed wood windows and doors are available in many construction exchanges and salvage shops. Salvaged doors are most often made from higher-quality solid wood. There is a trade-off, however, in that older pieces, especially single-glazed windows, may lack energy efficiency. If there is paint present on the old window or door, testing for lead should be done before any stripping or sanding. Finding a good fit is also a critical issue if looking for replacements or if the openings have already been constructed; old windows and doors may need additional weather stripping for insulation.

Traditional wood-framed windows and doors are an excellent choice for their solid construction and, thereby, insulating properties; for their resistance to condensation when used with double or triple glazings; and for the fact that they are mostly made from renewable, natural materials (wood and glass). New windows and doors may be made from solid wood, engineered wood, or have veneers; look for FSC-certified wood content for each option. Avoid formaldehyde-based binders and outgassing adhesives in engineered wood and laminates.

Factory-finished wood windows are usually best because they'll have time to outgas; specify low-VOC finishes. Window finishes are tricky to apply, and protection from the elements is imperative to avoid rot, warping, and cracking over the years. Outgassing affects air quality, but if the process is allowed to occur outdoors, it will be easier on a sensitive client. On the other hand, doors are easily finished on-site, and the interior side might be done with a healthful, natural oil or wax. Be certain to specify a finish on the exterior that is earth-friendly and that will stand up to the weather.

Specify locally harvested species of wood, and request reclaimed planks or deadwood from a nearby forest. Although these choices will lack FSC certification, the carpenter should be able to verify the source for maximum sustainability. Local work also ensures there will be minimal transportation, further conserving fossil fuels. Specify glues and finishes that are low-VOC, low-odor, water-based, and formaldehyde-free.

There are many other options for windows and exterior door materials, but most have environmental shortcomings. Solid vinyl, vinyl-core, or vinyl-clad frames are not eco-friendly; the perils of vinyl manufacturing and exposure to PVC phthalates are many. Aluminum windows are inexpensive, and recycled aluminum is being used in some window and door manufacturing, but even double-paned aluminum-clad windows lack insulating properties and encourage condensation problems.

Another option is fiberglass with an insulated core. Fiberglass is basically made from glass, so it's easier on the environment. But neither the core nor the fiberglass is readily recyclable, and the core may be mostly unfriendly polystyrene.

Steel is used for exterior doors (but not usually windows) because of its security and superb durability, and recycled steel is sometimes a component. However, most residential applications are made with a polystyrene core; solid metal is too heavy. Without the synthetic insulation (of a not-so-natural origin and even more uncertain environmental future), the metal door would also be prone to condensation and would transfer heat and cold too readily, thereby falling short in energy efficiency. Steel doors are most eco-friendly if reclaimed or if made from 100 percent recycled steel over a natural core material such as wood or biocomposite board.

The glass in doors and windows is made from common sand and is gentle on the earth, but a single-pane type is not energy-conserving. Adding storm windows is the simplest method of improvement and may pay back quickly in lowering utility bills. Double or triple glazing (two or even three panes of glass sandwiched together) greatly improves on the storm window idea by trapping air between tightly sealed, closely sandwiched panes, forming insulated glass units (IG units). Glass is reassuringly green, as well. Although it does require high heat to be manufactured, it can be recycled indefinitely, and it introduces no toxins to the home and the environment.

Low-emissivity (low-e) coatings such as silver oxide let in as much as 95 percent of the visible light while reducing ultraviolet light penetration that can fade fabrics and furnishings. Low-e coatings also control heat loss by reflecting infrared energy back inside, keeping the house cooler in summer and warmer in winter. "Superinsulator" argon and krypton gases—they are nontoxic and have no odor—are sometimes pumped in between insulating glass panes. The client might also be interested in electrochromic windows that tint and shade automatically, or windows that contain blinds between the

This garage door offers ample day-lighting into this space which also features low-VOC paint and 25 percent fly ash concrete flooring.
© 2005 Aaron Blake.
Designer: Christina Davis.

panes (no dusting necessary). Many of these chemical engineering or manufacturing "advancements" are difficult to analyze as being pro- or antienvironment. A small amount of not-so-green coatings, for instance, might drastically reduce heating and cooling needs, energy consumption, and thus fossil fuel use for decades, but the effect on air quality and the chemical risks are still unknown.

Two independent rating systems remove much of the guesswork about the energy efficiency of any given window or door:

- A third-party nonprofit, the National Fenestration Ratings Council (NFRC), certifies, rates, and labels window products for thermal properties, how well solar radiation is blocked, how much light shines through, the rate of air leakage, and condensation resistance. Some states now require that windows be NFRC-labeled.

- ENERGY STAR, a U.S. government-sponsored energy-efficiency initiative, goes a step further by identifying windows and doors that are well-suited for a particular climate zone that have been labeled by the NFRC. Its logo appears on approved products.

Another helpful guide is the Window Selection Tool, an online energy costs calculator (www.efficientwindows.org), which allows for comparison of energy costs and savings between window types. It's maintained by the Efficient Windows Collaborative, whose members include educational institutions, research organizations, and industry representatives. The calculation takes into consideration the regional location of the house, average public utility rates, window frame and fenestration specifics, ENERGY STAR certification, and whether it's new construction or remodeling. In addition, state-by-state fact sheets are available that recommend NFRC ratings for the particular region and that list any mandated labeling or certifications.

Where Does It Come From?

- Windows are primarily made from glass, which is manufactured through the melting of common sand (silicon dioxide).
- Sealed double or triple glazings may have argon or krypton gas between panes.
- Glass may be treated with a variety of low-e coatings (often made from silver oxide) or synthetic tints.
- Exterior door and window frames may be made from a wide variety of materials, including but not limited to wood, PVC-vinyl, steel, aluminum, fiberglass, and polystyrene.
- Doors and windows are usually factory-finished.
- Reclaimed doors and windows, especially older ones, are usually made from wood.
- Older painted doors and windows may have lead-based paint.

Installation

Specify insulation around every window and door frame, since these are often the areas of greatest heating and cooling losses. Magnetic seals, good hardware, and adequate weather stripping on exterior doors will ensure tight seals all around.

Maintenance

Exterior doors and windows need little maintenance except to keep the finishes and weather stripping in good condition. Advise the client to do an annual check of airtightness around all windows and doors; many electric and gas utilities offer energy audits that include this service for free or at little cost.

Where Does It Go?

Glass can be recycled indefinitely, and will eventually become sand again through erosion. Wood, steel, and aluminum frames may be recycled or even reused. Mesh from screens can be recycled if made from metal; fiberglass recycling may become more accessible in the near future. PVC-vinyl and plastic may or may not be recycled, do not decompose well, and leach toxins.

Spec List

Specify:

- Optimal window positioning to benefit from solar gain and natural light
- Low-emissivity glass
- Krypton- or argon- filled panes, especially in colder climates
- Double- or triple-glazed windows
- Different window types for different directional orientations and placements
- FSC-certified wood doors and frames
- Factory finishing *or* on-site finishing with all-natural or low-VOC, formaldehyde-free, water-based products that are free from heavy metals
- High-quality insulation around all window frames and doors
- Tight seals around all windows and exterior doors
- Casement or awning windows, rather than double-hung or sliding, for tighter seals

Avoid:

- PVC or vinyl, either solid or clad
- Aluminum or steel windows
- Synthetic foam cores
- Doors and windows with lead-based paint

HARDWARE

Almost all door and window hardware is made from metal, often steel or brass, because it can be formed to any configuration, is incredibly durable, and provides a tight closure mechanism that gives security against intrusion and weather (see Metals, page 129). Window hardware is most often supplied by the window manufacturer and may already be installed on the components. This preinstallation also ensures a perfectly tight fit, a prerequisite of energy efficiency and excellent fenestration ratings. Specify recycled metal content in the preinstalled hardware, whenever possible.

Door hardware, in contrast, is almost always purchased separately from the door itself. A few companies specialize in manufacturing door hardware from recycled metal, especially steel from minimills. These manufacturers are often smaller and may do more customized, decorative pieces as well. Whenever possible, look for door hardware that has high recycled content.

Salvage shops often feature door hardware. This is a terrific option for replacements and remodeling, especially if the client appreciates reuse. Sometimes it is difficult to find enough matching pieces for an entire job, but with careful design, an eclectic combination may be appealing.

A local blacksmith crafted this recycled-content metal-door hardware.
Photo by David O. Marlow.
Designer: Associates III.
www.associates3.com

Some doorknobs are made from decorative glass, crystal, or ceramic (porcelain), especially vintage ones. Glass is a safe, eco-friendly, cradle-to-cradle material. Ceramic also has green properties: It is made mostly from common clay, is inert once fired, and breaks back down into minerals at the end of its life cycle. Crystal knobs pose no known risk to occupants since they don't deteriorate like flaking paint and can't be eaten or inhaled. On the other hand, it is made with lead oxide, and lead contamination is a serious risk for those who ingest or inhale it and for those who work with it in factories. If the existing knobs are crystal, there's no need to replace them, but the beauty of new crystal is hard to justify in a green home because of the hazards for workers. Nontoxic glass imitates the look of crystal well, and it is much safer.

Where Does It Come From?

- Window and door hardware is made primarily from metal such as steel.
- Doorknobs may be made from glass, crystal, metals, wood, or ceramic (porcelain).
- (Lead) crystal contains lead oxide, a known toxin to humans.

Where Does It Go?

The hardware on windows and doors frequently outlasts the life span of the house, and hardware is often salvaged. Steel and glass can be recycled indefinitely, and a strong market exists for both. Crystal has a very long life span, but the hazards of disposal are undefined, and the lead may leach into water or soil eventually.

Spec List

Specify:
- Window and door hardware that has high recycled-metal content
- Decorative parts made from glass, ceramic, wood, or metal
- Antique or salvaged or reclaimed hardware

Avoid:
- Lead crystal

RESOURCES

Efficient Windows Collaborative: www.efficientwindows.org
Home Energy Saver (home energy audit), Lawrence Berkeley Lab: http://hes3.lbl.gov
National Fenestration Rating Council: www.nfrc.org

finishes

*Drawing: Donna Barta-
Winfield.
Design: Maggie Tandysh,
www.associates3.com.
Photo: David O. Marlow.*

Finishes—treatments for walls, ceilings, and floors—are where we move practical *structure* into the realm of a personally detailed, carefully crafted, individually tailored *home.* And our preference as green designers, along with that of our clients, is that the process and the materials be earth-sensitive.

A good relationship with the contractor and architect will ease the transition to eco-friendly finishes, especially if the building envelope was not planned with strict green standards in mind. There are many construction-related questions to be answered before the finishes can be specified, among them: Will you be determining the type of plaster used, or will the builder? If the client prefers recycled glass tile, will you be able to specify the substrate, or is it already in place? In some instances, allowing the structure to become the finish—exposed wood beams, concrete floors, or unpainted plaster—might be the best environmental choice because it uses fewer resources altogether.

When remodeling and redesigning, investigate the existing structure and the land with an eye toward minimal destruction and optimization of what exists. The beauty of most green finishes is that they are inherently adaptable to multiple applications. Reclaimed flooring becomes paneling; recycled glass bottles show up in countertops, floors, or shower surrounds. Because so many finishes can be used in so many ways, this chapter will cover only the basics for floors, walls, and ceilings, hence should only be regarded as a starting point.

Plaster and Gypsum Board

Plaster is a fundamental building and design material. Earth, gypsum, and lime all have been used for thousands of years to protect, finish, and beautify interiors and exteriors, and centuries-old plastered structures have survived brutal natural disasters on every continent. Plaster both contributes to the structure of the wall and provides a finished veneer or topcoat. It has terrific thermal properties, staying cool in extreme heat but also insulating against cold. As a bonus, plaster is fireproof, making it an ideal material for high-risk mountain and desert communities.

Clients with chemical sensitivities will appreciate mineral-based plaster (without synthetic additives) because it's basically inert once dry. Walls made of plaster breathe and adapt marvelously to climate changes within a building by allowing water vapors in and out, improving indoor air quality. This same attractive feature also allows plaster to "exhale" chemicals, so it's important to specify nontoxic, nonoutgassing materials in the plaster mix, as well as in the underlayments and substrates.

If the plaster is mixed on-site, there's little waste to end up in the landfill. Depending on the type used, a plaster wall may lend itself to many environmentally friendly finish options: paint it, tint it, apply a clearcoat finish or beeswax, or just leave it as is. Consider specifying plaster that allows the structure to become the finish, as it is a wonderfully waste-free, eco-friendly principle.

Gypsum board evolved from gypsum plaster, and use quickly gained preference in the late twentieth century for their preformed, ready-to-finish convenience. Gypsum board (drywall) is the most common material used in new construction for walls. The smooth surface takes almost any finish well. That convenience, however, comes with an environmental price: on-site construction waste and postindustrial debris is piling up in landfills, and the United States has been slow to begin recycling and reclamation efforts. Most gypsum board contains chemicals and additives intended to enhance particular properties, but this may cause unintended environmental and health repercussions as well.

While all mineral-based plasters and wallboards have some earth-friendly characteristics, they vary greatly in the amount of embodied energy and waste generated. The following will help determine the best options available.

GYPSUM PLASTER

Gypsum plaster is also known as plaster of paris, named for the once-abundant Parisian gypsum beds. It was widely used in the twentieth century, but it has been around since ancient Egyptian times and is what most people think of as plaster.

The main component, hydrous calcium sulfate (also called calcium sulfate dehydrate) is an abundant mineral that is mined, dehydrated at about 300°F into a powdery substance (hemihydrate gypsum), then remixed with water for application to walls or for joint compound. This crude or "virgin" gypsum has some environmental drawbacks in that it's nonrenewable, mined, and usually transported long distances.

Synthetic gypsum, also called recycled or by-product gypsum, is recovered from legislation-mandated power plant "scrubbing" of fossil fuels and from production of titanium dioxide. The recovered gypsum, therefore, fills an eco-niche by reducing waste and landscape destruction. The use of synthetic or recycled gypsum is a rapidly growing trend worldwide. The term sometimes refers to that which is recovered post-construction from drywall scraps, so always inquire as to the source material. Synthetic gypsum usually has a higher level of purity than that which is mined.

Both crude gypsum and synthetic gypsum need only hydration to be made into plaster. These plasters are suitable only for interiors because rain and weather will erode them. Gypsum plaster can be built up on lath to become the structural wall element, or simply applied as a veneer on top of a structure such as gypsum board. The beauty is that natural mineral- or vegetable-based pigments can be added directly to the mix, so other finishes like paint aren't necessary. Gypsum is a superb surface for virtually every type of wall treatment; once it has set, is basically inert. All are characteristics that lend longevity to the finish.

Fact Check

- Mineral gypsum is very safe for humans. It is used in orthopedic casts, food, and toothpaste.
- The average person will consume 28 pounds of mineral gypsum in a lifetime.

Source: National Gypsum, www.nationalgypsum.com.

Other minerals, such as lime, may be added to gypsum plaster to prevent shrinkage and cracks. Crystalline silica—a ground-up version of the most common mineral, quartz—also shows up on the ingredient lists as a drying agent. Although long-term, heavy, unprotected, and repeated exposure to the dust causes silicosis (a form of cancer), the risk to inhabitants of a plaster-walled home is miniscule. However, many gypsum plasters today also contain harmful fungicides, setting agents, and other chemicals, negating some of the eco-benefits. Specify natural gypsum plaster with no or low-VOC additives, if possible.

A Word of Caution

Existing gypsum plaster, especially that which is older, may contain trace levels of arsenic (*Journal of Light Construction*, July 2004; www.jlconline. com) or vermiculite that was contaminated with asbestos from mines (*Environmental Building News*, March 2000; www.buildinggreen.com). Testing and/or abatement of hazardous materials should be done before sanding, remodeling, deconstruction, or demolition to protect both the workers and the occupants.

Where Does It Come From?

- Gypsum plaster is primarily made of powdered gypsum mixed with water in varying formulas.
- Plaster may also contain chemical epoxies and/or plastics, fungicides, setting agents, drying agents, binders, and fillers.
- Quartz or crystalline silica is often used in gypsum plaster mixes as a drying agent.
- Lime and other inert minerals may be used in plaster to prevent shrinkage and cracking.

Installation

Specify that plaster be mixed on-site in the precise quantities needed to limit waste. There are two basic application methods, depending on the chosen substrate:

- *Veneer plaster.* One or more thin layers of specially formulated veneer (also called thin-coat) plaster is applied, each approximately one-eighth-inch thick, over blueboard or similar backing intended for such a purpose (see Gypsum Board, page 185).
- *Plaster over lath.* Two or more coats of gypsum plaster go over wooden, metal, or gypsum lath. The first coat is called the basecoat or scratch coat, which is scratched to rough up the surface in preparation for the next one; the second is called the brown coat; the third, the finish coat. A simpler two-coat system may

This straw-bale wall, featuring a truth window, is finished with integrally colored gypsum plaster. Photo courtesy of Kelly Lerner, www.one-world-design.com.

also work and will use less product—and less natural resources. The final depth of the plaster varies. Eco-friendly choices for lath include FSC-certified wood, recycled steel, or possibly blueboard that is made of synthetic or recycled gypsum.

Traditional wooden lath may expand and contract due to moisture within the wall and plaster, so metal lath may be a more durable choice. Another alternative is gypsum lath with an absorbent-paper face. Specify high recycled-paper content when using gypsum lath.

The plaster, if free of VOCs and additives, may be left unfinished—the best option for those with chemical sensitivities. The final coat may also be sanded or polished.

Maintenance

Care should be taken to keep the walls dry and clean, as they will deteriorate if wet, or "chalk" if scuffed. Fortunately, plaster can be easily patched or sanded to fix damage. Overall, natural or low-VOC gypsum plaster is a good long-term, highly adaptable choice for a home that is eco-friendly, as it promotes good indoor air quality.

Where Does It Go?

Leftover plaster mix can be used on another application or taken to a construction salvage exchange. The mineral gypsum in the plaster is not considered harmful to the environment. Chemical additives (not preferred) could leach into land or water upon disposal.

Paint and wallcoverings are difficult to separate from plaster, and plaster is difficult to separate from the wall, so plaster deconstruction and recycling isn't yet feasible. Drywall scrap recycling may be required in some parts of the world by 2010, including Canada and the European Union, so it's possible that a process will be designed to deal with deconstructed plastered walls in the same manner (see Gypsum Board, page 185).

Spec List

Specify:
- Natural gypsum plaster mix *or* recycled/synthetic/byproduct gypsum mix
- Wooden lath, preferably reclaimed or FSC-certified Recycled steel or metal lath
- Natural gypsum or recycled gypsum lath with recycled paper face
- Low-VOC additives, if any
- Adequate dry time between coats

Avoid:
- Remodeling, sanding, demolition or cutting of existing plaster without first testing for hazards (arsenic, lead paint)
- Fungicides, chemical agents, or synthetic additives
- Water or high humidity in direct contact with walls

RESOURCES

The Natural Plaster Book: Earth Lime and Gypsum Plasters for Natural Homes, Cedar Rose Guelberth and Dan Chiras (Gabriola, BC: New Society Publishers, 2003)

PORTLAND CEMENT PLASTER

Cement plaster is made from portland cement, sand, lime, and water. The most likely places to use cement plaster indoors are basements, fireplaces, and masonry walls. Concrete or masonry can be covered with cement plaster if clean and free of debris, and the cement can then be painted or sealed. It is, however, uncommon to see large expanses of cement plaster indoors. The relatively cool temperature of the cement plaster, especially in warm, humid environments, may cause condensation and moisture problems indoors that lead to mold and compromised indoor air quality.

LIME PLASTER

Lime plaster is an ancient building material, dating back several thousand years—perhaps older than all other plasters except earthen types. It's distinct from cement plaster or stucco, treatments are usually reserved for exteriors that include portland cement as an ingredient.

Lime itself is not a naturally occurring substance. It is derived from mined limestone (calcium carbonate), which is found in abundance worldwide. The rock is then crushed and fired in a kiln at a very high temperature between 1600°F to 2100°F. The product is then labeled "quicklime" (calcium oxide). Quicklime in turn becomes lime putty through the addition of water; the hydration process is referred to as *slaking*.

Lime putty is the main ingredient in lime plaster; once the putty has achieved the right consistency, it's dehydrated to form a mix, then again combined with sand and water to form the plaster. It may also be thinned with water alone to produce a wash.

The process for making lime plaster is lengthy and quite energy-intensive. What may tip the eco-scales in its favor, however, is how lime plaster reverts back to being calcium carbonate when it dries. It starts out as limestone, and it will return back to the earth as the same substance.

Lime plaster is basically rock solid and may last for centuries with regular upkeep. The inert nature of lime plaster, along with its purity (no chemical additives are needed) makes it a healthy option for a green home. Like earthen plaster, lime plaster is also vapor-permeable, but it resists cracking and eroding better. It is the hardest and most durable of all interior finishes and can be used in very humid indoor climates. Lime plaster can be applied directly on earth walls or masonry of all types, added as a final coat over earthen plaster, or applied on traditional drywall as a topcoat. If color is desired, natural mineral or vegetable pigments may be added to limewash or plaster. If marble dust is added to plaster and the finish is polished, it's called Venetian plaster (see page 181).

These straw-bale walls were finished with earthen plaster, the house-fused glass decorative windowpanes were by a local artisan. Photo courtesy of Kelly Lerner, www.one-world-design.com.

Where Does It Come From?

- Lime and lime plaster are made from mined limestone that is crushed, fired, and rehydrated (slaked).
- Limewash is a water-thinned version of lime plaster.
- Crushed or powdered marble may be added for hardness and sheen.
- Natural pigments add subtle color to limewash.

Installation

Lime putty powder, when rehydrated, "boils" and is extremely caustic. The plastering process, from start to finish, may be lengthy. After an extended period of carefully guarded slaking—days or sometimes weeks, depending on the plasterer's preference—sand is added to the lime putty. Marble can be mixed in for sheen, or mineral pigment for color. The plaster is then troweled or harled (see the sidebar, "The Art of Plastering") onto the walls, smoothed or textured, and left to dry. Daily misting, especially in dry climates, ensures proper curing; weather may greatly affect the outcome and time needed to set.

Maintenance

A lime plaster finish is practically eternal, especially if a new topcoat or wash is added when the surface starts to show minor signs of deterioration. Once hardened, it would be a chore to effectively deconstruct. And the beauty in a fresco or similar plaster treatment is so timeless—Michelangelo himself used it—few would ever attempt to destroy it. An experienced artisan may perform touch-ups if needed. Wallcoverings or paint over lime plaster are not recommended, as the alkalinity of lime may leach through and cause spotting.

Where Does It Go?

Lime plaster, like limestone, will eventually disintegrate naturally back into the earth.

Spec List

Specify:
- Lime without synthetic additives
- Natural/mineral pigments

Avoid:
- Wallcoverings or traditional paint on lime plaster

The Art of Plastering

Lime plaster lends itself readily to eco-friendly interiors with simple mineral pigments and sculptural detailing. Expert plasterers are considered nothing less than artists in many parts of the world. Some use a Scottish method called "harl" in which the lime plaster and pebbles are "thrown" with a special tool. In the Mediterranean region, experienced artisans developed the fresco technique where pigment is ground into water then painted directly onto fresh, damp lime plaster. The English word "cartoon" comes from the ink-on-paper outline that is first traced onto the wall for guidance prior to painting; "graffiti" is derived from the Italian term meaning a carved or scratched plaster design on the wall. Any or all of these methods may be employed for a highly decorative touch in the home that won't compromise the environment. Limewash, a thin mixture of lime putty and water, is an excellent topcoat; adding mineral pigments will give it a soft color.

RESOURCES

The Natural Plaster Book: Earth Lime and Gypsum Plasters for Natural Homes, Cedar Rose Guelberth and Dan Chiras (Gabriola, BC: New Society Publishers, 2003)

VENETIAN PLASTER

Venetian plaster, also called Italian plaster or Venetian stucco, was developed on its namesake island in the 1500s. Artisans developed the technique and materials to imitate the polished beauty of marble. Venetian plaster is made of lime (see Lime Plaster, in previous section) and marble dust, applied in several thin layers, then burnished, sanded, or polished. In this way, the beauty of natural stone, without the weight or expense of real marble, was achieved.

Traditional Venetian plaster is an earth-friendly, mineral-based option that dries to an inert, no-VOC, nonallergenic surface. The lime and marble or mineral content varies by blend. Synthetic acrylic resins or pigments are often added, but all-natural products are preferred for green homes. Check with the manufacturer for details regarding the content of the plaster mix. Specify low-VOC finishes for bathrooms, kitchens, or high-use areas to protect the finish from stains.

Where Does It Come From?

- Venetian plaster is made from a mixture of lime and marble.
- Sometimes pigments and synthetic resins are added.

Installation

Venetian plaster application is similar to that of lime plaster (see Lime Plaster, in previous section). As the final coat is being applied, before the first sections are completely dry, the surface is burnished by hand or with power tools.

Maintenance

Venetian plaster may be patched by an expert, but the surface ages gracefully and requires virtually no upkeep.

Where Does It Go?

Lime and marble will break down naturally in the environment.

Spec List

Specify:
- Venetian plaster with natural lime, marble, or mineral content
- Cementitious resin
- Low-VOC binders and adhesives
- Natural mineral pigment

Avoid:
- Binders that outgas high levels of VOCs

RESOURCES

The Natural Plaster Book: Earth Lime and Gypsum Plasters for Natural Homes, Cedar Rose
   Guelberth and Dan Chiras (Gabriola, BC: New Society Publishers, 2003).

EARTHEN PLASTER

Earthen or "mud" plaster is as ancient as humankind, has the permanence of rock, and yet has the modern look and feel of suede. Although more traditionally used on homes built from straw bale, cob, adobe, or rammed earth, mud plaster can also be applied over drywall. It provides a natural, breathable, no-VOC surface that adapts to humidity and adds thermal insulation.

   Earthen plaster has the least embodied energy of any building material. The best recipe for durability lies in the regional soil, which is already adapted to the home's particular environment. Plus, it's literally dirt-cheap if the home site has suitable clay available and the earthen plaster can be made with it. But before proceeding, specify that the soil be tested for contaminants from nearby sites, if there is any doubt as to its healthfulness and suitability for the project.

Traditional earth plaster recipes include some or all of the following ingredients, all available at little or no charge: clay dirt, sand, straw, and cooked flour paste or manure. Commercial clay plaster mixes may be purchased, along with sanded primers and special sealants, for application as a veneer over existing paint, wallboard, gypsum plaster, or even wallpaper. The primary ingredients in the purchased clay plasters are earth (clay) mineral pigments, and borax. Primers and sealants, available from the clay mix suppliers, are specially designed for eco-friendly homes and will usually be nontoxic, solvent-free, and low- or no-VOC. Although clay mixes are essentially all-natural choices for a green home, they require off-site excavation and shipping and, therefore, add embodied energy through transportation.

Unfinished earth plaster is best suited for dry ecosystems and well-ventilated home environments, as constant moisture or humidity will compromise the plaster integrity. Commercial sealants solve most moisture-related problems for the purchased clay plaster veneers.

Where Does It Come From?

- "Homemade" earthen plaster is made from clay earth and natural additives such as sand, straw, and cooked four paste or manure.
- Commercially made earthen plaster mixes usually include borax, derived from naturally occurring borate.
- Sometimes synthetic resins are added to commercial mixes.
- Mineral pigments may be added to "homemade" or commercial earthen plaster.

Installation

Seek out expert installers to find just the right blend of ingredients, savvy application techniques, and expertise to determine time of year or weather that is best for plastering in the region. The best approach will also depend on the particular substrate:

- Dry and clean cement stucco, unsealed lime or earth plaster, and unsealed masonry are ideal for earth plaster or clay mix.
- Unfinished walls of earth, straw, building-form blocks, concrete, or rough-surface masonry require a basecoat or brown coat of lime plaster, fibered cement, drywall, or plaster.
- Sealed, finished, or painted surfaces; smooth plasters; blueboard; or smooth stone work best with a primer.

Earthen plasters may be mixed up to a day in advance to maximize the water absorption into the clay particles. Specify a minimum of two coats: one as a base (it may be slightly thicker depending on the surface underneath) and the second as a topcoat. The clay may also be used in place of traditional joint compound on drywall or blueboard. The final coat may be smooth or rough, depending on client preference, then

This bathroom was constructed with earthen plaster walls and features limestone tile flooring, skylights for daylighting, and a woven reed mat ceiling.
Photo courtesy of Kelly Lerner, www.one-world-design.com.

left natural in color or washed with a clay slip or alis (clay and sand in equal proportions mixed to the consistency of yogurt), with or without pigment.

Purchased clay mix must be allowed to dry completely between each coat. It will not require a finish, except in humid or moist environments, to protect it from water. If a sheen to the topcoat is preferred, casein or milk paint works over the alis to finish it, as do beeswax, clay wall paints, or commercial, all-natural wax-oil treatments.

Maintenance

Excellent ventilation and air circulation are the keys to sustaining earth plaster, especially if the room is occasionally humid. Exhaust fans or windows that open should be specified if not already present in the home design. Minor plaster cracks and blemishes that develop are easily patched with more clay plaster mix or earth and water.

Where Does It Go?

Earthen plaster is one of the best examples of a cradle-to-cradle building material. From the dirt to the house and back into dirt again, the plaster will naturally decompose.

Spec List

Specify:
- Earthen plaster made from locally acquired soil
- Purchased earthen plaster mixes made from clay
- Primers made with all-natural ingredients (clay, sand, borax)
- Sealants made from beeswax or all-natural oils
- Natural mineral or vegetable pigments
- Fair weather for application, excellent ventilation, and adequate drying time between coats

Avoid:
- Excavation that may cause drainage problems or damaging scars on the landscape (if soil is acquired locally)
- Water in direct contact with the walls

RESOURCES

The Natural Plaster Book: Earth Lime and Gypsum Plasters for Natural Homes, Cedar Rose Guelberth and Dan Chiras (Gabriola, BC: New Society Publishers, 2003)

GYPSUM BOARD: DRYWALL, WALLBOARD

Soon after World War II, labor-intensive gypsum plaster fell out of favor and was replaced by prefabricated wallboard—plaster sandwiched between paper—that is cut to fit. Gypsum wallboard is now the overwhelming choice for the vast majority of conventional American homes and offices. Typically, the architect or builder specifies this material, so if the client and contractors are willing, select the most eco-friendly type.

Gypsum board is also called gyp board, plasterboard, drywall, or Sheetrock (depending on its purpose and, sometimes, the regional dialect). Other products, including substrates and underlayments, also fall into the general category of gypsum board. Blueboard serves as an underlayment for plaster and has an absorbent blue paper surface. Greenboard, designated for building trades by its color, is water-resistant and used in wet areas. Gypsum ceiling board, 1/2 inch in thickness, is slightly thinner than that used for walls (usually 5/8 inch).

While the gypsum itself is an abundant natural material, wallboard not only loses the plaster artisan's touch but many of the environmental benefits. Gypsum board scrap is piling up in landfills, and the chemical additives leach into the earth (see the sidebar, "Addressing Wallboard Waste"). Look for U.S. manufacturers to start recycling it soon, following the lead of Canada and Europe where the construction preferences are already changing in response to this dilemma.

Recycled or synthetic gypsum wallboard is usually made (in the U.S.) from post-industrial byproducts, such as from gypsum wallboard manufacturing and from "scrubbers" in fossil-fuel-based power plants. The reclaimed gypsum is often of higher purity than raw ore. Gypsum reclamation may actually consume less energy than the mining and transportation of the mineral, especially if the gypsum reclamation plant is located near the power plant.

Where Does It Come From?

- Gypsum board, manufactured from mined calcium sulfate, usually has a paper face.

Addressing Wallboard Waste

Drywall is the material of choice for American homes, mostly for its convenience. It can be cut it to fit, and no drying is needed, as is for plaster. Herein lies the problem: prefabricated slabs aren't one-size-fits-all, and the wallboard waste generated by residential construction is overwhelming.

- The United States produces an estimated 30 million tons of drywall annually, and 3 to 5 percent of the gypsum used in the wallboard manufacturing process emerges as waste at the wallboard plant.
- More than 95 percent of U.S. building interiors use some form of gypsum-based wallboard.
- The average new home contains more than 7 tons of gypsum. In construction and renovation, when drywall is cut and placed into position, 10 to 12 percent ends up as scrap. A 2,000-square-foot house construction project may generate one ton of wallboard scrap.
- It is estimated that 1 percent of the total waste stream in North America is scrap gypsum.

Source: "Stop Landfilling Drywall," *Pollution Engineering,* March 1, 2003, www. pollutionengineering.com; "Interior Finish Systems: Judging a Building by Its Inside Cover," *Environmental Building News,* November 2000, www.buildinggreen.com; *Minerals Yearbook* (2003), USGS, http://minerals.usgs.gov; and New West Gypsum Recycling, www. nwgypsum.com.

- Gypsum board may contain chemical additives such as fungicides, adhesives, or vinyl.
- "Recycled" or "synthetic" gypsum board is made from industrial by-product gypsum.

Installation

The paper on wallboard has been known to attract mold that compromises indoor air quality, human safety, and structure, especially in situations where vapors become trapped. Most gypsum board manufacturers add fungicides and similar chemicals to control this. Environmentally speaking, the fungicides are not desirable, but the risk of mold in the home is much greater without them. It may be in the client's best interest, especially if the climate or home site is damp, to allow for some fungicides. It is also possible to specify gypsum board without the paper sheath (recycled paper content is available), but the lack of it usually mandates the use of chemical binders in the gypsum. Consult with the manufacturer for details as to the chemical content of the fungicides, then discuss the options and risks with the client.

The best medicine for mold control, especially if it has been decided that the gypsum board should not contain fungicides, is prevention. Work with the contractor to ensure that quality construction materials, drainage, and structure breathability are built in so that water and humidity are not trapped underneath the surface or against the wall.

Waste management is a critical factor when using drywall (see the sidebar, "Addressing Wallboard Waste"), and careful measuring and planning will eliminate as much scrap as possible. Design wall heights to work with gypsum board sizes, if possible, and use leftover pieces in closets, basement stairwells, or other places where joints will be less visible.

Specify recycled-content paper tape for joints, and low-VOC or natural gypsum joint compound to bridge the gaps. Drywall should then be plastered, painted, or covered. High humidity will cause gypsum-based surfaces to deteriorate, so a water-repellent finish such as tile or paint is typically used in bathrooms, laundry areas, and kitchen sink backsplashes.

Maintenance

Drywall is never left without a finish because of the unsightly joints and the susceptibility to moisture. The boards will warp or degrade if exposed to standing water, high moisture, or constant humidity, so the most important maintenance consideration is a quality finish. Almost any drywall texture, plaster, paint, or wallcovering may be applied over wallboard to protect it.

Minor damage can easily be patched with taping and more plaster or joint compound, but moldy sections of drywall should be replaced immediately.

Where Does It Go?

In some locations, where soil conditions allow, crushed gypsum may be used as a soil conditioner. If there is no construction-waste recycling for wallboard available in the region, talk to the contractor about pulverizing leftovers into pieces smaller than one-half inch (by hand or with power tools), then mixing them into the topsoil.

Currently, wallboard can't be recycled once it has been used in the home, but the burden on landfills may drive the demand for more wallboard recycling options in the future. In the landfill, gypsum board and the paper envelope will break down, but paint, chemical adhesives and other manufactured materials may not.

Spec List

Specify:
- Wallboard purchases in precisely measured amounts, the same as room height, to eliminate waste
- High gypsum content (natural or synthetic/recycled)
- High natural material content (in addition to gypsum; sand, quartz, etc.)
- Recycled paper sheathing or no paper sheathing with minimal additives
- Low-VOC joint compound, preferably gypsum-based plaster
- Recycled-content paper for joint tape and/or acoustical sealant
- Reuse of construction scrap on-site
- Small amounts of ground scrap be incorporated into topsoil if allowable by code
- Scrap recycling (look for wallboard recycling programs in the future).

Avoid:
- Powdered joint compounds with antifreeze, vinyls, preservatives, biocides, or that outgas VOCs
- Chemical additives to wallboard, especially those that may give off VOCs
- Wasteful drywall purchases or installation methods

RESOURCES

New West Gypsum Recycling: www.nwgypsum.com
USG Corporation (USG): www.usg.com
See also Gypsum Plaster, page 174

Tile

The definition of "tile" covers a broad spectrum of materials that are installed in geometric shapes or flat pieces. Tile may be made of ceramic, porcelain, terra-cotta, or earthenware (all of which are types of fired clay); new glass or recycled glass; cement; stone; or a mix of minerals in a resin-based conglomerate, called terrazzo.

This bathroom features slate tile flooring and tub surround. Photo courtesy of Kelly Lerner, www.one-world-design.com.

Tile is specified for flooring, shower surrounds, walls, ceilings, and backsplashes because of its high durability and less frequent replacement requirement. Tile has wash-with-water maintenance and inert properties that promote healthful indoor air quality. Most tile will resist mold and stains, and is fireproof, won't outgas, or break down in water.

Tile does have some drawbacks as a truly environmental choice. Though it's usually made from widely available natural materials such as clay, sand, or stone, these are non-renewable. Tile may contain a number of less desirable materials such as synthetics, recycled postindustrial or postconsumer compounds of questionable origin, or rare minerals. Even simple clay excavation will cause water quality issues and scar the landscape. The raw materials might be quarried at a distant location, then transported to a tile factory for manufacturing and firing. Many types of tile are fired or baked at very high temperatures. All of this occurs before it is shipped to the retailer or distributor, then again to the site. The whole tile-making process results in high embodied energy.

Some tiles have glazes, which although inert once fired may contain toxic chemicals that are risky to the factory workers, the earth, or the atmosphere. Historically, tile glazes were composed of radioactive materials, asbestos, or lead, but these are now banned in the United States; however, they may still be found abroad. (Note: If the tile has an MSDS, it has been approved for import.)

All negative characteristics considered, tile still makes sense for use in an ecologically oriented home, for two reasons. First, it's healthy for the occupant and is neither a source of contaminants that outgas (if installed with healthy materials) nor a "sink" where they will collect. Second, tile is extremely durable and could easily outlast the house.

Currently, there's no independent certification for tile and no easy-to-follow green standards. As a guideline, look for tiles that are manufactured regionally, such as those made by a local artisan. If no such option exists, broaden the search. Specify natural materials or those with positive environmental impact such as recycled glass. Then consider the underlayment in the equation, as well as the mortar, mastic, grout, and sealants; any or all may contain unhealthy chemicals. The best choice for the client and the environment will involve a careful weighing of many factors: the tile content, the manufacturing processes used, the distance shipped, and the methods and substances needed for installation.

CERAMIC AND QUARRY TILE

The terms "ceramic," and "quarry" loosely refer to almost any type of tile that is made of clay and is fired. The definitions were once distinct: porcelain and ceramic were made from finer clay that was glazed, while quarry tile (glazed or unglazed) was larger than 6 inches square, and terra-cotta was unglazed and reddish in color. Now, almost any tile made from fired clay is called ceramic. In addition to clay, the tile might contain materials reclaimed from the tile manufacturer, glass, stone, or other natural and manufactured substances.

Clay: The Main Ingredient

Humble, seemingly abundant (albeit nonrenewable) clay is the primary ingredient in most ceramic tile. In fact, 650 million square feet of ceramic tile is produced in the United States each year—enough to pave the entire island of Manhattan.

Source: Ecology Action, www.ecoact.org.

Conventional ceramic or quarry tile provides a durable, water-resistant, low-maintenance surface. It's fireproof, bugproof, and moldproof. In its unsealed state, it won't outgas VOCs, and glazed tile won't absorb contaminants and reemit. It's also effective for energy-efficient passive solar storage or radiant heat systems. Tile can outlast multiple installations of other materials. As testament to their longevity, mosaics installed on walls, fountains, and domes by Islamic and Roman artists more than a thousand years ago still showcase vivid color and pattern today.

For most residential applications, a sealant will be needed on the unglazed surfaces to protect it from dirt and stains. The tile will also absorb tiny amounts of contaminants, depending on the porosity.

If the client has chemical sensitivities, choose factory-glazed tile. A glaze becomes inert when fired, so it won't outgas and it provides a waterproof, impervious surface that is easy to keep clean. The drawback to the glazed tiles, however, is that many are manufactured in developing countries, where workers might have few protections against the highly toxic chemicals and metals used in standard glazes. Lead, cadmium, and radioactive metals are considered hazardous to consumers, as well, and are banned from use in the United States, most of Europe, and many other countries. These substances are still occasionally found in the glazes on handmade tiles and cookware from nonregulated countries. Although all regulated imports and domestic tiles will have an MSDS that will help determine the properties of the tile itself, it may be difficult or impossible to know the environmental practices of a manufacturer.

In general, it's difficult, if not impossible, for a designer to know the exact content of most ceramic tile, other than the hazardous components listed on the MSDS. All

This bathroom features recycled glass tile flooring and tub surround.
Photo courtesy of Oceanside Glasstile, Christopher Ray Photography.

other ingredients and processes are proprietary. For this reason, specify tile from manufacturers or dealers with environmental policies. Look online for published company guidelines that set internal standards for lowering factory emissions and waste, improving recycling rates for raw and scrap materials, and protecting human safety.

GLASS TILE

Glass, made primarily from incredibly abundant sand (silicon dioxide) is terrific for making tile and provides an inert, easy-to-clean surface. Recycled glass tile, growing in popularity, is made from postconsumer and postindustrial waste bottles, windshields, and windowpanes. The amount of recycled glass content varies considerably, from incidental to 100 percent.

It's difficult not to appreciate the concept of recycled glass tile for the simple fact that it takes briefly used beverage containers, along with other types of glass, out of the wastestream and makes them into semipermanent design materials (see the sidebar, "Bottleneck," under Countertops, page 317). The manufacturing for glass tiles is straightforward: ground-up glass, called cullet, is poured into molds (sometimes mixed with metallic oxides for color), then fired or melted and shaped. No glaze is needed; glass is impervious without it. Subtle variations in color only add to the charm. Pure glass tile is generally less energy-intensive to manufacture than ceramic, as the glass is melted or heated at an even lower temperature ("sintered"), not fired. Glass is also popular in terrazzolike tiles that use concrete as the matrix (see Terrazzo section, page 217).

STONE TILE

See Masonry, Chapter 7.

METAL TILE

See Metals, Chapter 8.

TERRAZZO TILE

See Terrazzo, page 217.

Where Does It Come From?

- Traditional ceramic tile is usually made of fired clay.
- Talc, cement, or other minerals may be added when making ceramic.
- Manufactured or recycled materials such as fly ash or glass may also be added.
- Tile may be glazed or unglazed; glazes consist of metals, pigments, and various chemicals, along with simple silicon dioxide—sand—that become inert when fired.
- Glass is made mostly from silicon dioxide (sand). Glass for recycled glass tile generally comes from postconsumer waste such as bottles and windshields.

This bathroom has durable natural stone and ceramic tile flooring and walls applied with low-toxic adhesives and nontoxic grout. This space also features a locally sourced glass shower enclosure.
Photo by David O. Marlow.
Designer: Associates III, www.associates3.com

- The recycled glass content varies greatly by manufacturer and product, even between particular colors of tile.
- Small amounts of metals and chemicals may be added to glass for color and texture.

Installation

The general methods for installing ceramic, glass, terrazzo, and other tile are similar. Manufacturer specifications will differ according to the design application and the particular tile, as will recommended underlayments, mortars, adhesives, grouts, and sealants. Aim for all-natural materials (such as with sanded grout), but if that option is not available, go with the least toxic, low-VOC, zero-solvent, minimal-additive material possible. Urge the installer to measure carefully, as well; it's easy to be wasteful and buy more tile than is needed. Tile cutting should be done outdoors or in an open area such as a garage or deck, preferably with a wet saw; the superfine ceramic or glass dust can be hazardous. Dry installation conditions are vital to give the tile a good defense against mildew or cracking.

- *Underlayment.* The weight and strength of the underlayment needed will be determined by the purpose and location of the tile surface: wall, shower stall, floor, or countertop. FSC-certified formaldehyde-free MDF or exterior-grade plywood are the greenest choices. Cement board, gypsum-based board, or cured-and-dry concrete are also possibilities.

- *Mortar.* Thickset mortar (greater than 1 inch deep) is ideal because the mortar itself provides the "grip" and so avoids the use of synthetic adhesives and mastics. Thickset can be done with simple portland cement, sand, and lime. Thinset mortar is more fragile and prone to cracking, so it usually has chemical and latex additives for flexibility. If thinset is the preferred method for the particular tile, opt for a water-based, additive-free, low-VOC variety.

- *Adhesives/mastics.* Mastic (a particular type of ceramic adhesive) and other tile adhesives are popular because they are cheap and make for quick installation: The tile is glued to the flat substrate and the grout filled in, but no mortar is needed. In general, mastics and adhesives are not the best choice for eco-friendly tile applications because they are manufactured from toxic ingredients and may outgas VOCs. Mastic also has limited applications; it can't be used in damp areas, with glass tiles, or on slightly uneven surfaces. If an adhesive or mastic is required for the particular application, specify a water-based, low-VOC type that has no petroleum base, no toluene, hexane, benzene, or other solvents.

- *Grout.* Simple grout made of portland cement, sand, and water (lime is optional) works very well in many residential applications, and mineral pigments may be added for color. Unsanded grout should be specified if the tile might be easily scratched (glass) or will have very narrow grout joints. Of the commercial blends available, specify additive-free grout. Be aware that commercial grout blends may contain a host of questionable ingredients and outgassing components, so look for those without synthetic latex or polymer additives.

Giving Grout a Good Name

Some of the most common complaints about grout are easy to address. Stains, for example, are much less obvious if the grout color is dark. Thinner grout lines and bigger tiles will alleviate mold by reducing the surface area of grout available to fungal growths. Either strategy will result in less cleaning and fewer grout repairs.

Maintenance

Tile, especially if glazed, is amazingly durable and needs little more than soap-and-water cleaning. Unfortunately, the tiny cracks and holes present in grout are prone to expansion and contraction by water and heat, leading to deterioration. Mold and mildew will move in and take up permanent residence in grout if the tile and the room are not kept dry. Good ventilation through windows and via exhaust fans is a must, as is regular cleaning of the tiled surface.

Unglazed ceramic, terra-cotta, frosted glass, or other more porous tiles are more susceptible to damage from stains, scratches, and general abuse (underfoot or on a countertop). In addition, the porous unglazed surface provides a sink for contaminants and bacteria. Glazed tile, on the other hand, is resistant to just about everything.

The grout around both glazed and unglazed tile, however, is more vulnerable and should always be sealed on-site after installation to prevent mold and stains. Specify a low-VOC, water-based, wipe-on sealant rather than a spray-on variety, as it will have fewer negative repercussions on indoor air quality.

It may be tempting to avoid the use of sealants, but the drawback will be that the grout, and then the tile, will deteriorate much more quickly and need replacement. Ultimately, if the tile falls apart and must be disposed of in a landfill, it's bad for the environment. Sealants also prevent mold, a concern to sanitary health and indoor air quality. The best method for prevention of tile degradation is a sealant applied immediately after the tile is laid, then reapplied as necessary.

The wall and backsplash of this kitchen are made of recycled glass tile. This space also features bamboo floors, fluorescent lighting, low-VOC paints, and radiant-heat flooring.
Used by permission of My House Magazine.
Photo by Mikel Covey.
Designer: Gail Madison Goodhue.

Advise clients that they need not replace tile or employ toxic cleansers just because the grout has become stained or dirty. Simple cleansers such as vinegar and water, borax, or baking soda, used with a stiff brush, make good cleansing agents. If mold is persistent, professional steam cleaning may help. Grout can be carefully removed and redone, as well, without removing the tile.

Where Does It Go?

Broken pieces of tile can be used in mosaics, underneath soil in potted plants for drainage, or tossed into the garden. Extra tiles may be saved as replacements for future repairs and breakage or taken to a construction recycling or exchange site. Consider using leftover tiles as decorative accents in other applications such as tabletops or trim, or donating them for crafts to youth groups, schools, or senior citizen centers.

Fired clay, mortar, and grout are similar to metamorphosed rock, and will eventually break up into inert rocklike pieces at the end of the tile life cycle. The glaze will also be inert. In some localities, porcelain and ceramic recycling exists for old toilets and bathroom fixtures; tile may be accepted there, as well.

Glass tiles have the most promising future of all. Those that are 100 percent glass can theoretically be recycled over and over, then will eventually become sand again.

Spec List

Specify:
- Tile made with unprocessed, all-natural clays or safe recycled materials such as glass
- Domestic tile, especially locally made
- Factory-glazed ceramic
- One hundred percent recycled glass tile or high recycled-glass content
- Natural backerboard, MDF, or underlayment (FSC-certified wood, plaster, gypsum, or concrete)
- Simple mortar from cement, sand, water, and possibly lime (no additives)
- Grout without added fungicides
- Low-VOC, water-based, wipe-on sealant
- Low-VOC, low-solvent, additive-free, latex-free mortar and grout

Avoid:
- Unregulated import tile
- High amounts of new glass added to glass tiles
- VOCs, solvents, fungicides, vinyls, or latex additives in mortar, grout, and sealants

RESOURCES

National Terrazzo & Mosaic Association: www.ntma.com
Tile Council of America: www.tileusa.com

Flooring

BAMBOO FLOORING

Bamboo is a popular green option for flooring as well as for other applications such as cabinets, wall paneling, and furniture. Some types of bamboo are harder than oak or maple, have the tension of steel, and are as versatile as wood. High-density versions work best for underfloor radiant heat systems. Unlike wood, which takes decades to replenish itself in forests, bamboo's earth-saving quality is that it can be cut and regrown every five to ten years.

A man can sit in a bamboo house under a bamboo roof, on a bamboo chair at a bamboo table, with a bamboo hat on his head and bamboo sandals on his feet. He can at the same time hold in one hand a bamboo bowl, in the other hand bamboo chopsticks and eat bamboo sprouts. When through with his meal, which has been cooked over a bamboo fire, the table may be washed with a bamboo cloth, and he can fan himself with a bamboo fan, take a siesta on a bamboo bed, lying on a bamboo mat with his head resting on a bamboo pillow. His child might be lying in a bamboo cradle, playing with a bamboo toy. On rising he would smoke a bamboo pipe and taking a bamboo pen, write on a bamboo paper, or carry his articles in bamboo baskets suspended from a bamboo pole, with a bamboo umbrella over his head. He might then take a walk over a bamboo suspension bridge, drink water from a bamboo ladle, and scrape himself with a bamboo scraper (handkerchief).

Source: *A Yankee on the Yangtze*, by William Edgar Geil (London: Hodder and Stoughton), 1904; World Agroforestry Centre, www.worldagroforestry.org.

All bamboo products, however, are not created equal. Pesticides, fungicides, and fireproofing chemicals may have been used on them, and many manufacturers employ urea-formaldehyde as the binder, acknowledged by the EPA as a known carcinogen to humans. Some bamboo flooring will exceed OSHA and LEED recommendations for allowable formaldehyde, while others fall well within acceptable levels. Formaldehyde-free is by far the best option; check the MSDS for details.

Bamboo flooring types are almost as variable as wood; solid or 100 percent bamboo, engineered, veneer, or strand products are available. Strand bamboo products are the latest innovations, which take strands, or individual fibers, and bind them with pressure, heat, and a resin. The resins usually contain a form of formaldehyde. Engineered and veneer bamboo flooring contains a core wood, which may or may not have been harvested from a certified sustainable forest. Rubberwood, which is harvested when the latex-producing tree is no longer viable, is popular as a bamboo core. The bamboo itself does not yet fall under established FSC guidelines, but look for FSC certification for the wood core (see Chapter 9 Wood).

One of the limitations of bamboo is that high moisture and humidity can cause it to warp or weaken. Therefore, it's a poor choice for bathrooms or applications in very wet climates. Manufacturers recommend it not be installed where humidity levels exceed 60 percent. Another is that color choices are limited, as bamboo does not take stain as easily but some manufacturers who use waterbased stains have had better success of late and this may continue to improve.

Until domestic production becomes reliable, transportation of raw materials from overseas is still a negative on bamboo's report card. Although it is grown in many developing countries and may provide opportunity for sustainable, economically viable commerce, as yet there are no certifying agencies that assure quality control, eco-friendly farming, or worker treatment. The best guideline is to purchase from a firm with sustainable management practices that manages its own forests abroad or buys from a single source. Demand for bamboo is booming; we can expect domestic sources to appear in the future.

In Demand as Food, Too

Bamboo is the sole source of food for giant pandas; each panda consumes 22 pounds a day. No wonder they grow so fast—the bamboo stalks, that is. Fortunately, commercial bamboo flooring is not the same species as the type favored by the endangered panda.

Where Does It Come From?

- Bamboo is technically a grass with a woody stalk; there are more than a thousand species worldwide. Most bamboo is grown in Asia, although U.S. sources are emerging as demand increases.
- Flooring, wallcoverings, and other residential applications may be made from solid or from engineered bamboo.
- Plantation practices vary greatly in their sustainability and ethics; no certification from the FSC or a third party is yet available.
- Engineered bamboo is layered like a laminate and may have rubberwood or another wood as the core (see Wood, Chapter 9); look for FSC-certified core wood.
- DDT or harmful pesticides are sometimes used on bamboo farms in countries where pesticide use is not as well regulated. Borate, a pest-inhibiting treatment that is generally considered safe around humans, is also employed.
- Urea-formaldehyde is frequently used in bonding agents for flooring planks. Formaldehyde-free bonding agents are less common.

- Other chemicals are sometimes added for mildew control, fireproofing, and pest resistance.
- Aluminum oxide and polyurethane are in standard factory finishes.
- Water-based acrylic stain may be added in standard factory finishes.

Installation

Bamboo must be allowed to acclimate to the home environment for several days prior to installation. While bamboo is touted to be more moisture-resistant than some hardwoods, humidity or water trapped underneath may compromise the integrity of the floor over time, so specify that the substrate be tested for moisture content beforehand. It should measure no more than 3 percentage points different from that of the bamboo. Relative air humidity of below 60 percent is recommended by manufacturers for bamboo installation, and some will void the warranty otherwise.

Concrete slabs require special consideration if they are to be the substrate under bamboo; they should be cured for at least 60 days, allowed to completely dry, and then

This stairwell is constructed of bamboo stair treads, risers, and nosings. This space also features a railing made from unpainted steel with a low-VOC clear sealer, and walls that are finished with no paint "tinted gypsum plaster". Sanger Residence, Bruce Millard architect. Photo by Bruce Millard.

be tested for moisture content. It may then be necessary to specify a vapor film to protect the flooring from seepage.

Depending on the particular flooring system selected, bamboo can be nailed, stapled, floated, or glued in the same manner as wood, over tile, wood, underlayments, concrete, and many other surfaces. A high-water-content adhesive is not recommended, so specify a low-VOC alternative.

Bamboo does not take stain well, so staining is not recommended unless done during manufacture. If specifying solid bamboo flooring with on-site finishing, also specify a low-VOC, water-based finish.

Maintenance

Bamboo can discolor in direct sunlight, especially at high altitudes where the solar radiation is intense. Draperies or UV-coated windows will minimize the effect. Occasional use of mild, nonabrasive, environmentally friendly cleaners, in addition to regular vacuuming and/or sweeping, will keep the floor looking bright. Oil soaps and damp mopping are not recommended.

Where Does It Go?

Bamboo with minimal amounts of binding adhesive, contaminants in the topcoat, or chemical treatments will biodegrade safely and quickly, much like wood. Engineered bamboo, with chemical binders, will not do as well. Bamboo can also be reclaimed, refinished, and reused in other applications.

Fact Check

- There currently are 35 million acres of bamboo worldwide (Solar Living Institute; http://store.solarlivingstore.com).
- Depending on the species, a bamboo "forest" can completely regenerate every 5 to 10 years. Some species grow more than a foot a day.

Spec List

Specify:
- Formaldehyde-free bamboo
- FSC-certified wood core
- Low-VOC finish (factory-finished is preferable)
- Low-VOC underlayment, adhesives, and binder
- Minimal use of adhesives
- Perfectly dry subflooring

Avoid:

- Formaldehyde in the underlayment, binder, or finish
- High-humidity weather for installation
- Chemicals added for mildew control, fireproofing, pest resistance and in finishes

RESOURCES

American Bamboo Society: www.americanbamboo.org

LEATHER FLOORING

Durable animal skins were probably one of the original flooring materials, along with grasses and dirt. Today, although some individuals are opposed to the use of animal products, leather flooring provides a soft, cushioned surface with terrific sound absorption, durability, and warmth. The surface breathes and gives with fluctuations in indoor temperatures and humidity.

Most animal skins are acquired by leather tanneries as a secondary product of the meat industry. Consultation with a sustainable/organic meat producer may provide leads to the tanneries that purchase from them. This step will ensure that the skins were obtained from a pesticide-free, all-natural environment.

The modern production and tanning of hides uses a large amount of water, some of it to wash chemicals from the skins. And those chemicals, especially chromium sulfate and certain dyes, are poisonous. In developing countries, which are the largest producers of leather, there are few controls to protect the safety of the workers or regulate the quality of the discharged wastewater. In addition, the chemicals used may cause clients with sensitivities to react to large expanses of new leather, which will outgas initially (think of that new-shoe smell, amplified).

Vegetable-based tanning processes, which rely upon natural tannins from rhubarb, tree bark, tare (vetch seed, a weed), and valonea (the beard of the acorn from an oak tree, that grows in Greece), are employed by a few companies. Natural vegetable and mineral dyes are popular with these tanneries. Specify leather from a company that specializes in these old-world methods. Local artisan leatherworkers might also be able to custom-make the flooring to specifications—thus providing a locally produced, more eco-sensitive product.

Recycled leather obtained primarily from clothing and upholstery scraps is an alternative for flooring. The leather will have already completed outgassing. (VOCs will still be a problem no matter where they outgas, but this will minimize the effect on a chemically sensitive client.) Most of the characteristic stretching of the leather will have occurred, as well. However, recycled leather flooring is not widely available; look for specialty artisans and producers.

Installation

Leather flooring is available in tiles or sheets. Leather is sensitive to humidity and temperature, so it should be acclimated for several days, then installed when the temperature is moderate. Leather is not recommended for damp areas. It can be laid similar to any resilient flooring, over concrete or underlayment, then glued, smoothed with a weighted roller, and tacked or covered with trim at the edges. Adhesive is necessary to prevent stretching and movement of the leather against the subflooring. Always specify low-VOC, solvent-free glues that work with the natural porosity of leather.

Manufacturers recommend several applications of carnauba or other naturally penetrating waxes or oils immediately after installation.

Maintenance

Light use enhances the patina of leather. Touch-ups with colored wax will hide some markings, but leather will not stand up to heavy abuse from heel marks or pet claws. Regular waxings or oilings are highly recommended to maintain the finish and protect the leather.

Where Does It Go?

Although leather and animal skins are, by their nature, resilient to deterioration from the elements, they will eventually decompose. Certain tannery chemicals, however, present an ecological dilemma. Although the chemicals are only barely present in the finished product, their use creates water quality hazards that have not been fully measured.

Spec List

Specify:
- Vegetable tanning and dyeing processes that rely on tare, rhubarb, valonea, and tree bark
- Locally tanned leather with minimal chemical processing or dyes
- Low-VOC, water-based glues

Avoid:
- Leather tanned with chromium
- Chemically dyed leather
- Solvent-based adhesives

CORK FLOORING

Cork is one of the best examples of a cradle-to-cradle resource. It originates as the bark of the cork oak tree, *quercus suber*, a species that grows primarily in Portugal and six other Mediterranean countries: Algeria, Spain, Morocco, France, Italy, and Tunisia. The bark is stripped from a tree every decade or so in a process that dates back 3000 years. Regular extraction does not harm the oaks, but instead ensures cork that is of top quality. The World Wildlife Fund proclaims it a prime example of harmonious interaction between humans and nature (www.panda.org). With the demand for eco-friendly products expanding, many cork producers are moving toward certification by the For-

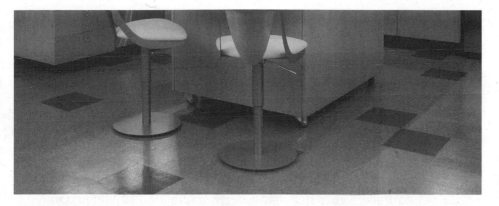

This kitchen has natural cork flooring.
© 2006 David Bergman.

est Stewardship Council (FSC), ensuring that sustainable yields and sound environmental practices will continue.

The environmental impact of shipping lightweight cork from Europe is slightly less than that of heavier ceramic tile or stone. The processing for cork is simple and green: slabs of bark from the tree, cleaned, and boiled. In the cutting room, the production of wine corks usually gets priority, while the remaining scraps are collected for other uses such as flooring and wallcovering (see Wallcoverings, page 224). There's virtually no waste.

Binder is added, and the cork is "baked" into a sheet. The composition of the binder depends on the manufacturer. While urea-formaldehyde was once common, some companies now opt for polyurethane or supposedly greener protein-based compounds (although the specifics are proprietary and sometimes difficult to determine). Avoid cork with vinyl or styrene butadiene backings or blends, as these are not environmentally friendly choices.

Cork's cellular structure, consisting of polyhedral (14-sided) hollow walls, gives cork its buoyancy in water and makes it comfortable underfoot. Cork has the pliability of linoleum, outstanding sound-absorption qualities, and bounce-back resiliency—up to 94 percent of the initial dimension—along with superb flaw-disguising qualities. And it's not a new flooring option—it's been used for over a century.

There's more. Suberin, a natural fatty acid inherent in cork, provides water resistance, has antimicrobial properties, deters pests (even termites), and is fire-retardant. Cork won't mold or rot like wood. It's antistatic and provides a nonslip surface that is especially appropriate for children or the elderly. The material is ideal for those with chemical sensitivities, as it does not outgas or shed microfibers that may irritate.

Rumors of a cork shortage may be unfounded; some say it's intended to drive up pricing for wineries. Still, cork production is limited by the relatively small number of trees, mostly growing in the handful of Mediterranean countries named above. The cork oak species only lives to about 150 years of age, and a new seedling needs at least 30 years to mature. Beverage cork recycling, another potential resource for flooring, has yet to catch on in the United States, but the trend is growing abroad (see the Fact Check, sidebar, page 204).

Cork is sometimes blended with synthetic latex (styrene butadiene). Synthetic latex is often just called "latex," or even "rubber," but it is not the natural substance derived from rubber trees (see Latex, page 362). Avoid cork flooring blends for this reason.

Cork Is Tops

- A French monk from the eighteenth century discovered the special ability of cork to stop up a bottle. Dom Perignon is famous not only for his champagne, but for the top that's fun to pop. Cork was widely used for bottling beverages before it was recognized as suitable for flooring, wall-coverings and other applications.
- Wine cork is readily recycled in Europe and Australia, but not yet in the United States.
- Guides Australia, a girl's club, has collected more than 75 million bottle corks for recycling into floor tile, sporting goods, and boat decking (www.guidesvic.org.au). Girl Guides in Canada is following suit.

Where Does It Come From?

- Cork is harvested from the bark of the cork oak tree, most often found in the Mediterranean region.
- Cork flooring is made from sheets of bark or pressed from scrap pieces.
- Binders may contain urea-formaldehyde or polyurethane, or may be protein-based.
- Cork flooring may be stained or left unstained. If finished in the factory, it may have an acrylic topcoat.
- Low-VOC, water-based adhesives are preferable, if needed.
- Cork-rubber flooring blends are usually a mix of recycled styrene butadiene (synthetic) rubber and cork granules.

Installation

Cork flooring comes in large sheets, square or geometric tiles, planks, or mosaics. Some have interlocking systems and backings that make it unnecessary to use adhesives, except perhaps in high-traffic areas or around the edges. The color spectrum available is comparable to wood flooring, and natural stains can be used to enhance or change the hue of unfinished cork. Tiles come in varying shapes and sizes, making it easier to fit sloping floors and odd angles.

Cork will expand in high-humidity locations and will contract or become slightly brittle in arid environments, so specify acclimation to the particular home space before installation—most manufacturers recommend at least 72 hours.

The suberin in cork makes it unnecessary to treat the floor with finishes or chemicals, but the life span and stain resistance may be increased by doing so. Specify that the finishing be delayed until five days or more after installation to further allow for acclimatization. Inconsistencies may then be sanded out. Specify a beeswax-based finish or a low-VOC, water-based polyurethane. Any factory finish should also be low-VOC and formaldehyde-free.

Maintenance

Cork is basically maintenance-free: vacuuming and sweeping are all that is necessary. Occasional, very light damp mopping is acceptable. Cork can be damaged by standing water, however, so advise the client to use a well-squeezed mop, never to allow the water to pool on the floor, and to put a towel under the bucket.

A cork floor can also be refinished with 00-grade steel wool on a floor sander.

Where Does It Go?

Cork is fully biodegradable, with the exception of any finishes or adhesives that might be used. Although it is possible to recycle cork from bottles, technology has not yet been developed to do the same with cork flooring.

Historical Cork

The use of cork in home design is timeless. Frank Lloyd Wright, eco-builder extraordinaire, used cork flooring in Fallingwater, the home that is now a historic landmark and museum in western Pennsylvania. (www.paconcerve.org/fw).

Spec List

Specify:
- Formaldehyde-free binders in the cork
- Minimal low-VOC adhesive backing or adhesive applied to subfloor
- Tiles that are interlocking and therefore need little adhesive
- Unfinished or factory-finished surface with low-VOC polyurethane
- Resin-oil primer and/or beeswax-based finish
- Natural pigment-based stains

Avoid:
- PVC-vinyl blends or backings
- VOCs and solvents in adhesives and finishes
- Synthetic rubber (styrene butadiene) blended into cork flooring

RESOURCES

Forest Stewardship Council: www.fsc.org

BIOCOMPOSITE FLOORING

An engineered panel product constructed from the stalks of the sorghum plant grown around the world for food. The stalks left over after harvest are heatpressed with a nontoxic adhesive to form lightweight, strong, unique Kirei board. This detail is from a photo by Mathais Brecher, Brecher Design.

Biocomposites, especially boards made from agricultural by-products, are expanding exponentially in popularity for home construction and design (see Wood and Biocomposites, page 157). They are manufactured from wheat or sorghum chaff, bagasse (sugar cane pulp), sunflower hulls, or a number of other "leftovers" from harvest and processing. Biocomposites are most commonly specified as substitutes for plywood, MDF, OSB, paneling, cabinet bodies and faces, or veneer. Agriculture-based biocomposites offer an annually renewable resource, from crop by-products available from crops already in production.

While not all ag boards possess the hardness or water resistance of solid wood, most varieties compare favorably to their respective engineered wood equivalents for purposes such as millwork, underlayments, backings, and casework. Where used as finish materials, the inherent grains, speckles, and color striations of the boards will add unique beauty to an environmentally conscientious home.

Biocomposites can be used for flooring, cabinetry, or wall paneling applications and are somewhat experimental and long-term results are yet unknown. Boards made from sorghum waste fiber are one option that is being marketed as durable enough for flooring. The sorghum crops, which are drought-tolerant and require little fertilizer or pesticide, are mostly harvested from northern China. The potential for a U.S. supply is still undeveloped; however, sorghum is already grown worldwide as a feed enhancer for livestock, for ethanol, and for sweeteners.

Ag board manufacturers are strategically oriented to please the eco-minded market, so most use low-VOC, formaldehyde-free binders, and some are experimenting with soy-based substitutes for MDI (see Wood and Biocomposites, page 151). Keep specifications for stains and finishes similar to those for equivalent wood products. In general, sorghum-based or other types of biocomposites are not recommended for bathrooms or laundry areas as they are not waterproof and may warp easily.

Where Does It Come From?

- Biocomposite boards are made from a variety of crop residues and agricultural by-products that include wheat, rice, barley, or oat straw; sunflower hulls; bluegrass or rye grass stubble; cornhusks and sorghum stalks; hemp; soybean plants; and bagasse (sugar cane pulp).
- Adhesives and binders may include low-VOC glues, outgassing solvents, formaldehyde, soy-based products, and natural or synthetic resins.
- Borate is sometimes used as a pesticide, especially in the manufacturing plant. Other residual pesticides may be present from the cropland.
- Finished biocomposite boards may have water-based finishes or solvent-based polyurethanes.
- Formaldehyde may or may not be used in manufacturing as a preservative or in the finish.

Installation

Biocomposite flooring can be stained, finished, installed, and maintained much like wood; check with the manufacturer for recommendations. Specify low-VOC, water-based adhesives and sealants in all applications. Unfinished biocomposite sawdust may be disposed of as mulch or tilled into soil. Scraps should be treated like wood construction waste and taken to an exchange. No biocomposite recycling has been developed yet.

Maintenance

Maintenance of biocomposites varies by the content. Consult with the manufacturer for suggestions as to periodic resealing. Otherwise, the material should be cared for much like wood. Where there's heavy traffic from shoes or pets, rugs may greatly prolong the life of the floor.

Where Does It Go?

Like wood, biocomposite boards decompose naturally, back into soil. Small amounts of binders, resins, stains, and finishes used within or on the board may also decompose, but will do so much more slowly.

Spec List

Specify:

- Boards made from 100 percent renewable grain (no plastics added, for example)
- Formaldehyde-free, low-VOC, water-based binders, sealants, adhesives, and stains
- Borate (if necessary), added for preservative or pest resistance

Avoid:

- Formaldehyde in the binder or finish
- Preservatives or pesticides (other than borate)

WOOD FLOORING

When thinking of natural elements in a home, the first that probably comes to mind is wood. It's a logical choice for homes with children, pets, or people with allergies, because unlike carpet, which may collect mold, dust, and pet hair, wood is simple to keep clean. If properly maintained and occasionally refinished, it can last the lifetime of a home and will be a superb long-term investment.

Wood has less embodied energy than nonrenewable, mined material such as stone, and it requires only cutting and finishing to be suitable for home flooring. Unfortunately, most wood grows slowly over many decades, making it a slowly renewable resource—a fact that was largely ignored by our ancestors who felled old-growth trees at alarming rates.

Although there have been improvements in recent years, forestry practices remain highly controversial and problematic. Single-species tree plantations are one way that

This home has recycled oak flooring that was removed from a demolition project in Kansas City. This space also features recycled metal stairs and railing and ample daylighting.
Photo courtesy of Rockhill and Associates.
Designer: Rockhill and Associates.

forest products companies have tried to meet consumer demand for wood, but they lack the vital biodiversity necessary to sustain a complex, healthy ecosystem. And the destruction of the tropical rain forests, at the rate of six football fields per minute, according to Greenpeace (www.greenpeace.org), is frightening.

Standing Tall

It has taken more than 2,000 years—and a lot of luck avoiding fire, disease, lightning and saws—to become the tallest tree in the United States. The Coast Redwood in Jedediah Smith Redwoods National Park soars over 300 feet tall and is close to 80 feet in girth (National Register of Big Trees, American Forests, www.americanforests.org).

To counteract traditional forestry practices that meet market demand at the expense of the environment, the Forest Stewardship Council (FSC) has developed chain-of-custody certification and environmentally friendly standards for the industry. Look for the FSC symbol on new wood flooring (see Wood, page 144).

Reclaimed Wood Flooring

For truly eco-friendly wood flooring, specify reclaimed wood from a local construction salvage yard, a dealer, or from a building planned for remodeling, deconstruction, or demolition. Locally found "used" wood prevents new logging, cuts out the long-distance transportation factor, and saves wood from disposal. Better yet, specify SmartWood-certified types to ensure the species, the logging methods, and the remanufacturing are all earth-friendly (see Wood, page 142).

Take time to investigate the source of the reclaimed wood to determine whether it is suitable for indoor use. If the flooring has been exposed to industrial chemicals or agricultural pesticides, for example, it's unsafe for residential applications. Reclaimed residential flooring from older homes is widely available and usually ideal.

New Wood Flooring

New wood flooring is an ecological choice if the species isn't threatened and the forestry practices are sustainable, but sorting through the criteria can be challenging. For example, it may appear more ecologically prudent to specify domestic wood because it requires less energy for transportation. All exotic (foreign) species are endangered, whereas some local forests might be. But the details may indicate otherwise. Look to the FSC for guidance. Its seal on the packaging will ensure that every effort has been made to apply sustainable forestry and to avoid depleting endangered ecosystems. The FSC takes into consideration the availability of the tree species, monitors conservation efforts within a company and along the chain of custody, and prohibits the use of genetically modified organism (GMO) species and certain pesticides. Other reputable and credible certification organizations exist, but none have gained the reputation of FSC for such thorough, unbiased methods.

There are three basic types of new wood flooring: solid, engineered, and acrylic impregnated.

- *Solid wood flooring* can be purchased prefinished or unfinished. If specifying FSC-certified and an eco-friendly finish, solid wood is an excellent green choice. Suppressed wood—small undergrowth trees that are thinned and culled to aid in forest fire prevention on public lands—may not yet be certified (due to technicalities), but it's another wise selection.

- *Engineered wood* uses a variety of chemicals in the manufacturing, and it's made of pressed layers (usually three-ply or five-ply) that run in different directions, which gives it added dimensional stability in humid conditions such as near bathtubs or sinks. Look for formaldehyde-free, FSC-certified products.

- *Acrylic-impregnated wood* is a popular choice for commercial installations such as gym floors, but it's not considered an ideal green choice for homes because synthetics are a major component. There are a few manufacturers of acrylic-impregnated products, however, that use FSC-certified wood.

Where Does It Come From?

- Wood flooring is made from both domestic and exotic trees.
- Reclaimed wood is culled from residential, commercial, and agricultural floors, walls, and structures. It may also be culled from rivers, lakes, streams, or from fallen trees.
- Sometimes wood floors are made from recycled (downcycled) wood scraps or sawdust with acrylics or resins added.
- Sealants are usually polyurethane. Resin-oil primers are an option.
- Floor finishes or stains may contain a variety of natural oils, resins, or pigments; solvents; chemical compounds; petroleum distillates; metal drying agents; formaldehyde; and sometimes water.

Installation

Wear spots, uneven edges, and inconsistent widths and lengths in reclaimed wood are all part of its beauty, but can make it tricky to install. The job is best done by a professional with expertise in reclaimed wood floor installation.

Specify that the installer do the cutting outdoors to keep sawdust down. There are three basic installation methods; the flooring choice and the "bones" of the house will determine which might work best.

- *Nailed.* Each piece is nailed, at an angle, to a subflooring, in a process often called "blind nailing." This is the most traditional way, and it needs virtually no adhesives, so VOC emissions will be minimal.

This home features 200-year-old reclaimed barnwood flooring with water-based sealer and low-toxic finishes. Photo by David O. Marlow. Designer: Associates III. www.associates3.com

- *Floating.* Engineered flooring or subflooring can be designed to attach to and support itself through interlocking pieces. This is the most obvious choice for use over a radiant heat system.

- *Glued.* The flooring (usually engineered) is glued to a subflooring, usually concrete or plywood. The adhesives chosen should be low-VOC to minimize health concerns.

Addressing Sawdust Concerns

Conventional floor sanding stirs up huge volumes of wood dust and particulate from the existing finish, which is hazardous. Container systems that are attached to the sander must be manually emptied and are an improvement on the conventional method of floor sanding, but the best method is to rely on a professional floor refinishing company that uses a sanding system with a hose that extends out of the house, usually to a collection unit inside of a vehicle.

Alternatively, if the existing finish is in reasonably good condition, there are some low-VOC, eco-friendly finishes that may be applied—no sanding needed.

Factory staining and finishing of wood flooring avoids VOC outgassing in the home. (The VOCs will outgas anyway, but this will minimize the effect on indoor air quality and will protect the client who is chemically sensitive.) However, choosing to finish on-site allows for greater control over the products used. Consider skipping the finish altogether if the house is in an arid climate, there are dry conditions in the home, there will be low foot traffic, and if the client desires a wood species that will develop a smooth patina with use.

Maintenance

Preserving the beauty and integrity of a wood floor is a simple task. Penetrating oils and waxes need to be reapplied occasionally, followed by a thorough buffing to shine it up. Stripping is a last resort if layers of grime have developed. Hard finishes, on the other hand, will last indefinitely if given a bit of TLC.

For both reclaimed and new wood flooring, advise the client to:

- Prevent scratches and marks by putting felt or floor protectors under all furniture, rugs, and appliances.
- Remove shoes in the house.
- Put rugs down in high-traffic or play areas. (Secure with nonslip backing or padding for safety.)
- Sweep with a soft broom or vacuum regularly (turn the rotating bristles off to avoid scratches).
- Use a bit of soap designed for use on wood floors and minimal water when a more thorough cleaning is necessary.
- Never allow water to pool on the floor; use a well-squeezed mop, and place a towel under the bucket.

If one piece of flooring has been damaged, it can be replaced to avoid problems. If refinishing the entire floor is necessary and the existing finish is compatible to it, specify an eco-friendly product that adheres with minimal or no sanding. Stripping the floor bare not only creates a mess, but the resulting debris can be hazardous to both the health of the worker and the client.

Where Does It Go?

A wood floor may be deconstructed, then salvaged for a similar or different use or downcycled into a wood-based product. Only wood that is rotten or has been permanently tainted with toxic substances is not suitable for reuse.

Spec List

Specify Wood That Is:
- Fallen on or thinned from the property
- Reclaimed
- Locally or domestically harvested, FSC-certified, and a nonthreatened species
- Suppressed (no certification is available)
- Rapidly renewable

Specify Finishes and Stains (either on prefinished wood or to be applied on-site) That Are:
- Water-based
- Made of natural (sometimes called food-grade) oils, resins, pigments, and waxes
- Low-VOC
- Formaldehyde-free
- Free of metallic hardening or drying agents (such as zinc)
- Solvent-free
- Protected from moisture before and during the installation

Avoid:
- Reclaimed wood of uncertain origin
- Chemically tainted wood (lead, arsenic, factory chemicals)
- Uncertified wood
- Rare or threatened species
- Solvent-based finishes
- Formaldehyde and other preservatives in the wood or finish
- Metal-based drying agents in the finish
- Engineered wood unless certified

RESOURCES

Forest Stewardship Council U.S.: www.fscus.org
Green Seal Floor Care Products: Finishes and Strippers: www.greenseal.org/recommendations.htm
SmartWood (Rainforest Alliance): www.Smartwood.org
See also Chapter 9, Wood and Composites.

LINOLEUM

Linoleum is both a brand name and a widely used term that is not brand-specific. In general terms, linoleum is made from linseed oil (from the flax plant), pine resin (or tall oil, a by-product from pine pulp processing), sawdust or wood flour, cork, and limestone. It is also used on desks, countertops, or walls. The material is available with an adhesive backing or without, and comes in sheets and tiles.

Linoleum is not vinyl, although in vernacular English, the term is used often, and mistakenly, for it. Resilient flooring is often made from PVC-vinyl, as well as a host of chemicals and petroleum-based compounds. The confusion began after World War II when the vinyl floor craze took over: both linoleum and vinyl were sold in rolled sheets or tiles, and the distinction was blurred and persists to this day. Similarities between the two end there.

For a time, linoleum wasn't manufactured in the United States (adding to the energy use for transport), but that is changing; the raw materials are available here, and the demand for this healthy, environmentally friendly flooring is booming. A leading manufacturer reported in 2004 that linoleum sales growth outpaced the overall floor covering market by more than double in five years (*Healthy Building News,* May 17, 2004; www.healthybuilding.net).

Linoleum is basically manufactured through mixing, pressing, and a curing or drying process that takes several weeks. High temperatures are not used—it's more like a slow baking—but it does consume energy. Linoleum is made from mostly renewable resources in an ecologically gentle process.

The drawbacks to this material are few. Linoleic acid oxidizes naturally, releasing a VOC that is rarely irritating, but the slight odor can drive the issue if the client has chemical sensitivities. The VOCs will taper off over time. Are the fumes harmful? It's unlikely, but the verdict is still out. On the flip side, linoleum's natural oxidation process is useful for preventing and eliminating bacterial growth, making linoleum the flooring choice of many health care facilities.

The flooring may easily last 30 years in high traffic, or decades longer with less wear and tear. Linoleum underfoot has comfortable resiliency. The dyed-through color hides minor blemishes and damage, and a sort of self-healing occurs to tiny cracks because of the "give" in the material. Kits with accurate color are available to patch small blemishes.

Where Does It Come From?

- Linoleum is mostly made from linseed oil, pine resin, sawdust or wood flour, cork, small amounts of pigment, and limestone.
- Linoleum usually has a burlap-type backing made of jute or sometimes hemp.

Unique Tribute of Linoleum

Are bright sunlight and fading an issue for the client in selecting a floor finish? Linoleum has a truly unique property that will counteract this problem. When kept in the dark, linoleum may experience natural yellowing, but the colors will brighten again when exposed to daylight.

- The finish, if there is one, is usually ultra-thin acrylic.
- Linoleum adhesives are chemical compounds; some are low-VOC, water-based, and formaldehyde-free.

Installation

Some manufacturers recommend linoleum not be used below grade or in bathrooms where moisture will stain it. FSC-certified wood-based underlayment or concrete are both acceptable subfloors. All subflooring cracks should be filled and bumps completely smoothed out, as the softer surface of linoleum shows imperfection. Specify that the floor must be perfectly dry before installation, according to manufacturer recommendations for moisture content. This is critical so that water isn't trapped that will degrade the integrity of the flooring.

The adhesives recommended for linoleum are not interchangeable with those for vinyl, so follow the manufacturer specs precisely. A low-VOC, water-based type is best. The small amount used may have an odor, but most linoleum adhesives list "no hazardous ingredients" on the MSDS and are not skin or eye irritants. Linoleum seam adhesives, however, may outgas and do include cautions for eyes and skin on the MSDS. Plan for good ventilation and airing out, both during and after installation.

Because linoleum usually comes in rolls or boxes of tiles, undoubtedly there will be extra, even after careful measurements. The extra tiles are handy to have around for replacing small damaged or worn-out sections, so advise the client to keep some. Leftover pieces might also be put to use in a bathroom or closet. Thin strips may be safely shredded for garden mulch, as linoleum is completely biodegradable, or they could be donated to a school or senior citizen art program.

Maintenance

Linoleum is best vacuumed or swept or occasionally cleaned with a barely damp mop. No chemical cleansers or finishes are needed. For cracks or tiny holes, patch kits can be purchased to match; they are made from simple nontoxic glue and ground-up linoleum solids. Very light sanding will also improve a damaged surface.

Where Does It Go?

Linoleum, with the exception of the thin acrylic coating and adhesive, is fully biodegradable.

Spec List

Specify:
- True linoleum, not vinyl, made from linseed oil and other natural materials
- Smooth, dry subfloor or underlayment
- Low-VOC, water-based, formaldehyde-free adhesives

Avoid:
- Vinyl flooring that is mistakenly called linoleum
- Seam adhesives

"RUBBER" FLOORING

The verdict is still out on whether recycled "rubber" flooring—not made from rubber trees but from synthetic, petroleum-based latex in recycled tires—is truly safe for residential applications. Most companies that market the products to homeowners claim low-VOC levels that meet indoor air quality specifications, but as with automobile tires, this flooring has a distinct odor. Additionally, the source latex from tires, which is rather spongy by nature, has been exposed to enormous amounts of toxins while rolling down the highways under someone's car. It seems unlikely that all dangerous compounds could have been removed.

Although there is redeeming value in recycling resources, and this product is frequently marketed as eco-friendly, its safety for interior use has yet to be determined.

Where Does It Come From?

- Recycled rubber/latex flooring is not made from natural rubber or latex (from rubber trees); it's made from recycled tire chips.
- Tires are largely manufactured from synthetic rubber, a petroleum-based product.
- Some "recycled rubber" flooring has as little as 5 percent recycled tire rubber.
- Rubber flooring may contain traces of heavy metals, chemicals, and other elements from its former life on the road. This is difficult to quantify because the content varies with supply.

Where Does It Go?

It may be possible to again recycle this rubberlike compound, but it will not break down in a landfill for innumerable years. Incineration of tires is highly controversial and may pose a serious human health hazard.

Spec List

- Because of its questionable content, recycled tire "rubber" is not a healthy choice for a home, even if it does prevent landfilling.

Fact Check
- Nearly 310 million new tires were produced in the United States in 2002 (Idaho Department of Environmental Quality, www.deq.state.id.us).
- More than 2 billion tires are stockpiled nationwide (www.rubberrecycle. com).

RESOURCES

Ohio Department of Natural Resources, Division of Recycling and Litter Prevention, "Recycling Tires": www.dnr.state.oh.us

CONCRETE FLOORING

See Concrete, page 111.

TERRAZZO

Traditionally, terrazzo refers to flooring that is made from small pieces of mineral (especially marble) in aggregate and cement or resin, often polished to a high sheen. Originally, the technique was designed to make use of waste marble and other rock chips from quarries, turning them into a product that mimicked expensive stone at a more affordable price. The Italians perfected the terrazzo technique and gave it the name we still use in English. In fact, they discovered that goat's milk intensified the beautiful color of the marble, making it the first all-natural terrazzo finish.

Modern terrazzo can be poured on-site, prefabricated into slabs, or manufactured into tiles that are laid in mortarlike ceramic or stone. It is made from chipped, ground, or sorted mineral or manufactured aggregate. The pieces are then bound together in a cement matrix, a modified cement matrix that contains acrylic additives, or a resinous matrix. Sometimes brass, metal, or manufactured forms are inlaid to produce beautiful patterns. The color and design possibilities are endless, and the final product can be specified to fall below the most rigid standards for VOC emissions.

Terrazzo is more common in commercial settings than residential, yet it offers many benefits for a healthy eco-home. It's superdurable and will easily last the life span of the house. For those with allergies or chemical sensitivities, it won't collect aggravating substances, and it's simple to sweep, vacuum, or damp-mop. If the terrazzo is made from postconsumer recycled glass, then the aggregate is nontoxic, zero-VOC, and stain-resistant. Another ecological plus is that the use of "waste" rock keeps valuable, mineral-based material from the wastestream.

Careful specifications will ensure that the aggregates in the terrazzo are environmentally sound. Recycled glass is an earth-friendly aggregate choice. Quarried rocks like marble or granite, especially if imported or rare, are less green because they are nonrenewable and have higher embodied energy from mining and transportation. Be wary of aggregates of other manufactured or recycled materials, as they may contain undesirable petrochemicals, vinyls, heavy metals, or other toxic or outgassing substances. Pigments that occur naturally in the aggregate stone, minerals, or recycled glass are better for home and earth than chemical colorants.

Cement and concrete are energy-intensive "binders" but are very long-lasting and made from relatively abundant natural resources. If admixture-free concrete is used, the hardened substance will be inert and not outgas. Cement terrazzo will need to be sealed, however, because it is porous and absorbs stains and dirt.

The resinous matrix for the aggregate is often made with epoxy, latex, polyester and acrylic, or a combination. This type of terrazzo will not need to be sealed, as the surface is basically impermeable. The complex composition of these resins, usually proprietary and not readily available to consumers or contractors, can be difficult to analyze for nontoxic properties or eco-friendliness and might contain chemicals that are harmful to the workers or emit VOCs after application. Careful investigation into ingredients and methods is warranted. Look for low-VOC, formaldehyde-free, water-based, or low-solvent binders.

Where Does It Come From?

- The agglomerate, also called matrix or conglomerate, may consist of stones, mineral chips, glass, metal, or any number of manufactured or natural materials.
- Minerals are often gleaned from postindustrial waste.
- Glass is usually postconsumer bottles and windshields.
- The binder may be cement, modified cement with acrylic additives, or a polyester/ epoxy system.

Installation

Poured terrazzo flooring systems require a heavy-duty, perfectly level, flat substrate, preferably made of concrete. Additional sand and cement underneath, in a metal grid system, are needed for cementitious terrazzos. Resin-based, thinset terrazzo systems do not require a sand-cement underbed.

Once the aggregate and resin are poured, on-site polishing is performed with power or (rarely) hand tools. Because the polishing process creates airborne particulates that are inhaled, it's critical that the resin matrix be nontoxic. Specify that all furnishings be removed from adjacent areas and that proper ventilation or vacuum systems be used to prevent contamination of other living areas.

Terrazzo tile may be laid like ceramic or stone; specify FSC-certified wood or agricultural fiber underlayment. (see Tile, page 188). Tile or cementitious terrazzo will need to be sealed. Specify a low-VOC, water-based type, preferably wipe-on (as opposed to spray).

Maintenance

The maintenance of terrazzo depends on the materials it's made from. Consult with the manufacturer for specifics. However, terrazzo flooring should never be cleaned with chemicals, harsh detergents, or abrasives. Advise the client to damp-mop with water and mild detergent, or simply vacuum or dust-mop. Cementitious terrazzo may need to be resealed, eventually.

Where Does It Go?

The natural terrazzo tile content will break down—ceramic, stone chips, and glass deteriorate into minerals. The binders, epoxies, acrylics, and other manufactured compounds may complicate the biodegrading of the terrazzo, slowing the process as a whole or by leaching contaminants.

Spec List

Specify:

- High recycled-glass content
- High (waste) mineral content, preferably not rare or imported types
- Cement matrix without admixtures
- Low-VOC, water-based, no odor resin or modified cement binder
- Low-VOC, water-based, wipe on sealer

Avoid:

- Manufactured aggregate content that may contain contaminants or harmful chemicals
- Outgassing binders or sealants

RESOURCES

Marble Institute of America: www.marble-institute.com
National Terrazzo and Mosaic Association: www.ntma.com

CARPET

"Where does it come from and where does it go?" are the questions to answer when considering the environmental impact of carpet, as most conventional carpet is not made from natural materials and won't easily decompose or biodegrade at the end of its relatively short useful life. Historically, natural animal and plant fibers were knotted or woven for floor coverings; large carpets were reserved for the wealthy. But along with cheap petroleum and post-World War II scientific "advancements" came the advent of 100 percent manufactured fibers. The price of carpet plunged, making it affordable and immensely popular.

The carpet industry was confronted when people began to complain of multiple chemical sensitivities (MCS) or sick building syndrome (SBS), then pointed at the floor. The suspects? The array of chemical carpet treatments (individually or in combination), even the primary materials, may have been outgassing. Tests on mice showed them getting sick and dying from exposure to the same.

Now, the Carpet and Rug Institute has implemented a voluntary-compliance Green Label program that tests and verifies the absence of many potentially harmful substances in certain brands of carpet, padding, and adhesives, especially as they affect indoor air quality. Green Label Plus meets the strict guidelines for the low-VOC emissions that were established for California schools and health care facilities. Although other chemical substances may be substituted for the ones that emitted higher levels of VOCs, the improvement is a step in the right direction for the conventional carpet industry.

Most carpet is still made with nonrenewable petroleum by-products, and most types can't be recycled. Natural fibers are a much more eco-friendly choice. Unfortunately for those with environmental preferences, all-natural carpet is an anomaly in the mainstream marketplace. Even those touted as 100 percent wool, the natural fiber of choice, are often chemically treated. Underneath, natural backings and paddings are even less common. Grasses and plant fibers such as jute, hemp, coir, sisal, and seagrass are more likely to be found in area rugs rather than wall-to-wall carpet.

This home has natural wool carpet with natural jute backing and a nontoxic polyurethane pad. Photo by David O. Marlow. Designer: Associates III. www.associates3.com

Fact Check

- Formaldehyde is no longer used in carpet manufacturing. The formaldehyde that outgasses from old carpet may come from other sources—for example, when home and garden chemicals come in on the soles of shoes.
- The latex used in most carpet backing and padding is synthetic and will have no effect on someone with a true latex allergy.

In greening a home where the client prefers carpet, go with all-natural types (no chemicals or synthetics) made from wool. Specify domestically made, if possible, to avoid transportation and the pesticides that are mandated with imports. Wool is already stain-repellent, fire-resistant, and extremely durable without any treatments. Jute, coir, and plant materials are generally not as long-lasting as wool and stain more easily, but they are completely biodegradable.

Next to all-natural carpets with no additives, all-wool carpet with minimal chemical treatments is a second-best choice. Avoid synthetic dyes. Because conventional carpet dyes are chemicals, the color choices for an eco-friendly home will be limited to nature's palette of subtle hues. Look for the Green Label Plus certification, then avoid additional stain repellents or mothproofings.

Another choice with commendable qualities would be natural fibers in carpet-tile form. The major drawback is that manufacturers of carpet tiles don't always use 100 percent natural materials, but they do predominantly feature wool, coir, hemp, and even corn in some of the blends.

Carpet Recycling

Carpet comprises up to 1 percent of landfills in the United States. That's almost 5 billion pounds total; and a huge proportion of it is nonbiodegradable nylon (Carpet and Rug Institute, www.carpet-rug.com). In an effort to keep the pileup down, several major carpet manufacturers have committed to diverting more than 27 percent of all waste carpet away from the landfills and into remanufacturing through the Carpet America Recovery Effort (CARE; www.carpetrecovery.org).

Other carpet manufacturers have committed to closing the loop in a different way. They've designed carpet squares so that they need little adhesive, and so that one tile—not the whole carpet—can be pulled up and replaced if damaged. A handful of companies even offer to take back the carpets for recycling at any point in the future—a truly valiant step toward environmental responsibility.

To locate a carpet recycler, contact the manufacturer or check out Earth 911 at www.earth911.org.

Who would ever imagine that the film on a glass windshield might someday be downcycled into carpet? It's happening, at least for commercial applications. Spurred on by the need for PVC-free carpet and by the burgeoning supply of recyclables, carpet is being made from PVB (nonchlorinated vinyls). No microbial agents are needed, the carpet won't mildew, and the PVB doesn't outgas or cause health problems. Carpets are also being made from downcycled PET plastic bottles or carpet manufacturing scraps. While all of these certainly merit as landfill-reduction strategies, they only stall the inevitable.

Don't forget to consider the carpet backing. Jute and natural latex are found on the underside of natural carpet fibers, while cotton and hemp are also used. Conventional synthetic carpets will typically have synthetic backings.

Where Does It Come From?

- All-natural carpet is made from natural fibers such as wool, silk, jute, coir, sisal, and seagrass.
- Synthetic carpet or synthetic-natural blends contain artificial fibers such as nylon, olefin, and acrylic.
- Carpet backing is often made from synthetic latex (called styrene-butadiene, SB latex or SBR); natural-fiber backings such as jute are less common.
- Padding may be made from PVC or vinyls, recycled carpet fibers, wool, jute, and camel hair or mohair.
- Carpet, padding, and backing may contain possibly toxic substances such as benzene, styrene, toluene, vinyl acetate, PVC, fungicides, mothproofing, stain-proofing, mildew inhibitors, antistatics.

The Truth about Carpets and Allergies

You'll probably want to specify another floor covering if anyone in the clients household suffers from allergies or MCS. Carpet's cushy surface serves as a superabsorbent sink for all kinds of airborne and footborne irritants: dirt, allergens, pet hair, dust mites and insects, water, even toxins on shoes carried in from the workplace or street. There is a small body of research that indicates carpet collects some irritants, thereby removing them from indoor air so that air quality is improved; but no one has addressed the fact that the offensive substances still end up between the client's toes. Even the most fastidious housekeeping can't remove it all; recent studies showed that considerable dust was still being extracted from carpet after 40 minutes of vacuuming (*Environmental Building News*, May 2003; www.buildinggreen.com).

Installation

Before removing old carpet, request that it be vacuumed thoroughly to eliminate as much dust as possible so it doesn't escape into indoor air. Specify that new carpet be installed in good weather so it can be aired out in the sun for a day before bringing it into the house. Sunshine and good air circulation will speed up any remaining outgassing.

- *Underlayment.* Specify FSC-certified, low-VOC, formaldehyde-free plywood or gypsum substrate.
- *Padding.* To enhance a carpet's life span, don't scrimp on the padding. The padding makes up half of the total weight or volume of some carpet installations, thereby providing a buffer against the hard floor underneath and lengthening the carpet's life span. Specify natural padding made from wool, jute, horsehair, or

similar materials. Specify that it be formaldehyde- and BHA-free (Butylated hydroxyl anisole).

- *Adhesives.* Use little or no adhesive to support optimal indoor air quality; opt instead for wooden tack strip or "tackless" strips along the walls. If adhesive is needed, specify a low-VOC, solvent-free, or water-based variety.

Another alternative is to purchase removable tiles with adhesive backings or corners, or carpet that is held in place through a hook-and-loop (Velcro) tape; the client will be able to lift the sections for easier cleaning, repairs, or replacement.

Maintenance

Avoid topical stain treatments that might outgas or flake harmful contaminants, and talk to the client about doing the same.

Carpet demands excellent care to extend its lifetime. Dust and other heavier-than-air toxins follow the course of gravity and will settle into the carpet, degrading the quality of both carpet and indoor air. The secret to maintaining carpet, especially an all-natural one, is simple: keep it clean and dry. Encourage the client to vacuum thoroughly at least once a week with a HEPA-filtered model. Natural products such as club soda or a tiny amount of mildly soapy water can be employed for stain removal. Cornstarch can be used as a blotter, or baking soda sprinkled for odor removal. Natural wool, especially, is prone to mold, so avoid wet-extraction cleaning methods.

Where Does It Go?

Nylon can be recycled, but the availability of such has not developed yet to serve the average carpet consumer and so most carpet still ends up in landfills. Wool, jute, coir, sisal, seagrass, corn, cotton, and silk carpet will all biodegrade. Some manufacturers have committed to accepting their carpet—one square to a whole houseful—back for recycling into new product. Urge the homeowner to keep the warranty and product information for future recycling and disposal options.

Spec List

Specify:
- One hundred percent wool carpet, domestically produced, free of dyes, additives, and all chemical treatments
- One hundred percent plant-fiber carpets (jute, coir, sisal, seagrass), free of chemical additives and dyes
- Carpet content that is recyclable/returnable to the manufacturer, especially if made from natural fibers
- Carpet tiles for easy cleaning and replacement
- Jute backing
- FSC-certified wood underlayment *or* gypsum substrate

- Tackless strip, tack strip, or Velcro-type fastening system
- Low-VOC adhesive backing
- Small amounts of water-based yellow or white glue, or low-VOC adhesives, applied to perimeters only
- Formaldehyde-free
- BHA-free
- Pesticide-free
- Recycled-content carpet
- Recycling of replaced carpet

Avoid:

- Manufactured fibers such as nylon
- Stain repellents
- Synthetic dyes
- Benzene, styrene, toluene, vinyl acetate, and similar chemicals
- PVC-vinyl, especially in the backing or padding
- Fungicides, mothproofing, stainproofing, mildew inhibitors, antistatics, or other chemical treatments

RESOURCES

Carpet and Rug Institute: www.carpet-rug.org

Wall Treatments

WALLCOVERINGS

If it's flat and can be hung vertically, it can be made into a wallcovering. Traditional paper is just one green option; there's also sisal, bamboo, linen (made from flax), hemp, jute, wood, fabric, cork, and more. That's a great environmentally friendly option for covering old paint or blemished walls or for simply adding texture and color to a living space.

The practice of finishing walls with rice paper may have begun in the Orient over 2000 years ago, but the concept of decorative wallpaper made its debut in Europe around the 1400s. Those with limited financial means used painted wallcoverings to mimic the luxurious tapestries, paneling, molding, and scrollwork that embellished the homes of the very rich. By the late 1700s, fashionable wallpaper was being printed onto rolls in mass quantity.

In the mid-twentieth century, PVC-vinyl became the wall "paper" of choice. Soft, pliable vinyl offered durability, scrubbability, and stripability, and it offered practical and affordable characteristics. It also had some frightening ones:

- PVC-producing factories poison the air, water, and soil—as well as the factory workers—with dioxins.
- Products made with vinyl outgas hazardous VOCs during manufacture, immediately after installation, during fires, and if incinerated improperly.

This space is host to columns with natural sisal wallcovering.
Photo by David O. Marlow.
Designer: Associates III, www.associates3.com

■ PVC and its softening agent, phthalate, have been implicated in causing a host of illnesses, ranging from respiratory irritation to cancer. *(Source: Environmental Building News*, www.buildinggreen.com)

There's another downside to vinyl that directly affects the indoor environment: it lacks breathability. Moisture trapped between it and the wall creates a breeding ground for mold. Open-weave wallcoverings are much more vapor-permeable, and plant- and animal-based materials are inherently more porous. Needless to say, there are few applications in eco-friendly home design where vinyl should be considered.

Nevertheless, vinyl still figures prominently in the "fabric" of most conventional wallcoverings and their backings and coatings. The growing public awareness of PVC toxicity and hazards is, however, quickly decreasing its popularity on walls—the market share has dropped more than 25 percent in recent years (*Environmental Design & Construction*, "Green by Selection," by Carole Beeldens, March 7, 2005; www.edcmag.

com). In an effort to camouflage PVC content, the word "acrylic" is often used instead of "vinyl"—it sounds more benign, but the substance is usually one and the same.

Some manufacturers have switched to other synthetics. It's a step in the right direction for human health, but still reliant upon petrochemicals and nonrenewable resources. Still others are offering new, greener options made from all-natural and recycled fibers.

Shrewd research into both the maker and the materials is warranted before introducing a client to any wallcovering option. Some companies offer natural fibers in a particular line of wallcovering, yet add vinyl to those products. Others feature a line of all-natural wallcoverings, but use synthetics and vinyl in all their other offerings. Specify coverings that are absolutely vinyl-free, not just made with a percentage of all-natural materials in the total composition.

Vinyl isn't the only issue, but it's the prevalent one with wallcoverings. Once that hurdle has been jumped, look at the potential life span of the product. Will the treatment last in the particular environment? Can it be wiped clean, or a single section replaced if soiled? Or if it's removed, will it biodegrade?

When an eco-friendly wallcovering has been found that suits the client's needs and tastes, consider any additives used on the paper or covering, along with the methods and products that will be used in installation. Water-based inks or dyes are best; heavy metals should be excluded in the manufacturer's specs. Look for vinyl-free, low-VOC, no-formaldehyde, solvent-free, and apply these same specs to strippers, lining papers, pastes, coatings, sizings, or backings. Avoid chemical additives such as stain repellents, biocides, fireproofings, and pesticides. (Borate is an acceptable mineral treatment that both repels insects and resists fire.)

Paper and Nonwovens

Wallpaper often carries an affordable price, and the selection of colors and patterns is infinite. The term "wallpaper" is used generically in English to describe many wallcoverings, including those made with no paper at all. The term is also often used to describe vinyl sheeting that contains no wood-fiber content.

That said, conventional wallpaper is often made from wood, but other all-natural, fiber-based paper coverings can be produced from rice, bark, cotton, linen (flax), straw, or parchment (animal skin). A truly green wallcovering might be derived from organically grown, pesticide-free, non-GMO crops, but such wallpaper has yet to be developed. Focus on specifying natural content with a minimum of processing or additives. Wallpaper with postconsumer and postindustrial stock may also fit the client's preferences and green objectives; look for a high percent of recycled content such as paper or sawdust. When specifying, be precise in the request for paper content.

Sometimes minerals figure into the content of wallcoverings, including clay, sand, and powdered stone, which add texture or color. Ceramic "beads" and glass "fibers," although manufactured, have mineral-like qualities. They add durability and scrubbability to the wallcovering, give off no VOCs, and cause no harm to the environment when disposed of, and so are considered eco-friendly.

Other manufactured substances such as polyester, rayon, and PVA may be blended into the natural mix. They might add slightly greater durability, but they subtract nonrenewable petroleum from the earth and are made through intensive manufacturing processes. Avoid synthetics in general. Lastly, specify water-based inks (or none at all) to avoid solvents and VOC emissions.

Value in Tradition

Zuber has been manufacturing wallpaper in France since 1797, using the traditional system that is quite eco-friendly. Every panel is painstakingly printed by hand using carved woodblocks and natural pigments, chalk, and sizing. The most elaborate wallcoverings require more than a thousand separate blocks and hundreds of colors. Zuber wallpaper in any home is priceless. Many older residences and historical sites throughout the United States that feature Zubers have hired restoration specialists to preserve their extraordinary beauty. The wallpaper has tremendous cultural value, as well; in 1995, the French government declared the blocks "Nationally Valuable Historic Monuments."

Wovens

Eco-friendly woven wallcoverings are made from a wide variety of fabrics (see Furnishings, page 328), grasses, and fibers, such as sisal, silk, raffia, linen, hemp, cotton, and others. Grasscloth is a traditional type of woven wallcovering that is defined as being made from ramie (a member of the nettle family), although imitations and those with vinyl backings are also common, so double-check the specifications for content. All natural-fiber wovens are intrinsically breathable, yet not all are suitable in high-humidity locations or near tubs and sinks. Water staining can be an issue.

Glass "yarns," which are made from common sand and treated with a modified starch, are the latest wallcovering innovation. The glass-based wallcoverings can be wiped clean; plus they meet stringent low-VOC requirements and are far more durable than traditional papers or fabrics. The surface can be painted over if it becomes badly soiled, eliminating the need for future removal. While the fabric is not all-natural, glass is inert like a mineral and will eventually revert back to silicon dioxide (sand) when it disintegrates at the end of its useful life cycle.

As with wallpaper, woven wallcovering backings are sometimes made from vinyl. Search for no PVC or vinyl, no added fire retardants, and no pesticide inhibtors (except borate), no waterproofing, or the use of other synthetics. Water-based dyes and inks are preferable, or none at all.

Cork

Cork wallcovering adds superb sound absorption to any room. It has natural microbial qualities, needs only occasional dusting or light spot cleaning, and is available unfinished or factory-finished with low-VOC waxes or polyurethane. In addition, cork has great thermal qualities, retaining heat or staying cool as needed. The only place that this wallcovering might not be ideal would be in a kitchen or other areas that get wet or soiled easily, as cork can't be scrubbed, and it absorbs oils and stains.

See also Cork Flooring, page 202.

Leather

It might not be the first thing that comes to mind to use as a wallcovering, but leather is extremely durable and can be applied in tiles or sheets. However, some people are opposed to the use of animal products, an obvious client consideration. And leather is usually processed with toxic chemicals in developing countries with few worker protections.

Leather wallcoverings require a period of acclimation before being installed, to avoid outgassing the tanning substances within the home. Research recycled leather, locally made, or processed with minimal dyes and chemicals, if possible. Reapplication of natural oils, waxes, or sealants may be necessary to protect the finish and maintain the desired patina.

Because the weight of the leather causes it to stretch over the years with the pull of gravity, a combination of fasteners and low-VOC adhesives are recommended when it's applied to walls.

See also Leather Flooring, page 201.

Wood, Bamboo, or Biocomposite Paneling

Wood paneling is a popular wallcovering, also showing up in wainscoting and beadboard. Bamboo and agricultural-waste biocomposites are catching on, as well, because they are more quickly renewable but have many of the same qualities as wood.

See also Biocomposite Flooring, page 206; Biocomposites, page 157; Bamboo Flooring, page 197; and Wood, page 139.

Installation

Depending on the particular material, wallcovering installation may require sizing, priming of the walls, adhesives/glues/pastes, stapling or tacking, and seam or edge treatments (such as extra adhesive or trim).

Specify natural glues and pastes whenever possible, or a low-VOC, low-odor, water-based type of synthetic adhesive if the former will not provide an adequate bond. In the same manner, specify low-odor, low-VOC, water-based primers. Avoid all products that contain formaldehyde or vinyl.

Maintenance

With proper care, fine wallcoverings made from quality materials may last for decades. Gentle dusting or occasional spot cleaning is all that is required. Consult with the manufacturer for specific recommendations.

Wood, leather, or cork will last longer than most fabrics or papers, and paneling may endure the full life span of a house. Although unsealed cork and leather may develop water spots, they may be spot-cleaned with mild detergent and water if they have been sealed. Some wallcoverings are easily removed if replacement or if a different wall finish is desired, depending on the type of material, the adhesive, and the substrate.

Where Does It Go?

If made with 100 percent natural fibers or material, wallpaper will decompose so easily that it could be shredded and used as garden mulch. Cork, leather, wood, and bamboo have potential for reuse or recycling, and will also break down quickly if disposed of.

Spec List

Specify:
- Wallcoverings made from all-natural fibers such as grasses and reeds
- Wallpaper made from all-natural paper (wood, rice, or other pulp)
- All-natural cork wallcoverings
- Leather wallcoverings that have been minimally processed with the use of natural tannins
- Wallpaper or wallcoverings made from high recycled-paper or fiber content
- Water-based inks or dyes
- Nontoxic, low-VOC wallpaper paste

Avoid:
- PVC-vinyl
- Heavy metals in the inks or dyes
- Formaldehyde
- Solvents in strippers
- Stain repellents
- Biocides
- Fireproofings
- Pesticides

Paint and Coatings

Wall color is one of the design changes most often requested by homeowners. Half of them will paint soon after moving in (2004 National Association of Realtors, "Profile of Buyer's Home Feature Preferences," www.realtor.org). As designers, we understand that paint color is more than just embellishment, there is psychological energy in a well-chosen hue.

Fundamentally, paint was designed to preserve and protect the surface and structure of a home. Architectural coatings, the most common type being paints, effectively seal out moisture and mildew, prevent abrasion and damage, repel dust, and provide a surface that may be occasionally washed or cleaned. Paint may last years with only minimal maintenance. These are sound ecological characteristics that also increase the longevity of a home.

This sunroom is finished with low-VOC wall paint and a water-based floor paint. The space also features citrus oil sealer, ample daylighting, and 100 percent cotton fabrics. Trudy Dujardin, Dujardin Design.

Evaluating paint for its environmental pluses and minuses is complex. The same chemical components that boost the durability of conventional paint may also outgas VOCs, irritate chemically sensitive individuals, pollute the air (both indoors and out), smell bad, or eventually chip or flake toxins. It's no small matter to consider when painting walls, where the large surface area covered with paint could have a significant effect on the health of clients and on the environment.

The push for cleaner air, both indoors and out, has motivated paint manufacturers to scrutinize the safety and health of their products, at least regarding one aspect: the

The Culture of Color

There's more to hue than meets the eye. Designers often overlook the powerful meanings and cultural interpretations possible when selecting the perfect color to pair with furnishings. Yellow may be sunny and upbeat to Westerners, but it signifies mourning in Egypt and Burma. Red is the color of weddings, prosperity, and good luck for most Asians. And in some parts of China, blue signifies little girls, while black is reserved for little boys. The paint colors the client prefers may have subtle or strong spiritual and personal significance.

VOC outgassing level (see VOCs, pages 241–2). The volatile organic compounds in paint present a special risk when indoors, since ventilation is more limited and soft surfaces such as furniture may provide a "sink" where they collect. (All furnishings should be removed for any interior paint job). VOCs also react with the atmosphere to form ozone. To deal with these problems, new architectural coatings that offer lower-than-ever VOCs, along with less odor, are constantly being introduced to the market. But eliminating VOCs is not the end-all answer to improving paint ingredients.

Standard architectural coatings may contain hundreds of other chemicals—preservatives, fungicides, drying agents, suspension agents, and more, so deciphering labels and MSDS warnings for the pros and cons can be challenging. Unless the paint has particular quantities of compounds that are deemed hazardous, the manufacturer is not required to put a warning on the label or MSDS for it. And the risks that exist when chemicals are mixed together are not always known. The result? A label will carry some warnings of known hazards, but the paint "recipe" is considered highly proprietary, and the rest of the contents remain a mystery to designers, contractors, and architects.

There are alternatives to conventional paint that are made from naturally occurring substances. Some have outstanding ecological characteristics and have been in use for decades or even centuries. But paints touted as being made from all-natural or organic ingredients are not necessarily benign in their effects on the environment and human health. Unlike organic produce, no labeling standards exist for coatings. Natural-ingredient paints may contain as many or more irritants and odors as conventional types, and may pose their own health or environmental risks. We recommend careful evaluation and trials of any paint, even those marketed as natural or organic, before selection and use.

If in a conundrum over paint, there are other possibilities. The materials used in wall construction or an existing finish will determine, as least to some degree, whether options besides conventional paint might be preferable from an environmental standpoint. If the walls have not yet been constructed, forgo paint altogether and specify no finish, a natural finish over plaster or wallboard, or a pigment added to the plaster. These choices have fewer VOCs and negative repercussions than conventional paint.

Faux Finishes

Faux finishes are decorative treatments, usually painted, that simulate "the real thing." Stone, metal, Venetian plaster, brick, and panoramic views can all be imitated with the use of other materials. Sometimes the intent with faux finishes is to replicate something more costly or rare such as marble tabletops or gilded trim. Other times the intent is purely whimsical, such as a landscape painted on the dining room walls.

There are possible benefits to using faux finishes in a green home, if they replace the use of a resource that would be less ecologically prudent. Instead of using a rare wood for trim, for example, a skilled artisan might be able to paint or stain a sustainably grown variety to look the part.

On the other hand, the faux finishing techniques might require the use of paints or other compounds that are not earth-friendly (see Artist Paints, page 243). It might make more sense to apply a nontoxic mineral-based plaster, for instance, than to mimic the look with layers of conventional paint.

Weigh the options before deciding on a faux finish for a green home.

Still, there will be many times when paint is the preferred finish, either because of economics (it's inexpensive), practicality (there is already a coat of paint on the wall), or client preference (the zero-VOC types may have the least irritating compounds). Quality paint does have some ecologically positive characteristics. Paint provides a cost-effective wall treatment that is easily "repaired" or covered with more paint if the décor, or the homeowner, should change. There's no demolition or deconstruction needed, just a few gallons and a brush. It will last for decades, if the surface was prepped well and the finished paint job is kept clean. In addition, the industry leaders now offer many options for more eco-friendly and people-friendly products.

When evaluating conventional paint options, steer toward those with the lowest amounts of harmful chemicals, especially VOCs that are a risk to homeowners, workers, and air quality. Specify low-VOC, water-based coatings without preservatives, biocides, or solvents whenever possible. Avoid certain chemicals (listed in this chapter) as particularly risky.

Careful surface preparation will ensure the longest life span for the product. Prudent sampling and precise estimating of the quantities needed will avoid waste, and leftover paint can be reused or recycled to avoid sending it to the landfill.

This information is a starting point for evaluating the seemingly infinite choices and combinations of paints and primers available. As designers, we can continually educate ourselves about the technological changes so that we can guide the client, the contractor, the architect, and the crew to better selection and proper disposal of architectural coatings.

Paint Composition Basics

All paints—the conventional type and alternative varieties—contain three basic elements:

- The liquid, called the vehicle, carrier, or solvent
- The pigment(s) and solids
- The binder, which keeps it all flowing together in liquid form

In addition to the basics, many paints contain additives to improve drying time, flow, mildew resistance, scrubbability, coverage, fade prevention, and more.

The *liquid carrier* is what gets the paint from can to wall, but then "disappears" through evaporation, leaving only the pigments and binder. In latex paints, water is the liquid. In oil-based paints, a variety of oils, alone or in combination, are used. Alcohol also appears as a carrier in specialty paints.

Pigments do the hiding or covering and the coloring. Titanium dioxide is the most common pigment used; it provides a bright white base with excellent coverage. Filler pigments such as clay, calcium carbonate or chalk, or other powdered minerals may be added to provide bulk at less cost. Other pigments may include simple mineral compounds (like iron oxide), organic compounds (plant-based), or synthetically derived substances. When combined with a liquid dispersion agent so they can be added to paint, they are called colorants or tints. Pigments and covering agents together are called solids.

Binders enable the pigment to "float" in the liquid and be applied to a surface. The content of the binder varies greatly among products, from simple casein in milk paint to highly complex mixes of chemicals. The pigment and the binder—what's left after the liquid evaporates and the paint dries—are together called the solids.

The typical range of *solids* in paint is 25 to 45 percent, with glossy luster having the lowest percent. "Dead flat" paints may have a pigment-to-volume ratio (see the sidebar, "Come to Terms," page 244) of as much as 80 percent, but 40 to 50 is more common (Rohm Paint Quality Institute, www.paintquality.com). Better-quality paint has a higher percentage of solids and will cover in fewer coats and last longer, making it the environmentally responsible choice. In most cases, the more expensive the line of paint (within a particular brand), the higher the solids content and the longer the warranty.

CASEIN OR MILK PAINT

Casein, the protein in milk, has been used since prehistoric times as a coating or binding agent. Cave drawings were done with a mixture of pigments, milk, clay, and lime. Similar paint is very common on early American furniture and walls. Today's milk paints are made of the same ancient materials, but usually come in a powder form that is mixed with water at the site. Milk paint (or casein paint, as it is sometimes called) is an ecological hero to many designers. Individuals who are sensitive to odors might find the wet-paint smell a problem; it dries quickly to an odorless, food-safe, completely nontoxic, biodegradable, durable, zero-VOC finish. Remove all furnishings before painting to lower the risk of VOCs settling into the upholstery and porous surfaces. Otherwise, the VOCs and odors will reemit later. There's virtually no waste because the precise amount needed can be mixed, and the leftover powder may be kept indefinitely in an airtight container for touch-ups or other projects. Casein paint dries to a hard, flat finish which is easy to maintain. And the slight variations in color from the natural mineral pigments are considered highly desirable. Although small amounts of nonrenewable minerals and energy-intensive lime figure into the composition, this drawback is certainly outweighed by the excellent preserving, beautifying finish that will potentially last for centuries.

A few companies offer premixed, liquid-form milk paint. However, like the milk we drink, casein-based conventional paint spoils rapidly, so the ecological positives are diminished by the preservatives that are required. There are also so-called milk or casein paints that are oil-based or formulated like latex paint that may include casein as an ingredient, but these are more comparable to conventional paints (see Conventional Paints, page 240).

Where Does It Come From?

- The liquid is water.
- The binder is the casein naturally found in milk.
- Pigments include naturally occurring metal oxides, salts, and clays.
- Lime is also added.

Installation

Remove all furnishings before painting to lower the risk of VOCs settling into the upholstery and porous surfaces. Otherwise, the VOCs and odors will reemit later.

Milk paint may be used on unfinished, uniformly porous surfaces such as gypsum plaster and wood. Previously painted surfaces and unfinished drywall with joints will need a surface prep coat as recommended by the milk paint manufacturer. The prep coat or primer will diminish the ecological characteristics overall but might be a good option if a milk paint finish is desired.

Mix the paint fresh on-site as needed so there will be minimal waste and spoilage. Leftovers may be covered tightly and refrigerated, but the paint will spoil in a matter of days.

Milk paint may be brushed, rolled, or sprayed on. Regular stirring (several times an hour) is necessary to keep the solids suspended. Clients should expect delicate color variations, even within a single batch. Although rigorous color standards are kept by most milk paint companies, the mineral pigments themselves will have natural, subtle differences that are reflected on the painted surface. Multiple coats will diminish these variations, but not eliminate them.

Because it is porous, unfinished milk paint is susceptible to stains and water spots. If the milk paint is applied near a tub or sink, a traditional water-based acrylic topcoat (per the manufacturer's recommendations) will prevent damage but will lower the environmental benefits of using milk paint. Natural penetrating oils or waxes may also be used as finishes; however, they will darken the color.

Small amounts of wet milk paint can be safely disposed of by pouring in the yard or down the drain. There is no need for disposal of the powdered form; it may be saved indefinitely for touch-ups or used on other projects. If the paint might become soiled from water, dirt, or oils from the skin, then the manufacturers recommend that a sealant or topcoat be applied after the paint dries to protect the surface.

Maintenance

Milk paint is porous and thus prone to water spotting and stains. The colors and surface will remain vivid and durable over many years, but the flat surface can't be washed.

Simple touch-ups may be done with more milk paint. Milk paint will not chip or flake like traditional paint, and age only enhances the rustic, natural beauty of it.

Where Does It Go?

Natural milk paint—in dry powder, with water added, or as a finish—is completely biodegradable. The painted surface is considered food-safe and has no known harmful effects throughout, even in the process of deconstruction, deterioration, or disposal.

Spec List

Specify:
- Dry milk paint powder made from casein, lime, clay, and natural pigments.
- Mix fresh paint daily on-site; small quantities of leftovers may be saved in a refrigerator overnight and used the next day.
- All leftover powdered base be saved for touch-ups or future projects.
- If milk paint becomes soiled, finish with a natural penetrating oil, beeswax, or water-based, low-VOC topcoat as recommended by the manufacturer.

Avoid:
- Latex, oil-based, or premixed paints labeled as containing casein.

SILICATE DISPERSION PAINT

Silicate dispersion paint is made from liquefied potassium silicate, which naturally reacts and binds with calcium salts, silica, ceramics, and some metals, forming a permanent coating on a variety of surfaces. (Liquefied potassium silicate is sometimes called waterglass, but the term also refers to sodium silicate.) Many materials will accept silicate paints and form an insoluble, crystalline, rocklike finish, including portland cement, limestone, marble, mortars, concrete, brick, terra-cotta, and iron, among others. Although it is most commonly used on exteriors because of its high durability, it's suitable for use on interiors, as well. Paint made with this substance has been around for more than a century, and has readily caught on in Europe where lime-plaster and rock walls are more prevalent than in North America.

Silicate dispersion paint is not suitable for wood or plastic, but with the correct primer (as recommended by the paint manufacturer), it may be used over paper-faced drywall. It is both permeable and durable, allowing air and moisture to "breathe" through the surface, and water will not damage it. The paint is completely noncombustible, odorless, VOC-free, and nontoxic, and the mineral-based colors are virtually fadeproof. It's perfect in a green home, especially for clients with chemical sensitivities.

The major drawback to silicate paints is the energy-intensive manufacturing. Potassium carbonate (also historically called potash), the chief ingredient in potassium silicate, is commercially prepared by a process of electrolysis and carbonation sequentially applied to mineral compounds. The potassium carbonate is then fused with silica, using high temperatures. The resulting potassium silicate compound is water-soluble and is blended with mineral pigments to form the paint.

Where Does It Come From?

- Mineral pigments are the primary coloring agents.
- Potassium silicate is derived from a complicated process involving electrolysis, carbonation, and high temperatures applied to mineral compounds.
- Water is the liquid carrier.

Installation

Silicate dispersion paint can be applied in basically the same manner as conventional paint, with brushes or rollers. The surface should be clean and free from oils or substances that might interfere with the natural bonding process. Because the paint is VOC-free, it poses no known risks to workers or inhabitants. One word of caution: Glass surfaces such as windows need to be protected to prevent permanent "etching" through a chemical interaction with the paint.

Maintenance

The dried and hardened silicate surface is less statically charged than traditional paint, so it repels dirt better. It is also water-resistant. Little upkeep is needed, and the surface may last for generations. Touch-ups and additional coats of silicate dispersion paint can be done on top of the preexisting silicate paint with no preparation except simple cleaning.

Where Does It Go?

Silicate dispersion paints bond chemically with the substrates. If the surface underneath the paint is limestone (calcium carbonate), for example, together they form a benign mineral compound that is also a carbonate. Any metal in the substrate and the minerals used as pigments will also safely decompose at the end of their life cycles. There are no known risks to the environment.

Spec List

Specify:
- Silicate dispersion paint
- Low-VOC primer, if needed
- Removal of all furnishings before painting the area, to avoid contaminating them with VOC's and odors

Avoid:
- Primers or paint additives that outgas

"NATURAL" OR "ORGANIC" PAINTS

There are many companies that promote their products on the premise that they are "natural," although there are no firm labeling standards for paints that use ingredients found in nature. So-called natural or organic paints, which are usually oil-based, usually contain natural oils, mineral or plant pigments, and plant resins. Some companies are strict about adhering to an all-natural policy, whereas others use fossil-fuel solvents and chemicals as needed, although in smaller quantities than in conventional paint. A few companies ride the proverbial fence, combining natural oils with traditional paint technology to produce conventional latex or oil-based paints that have slightly more eco-friendly characteristics (see Conventional Paint, page 240).

If the manufacturer chooses to rely on truly natural ingredients, the contents might include dammar resin, turpentine, natural-rubber latex, carnauba wax, or tung oil (all derived from trees). Shellac (made from insect secretions), citrus extracts such as d-limonene, vegetable oils, and beeswax may also figure into the compositions. Heavy metal pigments are excluded from the formulations. Calcium carbonate (chalk) or talc is often preferred over titanium dioxide as the covering agents for natural paints.

Natural paints may seem like a natural choice for the environment and the client. Although simpler, more naturally derived substances are assumed to be benign, that's not always the case. Lead, for example, is a metal found in nature, but it can be lethal to humans. In the same respect, not all natural paint ingredients are nontoxic or have fewer VOCs and less smell. Oils such as d-limonene (known to cause skin rashes) and turpentine have significant odors that can be irritating to those with sensitivities. Like their manufactured counterparts, these organic compounds will outgas; but it hasn't been determined whether natural VOCs are less harmful than manufactured ones. Some naturally derived oils and resins are under scrutiny for other more serious health risks, as well. Still, common vegetable oils such as castor (also called ricinus), soybean, canola, and safflower have virtually no smell and are obviously less problematic, so they are the safest choices. If the natural paint contains compounds not easily recognized, spend the time to investigate them and understand the risks.

There is one more distinct advantage in specifying natural or organic paints. The manufacturers are more forthright in revealing ingredients, as these substances are their source of pride. Conventional paint companies keep the compositions secret, for the most part, unless they are required by law to reveal a particular risk.

A "sniff test" and a painted patch within the home are prudent moves on behalf of the client if choosing an oil-based natural paint. Keep in mind that various colors have distinct smells because of the reactions between ingredients and different blends used to keep the mineral pigments in suspension.

Improved Paint Sampling

Choosing interior paint color must take into consideration numerous factors: the paint luster, interior lighting, daylight (or lack of it), adjacent furnishings and flooring, the surface texture, and the size of the space. Sampling in the location to be painted is optimal for accurate selection, and is especially important if odor or chemical sensitivity needs to be tested. Until recently, paint colors were chosen using small paint chips as a starting point, then a few brushstrokes, from quart- or gallon-sized "sample" cans, were applied to the wall. Needless to say, the amount of paint wasted through trial and error was significant.

In their charge to make the process easier and more cost-effective for consumers, manufacturers have been developing more user-friendly sampling media. The resulting decrease in waste generated is good news for the environment, as well. Paint chips have graduated to paint sheets, large "painted" papers, some of which are poster-size and even stick to the wall. Smaller cans and pouches of paint colors are another recent innovation that makes it simple and less expensive to "try them on" with far less waste. It's a win-win situation for the designer, the client, and the earth.

One advantage over conventional paint is that the manufacturing of natural or organic paints is usually less intensive, with fewer chemicals and manufactured compounds and generally less processing. The risks listed on the MSDS may also be more straightforward, and less numerous. Natural or organic paints may have the upper hand over their conventional counterparts in another way: because the substances are derived directly from plants and minerals, they usually break down better at the end of their life cycles.

Where Does It Come From?

- Plant-based oils are the primary carrier for natural paints, including but not limited to: turpentine, tung oil, d-limonene, safflower oil, and castor oil.

- Resins and binders are usually plant-derived as well, and may include dammar, shellac, carnauba wax, and beeswax.
- Pigments are mineral-based and plant-based.
- Calcium carbonate is a common covering agent.
- Some companies use petrochemicals or synthetics in combination with the natural ingredients.

Installation

Remove all furnishings before painting to lower the risk of VOCs settling into the upholstery and porous surfaces. Otherwise, the VOCs and odors will reemit later.

Natural, oil-based paints may be used wherever conventional paint might be applied: on wood, drywall, metal, and plaster, among other surfaces. A test spot will determine suitability. Because the paints are made with mineral pigments and oils, a perfectly consistent color should not be expected; rather, the paint displays variations that add to the earthy quality of the finish. Cleanup will require a compatible solvent, which may negate some of the environmental positives; consult with the manufacturer for specifics. (see Conventional Paint, Installation, page 240.)

Maintenance

Natural paints need little maintenance or upkeep, similar to their conventional paint counterparts, although their scrubbability is limited. Future touch-ups may be tricky because some natural paints don't store well, and good color-matching technology may be limited.

Where Does It Go?

The oils, pigments, and resins found in many minimally processed natural paints will break down much faster and more safely than complex chemicals found in conventional paint. Leftovers should never be dumped down the drain or thrown out with regular trash, as the solvents and oils may be flammable and therefore should be treated as hazards.

Spec List

Specify:
- All-natural plant-based or mineral-based oils and pigments; food-grade, when possible
- Low-VOC additives
- Removal of all furnishings before painting the area, to avoid contaminating them with VOCs and odors
- Proper disposal of leftovers as hazardous waste at cleanup and completion

Avoid:
- D-limonene or odorous paints if client is sensitive to such

CONVENTIONAL PAINT

There are several factors to consider when judging a conventional paint: the VOCs, the chemical additives, and the choice of latex versus oil, among others. At first glance, it would seem the choice of liquid vehicle is obvious. Water is better than oil, right? Mostly so. Water certainly provides an earth-friendly base for paint that is natural, renewable, and that cleans up with more water. Although quantities of paint should never be dumped down the drain, the small amount left on a brush may be rinsed at the sink.

There's another reason for the preference for latex over oil. Latex paints—almost all of them water-based—generally outgas far less than solvent-based paints. The water carrier naturally evaporates without giving off VOCs. Solvent-borne paints, commonly called oil-based, are made with natural or manufactured solvents. They also dry when exposed to air, but in the process, give off VOCs (see VOCs, page 241–2). In addition, oil-based types require yet another outgassing solvent for cleanup. Latex has fast become the preference over oil-based, both for its simpler cleanup and its less-noxious odor.

The drawback to latex? To enable water-based paints to dry effectively, not spoil, and avoid mildew, the manufacturers add drying agents, preservatives, fungicides, suspension agents, and a host of other chemicals. So while oils outgas as a result of their solvents, latex paints introduce other chemical issues. Both types will emit the most VOCs immediately after application, then taper off. However, VOCs can settle in fabrics and carpet, and the effects may be longer term. If a client has a sensitivity to a particular chemical, then scrupulous label-checking, even for water-based and low-VOC paints, is warranted.

This space has low-VOC Safecoat paint, along with organic bedding and art from a local artisan. Photo courtesy of Cheryl Terrace, Vital Design, Ltd., vitaldesignltd.com.

VOC Labeling for Paint

Cleaner air indoors and out, along with the obvious ease of use, are the motivating forces behind the popularity of today's latex paints. This is reinforced by legislation. Some governing agencies, such as the State of California and the European Union, have put limits on the VOCs allowed in paint, and have strict labeling requirements.

The standards for labeling paint as "low-VOC" vary according to locale and type of paint. While "low-VOC" and "low-odor" are often used interchangeably, they are not equivalent. Low-VOC paints emit less, but there still may be components in the paint that give off objectionable odors. And don't assume that because a paint is labeled "low-odor" that it is low in VOCs; it may simply have less odor than a different type or line of paint.

"Zero-VOC" is another common claim by paint manufacturers, but it isn't as clear a definition as it first appears. The method used to measure VOCs (EPA Reference Test Method 24) only works to approximately 5 grams per liter (g/l); below that, the compounds can't be accurately assessed. So zero-VOC or no-VOC paint does perhaps outgas, albeit immeasurably. Keep in mind that these standards were meant to measure the VOCs' effect on ozone and low-level smog; toxic chemicals that outgas but do not contribute to ozone are not considered in the VOC total. There could still be odors or vapors from dangerous substances in low-VOC paints. Be certain to ventilate well, whatever the product used.

Other Considerations

Whatever the variety, oil-based or latex, there are other factors to consider. In general, the higher-gloss paints contain elements that raise the VOC level; conversely, so-called dead flat paints almost always have the lowest levels. If the colorant is solvent-based, deep colors will increase the VOC emissions slightly. Specify natural food-grade or mineral-based pigments.

The typical binder for conventional paint is an acrylic such as polyvinyl acetate (PVA). Acrylics are petroleum-based, energy-intensive, and generally nonrenewable. Their complex chemical makeup also breaks down very poorly upon disposal. The production of acrylics creates an abundance of waste and by-products, as well.

Titanium dioxide production is yet another downside to conventional paint. The compound has replaced lead, a known toxin and significant health threat, as the number-one choice for covering power and whitening pigment. Titanium is the fourth most common element on Earth, yet the manufacturing process for it is anything but environmentally favorable. Synthetic and natural rutile (a titanium compound) are

VOC Guidelines for Paints

	Flat g/l*	Nonflat g/l
Regulations		
United States (effective 9/13/99)		
Interior	250	380
Exterior	250	380
California South Coast Air Management District	250[1]	420[2]
Voluntary Standards		
Green Seal Standard		
Interior	50	150
Exterior	100	200
Canadian Environmental Choice Program	200	200
European Community Eco-label	30	200

*To convert grams per liter to pounds per gallon, multiply by 0.0083.
1. Allowable levels scheduled to decrease to 100 g/l in 2001, and to 50 g/l in 2008.
2. Value based on resin type; no nonflat category listed.
© 1992–2006 BuildingGreen, Inc., www.buildinggreen.com

combined with the titanium-rich slag from pig iron smelting. The complex manufacturing is best understood by a chemist, as it involves high temperatures, chemical washes, and reductions. The process contributes to pollution and is hazardous to workers. Other pigments like chalk and clay are usually considered secondary fillers because they don't cover as well nor last as long, but are occasionally used as primary pigments. Yet the mining of clay and chalk also has drawbacks and health risks for workers. The decision for or against titanium dioxide in paint, from an environmental standpoint, is a complicated one.

Heavy metals are hazardous additions to paint, too, usually showing up as pigments or in colorants. Lead was banned from use in architectural coatings in 1978, then mercury followed suit and was banned from interior paints in 1992. Artist paints and colorants (see the sidebar, "Artist Paints") may contain cadmium and chromium hexavalent (also called chromium VI). Specify that all paints be free of these, and use extreme caution when removing old paint that could be contaminated with lead or other substances.

Formaldehyde-based resin is still found in some paints, and should be avoided. Formaldehyde also appears as a biocide, along with copper, arsenic, phenol, and ammonium compounds. While such additives are intended to prevent mold, mildew, and wet-paint spoilage, they are associated with numerous health risks and can trigger reactions in those with chemical sensitivities. Specify paint that is mixed "fresh" and biocide-free.

Artist Paints

Artist paints, lacquers, and thinners are commonly used for faux finishes and murals. Generally speaking, artist paints are highly concentrated and may contain a wide variety of toxins such as petrochemicals, heavy metal pigments, or VOC-emitting solvents. These paints and associated chemicals have limited applications within a green home.

There may be occasions where a faux finish is a better choice than the rare or nonrenewable natural material that the client desires (see Faux Finishes, page 232). To minimize these negative effects, encourage the use of nontoxic paints or finishes such as plaster, mineral pigments, lime washes, or milk paints. Specify water-based products whenever possible. Avoid all sprays, as the airborne particulates are especially harmful to air quality. If the client is sensitive to odors, it may be possible for the artist to do a mural in the studio on a canvas, then transfer it to the home after it has had time to dry and air out.

Remanufactured Paint

Leftover paint that would otherwise end up in hazardous waste disposal sites is now being collected by manufacturers and remade into useable new product. It's a noble effort on behalf of the environment. The companies sort the used paint by type (oil or latex, interior or exterior), test it to determine its particular properties, then mix it with compatible products. Some locations add the recycled paint to new paint for even better quality remanufactured blends.

The final product is usually tested for VOCs and is suitable for many uses, even though the color choices are limited to gray, beige, or muted colors. Because the chemical content is still unclear, remanufactured paint is best used where human habitation is limited (storage areas, garages) or where it will not affect someone with chemical sensitivities (exteriors). As remanufacturing technology improves, low-VOC and specialty paints will become more available.

Fact Check

- An aggressive recycling program in the Canadian Maritime Provinces and Quebec collected close to 2.5 million kilograms (approximately 2,500 U.S. tons) of used or leftover paint in 2003 (www. peintureboomerang.ca).

Recycled Paint

Many communities have drop-offs that divert leftover paint from the landfills, then some are made available to the public through "swaps." The rest of the collected paint is usually sorted (interior or exterior, water or oil base) and then mixed with similar types. The resulting unpredictable shade of gray is often used for graffiti abatement, community restoration projects, even park shelter finishes.

A few locations make the remixed paint available to consumers at a nominal charge. Unlike remanufactured paint that undergoes testing, meets certain safety standards, and is usually labeled as to the VOCs and basic chemical content, VOC emissions and other details about these recycled paints are not known. While the community recycling program certainly prevents waste, the remixed paint is a poor selection for a healthful interior and is best left to lower-risk exterior projects.

The Yes List

With so many things on the no list, what's left for a project team to choose from if conventional paint is the client's preference? Fortunately, there are companies that strive to manufacture quality products and leave the hazards out of their formulas. Additionally, the independent nonprofit Green Seal certifies and puts its mark on products that vol-

Come to Terms

Here are clarifications of a few confusing paint terms.

- *Latex.* Although it once referred only to the material derived from the rubber tree, the term is now used to describe a wide variety of synthetic resins that remain elastic or pliable. "Latex" paint, however, is not made from rubber (National Paint and Coatings Association, www.paint.org).
- *Enamel.* In days gone by, enamel paint was the glossy, oil-based variety. Because it implied durability, enamel came to be used by manufacturers to describe almost every paint: water-based, oil-based, glossy, or even flat. "Enamel" now basically means "paint" (Rohm and Haas Paint Quality Institute, www.paintquality.com).
- *PVC.* This abbreviation usually refers to PVC-vinyl in common speech, but PVC-vinyl is almost never used in architectural coatings (although vinyl-acrylics are). The initials mean something quite different to someone in the paint industry. PVC is pigment-volume concentration, the relative volume of pigment as compared to binder. A high-PVC ratio will usually be lower in VOCs, at least in conventional paint (Rohm and Haas Paint Quality Institute, www.paintquality.com).

untarily comply to rigorous standards and testing. Items marked with Green Seal not only leave out high-risk ingredients, they satisfy criteria for high quality.

Evaluate the MSDS carefully for each brand or style of paint being considered. Then consult with the client to avoid known allergens or chemical sensitivities. Specify the paints and primers best suited to the project with the least amount of known hazards. Specify the highest quality of paint possible; less-frequent repaintings will be cost-effective and environmentally friendlier.

Educate the client well as to effective maintenance and cleaning of the painted surfaces. Help the client establish optimal storage solutions for leftover paint, along with earth-friendly disposal methods when leftovers kept for touch-ups are finally unuseable. Finally, clients need to know how to get a good paint match in the future so complete repainting can be avoided.

Where Does It Come From?

- Conventional paint, with few exceptions, is usually made from hundreds of petrochemicals and synthetic oils, resins, and binders. The exact composition is usually proprietary and not completely revealed on the label.
- Energy-intensive manufacturing is common.
- Water-based paint uses water as the carrier; oil-based paint uses manufactured solvents.
- Water-based paint, often called latex, is not made with natural rubber but rather manufactured, flexible synthetic latex compounds.
- Colorants contain a mixture of mineral pigments and solvents.
- Other chemical additives may include those that serve as drying, flow, and suspension agents, and preservatives and biocides.

Installation

The first step to keeping a home safe and green, before a paintbrush is lifted or can opened, is to remove all furniture, rugs, and décor from the area (drop cloths will protect from spills but not VOCs). Paint will emit VOCs, and they will permeate the surfaces of these items. Soft goods work as "sinks" that collect airborne molecules, then possibly chemically react with them or outgas for an indefinite period. Be certain the paint is completely dry and odorless before returning the furnishings to their places.

Primer is the key, and often the most overlooked, step to adequately prepping an area for paint, especially if the surface has never been painted (new drywall or wood, for example). Professionals agree that it greatly improves adhesion of the finish coat and thus the paint life span, which is wise ecologically because it avoids paint reapplication in the future. Color changes and deep hues require fewer coats of paint with a primer. Stains, odors, mold, uneven texture, cracking, and peeling may all be prevented using primer. Primers also improve water, stain, and mold resistance in the future.

A primer must be used over unsealed surfaces such as masonry or concrete, or if covering a nonporous surface. Lead-based paint and outgassing surfaces may successfully be covered with primer, as well. And if a change from oil-based paint to a new water-based latex paint is desired, a primer will help make the transition.

Getting the Lead Out Safely

Lead was banned from use in architectural coatings in 1978; before then, it was a popular drying agent and white pigment. Microscopic amounts of lead in the bloodstream, from simple sources such as paint chips and dust, can be toxic and cause illness or even death.

If the house was built before 1978, there is a chance that renovations such as sanding, scraping, deconstruction, or demolition will expose both the workers and the occupants to this serious hazard. Approximately 7.7 million repairs or renovations occur each year in older housing containing lead-based paint (EPA, www.epa.gov). Professional testing should be done before any such work is undertaken, and all necessary precautions and protection used if lead is found. Where large amounts of lead are present, professional abatement is recommended.

For more information on lead hazards go to EPA, www.epa.gov/lead, or call the National Lead Information Center (NLIC), 800-424-5323.

Unfortunately, typical primers often contain some of the most noxious chemicals and are the worst culprits for outgassing VOCs. It's imperative to seek out the least toxic, least outgassing primer possible for the specific surface or problem to be dealt with. Rely on reputable manufacturers that formulate products to have low VOCs, be formaldehyde-free, be water-based (when possible), and use minimal additives. If the priming step is not within the scope of the interior design specifications, then be certain to present these healthier primer options to architects and contractors beforehand.

Fact Check

- Americans each buy about two gallons of paint every year.
- The sheer volume of paint manufactured is staggering: roughly three-quarters of a billion gallons of architectural coatings are sold annually in the United States, and more than half is for interiors (National Paint and Coatings Association, www.paint.org).

Specify brush or roller applications. Sprays only aggravate air quality issues, both indoors and out. Specify that conventional paint be applied when dry time will be short (good weather) and when ventilation can be enhanced (windows or doors opened). The workers and homeowners will be exposed to fewer VOCs and less odor, and the offending substances can dissipate.

Maintenance

Water-based paint cleans up with water. Measurable leftovers should be poured back in the cans or containers, then kept for touch-ups and stored in a place that has a constant, cool temperature, away from living areas. Record the date and location on the lid.

If leftover paint will not be used, encourage donation to a graffiti-abatement program, a community restoration project, a local nonprofit, or a theater program. There may also be recycling or remanufacturing options in the area. If a paint container is virtually empty, the residue should be allowed to completely air-dry outdoors, away from pets and children. Steel paint cans are recyclable in most places, or there may be requirements to dispose of them as hazardous waste (local rules vary).

Where Does It Go?

Conventional paint is a complex substance designed to resist deterioration within the home. Those same chemical enhancements that make it last also keep it from naturally biodegrading, and it is usually treated as hazardous waste. The water and solvents will evaporate and the solvents will outgas VOCs that contribute to ground-level ozone. Most other ingredients will remain in landfills or on painted surfaces for indefinite periods—years, decades, perhaps even centuries—and the future chemical hazards are largely unknown.

Spec List

Specify:
- Green Seal-certified paint
- Conventional paint if other paint or finish options are not possible
- Water-based or natural plant-based oils in the base
- Zero- or no-VOC paint
- Low-VOC paint
- Formaldehyde-free
- Preservative-free (paint mixed fresh, if possible).
- Low-VOC, formaldehyde-free, water-based, minimal-additives primer, if needed to deal with surface problems, prep, deep colors, or color changes
- Conservative paint sampling
- Recycling of leftover paint, or proper storage for potential touch-ups

Avoid:
- Preservatives
- Biocides, fungicides, mildew preventatives
- Formaldehyde
- Lead and other heavy metal pigments or drying agents, especially: chromium hexavalent, cobalt, cadmium, mercury
- Recycled or remanufactured paint for projects indoors

RESOURCES

National Coatings and Paint Association: www.paint.org

The Natural Paint Book, by Lynn Edwards and Julia Lawless (New York, NY: Rodale Books), 2003

Rohm and Haas Paint Quality Institute: www.paintquality.com.

Overview: Stains, Finishes, and Adhesives

As designers with ecological sensibilities, our duty is to find the best possible products for the tasks at hand while causing the least amount of harm to the client, the construction team, and to the earth. It's impossible, within the scope of this book or any other, to discuss and adequately analyze every substance used to tint, glue, or coat materials used in residential interiors.

The world of chemicals available for design and construction is both astounding and frightening. It would be easy to blame the manufacturers for the undesirable aspects of these highly complex compounds. But as consumers, we continually demand "better" compounds that adhere under every condition, color every surface consistently, and finish every material with eternal durability—often to the eventual destruction of our health and our world.

Yet it's not all gloom and doom. Many companies are committed to providing quality products that balance consumer needs with those of the earth. And there are still simple, eco-friendly choices for many applications.

Whenever a stain, colorant, finish, adhesive, or stripping agent is to be used, research the contents of the proposed product thoroughly. Request the MSDS from the manufacturer, distributor, or retailer, or go to the company Web site and print it out. Look for simple compounds with few ingredients, as multiple chemicals might interact and cause hazards that haven't yet been evaluated. Also look for products that have the fewest known health risks or recommended precautions. If the product is listed as having ingredients that are carcinogens, reproductive toxins, or other serious health risks, seek out a more benign product. In general, risks to human health are also risks to environmental health, as well.

Request a sample if the client is sensitive to chemicals or odors. After selection, specify that every precaution for use is precisely followed by workers, including recommendations for disposal. Finally, provide the client with instructions for maintenance.

Without going into great detail about each chemical used and every possible outcome, the following overview and spec list will be a guide for specifying stains, finishes, or adhesives. For more information on the best products to use with a material such as wood, metal, or concrete, consult the chapter or section in this book that covers that particular material.

Stains, Colorants, and Tints

Most synthetic colorants are solvent-based, made from petroleum-based compounds that evaporate when drying. Even though the amount of colorant, stain, or dye used might be miniscule, the solvents and other chemicals may contribute to outgassing, VOCs, toxicity levels, and odor (see VOCS, pages 241–2). Although a product such as paint may be advertised as being zero-VOC, when a colorant or another additive is added, the level changes, perhaps for the worse. Deeper hues, if made with solvent-based colorants, may outgas more than lighter ones.

The greenest choice, by far, is to specify that the material be left in its natural state, no color added. The next best would be to specify natural mineral pigments, natural penetrating oils, or water-based vegetable dyes. Food-grade or mineral-based colorants are safe at any concentration level.

Avoid heavy metals such as chromium, lead, and uranium (the latter was once commonplace in yellowish colorants). Because other countries may lack restrictions against the use of known harmful substances in dyes, paints, and glazes, avoid painted objects such as souvenir tiles that have not been imported through regulated channels.

Finishes, Sealants, and Topcoats

As with colorants, the safest, greenest choice usually is to use no finishes, sealants, or topcoats at all. Many natural materials need no assistance to maintain their durability and beauty. Others, however, will deteriorate rapidly if not protected against moisture, dirt, stains, mold, or insects. It's ecologically prudent, for example, to seal grout rather than risk replacement of an entire section of tile. Sometimes the finish protects the client, as well. Mold, VOCs, and odors can be controlled through the application of effective, nonporous sealants.

Factory-finished products keep many offending odors and harmful VOCs out of the home because the material will have extra time to outgas before being installed. (Although the outgassing will still be harmful to the environment, this minimizes the harm to the home's occupants.) But specifying on-site finishing or sealing allows for greater control over the application method and the substances used, possibly improving the ecological balance and the health of the home.

All-natural waxes and oils provide porous, breathable protection for many surfaces. They'll usually need regular reapplication, however. Some finishes such as silicate dispersion paint chemically bond with the substrate (usually mineral-based products) and become completely inert and safe when dry. Borate, a mineral, can be added to a finish or treatment to provide resistance against pests and fire.

If a nonporous or "hard" finish is desired, specify the least toxic product that contains no formaldehyde, low amounts of solvents, low VOCs, and is water-based. Avoid chemical biocides. Zinc was once popular as a hardening agent in floor finishes, but its use has been found to be toxic to aquatic life, so it should also be avoided.

The method of application may be as important as the ingredients in the finish. Specify "no spray-on sealants" unless otherwise applied within a spray booth by the manufacturer. Alternatives can be wiped, brushed, rolled, or poured on. The use of sprays will directly affect air quality and may be particularly irritating to a chemically sensitive client.

Adhesives and Glues

In the world of adhesives, there are particular distinctions made by manufacturers that work as guidelines for specifying more eco-friendly products.

- *Paste* is usually made from a base of flour and water.
- *Glue* is usually made from animal products (casein, hide) and plant sources (natural rubber, cellulose, paste).
- *Adhesives* (synthetic) may be made from any number of synthetics: epoxy, cyanoacrylate, contact cement, hot melt, polyurethane, polyvinyl acetate (PVA), resin, resorcinol, silicone, or urea formaldehyde.

Although the terms are often used interchangeably, these definitions are a place to start when looking for earth-friendly products. In general, paste and glue will be the most benign substances, and can be used with many porous, natural materials such as unfinished wood, wallpaper, or cork. Adhesives, on the other hand, offer grip for non-porous surfaces or more difficult applications such as stone, tile, or finished bamboo. Always consult the MSDS to ascertain the content of pastes, glues, and adhesives.

Some interior design materials have peel-and-stick backings. The factory-applied, extremely thin coat of adhesive, especially if found only on the material's perimeter or in small spots, may need considerably less adhesive than would an on-site application. This may be helpful to a client with sensitivities to odors or chemicals. Choosing the adhesive, however, allows for greater control over the product content, and it may be possible to find one that has less odor than the preapplied backing does.

If glue or paste won't provide a bond that's durable enough, specify synthetic adhesives that have low-odor and low-VOC levels. Look for companies that specialize in manufacturing low-toxic, environmentally safe compounds, especially if the products meet more rigid air quality standards and specifications for schools or health care facilities. Tack strips, staples, decorative studs, nails, trim pieces, or screws may reduce the amount of adhesive needed, as well.

Spec List

Specify:
- No colorant, tints, or dyes added
- Light colors (as opposed to dark) if synthetic colorants are to be used
- No finish, if material integrity or durability will not be sacrificed
- Low- or zero-VOC
- Low-odor
- Factory-finished materials if client sensitivity to odors or on-site outgassing is an issue
- Nails, staples, tacks, trim pieces, and so on, to reduce the amount of adhesive needed
- Solvent-free, water-based, *or* natural-oil-based
- Natural plant-based, animal-based, or mineral-based dyes, oils, waxes, and finishes
- Animal- or plant-based pastes or glues (as opposed to chemical adhesives, when possible)

- Formaldehyde-free
- Natural borate preservatives or pest controls
- Brush-on, wipe-on, or pour-on substances

   Avoid:
- Heavy metals such as chromium, lead, cadmium, or mercury
- Metallic hardening or drying agents such as zinc
- Sprays
- Solvent-based formulas
- Biocides
- Compounds that require chemical solvents or thinners
- Factory finishes of unknown content

RESOURCES

"Choose Green Report: Wood and Stains," Green Seal, www.greenseal.org
"Lowes Guide to Glues and Adhesives," www.lowes.com

CHAPTER 12

specialties

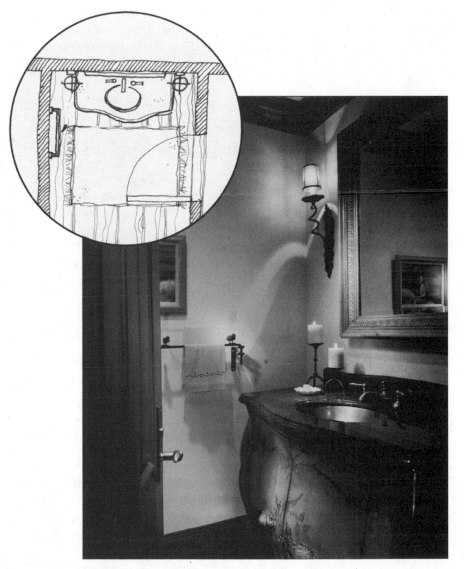

Drawing: Donna Barta-Winfield.
Design: Kari Foster,
www.associates3.com.
Photo: David O. Marlow.

Shower Enclosures

When it comes to shower enclosures, the greenest choice is to have none at all. Citizens in many parts of the world do not have enclosed shower stalls, but rather leave at least one side open. In some places, the shower is defined by nothing more than the bathroom or bathing area walls, a drain on the floor, and the shower head on the wall. For added privacy, the shower may be designed with a partial wall or be situated so that there is a visual barrier. By eliminating the enclosure, it will simplify the design and use fewer materials. The open-sided design is also particularly functional for those in wheelchairs or with limited mobility.

Tempered glass, which is specially heated and cooled ("annealed") to resist breakage and which is five times stronger than typical glass, is common for shower stall walls. The edges are either defined and protected by metal trim with metal towel bars attached, or frameless glass is available and is more environmentally friendly because it

This bathroom has a shower door of frosted, frameless glass.
The space also features a green slate countertop, recycled glass
tile in the shower, anigre wood cabinetry, a wood ceiling from a
reforested area, fluorescent lighting, and low-VOC paint.
Used by permission of My House Magazine.
Photos by Mikel Covey.
Designer: Gail Madison Goodhue.

can be easily disassembled for recycling. Powder-coated, recycled steel, or recycled aluminum are the best green choices for frames.

Where Does It Come From?

- Tempered glass is made from common sand (silicon dioxide).
- Metal frames are made from mined metals or alloys, and are often powder-coated.

Where Does It Go?

Tempered glass can't be recycled along with beverage glass or in the same manner, so it poses a special challenge for the recycling industry. However, new products that use a cold-cast process, such as recycled glass and concrete countertops, may incorporate recycled tempered glass from shower surrounds, windshields, and other sources.

Installation

The contractor must provide a level finish surface where the door is being installed. To seal against leaking, a slightly concaved bead of caulking is normally used. Specify a water resistant, non-toxic caulk to seal the installation against the finished surface; this will provide an excellent initial and permanent adhesion. Also request that masking tape be used to prevent the caulk from trickling into the grout joints.

Maintenance

Shower doors typically do not encourage the development of mold and mildew, which is more prone to occur with shower curtains. Daily use of a squeegee and adequate air circulation will deter mold and the shower will dry faster. Utilize a non-toxic glass cleaner and address potential buildup with a solution of half water and half distilled white vinegar, or a non-toxic spray that is made for this purpose.

Spec List

Specify:
- No shower enclosure *or* frameless glass
- Metal frames with powder coating or no finish at all (if metal won't rust)

Closets and Shelving

See Cabinetry, page 322.

Fireplaces and Stoves

Humans first relied on fire for existence: it provided security, warmth, light, and the ability to cook food. Today, a fireplace or stove can serve as a primary or supplemental source of heat for the home, or even as the primary one, especially where utilities are costly; some types have a cooking surface or oven. But more often than not, the modern hearth is valued for its aesthetics and for "psychological warming."

Fireplaces and stoves are usually built from a combination of some of the following materials: all-natural stone, cast iron, enameled steel, brick, clay, cement or concrete, tempered glass, or ceramic. Intrinsic to stove and fireplace design is that the materials must be noncombustible, not outgas, and be extremely durable. Some fireplaces and stoves are made from cast iron or steel that may incorporate recycled metal. Soapstone is another desirable material, preferred for many stoves because of its high thermal efficiency and radiant qualities.

Older stoves or cheaply manufactured ones will burn fuel inefficiently, causing air pollution and wasting valuable natural resources. In addition, the poor combustion creates carbon monoxide, nitrous oxides, and particulate matter, among other health hazards. Many municipalities have strict ordinances that forbid wood burning on those days when air quality is predicted to exceed federally regulated standards, unless the home has no other source for heat or cooking.

The fuel choice for the stove might be dictated by local availability, air quality restrictions, or the client's desire for innovation and super energy efficiency. Will the fire be a primary heat source in an off-the-grid home, or just be used as a secondary heat source on cold winter days? Or will it be used only occasionally, for ambience? The client may desire an oven or a cooktop as a feature. There are even stove designs that may include hot water heating units.

EPA Certification

In 1988, regulations governing wood stoves went into effect. All those sold in the United States must have certified emissions below 7.5 grams of smoke per hour, and many newer stoves and inserts have even lower emission rates. Catalytic stoves must have emissions less than 4.1 grams per hour. The regulation does not govern fireplaces.

FIREPLACES

Used as the primary source for indoor heat and for cooking until the twentieth century, fireplaces were found in almost every home. Today, many are built for ambience alone. In terms of green design, they are rarely effective—a typical fireplace actually draws heat *out,* up to 24,000 cubic feet of warm air to the outdoors—increasing energy consumption and heating bills in the winter (Energy Efficiency and Renewable Energy, "Energy Savers," www.eere.energy.gov/consumer/tips/pdfs/energy_savers.pdf). Therefore, installing a conventional wood-burning fireplace is never the best environmental choice; however, a stove, masonry heater, or fireplace insert greatly improves energy efficiency and still provides a warm, inviting focal point. If the client has an existing fireplace, consider retrofitting it with an insert. It will warm the immediate "zone" efficiently in the winter, lower utility bills, and, ultimately, save energy.

To improve energy efficiency in an existing home, upgrade to an insert. Have tempered glass doors along with a heat-exchange system or blower. Specify caulking around the hearth—use a noncombustible, low-VOC caulk designed for this purpose. Check the damper for a tight fit and replace it or the seal, if needed.

FIREPLACE INSERTS

Fireplace inserts are usually made of cast iron or stone for added radiant heat and thermal properties. Inserts are designed to be retrofitted to existing fireplace openings, with a damper that will control airflow and a special box design that will maximize thermal properties. An insert will drastically improve the energy efficiency of the existing fireplace. A chimney liner or slight modifications to the firebox may be necessary to accommodate an insert.

MASONRY STOVES OR HEATERS

A masonry heater or stove is made of stone, brick, and ceramic with some cast iron, is often assembled on-site and is usually freestanding. It works by burning a very hot fire for a short time with doors closed. The design of the heat exchange channel and chimney causes most gases to be completely consumed before exhausting through the

BTU Defined

A BTU is a British thermal unit, which is approximately as much heat as is given off by the burning of a match. Technically, it's the amount of heat needed to raise the temperature of one pound of water one degree Fahrenheit. The more BTUs, the warmer the output.

They may be small, but they add up: a single U.S. house consumes about 100 million BTUs a year, and about half of that is for heating (Home Energy Saver, http://hes.lbl.gov/hes).

chimney. The high temperatures absorb into the masonry, which in turn releases radiant heat into the home for many hours. The whole process is superefficient, using very little fuel. Masonry heaters produce almost no ashes, smoke, or creosote. And because the burning is enclosed, these heaters won't dry out the air, or the skin and sinuses, as fireplaces and conventional stoves do.

Masonry heaters are designed to fit, so their customized designs have higher price tags. But if the unit is well situated in a moderately sized home with an open floorplan, the entire space may be heated with one stove. Small baking ovens, cooktops, water heaters, and warmed benches may be added as customizations.

FUEL

Each stove is designed for one type of fuel only. Fuel type, cost, availability, and ease of use may be especially important considerations if the client intends to reduce reliance on public utilities. If the main purpose of the stove is to serve as backup heat, avoid those that are dependent upon electric controls or blowers, as they pose an unhappy dilemma should there be a power outage in winter.

If the client wants the occasional ambience of a fire and has a standard fireplace that is rarely used, or lives in a municipality with wood-burning restrictions, natural gas may be an option. Natural gas and propane are accessible and reliable sources: just flip a switch and the ceramic "logs" ignite. But they are not the best fuel choices, ecologically speaking, for most situations, as they are nonrenewable resources.

Biomass fuel is a superb option if it's locally available. The pellets are made from corn and other agricultural by-products, or sawdust and waste wood from sources such as furniture making and construction, all held together with a natural, safe-to-burn resin. Because biomass is new to the green marketplace, it's not readily available everywhere. Some environmentally conscientious consumers have formed local biomass co-ops and built storage silos, enabling them to buy in bulk and guarantee a steady supply.

The major drawback with pellet stoves, however, is that almost all are dependent upon electricity and won't be usable during a power outage (a rare few have battery backups). Still, the stoves are incredibly energy-efficient—so much so that the EPA does not regulate them. And the fuel is made from annually renewable or recycled sources.

Another agricultural by-product may be used in a specially designed fireplace: denatured alcohol, also called methylated alcohol. Crops such as corn, beets, and bananas may be used to manufacture the fuel, which is a denatured version of 100 percent ethanol alcohol. The fireplace requires no hookup to gas or electric lines, no chimney or flue, and doesn't even require a permanent fixture. The consumer simply purchases the fuel, decants it into the special burner, and ignites it. The fire produces a warmth and aesthetic similar to natural gas. There are no residue or ashes since it burns clean, and no special ventilation is required since the only by-products are heat, steam, and carbon dioxide. Because the alcohol-burning fire is a patented technology not widely available, the fireplace and equipment designed for it must be purchased and shipped from the supplier, thereby raising the embodied energy.

Variations on the alcohol stoves have also been emerging that rely on small canisters of fuel, much like fondue pots or food warmers. Sugarcane or corn is commonly used to make the alcohol-based gel fuels. While these stoves are usually much smaller than conventional fireplaces, they may be an eco-friendly alternative for a client who desires the ambience, heat, and flickering light.

Where Does It Come From?

- Fireplaces, stoves, and inserts are made from a variety of noncombustible materials such as all-natural stone, cast iron, enameled steel, brick, clay, cement or concrete, tempered glass, or ceramic.

This Tulikivi masonry soapstone oven provides heat for the entire home. The space also features solid wood furniture and natural clay plaster.
Photo by Laurie E. Dickson.
Architect: Baker Laporte & Associates.

- The fuel may be wood, pellets made from agricultural and wood by-products, natural gas, propane, denatured alcohol, or alcohol-based gels.

Installation

The installation and specification of an EPA-approved, energy-efficient stove, masonry heater, or insert is best done by a certified technician. The technician will ensure proper clearance between the venting system and fuel, protection of the floor and surrounding spaces, and assembly of the appliance. The technician will also be aware of codes that exist regarding placement of the stove or insert, restrictions for burning, and air-quality regulations.

Maintenance

If the client has a preexisting fireplace, make certain they know to keep the damper closed when it's not in use. Leaving a damper open in the winter is like forgetting to shut a window.

The most important component of fireplace and stove maintenance is chimney inspection and sweeping, usually recommended on an annual basis. Proper wood selection also enables the stove to burn efficiently with the least amount of creosote buildup. Scrap wood should not be used if the origin is unknown; it may have been treated with or exposed to chemicals. Advise the client to avoid painted or treated wood of all kinds.

Although uncommon, some newer stoves have catalytic converters to keep the emissions cleaner, much like cars. These stoves require a more rigorous cleaning schedule and will need replacement of the converter every few years.

Clean Sweep

Creosote is an oily, tarlike substance that's left over in the chimney after burning wood, and the buildup can ignite. Some wood species produce much more creosote than others, so careful fuel selection is important. Efficient burning reduces creosote, too. Annual inspection and cleaning by a certified sweep will further eliminate the risk of a chimney fire.

Where Does It Go?

The materials in stove construction are made to last for generations. Almost all components—steel, iron, stone, brick, clay, ceramic, and glass—can be recycled, reused, or will eventually decompose.

Natural gas burning produces methane, but no particulate matter. Wood and bio-mass fuels produce carbon monoxide, nitrogen oxides, particulates (ashes and smoke), and other substances. Efficient burning improves air quality through more complete combustion of gases and particulates.

Spec List

Specify:
- EPA-certified wood-burning stove or insert
- A masonry heater *or* a fireplace insert *or* a freestanding stove
- Wood or biomass fuel

Avoid:
- Conventional fireplace installations without efficient inserts
- Poor-quality wood that burns inefficiently *or* contributes to creosote buildup
- Wood that has been treated or painted in any way, or scrap wood of unknown origin

RESOURCES

Chimney Safety Institute of America: www.csia.org
Hearth Education Foundation: www.heartheducation.org
Hearth, Patio & Barbecue Association: www.hpba.org
Masonry Heater Association of North America: www.mha-net.org
National Fireplace Institute: www.nfcertified.org

CHAPTER 13

equipment: appliances and office equipment

Drawing: Donna Barta-Winfield.
Design: Donna Barta-Winfield,
Annette Stelmack,
www.associates3.com.
Photo: David O. Marlow.

Appliances

When specifying appliances, energy efficiency and water usage are increasingly the most important criteria for determining their environmental impact. The natural resources conserved through a wise appliance selection will translate into real savings through decreased monthly utility bills for the client, as well. Green-built homes that rely on alternative energy sources usually require lower electrical loads and therefore need energy-conserving appliances.

Washers, dryers, refrigerators, and freezers (called "white goods" in some regions) are responsible for about 20 to 30 percent of the average home's energy bills. They are the principal consumers after the heating and cooling systems and the water heater. Even when they are not in use, the standby energy consumed by the accessory clocks, timers, and power-indicator lights on appliances may account for up to 20 percent of the total.

Newer models use far fewer natural resources than those of just 10 years ago. There may be local or national incentives to purchase more efficient equipment, as well. Some states or municipalities now require front-loading washers, which use far less water than top-loading washers. Public utilities are struggling to keep up with the ever-burgeoning demand for more power and water, and so tax breaks and rebates are not uncommon for homeowners who replace old refrigerators or other appliances.

Two common labeling programs make it easier to distinguish the more eco-friendly appliances from the rest. Since 1980, all washers, dryers, refrigerators, dishwashers, and freezers in the United States (along with heating and cooling equipment) have been required to bear a yellow-and-black EnergyGuide label that enables consumers to compare energy efficiency between brands and models. The label indicates the estimated operating cost and energy use of that model in comparison to those with the highest and lowest figures. There's no special designation, however, for those appliances ranked best, nor does EnergyGuide judge appliances for water usage or other nonenergy-use factors.

The ENERGY STAR label takes off where EnergyGuide leaves off. ENERGY STAR is a partnership between industry and the U.S. government (through the EPA) that labels and promotes energy-efficient products. The program began in 1992, and now the blue-star logo appears on those appliances that excel in energy efficiency. The first products to be labeled with ENERGY STAR were computers. Now ENERGY STAR qualifies heating and cooling equipment, major home appliances, lighting, home electronics, and office equipment; its stamp of approval is even found on new homes built with the most energy-efficient appliances and equipment. Utilize both labeling systems for research and comparisons between models, as they differ dramatically between brands and models.

In spite of the measurable advantages to purchasing new, resource-efficient appliances to replace older models, there's still an environmental trade-off. Appliances consume great amounts of raw materials in the manufacturing, transportation, and even packaging, which add up to a large amount of embodied energy. Not all parts of all appliances can be recycled, or are. Carefully evaluate whether immediate appliance replacement makes economic and environmental sense, or if waiting might be more prudent.

This kitchen features ENERGY STAR appliances and FSC-certified cherry flooring.
Photo by Emily Hagopian, www.essentialimages.us.
Architect: Michael Heacock.

REFRIGERATORS AND FREEZERS

The refrigerator was designed as a solution that would keep food from spoiling, and it was a substantial improvement on cellars stacked with snow, and iceboxes that required regular ice deliveries. Although invented in the 1920s, the refrigerator didn't gain popularity until after World War II. Now it's arguably the most important appliance we have, finding a place in every American household and a large percentage of homes worldwide.

There are many specialty features available on refrigerators: icemakers, filtered drinking water, television screens, and electronic message boards. Refrigerators are already the greatest electricity consumers in most households, and these features increase the usage. The sheer size of a refrigerator necessitates the consumption of large amounts of steel, plastic, glass, and metal in the manufacturing. Refrigerators give off the most CO_2 of any appliance and are the toughest to recycle because of the coolants that must be extracted by law.

There are ways to improve a refrigerator's environmental performance. New models may need less than a third of the electricity of those built 30 years ago. To receive the ENERGY STAR label, full-size refrigerators must exceed the federal standard set for energy efficiency by at least 15 percent; freezers, by 10 percent, and compact models, by 20 percent. In general, freezer-on-top models offer the most space with the least energy consumption, and side-by-sides use about 10 percent more electricity (Rocky Mountain Institute, www.rmi.org). Ever-popular icemakers raise energy use by about 10 to 20 percent and reduce the usable cubic footage.

Evaluate how many cubic feet are really needed for daily use. Many people want a second or "extra" refrigerator, or additional freezer. One possible solution is to use a larger refrigerator, which is more efficient than two smaller ones. If a second freezer is needed, a chest freezer is slightly more efficient than an upright one. But will the second appliance be used only occasionally for parties? Efficiency measures only matter if the extra appliances are really needed and are used wisely.

Disposal of the old refrigerator or freezer, because of the hazardous coolant within, is an important environmental issue. Refrigerators originally used even more toxic coolant gases—such as ammonia, methyl chloride, and sulfur dioxide—than they use now. Then, in 1929, Freon, the trade name for halogenated chlorofluorocarbon (HCFC) or chlorofluorocarbon (CFC) gas, was first put to use. Later it was discovered that Freon destroyed the ozone layer. Laws effective since 1992 require all ozone-depleting refrigerants to be recovered by a certified agency during the service, maintenance, or disposal of any refrigeration or air conditioning equipment. If the existing refrigerator or freezer is to be replaced, locate a certified refrigerator service company to recover the coolant, and inquire to make certain they will have the remaining steel and materials recycled.

Fact Check

- In the United States, we throw away almost 8 million refrigerators and freezers each year.
- Four million pounds of ozone-depleting chemicals escape from appliances at disposal, annually. The harmful gases may survive for as long as 150 years in the stratosphere.

Source: EPA, www.epa.gov

RANGES, COOKTOPS, AND OVENS

Gas or electric? It used to be the only question a person needed to answer when purchasing a kitchen range. Now, simple four-burner stoves are less and less the standard in the modern American home. Down-vented grills, built-in slow cookers or fryers, convection ovens, and sophisticated temperature controls are just a few of the options available, as well as the smooth cooktop.

Because the United States has no minimum efficiency standards for cooking ranges, manufacturers have not been challenged to come up with better resource-conserving

This kitchen features a refurbished stove. The space also showcases ENERGY STAR appliances and locally made, FSC-certified cabinets.
Photo by Ed Hershberger.
Designer: Georgia Erdenberger, Czopek & Erdenberger.
Architect: Nathan Good, Good Architects.

technology. EnergyGuide does not label kitchen ranges, and ENERGY STAR does not rate them. The selection of gas or electric, therefore, is usually based on a personal preference. Both gas and public electricity are, unfortunately, reliant on nonrenewable fossil fuels. Gas (natural or propane) will use less energy overall because it is delivered directly to the home, as opposed to electricity that must be produced at power plants and then routed to the home. A gas range requires that the house be equipped for it, and it's imperative that there be adequate ventilation through an electricity-powered duct to the outside. If the client's home has a renewable alternative energy source such as solar, an electric range might be preferred.

Gas ranges today have electronic ignition to eliminate the need for an ever-burning pilot light. While this results in gas conservation, there's still a small amount of standby electricity used. Electric ranges, either smooth or exposed-coil, heat up slower, but electric ovens are sometimes favored because they cook more evenly. Hybrid ranges that combine a gas stovetop with an electric oven are becoming a popular solution for those who want the best of both worlds.

Convection ovens are a green choice because they speed up the cooking process yet consume one-third to one-half less energy by circulating hot air throughout. Self-cleaning ovens are generally more efficient because they have higher insulative properties and better seals on the oven doors. The self-cleaning feature itself, however, is energy-intensive, so advise the client not to use it more often than is really needed.

Cast-iron solid disk elements on rangetops are slower to heat up, and use more energy, so they are less than ideal for an eco-friendly kitchen. Other innovations include halogen-bulb cooktops with glass-ceramic surfaces, and magnetic induction units that work by generating heat when the placement of an iron or steel pan on it activates an electromagnetic field (the surface remains cool throughout cooking). Halogen cooktops are about 80 percent more energy-efficient than most conventional ranges; and induction stoves, 70 percent. Both are more expensive up front and less familiar to consumers. In addition, induction ranges require the use of steel or iron pots and pans.

One way to maximize energy conservation is to consider whether there might be a more efficient way to cook the food or meal. Ovens are especially consumptive energy users, as a large amount of space and steel must be heated up, even for a small meal. And when the oven or stove releases heat into the kitchen air, the air conditioning works harder, as well. In general, a smaller appliance will concentrate the heat where it's needed and lose less of it to get the job done. Pressure cookers speed up the process on the stovetop, reducing energy use by 50 to 75 percent. Slow cookers, toaster ovens, and even microwaves offer significant energy savings, especially when cooking a small meal. The choice of appliance and method for a particular cooking task may, after all, have the greatest environmental impact.

RANGE HOODS AND DOWNDRAFT VENTILATION

Proper kitchen ventilation, especially with a gas range, is required by building code in many areas, and should never be overlooked. Range hoods that simply circulate air through a charcoal filter are common in conventionally built houses. A much better option for home health is a hood that vents to the outside and rids the air of the cooking and combustion by-products such as carbon monoxide, carbon dioxide, moisture, and VOCs. Specify a fan designed for the particular range size to optimize airflow but not overdo it. Updraft vents are much more energy-efficient than downdraft types, although advancements in technology are improving the latter.

MICROWAVES AND SMALL APPLIANCES

Large families were once the norm. Today there are cookbooks devoted to meal preparation for one person. When the quantity of food to be cooked is small, choosing a smaller appliance over the use of a larger oven or the stovetop can save energy, time, and even cleanup. But it's not an exact science, as the temperature of a stove burner or the setting on a microwave affects the energy consumed.

Microwaves can be especially effective at reducing energy consumption, as they are oriented toward speedy reheating and small-meal cooking, and they don't radiate heat. In addition, the food may be cooked on a plate or in a bowl that doubles as the serving dish, eliminating hot water and power needed for dishwashing. Slow cookers, pressure cookers, toaster ovens, and electric teakettles are also energy-saving appliances.

As always, there is an ecological exchange: a small appliance that is rarely used or that is a luxury item is a waste of raw materials. Small appliances are often thrown away when components break or cease to function, because repairs may cost more than a new appliance or parts maybe difficult to secure. Few small appliances are recycled, as they have numerous small plastic and metal parts that are difficult to disassemble.

Typical Appliance Energy Consumption*

Appliance	Watts**	Energy Use	Use Time	kWh per Month	Cost of Use per Month (based on $.09/kWh)
Blender	400	0007 kWh/min.	Twice a week for 1 minute each	**	**
Bread machine (single-loaf)	400 (while baking)	.4 kWh/hr. (one loaf)	Twice a week	3.2	$.29
Coffeemaker (drip, brewing)	1000	.25 kWh/use (15 min.)	Every day	7.5	$.68
Coffeemaker, warming	70	.07 kWh/hr.	Every day for 2 hours	.4	$3.60
Deep fryer, small	600	.6 kWh/hr.	4 times a month for half hour each	1.2	$.11
Dishwasher (not inc. water heating)	1200	1 kWh/load	4 loads/week	16	$1.44
Dishwasher, high energy-efficiency (inc. electric hot water heating)	1500	2 kWh/load	4 loads/week	32	$2.88
Electric skillet	1200	1.2 kWh/hr.	Once a week for ½ hour	2.4	$.22
Food processor	350	.35 kWh/hr.	Twice a week for 3 minutes each	.14	$.01
Freezer, chest (15 c.f.)	350	1.3 kWh/day	—	39	$3.51
Freezer, upright, frost-free	450	2.8 kWh/day	—	84	$7.56
Microwave, (.7 c.f.)	700	.7 kWh/hr. (at high power)	Every day for 15 minutes	5.3	$.48
Oven, 350 degrees	5000	5 kWh/hr.	4 times a week for ½ hour	40	$3.60
Refrigerator/freezer, frost-free (17 c.f.)	500	.57 kWh/day	—	17	$1.53
Slow cooker	200	1.8 kWh per use (9 hours)	Twice a month	3.6	$.32
Toaster	1100	.055 kWh/use	Every day	1.7	$.15
Toaster oven, broiling	800	.57 kWh/hour	Once a week for 10 minutes	2.3	$.96

*Although appliances and home equipment vary greatly in the amount of electricity they use, this chart helps analyze the best places to cut back. The wattages listed were taken from the nameplates on various appliances.
**A watt is a unit of energy; a kilowatt is 1000 watts. Multiply the kW times the hours of operation to get the kWh (kilowatt hours) used.
Source: Misty M. Lees, "The Kitchen, Unplugged," *Natural Home*, September/October 2004.

Determine which small appliances might be best suited to the household needs and have the least impact on the environment. Factor in the frequency that they might be used, the typical energy consumption per use, and the life span of the appliance.

DISHWASHERS

Most American homes now have a dishwasher. Newer models save considerable water over handwashing, often cutting the amount in half. Yet water conservation is only part of the total picture when it comes to resource consumption. Dishwashers also rely on electricity to run the motor and more energy to heat the water (gas or electric); the appliance accounts for 1 to 2 percent of home energy use. With an average life span of only 9 to 12 years, the amount of metal and plastic used to make the appliance is also a serious consideration, as not all of it will likely be recycled (Consortium for Energy Efficiency, www.cee1.org).

When selecting a dishwasher, there are a few specifications that will optimize energy and water efficiency. Booster heaters within the dishwasher allow the consumer to set the home water heater temperature lower but still use a sanitizing rinse in the dishwasher. "Light wash" or "energy saver" features usually reduce the wash time and dry time, and are ideal for most loads. Air drying cuts out the heater, and those that use the fewest gallons of water per load are usually the most energy-efficient. ENERGY STAR-labeled dishwashers ensure top performance in energy conservation. If there is a solar hot water heater or solar power in the home, it will reduce the overall effect on the environment, as well.

GARBAGE DISPOSALS

Although standard in almost every kitchen today, the garbage disposal unit is not a green addition. Contrary to popular opinion, conventional disposals (also called disposers) don't return organic waste to nature. The bits of food must first go through the sewage system, adding to the ever-growing burden on water treatment plants. (For septic systems, garbage disposals may also create undue organic loads.) What might otherwise be "nutrients," if they were composted, actually contribute to algae bloom and other undesirable conditions in our wastewater systems, so they are chemically and biologically managed. The end result, when food is washed down the drain, is that the organic matter never really gets back to the earth. Moreover, a garbage disposal unit requires the use of water and electricity to function, and is made of numerous metal and plastic parts that can't be easily separated for recycling.

Alternatively, there are some disposal units that are propelled by water pressure, not electricity. While these certainly cut down on energy use and therefore are more eco-friendly than conventional disposals, increased organic waste in the water is still an issue.

The optimal way to handle kitchen food waste is to develop a compost system. Urban dwellers might not have the garden to implement composting, so many waste management districts are taking a new approach: they collect kitchen scraps and food-soiled paper with yard debris, all of which is recycled into compost. In some places, a special collection bucket with tight-fitting lid is supplied to each household. The resulting compost is sanitized, and even resold in some places.

This kitchen has ENERGY STAR appliances and features sustainably grown mahogany cabinets and bamboo flooring. Photo by David O. Marlow. Architect: Poss Architecture.

Garbage disposals may be required by code and are standard in modern construction. If there's an existing disposal unit, there's no need to get rid of it, but there are better ways to deal with food scraps.

WASHERS

The washer may be the largest water guzzler in the home, yet great strides have been made in technology to reduce the amount of water needed to do the job well. The most well-received change is the shift from conventional top-loading washers that fill completely with water to front-loading or horizontal-axis models that use a minimum of water, tumbling the clothes rather than agitating them. Top loaders use about 40 to 50 gallons of water in order to saturate and cleanse properly, but front loaders need only about a third to half as much. The front-loaders are more expensive to purchase, but the typical American household will save 7,000 gallons of water a year (Consumer Energy Center, www.consumerenergycenter.org).

> **Fact Check**
>
> ▪ The water saved by front-loaders is so substantial that the "thirsty" state of California has mandated strict regulations for residential washers: all new models must be horizontal-axis types beginning in 2007 (California Energy Commission, www.energy.ca.gov). Other states are following suit.

Approximately 95 percent of the energy used to wash clothes is for heating the water, so front-loaders reduce that need substantially, as well. In addition, the front-loader's improved spin cycle removes more water from the clothes and thus cuts the amount of energy consumed by the dryer, or the time on the clothesline. A study of 204 families that switched to front-loaders found they lowered energy use by 56 percent (Department of Energy, www.energy.gov).

ENERGY STAR has devised a system by which it rates washers for modified energy factor (MEF), a figure that evaluates washer tub capacity along with the energy consumption for both the washer and the dryer (i.e., time needed to remove the remaining water from the clothes and then dry them). The higher the MEF, the more efficient the washer.

Beginning in 2007, the MEF standards will be increased. Washers will also be evaluated for water consumption, labeled with a "water factor" (WF). The lower the WF, the less water is needed for the standard wash cycle. All ENERGY STAR washers, beginning in 2007, will be required to use less than eight gallons of water per cycle per cubic foot of capacity.

Although the precise MEF and WF figures may not be on the product label, ENERGY STAR-certified washers will meet high MEF standards (and maximum WF standards, by 2007). Specify ENERGY STAR qualification for all washers.

DRYERS

Specifying a dryer is not as straightforward as specifying a washer. Dryers are not required to display an EnergyGuide label, nor are they certified by ENERGY STAR. Most dryer models use similar amounts of energy to get the heating and tumbling done. In fact, the truly eco-friendly way to dry clothes is not to use a dryer at all, but to hang them out (see the sidebar, "On the Line"). Next to that, removing as much water as possible in the spin cycle of the washer will cut dryer time; using front-loading washers will also help.

The choice of gas or electric will be influenced by the client's preference, the available public utilities, the cost, and whichever dryer system is already in place (220 outlet or gas hookup). In general, gas dryers are slightly more efficient, although the availability of alternative electrical power might sway the decision in favor of an electric dryer. Good controls on the dryer will help energy conservation efforts; look for automatic shutoffs and moisture sensors. Timers are the poorest controls, as they may overdry before shutting off. Thermostats that sense air temperature do a fair job of determining when clothes are dry, improving on timer efficiency by about 10 percent; but moisture sensors excel at about 15 percent over timers (ACEEE, www.aceee.org).

On the Line

Clotheslines were once the only way to dry clothes, and they are still the most environmental way. Ironically, in many communities that are otherwise quite progressive, clotheslines have been banned as unsightly. Most of the 35,000 homeowners associations in California—the very state that has mandated all new washers be conservational front-loaders by 2007—have blacklisted clotheslines.

It's estimated that 30 million tons of coal could be saved every year if every American switched to hang-drying their clothes. Project Laundry List, an environmental coalition, calls the idea a "revolution." Best of all, it only costs a few dollars for the equipment, which will last for years. Even by using a clothesline part of the time—when the weather is favorable or the humidity low—the energy savings, along with personal satisfaction, is high.

Source: Project Laundry List, www.laundrylist.org.

Where Does It Come From?

- Appliances are manufactured from a wide array of materials, including stainless steel, plastic, cast iron, copper, ceramic, and glass.
- The energy supplied to run appliances comes from a variety of sources, including the burning of coal and fossil fuels, nuclear power, hydroelectricity, solar energy, wind power.
- The heat source for some appliances may be fueled by natural gas, propane, kerosene, heating oil, or wood.
- Many appliances also consume water and create wastewater.

Installation

Make certain that all appliances have the proper clearances suggested by the manufacturer for air circulation, secure hookups, and adequate ventilation. Position refrigerators and freezers away from heat ducts and bright sunlight, and away from warm appliances such as stoves and dishwashers.

Maintenance

Replacement of an appliance is a major decision that directly impacts the environment, especially if the existing appliance wastes water or energy yet still is usable. Although most appliances can be recycled for the large amounts of steel, there will be many components that end up in the landfill. Simple replacement parts such as refrigerator drawers or dishwasher door handles can often be found online, through the original manufacturer, parts retailers, or even auction sites. If the appliance is otherwise in good condition and is moderately energy- or water-conserving, it might be best to wait to replace it. On the other hand, if energy or water use could be greatly improved and the appliance could be recycled, it might be time for a better model.

Keep all appliances clean and free from dust that can hamper motors or moving parts. Using only biodegradable, eco-friendly and safe detergents, soaps, and cleansers in or on appliances helps in three ways: the substances are less corrosive and abrasive to the appliances, they don't have toxic fumes or chemicals to harm humans, and they don't destroy the environment.

The following are general tips to aid the client in maintaining the appliances in the home and to maximize energy and water efficiency.

Kitchen Appliances

- When cooking, use the smallest pan, the smallest burner, the smallest oven (if there are two), or the smallest and most energy-efficient appliance for the job. A too-big appliance for the job will give off wasted heat. Match the pan size to the burner to optimize efficiency. Flat-bottomed pans work much better with smooth surfaces and electric elements.
- Turn off the oven or the electric burner a few minutes before the cooking is complete; the radiant heat will continue to cook the food.
- Defrost foods in the refrigerator a day ahead, rather than using an appliance such as the microwave or oven to defrost them.
- Keep preheating to a minimum.
- Keep the oven door closed; using the oven light to check the food prevents heat from escaping.
- Use the self-cleaning feature when the oven is already hot from cooking.
- If a part is loose or damaged, replace the seal on the refrigerator, freezer, or oven to maximize thermal efficiency.
- Set the water heater temperature at 120 degrees, no higher, if the dishwasher already has a heat booster.
- Avoid rinsing dishes unnecessarily before loading the dishwasher.
- Use the shortest dry cycle time on the dishwasher—or none at all, and hand-dry the dishes.

Laundry Appliances

- Use the coolest water setting possible.
- Use the lowest water-use setting possible.
- Use the maximum spin cycle to lessen dry time.
- Wash only full loads.
- Hang-dry clothes whenever possible.

Where Does It Go?

Most of the energy expended in running appliances can't be "replaced" and comes from sources such as coal and natural gas. Homes or communities with renewable solar or wind power are much better off because the energy source is continually renewable. Water used by appliances is somewhat renewable, although the demand in the United States has outpaced sources such as aquifers and even natural rainfall. Anyone who has lived in the western states knows well the struggle to obtain enough water to sustain a conventional American lifestyle.

One of the heaviest burdens on the environment, outside of energy and water consumption, is the "death" of an appliance. Most appliances are made from a variety of natural and manufactured materials, including some that can be recycled easily; the EPA says that 95 percent of refrigerator materials are eligible for recycling. Washers, dryers, and refrigerators all contain enough steel and other metals to make them worthwhile for scrap businesses and disassembly, which shred the appliances and sort the debris magnetically. Many smaller items such as microwaves, however, get tossed out with the trash because the metal content is less than 50 percent.

In Europe and other places where landfill space is severely limited, recycling is mandated in some jurisdictions, especially for equipment with toxic components such as coolants, heavy metals, or cathodes. Appliance manufacturers there are required to build appliances so they last much longer and contain no banned hazardous materials or heavy metals. In some cases, manufacturers must establish an end-of-life plan for the equipment or take back the used appliances.

Until stricter manufacturing and recycling standards are established in the United States, the best ecological policy is to specify top-quality household equipment that will last long, use few natural resources in its operation, and that can be recycled.

Spec List

Specify:
- ENERGY STAR appliances
- Appliances with the best efficiency, as rated on EnergyGuide labels
- Maximum water-conserving features
- Front-loading washers
- Dishwashers with hot water boosters and shorter wash and dry cycles
- Recycling of all old appliances that are being replaced

Avoid:
- Unneeded or luxury features on appliances
- Purchases of appliances that the client might not use fully, or use at all
- New garbage disposal systems, unless required by code

Computers, Printers, and Office Equipment

Modern home offices usually have one or more pieces of electronic or computerized equipment. Computers are part of daily life; well over half of all American households own one (U.S. Census Bureau, 2000; www.census.gov), and the number is continually growing. Printers, faxes, and other peripheral office equipment are practical necessities for those who work full- or part-time from their homes, as well as for students.

There are advantages to having home office equipment, especially a computer. Working from home saves fuel that would be lost through commuting. In 2000, the number of people who worked from home was over 4 million (Energy Efficiency and Renewal Energy, www.eere.energy.gov). Part-time home office users allow for shared, more efficient use of space and equipment at the main job campus, as well. Stay-at-home parents juggle child-rearing and work through the addition of a home office, thus providing a presence for their children that might otherwise be missing. The positives of home offices can't be denied.

The flip side is that all this office equipment consumes vast quantities of nonrenewable materials, and improper or unprotected exposure to some of them is quite toxic. A computer is made from more than 30 different minerals, and telephones contain more than 40 (National Mining Association, www.nma.org). Lead, cadmium, mercury, and other toxic materials are among them. Unfortunately, computers and electronics often become technological dinosaurs in a matter of a few years, and replacement components, even batteries, are so difficult to obtain or so expensive that it's easier and cheaper to purchase all-new equipment. Many outdated computers, faxes, printers, phones, and scanners end up in the trash, where those hazardous materials leach into soil or groundwater. Electronics are a significant source of hazardous waste such as mercury and lead, and the European Union estimates that electronics disposal is growing at a rate three times faster than regular municipal solid waste (EPA, www.epa.gov). The statistics may be even higher in the United States.

Office equipment and computers consume energy as well as natural materials. A desktop computer with a cathode ray tube monitor uses about the same energy as two 100-watt light bulbs; laptops use a bit less. Most computer manufacturers have the power-down or "sleep" function, the only feature necessary for ENERGY STAR quali-

Fact Check

- Americans discard 100 million cell phones, computers, and other electronic devices every year.
- At least 60 million PCs have been landfilled already.
- Another 250 million computers will be obsolete by 2009; that's 136,000 a day.

Source: "E-gad!" by Elizabeth Royte, *Smithsonian Magazine*, August 2005.

fication to date. The amount of energy conserved with the feature is significant; an ENERGY STAR computer will save an average of 70 percent over one that doesn't meet the strict criteria, and other office equipment with power-down modes may save 90 percent.

Whenever possible, upgrade or repair office equipment rather than replace it. Or consider a used or refurbished model, as long as it meets ENERGY STAR criteria. By doing so, the need for disposal or recycling is delayed and valuable raw materials are conserved.

Where Does It Come From?

- Computers and office equipment are made from a wide variety of materials, but the bulk is metal, plastic, glass.
- Computers and office equipment often contain hazardous materials such as heavy metals, vinyl, and toxic chemicals.
- Computers and office equipment rely on electricity for power.

Maintenance

Keep the computer, printer, and other office equipment turned off when not in use— although older models didn't handle shutdowns well, it's no longer a problem. Activate automatic shutdown and power-saving features on the computer. Turn off the power strip or unplug the adapter, as well. Clocks, power-indicator lights, and similar devices use standby energy, which can quickly add up to 1 percent or more of the residential total.

Rechargeable batteries are much more eco-friendly than disposables. Locate battery and printer cartridge recycling options.

Where Does It Go?

In the best of situations, home office equipment will be recycled. Approximately 1 billion computers will be potential scrap by 2010 (Consumer Reports Greener Choices, www.eco-labels.org). Yet the recycling of computers and electronics has had poor economic value until recently. The thousands of different plastic components, benign by comparison to the toxic heavy-metal parts, are still the most challenging to recycle, according to the EPA (www.epa.gov). The process requires disassembly of hazardous components, and this job has frequently been relegated to the lowest economic rungs of society, such as citizens (including children) of developing countries and prisoners. Without protective gear or fair labor standards to protect them, they are at high risk for poisoning, cancers, and other work-related ailments.

Recently, there has been positive movement by manufacturers, government, and public-interest organizations to make electronics and computers greener and to make recycling an economically feasible industry. Some states require retailers and manufacturers to take back used equipment for recycling, and there are new laws and incentives to reduce the amount of toxic lead, brominated flame retardants, and other toxic materials used to make electronics. New initiatives prevent the export of hazardous computer components to developing countries, the disposal of waste equipment in municipal landfills and incinerators not equipped to handle it, or the use of prison labor for dismantling hazardous components.

In addition, manufacturers are being pushed to make it easier for consumers to upgrade, fix, or replace parts in the equipment. In the past, parts, batteries, printer cartridges and similar components were expensive, model-specific, and difficult (if not impossible) to procure. The consumer had few motivating factors, other than individual eco-conscientiousness, to recycle broken or unusable components. Now, manufacturers are working to provide postage-paid recycling packages for the consumer along with easier replacements for many parts and components. Pursue electronics recycling, whenever possible.

Spec List

Specify:

■ ENERGY STAR power-down features

■ Upgrades, if possible, rather than replacements of office equipment

■ Recycling of all components

Avoid:

■ Throwing any office equipment in the trash; many pieces contain hazardous materials

RESOURCES

American Council for an Energy-Efficient Economy: www.aceee.org
American Water Works Association: www.awwa.org
Earth911.org
EnergyGuide: www.eere.energy.gov/consumer/tips/energyguide.html
ENERGY STAR: www.energystar.gov
EPA, Water Efficiency Measures for Residences: www.epa.gov/owm/water-efficiency/resitips.htm
H$_2$ouse.org
Project Laundry List: www.laundrylist.org
U.S. Department of Energy, Energy Efficiency and Renewable Energy: www.eere.energy.gov

mechanical: plumbing

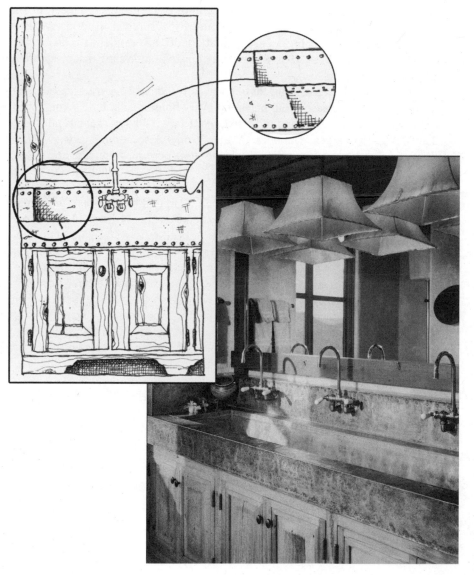

Drawing: Donna Barta-Winfield.
Design: Donna Barta-Winfield,
Annette Stelmack,
www.associates3.com.
Photo: David O. Marlow.

I n most cases, green interior design specifications are oriented toward the materials being used for the production of a finish, furnishing, or fixture. Environmentally con- scientious plumbing, on the other hand, requires a keen eye toward consumption of one particular natural resource: water. The toilets, sinks, showers, and tubs in our home affect how much water we use—or waste—every day.

Water has gone from the most common substance on Earth to being perhaps the most valued one. The booming human demand for water, especially in regions where freshwater is precious, has stretched many supplies to their limit.

While interior residential use is only a portion of the total—agricultural and indus- trial needs are far greater—every drop matters. Americans are especially "thirsty," with residential use totaling 92 gallons per day per capita (350 liters, residential). That's com- pared with 52 gallons (200 liters) in Europe and only 5 gallons (20 liters) or less in sub- Saharan Africa, where it's barely enough for survival (World Water Council, www.worldwatercouncil.org). Only a portion of U.S. residential consumption is for drinking water, however; 78 to 85 percent goes to our washing machines, showers, toi- lets, and dishwashers.

It's possible to make a big difference with little changes. Residential water con- sumption could decrease by 30 percent if every household in the United States were to install water-saving toilets and other fixtures. That's 5.4 billion gallons per day or almost 2 trillion gallons a year (American Water Works Association, www.awwa.org). New sinks and showers use less water, giving the same perceived pressure and cleansing abil- ity. And improved toilet design has cut each flush from 7 gallons down to 1.6 gallons or less.

There are changes that can be made on a larger scale, as well. On-demand, recir- culating, graywater, and solar hot water systems drastically cut back the amount of en- ergy used, and they are relatively easy to retrofit to existing plumbing. On-demand water heaters replace conventional tank types, and do the job by flash-heating water across a small system as it's needed, rather than keeping gallons of hot water stored on standby for occasional use. Recirculating systems can capture heat from shower and tap water as it drains, then redirect the warmth to hot water pipes on their way to the spigot. Solar-dependent hot water heaters conserve electricity. And graywater systems—plumber-installed, or those that are simply dependent on the client's habits— keep less water from going down the drain and put more directly into landscaping.

Fact Check

- Ninety-seven percent of the Earth's water is saltwater and 2 percent is frozen, leaving only 1 percent fresh water for human use.
- The U.S. has freshwater resources totaling about 660 trillion gallons, and Americans tap into about 341 billion gallons of those resources every day.

Source: American Water Works Association, www.awwa.org.

Water districts benefit, too. With conservation measures at the individual level, the infrastructure lasts longer and won't need replacement as soon. To encourage residential water-use cutbacks, many districts offer rebates for replacement toilets and more efficient plumbing.

Adding Up Savings

Interested to see what kind of savings a few changes in the plumbing might make? The Water Budget Calculator at www.h2ouse.org helps determine what the client's water use and utility bill would be if toilets, showerheads, faucets, and the washing machine were replaced with high-efficiency options.

While it is always wise to replace an inefficient toilet or showerhead, deciding whether to replace or to refinish damaged tubs and sinks is not a clear-cut issue. Many older fixtures with simple rust or small chips can be repaired or refinished, adding decades to their longevity. But the drawbacks to refinishing are significant. The chemicals used to etch the surface in preparation for the refinishing, such as hydrofluoric acid, are noxious to humans and may also corrode existing pipes. The room in which the refinishing is done must be well ventilated for the safety of the worker, who should wear protective clothing and ventilators. Needless to say, the whole process is tough on indoor air quality and should not be attempted in a home where a client has chemical sensitivities. It is possible, although much less economical, to remove a fixture, refinish it off-site, then replace it.

A great deal of materials and energy goes into the manufacturing of each fixture made from cast iron, ceramic, steel, acrylic, or fiberglass. Plus, plumbing fixtures can be heavy burdens on landfills. The decision to replace or refinish a tub or a sink is a tough one. Either choice has a negative effect on the environment. If a fixture must be removed, look for salvage or recycling possibilities. If refinishing is the preference, consult with subcontractors to find the least toxic, longest-lasting product and method (ask for the warranty specifics), then take every precaution to ensure the safety of workers and clients.

Toilets, Urinals, and Bidets

There are a number of technologies available to help cut water usage by toilets, most of which demand that we rethink the way we flush. The toilet is the single largest consumer of water, guzzling down more than a fourth of the total in every household

(H2ouse.org, www.h2ouse.org), and the simplest, most important way that Americans could conserve water is to replace all of the old toilets.

All toilets manufactured for use in the United States must now flush with less than 1.6 gallons of water. These types, typically called ULFs, for ultra-low flush, initially were unpopular, as many needed double-flushing that counteracted the intended water savings. But they've come a long way, and good design has resolved the issues. Homes with ULFs do not flush more often, on average, than those without, according to the AWWA (www.awwa.org).

If the project is a remodel, reducing home water use by 20 percent may be as simple as replacing the old fixture with a newer, greener one that has a 1.6- or 1.4-gallon flush (AWWA, www.awwa.org). To discover the age of a toilet, look under the tank lid to find the date stamp. The older it is, the bigger the flush. Before 1994, when ULF models became a requirement in the United States (see the Table 14.1, "Energy Policy Conservation Act," page 286), toilets used anywhere from 3 to 7 gallons per flush. A new toilet (the marking on these should be behind the seat) will use only 1.6 gallons, or as little as half of that if it's a dual-flush. Each ULF saves 14,000 to 17,000 gallons of potable water every year (H2ouse.org, www.h2ouse.org), cutting household water use by a fifth.

Fact Check

- In a study done by the American Water Works Association (AWWA), toilets used the most water daily (20.1 gallons per person, on average) in households without water-saving features in plumbing fixtures. Clothes washers were next, at 15 gallons.
- In households with ULFs, the toilet came in fourth, behind the washer, the faucets, and the shower, reducing the total gallons flushed to 9.6 per capita per day (www.awwa.org).

If the client does not yet want to replace the toilet, either because it is rarely used or has a flush capacity of just slightly more than 1.6 gallons, an add-on control can be purchased that will reduce water consumption. The mechanism allows the user to push the handle down for 1.5 gallons, or up for the full flush. It can be retrofitted on most models that have the flush lever on the front.

Even better for water conservation are dual-flush toilets. On most dual-flush models, the handle can be levered or rotated by the user, to provide more water or less, as needed. Some incorporate two separate buttons. The lighter flush gets used about 80 percent of the time, consuming 25 to 50 percent less water, and most households with dual-flush toilets will cut water used in toilet flushes by 50 percent overall. These toilets are new to the United States, but are already mandated by law in many parts of the world.

Public restrooms have long since made use of toilets with pressure-assisted flushes, but residential use is limited. Compressed air inside the tank provides 20 to 45 percent more efficiency than the ULFs. The most often cited drawback of pressure-assisted flush models is the increased noise.

Waterless urinals rely on an oil-and-alcohol mixture in the sanitary-chamber drain for cleansing, and to keep sewer gases from entering the home. The cartridge needs to be replaced after several thousand uses, and the usual bowl cleaning is necessary on a regular basis. Odor, however, is not an issue, as urine is odorless until in contact with water. Almost all waterless urinals are for male use; although urinals for women do exist and are fairly common in some parts of the world, they have never caught on in this country.

There is also a type of hybrid sink-toilet bathroom fixture that routes the wastewater from of the bathroom sink to the tank of the toilet. Because sink use does not provide adequate water to keep the toilet tank full, supplemental freshwater is also plumbed in. The graywater (see Graywater, page 288) is then recycled into the flush, with reported savings of another 5 gallons a day.

Although some municipalities formally exclude composting and incinerating toilets in building code, the units are commonplace in remotely located cabins and homes where there are no sewer lines. They also eliminate the need for costly septic system construction and maintenance. Composting types turn human waste into usable compost, yet look like conventional toilets and are not unsanitary or necessarily more odorous. Self-contained composting units are the least expensive but must be emptied frequently; the price increases with a full composting system that has greater capacity or that serves multiple toilets. Composting systems need to be emptied only about once a year, and the compost removal is designed to be inoffensive, mostly odorless, and simple enough for the homeowner to do. The compost may then go directly into the landscaping.

Toilets and bidets have gone high-tech, with heated seats, motion detectors, and other automatic sensors that are very popular in some parts of the world, but less so in the United States. Few of these options do anything to conserve water, and almost all require electricity (although solar-powered toilet features are emerging) and more electronic parts. Unless the client has a family member with a limited mobility where motion detectors or automatic sensors would be helpful, these "supertoilets" should be considered luxury items, as they offer no environmental benefits.

Toilets and bidets are usually porcelain/ceramic, which is sanitary, weighty, and very durable. Fiberglass and acrylic are also available, but not as easily recycled. Stainless steel is another option that is high-style and completely recyclable.

Plastic, wooden, and vinyl seats and lids are available. Wood is difficult to keep clean, as the finish wears down and tiny cracks can develop. Plastic and vinyl are by far the most popular for their lightweight and sanitary properties. PVC-free seats and lids are commonplace for babies and nursing care facilities, but not yet standard for typical residential applications, so consult with the manufacturers to see if they offer it.

When replacing an old toilet fixture, investigate the recycling options. The porcelain can be recycled into road base; check with the local waste management or recycling authorities, which might even pick it up curbside. The Virginia Oyster Heritage Program has used recycled porcelain toilets and sinks to restore oyster beds (Virginia Department of Environmental Quality, www.deq.state.va.us).

Saving Paper or Water?

The production of tissue paper, which includes toilet paper and facial tissue, is a voracious consumer of wood pulp. And don't forget the cardboard rolls. Although a large percentage of toilet and tissue paper comes from recycled sources, Americans still have a long way to go to reduce their dependence upon trees for paper needs. If every household in this country replaced a single roll of virgin-fiber paper towels with one made from 100-percent recycled fiber, 544,000 trees would be saved (National Resources Defense Council, www.nrdc.org).

An alternative that is less popular in the United States but is very popular in other parts of the world is the bidet. While paper is conserved, water use is increased substantially. The environmental winner is a toss-up. More trees and more paper manufacturing, versus more water and another fixture? The choice will be up to the client.

Lavatories and Sinks

Lavatories and sinks have typically been made from enameled cast iron or ceramic (also called porcelain or fireclay), with stainless steel also popular for kitchen sinks. Carved stone, cast concrete, copper, bronze, aluminum, enameled steel, and a host of synthetic resins are also possibilities; and glass is a newer option for bathroom basins. With the exception of synthetic resins and acrylics, which are rarely good choices in an earth-friendly setting, all of the aforementioned basin materials have some eco-friendly characteristics. They can be recycled (although some will inevitably be downcycled), all are nontoxic, and none will outgas. Sanitary characteristics are implicit in the design of any kitchen or bathroom sink, as they are in constant contact with hands, dishes, and food. All sinks have extremely long life spans and may outlast the house itself, although each type of material has its particular weaknesses.

Cast concrete is growing in popularity because it can be custom-designed to any shape or configuration, often integral with the countertop itself. A skilled artisan is required to craft concrete into basins and tubs, however. Although the concrete gains a desirable patina and hairline cracks over time, sealing, finishing, or waxing is recommended as a protective coat. These processes are usually done off-site. Carefully weigh the pros and cons of particular finishing techniques and products, as some emit fewer VOCs but are not as long-lasting. Specify low-VOC products whenever possible.

Copper requires constant maintenance if your client wants a new-penny shine, but scrubbing and polishing is hardly necessary, as a warm, attractive patina will develop over time, which may be more desirable. Enameled steel and cast iron may eventually crack, craze, and rust, yet they excel in durability and can be recycled. Porcelain or

This bathroom sink was handmade from pottery; the faucet came from a deconstructed house. The space also features strawbale wall plaster (an earthen mix of straw, sand, and clay), American Clay on the alternate wall, a mirror recycled from a deconstructed house, and wheatboard cabinetry.
Photo by Meghan Hanson.
Architect: Carney Architects.

fireclay may also lose some of its sheen and glaze over time, especially if subjected to abrasives. Glass is a perfect choice for bathroom sink basins where breakage isn't a risk, but not in kitchens where contact with heavy cookware could crack or break the glass.

Consider installing an undersink collection system for graywater. The rinse water from the kitchen or bathroom sink can be harvested for use in the landscaping (see Graywater, page 288). There's even an innovation that combines the bathroom sink with a graywater catchment and filtration unit so that wastewater can be reused to flush the toilet.

See also Fittings, page 287.

Showers and Tubs

Next to older toilets, showers are usually the biggest water consumers, accounting for about 20 percent of total indoor use (EPA, www.epa.gov). Some older, conventional showerheads flow at a rate of 5 gallons per minute (gpm) or more—that's 50 gallons for a 10-minute scrub-down—which also exceeded many water heater capacities.

Most of the "enhanced" bath fixtures, which are the latest on the list of must-haves for many upscale homes, use inordinate amounts of water. A full-body spa-type shower tower with multiple nozzles could consume as much as 60 to 100 gpm, even though each nozzle outputs less than 2.5 gpm as mandated by the Energy Conservation Policy Act (see Table, "Energy Policy Conservation Act"). "Rain" or "downpour" showerheads sold in the United States also comply with the 2.5 gpm law, but because there is only one nozzle, they might be the one luxury that is still water-conservative. Whirlpool and luxury baths have extra-large capacities—to fill one up, it might require 225 gallons of water.

By encouraging clients to select only water-savvy bath fixtures, high environmental standards are maintained. Newer showerheads use as little as 1.2 gpm, cutting the new standard by half or more, with more than adequate water pressure. Some come with a shutoff knob that makes it easy to stop the flow while sudsing up.

Tubs are an integral part of many bathrooms, but significantly more water is needed per use than for the typical shower. If the client chooses to limit the tub size, or reduce the frequency of baths and take showers instead, the water savings will increase. Specify a standard-size tub, or bathrooms with a shower only.

Energy Policy Conservation Act

Faucets: The maximum water use allowed by any of the following faucets manufactured after January 1, 1994, when measured at a flowing water pressure of 80 pounds per square inch, is as follows:	
Faucet Type	Maximum Flow Rate (gallons per minute or per cycle)
Lavatory faucets	2.5 gpm
Lavatory replacement aerators	2.5 gpm
Kitchen faucets	2.5 gpm
Kitchen replacement aerators	2.5 gpm
Metering faucets	0.25 gpc
Showerheads: The maximum water use allowed for any showerhead manufactured after January 1, 1994, is 2.5 gallons per minute when measured at a flowing pressure of 80 pounds per square inch.	

Note: Water efficiency standards established by the Energy Policy Act of 1992; www.epa.gov/owm/water-efficiency/wave0319/append_b.htm.

This bathroom features a salvaged claw-foot tub and stone pebble flooring hand picked from the beach just outside the home. Photo by Ed Hershberger. Designer: Georgia Erdenberger, Czopek & Erdenberger. Architect: Nathan Good, Good Architects.

One-piece or complete-ensemble shower and bathtub combinations are commonly made from fiberglass or acrylic. Although they offer durability and an easy-to-clean surface, these materials are not eco-friendly choices because they are manufactured with large amounts of chemicals and energy, and they can't be recycled. Some outgas and carry a significant odor when first installed. It's better to specify a tub from a material that can be recycled, such as cast iron or enameled steel. Consider a vintage tub, lavatory, or sink.

Fittings

In 1992, legislation was passed that required water-conserving features be included in all new faucets, showerheads, and toilets. Most kitchen faucets now have water flows of less than 2.5 gallons per minute (gpm) and bathroom sinks, less than 1.5 gpm (see page 286, "Energy Policy Conservation Act"). The latest, most water-efficient models save even more.

The "technology" behind many of these improvements is quite simple. Water flow is reduced by decreasing the supply or delivery pressure, either by installing flow restrictors (usually aerators) or controls. The easiest way to increase water conservation is to install an aerator on the end of a sink faucet. The device mixes water with air, increasing pressure. Most faucets can be retrofitted, cutting water use at that point by half or more. If working on a renovation project, check to make certain all kitchen and bathroom faucets have aerators. This simple improvement costs only a few dollars yet reaps huge results, reducing water utility bills and water consumption.

Directional or swivel spray heads on faucets serve a function similar to aerators by increasing water pressure and air mix while improving accuracy for rinsing and for sink cleanup. Faucets that shut off when touched or tapped allow the user to easily restrict water flow and maintain the temperature while hands are busy brushing teeth or rinsing dishes. Automatic and infrared sensors provide the same function, although they rely on electricity and require a few more electronic components. They may be particularly useful in households with small children or for those with limited mobility.

Faucets and other plumbing fittings are made from a variety of metals, including bronze, cast iron, aluminum, brass, chrome, steel, and copper. Many have recycled content; check with the manufacturer for specifics. Glass, ceramic, and acrylic are often used for handles; both glass and ceramic have earth-friendly characteristics, but might not last as long as metal because they are prone to breakage.

Graywater

Although sewer lines are outside the realm of interior design, encourage the architect and contractor to rethink where the wastewater goes. A few alterations to typical plumbing will send graywater to the landscaping instead of the sewer, reclaiming water that is a scarce resource in many regions. And graywater does more than nourish the flowers. The longevity of home sewer and septic systems is increased, as well as that of the sewage treatment infrastructure, when the load is reduced. Graywater diversion will even decrease the energy consumption of wastewater treatment facilities. The

Shades of Gray

Residential graywater is that which is left over after dishwashing, bathing, laundry, and light cleaning. (Note: The term graywater has two meanings and is not to be confused with reclaimed runoff from landscaping and roadsides.) Blackwater is waste from toilets, softeners, septic systems, and pools.

This bathroom features a reclaimed pedestal sink.
Photo by David O. Marlow.
Designer: Associates III, www.associates3.com.

client also will gain an increased awareness and appreciation for the amount of water expended and conserved.

A graywater reuse system can be simple if the client chooses this path. In fact, it requires only a change in thinking on the team's part; plumbing alterations are optional. At its simplest, it's a philosophy of "don't let it run down the drain." The homeowner can collect the kitchen sink or shower rinse water in a small bucket, then carry it to the outdoor or indoor plants. An integral system requires that the plumber route all of the drains that capture graywater (sinks, washer, tubs, and showers) to a purchased or custom-designed filtration system, mulch, or leach field. The debris is captured, then the graywater is sent straight to the home's landscaping or to a holding tank for such use at a later time. It is also possible to send graywater to the toilet tank for use in flushing. Check with building codes to see if graywater plumbing systems are allowed.

Where Does It Come From?

- Water is obtained from a number of renewable and nonrenewable sources, such as lakes, rivers, and aquifers.
- Some graywater may be collected for reuse from sink basins, washing machines, showers, and tubs.
- Plumbing fixtures can be made from concrete, stone, glass, ceramic, cast iron, steel, copper, acrylic or other plastics, and wood.
- Fittings are generally made from durable metals such as steel, cast iron, copper, and brass.

Installation

If the residence is new construction or a major remodel, recommend or specify the installation of systems that save water and energy, such as solar water heaters or on-demand water-heating systems. Confirm that all architect and contractor specifications include hot water pipe insulation to minimize thermal loss.

Maintenance

Advise the client to choose quick-to-disintegrate paper products, preferably with 100 percent recycled content. They're better for the environment, and sewer/septic systems.

Flushing less often may be a difficult topic to discuss with a client, but it's an earth-wise concept worth mention. Other ways to save water include shutting off the flow while soaping up in the shower, brushing teeth, or shaving.

Encourage use of earth-sensitive, biodegradable, and healthy bathroom and kitchen cleansers such as vinegar, borax, and simple soap. Recommend that caustic bowl cleaners be avoided; they are ecologically hazardous, toxic, and can damage the tank and its parts, causing leaks.

Timely repairs will save money and conserve water. According to various industry guesstimates, up to a quarter of all households have running toilets or dripping faucets. In fact, up to 8 percent of all residential water consumption may be accidental, primarily from leaks (Saving Water Partnership, www.savingwater.org).

Where Does It Go?

Porcelain fixtures such as toilets and sink basins are sometimes recycled into road base; check with the waste management district to see if there is a porcelain recycling program.

Water Saving Tips

- Run your washing machine and dishwasher only when they are full and you could save 1000 gallons a month.
- Use the garbage disposal sparingly. Compost instead and save gallons every time.
- When you shop for a new appliance, consider one offering cycle and load size adjustments. They are more water and energy-efficient than older appliances.
- Before you lather up, install a low-flow showerhead. They're inexpensive, easy to install, and can save your family more than 500 gallons a week.
- Turn off the water while you brush your teeth and save 4 gallons a minute. That's 200 gallons a week for a family of four.
- Make sure there are aerators on all of your faucets.
- Listen for dripping faucets and toilets that flush themselves. Fixing a leak can save 500 gallons each month.
- If you accidentally drop ice cubes when filling your glass from the freezer, don't throw them in the sink. Drop them in a houseplant instead.

Source: http://www.wateruseitwisely.com/index.shtml

Spec List

Specify:

- Water-conserving faucets, showers, and toilets
- Graywater recycling, whenever possible
- Recycling of old fixtures, if possible
- Smaller tubs
- Fewer nozzles in showers and tubs to reduce the water consumption per use
- Cast iron, steel, glass, ceramic, or other recyclable materials be used for all tubs, toilets, sinks, and shower stalls
- Vintage tubs, lavs and sinks

Avoid:

- Larger tubs
- Full-body or multiple-nozzle shower systems

- Reuse of fixtures that are not water-conserving (don't send them to construction exchanges; instead, recycle the materials)
- Acrylic or fiberglass tubs, sinks, shower stalls, and toilets that can't be recycled

RESOURCES

American Water Works Association: www.awwa.org

Create an Oasis with Greywater: Your Complete Guide to Choosing, Building, and Using Greywater Systems, Art Ludwig (self-published; 2002); www.oasisdesign.net.

EPA, "Water Efficiency Measures for Residences," www.epa.gov/owm/water-efficiency/resitips.htm

H_2ouse.org

CHAPTER 15

electrical: lighting and light fixtures

Drawing: Donna Barta-Winfield.
Design: Donna Barta-Winfield,
Annette Stelmack,
www.associates3.com.
Photo: David O. Marlow.

The advent of electricity in the home began a revolution. The flip of a switch and—voila!—a bulb comes to life. We no longer marvel at the process when it occurs. In fact, we expect nothing less.

The simple convenience that we now take for granted was developed out of sheer necessity, from the critical need to provide safe navigation in dim shelters and at nighttime. Primitive types of illumination once consisted of simple wicks in oil, candles, and lanterns. In the late 1800s, Thomas Alva Edison, building on the work of Englishman Joseph Wilson Swan, developed the lightbulb. The rest is history. Today, 100 percent of U.S. homes rely on electricity for lighting (Energy Information Administration, www.eia.doe.gov). Candles, oil lamps, and lanterns are still used in modern homes, but for their rustic or aesthetic qualities, not their convenience or practicality.

As designers we focus on specifying decorative lighting. The remaining residential electrical systems are specified by the architect, or mechanical/electrical (ME) consultant, or lighting consultant. To realize the highest energy efficiency, it is imperative to work closely with a qualified consultant. Lighting affects each room's mood, color, warmth, safety, and even the arrangement of furnishings, so it's a critical element of the design. The lighting layout and illumination needs should be carefully planned to maximize the placement and efficiency of the fixtures and underlying electrical systems.

The materials used in manufacturing light fixtures do affect the environment, but choices are limited somewhat by the constraints of technology. Yes, all fixtures must have electrical conductivity (wires and metal) and a protective, transparent surround (glass) that can withstand certain temperatures. But more than wise choice of materials for the light fixture, what lighting needs is to be energy efficient in order to be eco-friendly.

Electric lights consume vast amounts of fossil fuel. Residential lighting (indoors and out) accounts for approximately 3 percent of all U.S. electricity consumption and approximately 9 percent within the home. Seventy percent of our electrical energy comes

Tubular Skylighting

They look like recessed electrical lighting, but they are really narrow, tubular skylights with domed caps and highly reflective walls that focus and intensify the brightness of natural sunshine. Even though these tubes work only when there's daylight, they'll cut down on energy costs considerably, especially if a room or closet has no window. Want to control the ambience? These skylight tubes may be "dimmed" with butterfly baffles (flaps that open and close). And they have less impact on heating and cooling costs than traditional skylights. Although the construction of these tubes relies on metals and manufactured coatings, the systems are sustained by the renewable energy of the sun—no electricity needed, ever.

This kitchen is afforded ample daylighting. The space also features ENERGY STAR appliances, low-VOC paints, wheatboard and fir cabinets, and 25 percent fly ash concrete floor.
© 2005 Aaron Blake.
Designer: Christina Davis.

from nonrenewable resources such as coal, gas, and oil, and another 20 percent is nuclear (Energy Information Administration, www.eia.doe.gov). The need for residential energy conservation is clear.

Well-designed rooms emphasize natural and reflective light sources. Once available natural light has been evaluated, determine the amount, placement and orientation of artificial lighting needed, or not, and thus, potential energy consumption or savings.

Types of Bulbs

Before selecting light fixtures, specify the bulb (sometimes called the lamp), as the most energy-efficient bulb for the job may not fit a particular light fixture's configuration. Incandescent bulbs have long been the most popular choice, but fluorescents use far less electricity and last ten times longer. In addition, bulb choice affects color perception, comfort, and even health.

INCANDESCENT BULBS

Incandescent bulbs use a tungsten filament, halogen gas filling, and a quartz-glass bulb. They've been the standard for years and are the cheapest. Their color rendering index

(CRI), or accuracy compared to true daylight, is almost 100 (see the sidebar, "Color by Number"). Soft white coatings eliminate much of the characteristic incandescent glare. But they are also the most inefficient bulb and will cost the client and the environment more in the long-term.

Incandescents last only 750 to 2000 hours, on average, which is a fraction of the life span for fluorescents. Moreover, some 90 percent of the electricity in an incandescent bulb used is wasted as heat, and these bulbs actually pose a fire danger if placed too close to fabric or paper shades. A brightly incandescent-lit room in the summertime may require extra cooling, pressing the energy efficiency issue further.

Halogen bulbs are a type of incandescent. Although a low-voltage halogen bulb is slightly more efficient than a conventional incandescent, the energy savings is negligible because the halogen transformer needs more electricity.

Color by Number

The color rendering index, or CRI, is a mathematical system to help compare different light sources for the color perception accuracy, specifically in relation to eight pastel colors. Daylight has a CRI of 100. An incandescent bulb comes close, and fluorescent technology may get above 90 (the range is from 50 on up).

CRI isn't a perfect indicator, however. Some bulbs will showcase certain color spectrums better than others. For the highest degree of accuracy, only bulbs with the same *color temperature* can be compared. Color temperature is the color appearance of the bulb and the light it produces, expressed on the Kelvin scale. "Warm white" or "daylight" compact fluorescent lightbulbs (CFLs) have color temperatures similar to incandescent.

Use CRI and color temperature as guides in selecting bulbs. After installation, help the client maintain the ambience *and* energy efficiency by supplying specification sheets or detailed notes on the selected bulbs for future purchases.

FLUORESCENT BULBS

Fluorescent bulbs cost more but give off only approximately 30 percent of the energy used as heat, making them much more energy-efficient than incandescents. They last an average of 20,000 hours each, ten times longer than their standard incandescent counterparts. The more expensive price tag will save energy and money, in the long run. And the newest compact fluorescent light bulbs, or CFLs, fit most standard fixtures and lamps.

A fluorescent bulb is a long, sealed glass tube that has electrodes at each end and is filled with a very small amount of mercury. The synthetic fluorescent coatings on the

This powder room cube features fluorescent lighting inside the walls. The space also features a 50 percent recycled content steel door and fiberboard walls.
Photo courtesy of © 2006 Robert Meier.
Architect: Locus Architecture.

inside surface of the glass are absorbed and illuminated when the mercury becomes vaporized by the electric current running through. Until recently, these very long bulbs were impractical for use in homes, as they required large light fixtures (sometimes seen in older kitchens and workshops).

New technology has eliminated practically all of the flicker and hum of those first models and most of the delay, but there are still a few drawbacks. Fluorescents do not have perfectly accurate color rendering. Because the light given off is different from that of incandescents, CFLs may be perceived as being less bright. A slightly higher wattage will compensate for the difference and still save energy.

Be sure to ask for the correct bulb for the application and fixture: CFLs should not be used in enclosed, recessed locations because the wattage necessary to generate adequate light within is so high that it can overheat. Adaptation fixtures have been designed to modify recessed lighting to accept them. Dimmer switches require special fluorescent bulbs; electronic timers and photocells may not function properly or at all. That said, CFLs are terrific choices for kitchens, bedrooms, and most living and play areas.

Mercury is a known toxin, so fluorescents require special disposal methods; check with the local waste management authorities for specifics. The largest source of mercury pollution, however, is from coal-burning power plants, and fluorescents reduce energy needed from them. To further diminish the environmental impact and home health risks, specify low-mercury bulbs (they have green end caps).

Bulb Conversion

If switching over from standard incandescent to fluorescent bulbs, here's a basic conversion chart to get started. The bulb box labels will also have this information.

- 60 watts incandescent = 15 watts compact fluorescent
- 75 watts incandescent = 20 watts compact fluorescent
- 100 watts incandescent = 26–29 watts compact fluorescent
- 150 watts incandescent = 38–42 watts compact fluorescent

Source: GE, www.gelighting.com

LIGHT-EMITTING DIODE BULBS

Light-emitting diodes, or LEDs, are one of the latest and greatest lighting technologies. LED bulbs work with a tiny semiconductor microchip that produces infrared light. They consume very little energy, and may last 100,000 hours. The CRI is quite low, color perception distorted, and cost is prohibitive, however, making them undesirable for most residential applications. The most common home interior uses today are for nightlights and accents.

Lighting Controls

The choice of bulb isn't the only way to reduce electricity use; there are numerous controls that can be designed into a home, such as dimmers, automatic daylight shutoffs, occupancy sensors and timers.

- *Dimmers* work with two different methods: either the person can control the amount of light needed, or the light itself adjusts according to darkness and daylight. Both can help reduce energy consumption. Lights that automatically brighten when there is less sunshine from windows may be counterproductive, by increasing electricity consumption at times when the light isn't needed. When used with incandescent lamps, dimmers allow for a softer start-up that may lengthen the life of the bulbs. Special fluorescent bulbs are required for dimmer use.

- *Occupancy sensors* "know" when a person has entered a room, making them user-friendly for those with disabilities, for small children who can't reach switches, and for shoppers with groceries. They also detect when there is no movement after a set period of time, so the light is automatically turned off. Some sensors work in tandem with timers, or can be set to dim rather than shut completely off. Either way, they can conserve electricity.

- *Automatic daylight shutoffs* prevent lights from coming on during the day, which can certainly save energy. Conversely, some automatic controls turn lights on, which may provide light when it's not really needed and thus add to energy usage.

- *Timers* on interior lighting will reduce energy consumption only when the occupant is unavailable (or has forgotten) to turn lights off. They are more useful for controlling lights in greenhouses, pet areas, or spotlights on artwork. (Exterior lighting often employs the use of timers and occupancy sensors to heighten security.)

Fixtures

Fixtures can contribute to energy conservation, as well. ENERGY STAR, a U.S. government-backed program aimed at improving energy efficiency for individuals and businesses (www.energystar.gov), certifies residential light fixtures. These fixtures will reduce electricity consumption by two-thirds. The technology is simple: the fixtures are nonregressive, meaning they won't accept traditional incandescent bulbs and are designed to accept only CFLs. ENERGY STAR fixtures also distribute light more efficiently and evenly.

ENERGY STAR fixtures must last 10,000 to 20,000 hours. If the light fixture is used for 3.5 hours a day, the bulb won't need changing for seven years. Each fixture saves the client an average of $60 in electricity bills per year. Used throughout the home, the savings can add up to hundreds of dollars, even thousands in the years to come. It all translates to less electricity needed, less energy used, and less natural resource depletion.

See also Lighting, page 358.

Where Does It Come From?

- Most electricity is generated by the burning of fossil fuels at power plants. Smaller amounts are created through nuclear fission and renewable wind, water (hydroelectric), and solar sources.

- Residential lighting consumes approximately 3 percent of total U.S. electricity, and 9 percent of the electricity in a home.
- Residential light fixtures rely on metal and glass for integral components; other pieces may be made of plastic, wood, or other materials.
- Bulbs are made primarily of glass with metal electrodes and fittings. They also may contain various types of gas or mercury.

Installation

Work closely with the lighting consultant and/or electrical contractors to determine the best placement, controls, and fixtures that will provide the desired aesthetics and will maximize energy efficiency. Make lighting choices with the client while choosing the colors and furnishings to optimize color perception.

Specify the most energy-efficient bulb and fixture for the job. Specifying CFLs wherever possible will reap long-term savings for both the client and the environment. Rarely, the infrared light emitted by a fluorescent bulb can interfere with electronic equipment that uses infrared technology (e.g., remote controls, wireless telephones). Consult with the electrician to ensure this won't occur.

Light Pollution

In many places, light pollution—misdirected, too-bright, and sometimes unnecessary light—is a very real problem. While well-planned lighting installation improves security and safety, too many fixtures, glare, or poor location can be a nuisance, or worse. Light pollution may actually decrease visibility if the source is too bright or focused incorrectly, impeding safety on roads, sidewalks, front steps, and yards. Natural aesthetics are disturbed. Diurnal rhythms of birds, plants, and animals may be upset, and the stars and natural landscape will "disappear" from view. Unwanted light in sleeping areas may aggravate sleep disorders or negatively affect health.

While most light pollution is caused by exterior fixtures, interior ones may also contribute to environmental and physical malaise. Carefully evaluate designs and plans to ensure that the light is directed on the intended subject alone, that it's not too bright, and that it doesn't "trespass" into areas where it's undesirable or unnecessary.

Maintenance

Help maintain energy efficiency by providing the client with a list of ideal bulb types and optimal wattage for each fixture. According to *Energy User News* (Energy & Power Management, www.energyusernews.com), the following are common misperceptions:

- Turning fluorescent lights off, even for short periods, saves energy, contrary to popular belief that they should be left on.
- Turning a light off does not shorten bulb life. Leaving it on when not in use will certainly lead to earlier bulb replacement.

Where Does It Go?

While large quantities of fluorescent bulbs must be handled as hazardous waste or recycled because of the amounts of mercury present, homeowners in most areas, can put fluorescents bulbs in the trash. Unfortunately, though the amount of mercury in an individual bulb may be tiny, the cumulative effect on landfills is large. In 2004, 142 million fluorescent bulbs entered the wastestream, and only 2 percent were being recycled (LampRecycle.org, www.lamprecycle.org).

Consult with the waste management district to learn if recycling or better disposal options for bulbs exist. Some districts collect them at hazardous waste or recycling sites. Recycling containers, mostly intended for places such as schools, hospitals, and commercial buildings where bulb disposal is frequent, may become more available to individual homeowners in the near future. To participate, the consumer must purchase a bulb-collection box that has prepaid postage, and then when it's full, send it off to the recycling facility.

Nonrenewable energy sources such as coal, natural gas, and oil can't be restored. Renewable sources such as wind power, hydroelectric, and solar are continually replacing themselves, but provide for only a small percentage of overall energy consumption. Residential electrical lighting consumes 3 percent of the total (Energy Information Association, www.eia.doe.gov), but this could be drastically reduced by about 66 percent if all incandescent bulbs were replaced with CFLs (ENERGYSTAR, www.energystar.gov).

Spec List

Specify:
- Compact fluorescent bulbs whenever possible
- LED bulbs and technology for small needs like holiday lights or nightlights

- Controls such as dimmers, occupancy sensors, daylight shutoffs, and timers if they will reduce lighting use
- ENERGY STAR fixtures

Avoid:
- Incandescent bulbs; use only when all other options are not adequate or adaptable to current fixtures
- Light pollution, by overlighting a location or misdirecting light
- Landfill disposal of fluorescent bulbs; encourage the homeowner to recycle

RESOURCES

Bulb Recycling: www.lamprecycle.org
ENERGY STAR: www.energystar.gov
Earth 911: www.earth911.org

CHAPTER 16

furnishings

Drawing: Donna Barta-Winfield.
Design: Maggie Tandysh, www.associates3.com.
Photo: David O. Marlow.

t's challenging to find residential furnishings that meet environmentally friendly criteria, as there are few such products widely available. It's much easier to locate and specify greener architectural materials, because the market for those has largely been driven by OSHA and USGBC LEED guidelines for commercial buildings and the benefits of compliance to them. Though there has been a trickle-down effect, boosting the availability of green residential building materials, no system has yet been established with the same effect on the world of furnishings.

NOTE
Unlike Chapters 6 through 15, which follow the CSI MasterFormat divisions, this chapter is organized to more closely follow the order in which a designer would work on residential furnishings.

Countertops

Countertops by definition are horizontal work surfaces. For kitchens and baths, they need to be both sanitary and durable. They must withstand daily household rigors and frequent exposure to water, and make an attractive design statement. Solid-surface or laminate countertops, traditionally made from petrochemically based synthetics, have until recently been top choices among the general population. When adhering to green design standards, however, these synthetics are to be avoided, as they are of questionable manufactured content, are from nonrenewable resources, can't be easily recycled or reclaimed, and don't break down well in landfills.

The growing market for earth-sensitive products has encouraged the development of numerous countertop options that meet the criteria for aesthetics and superior durability in the home. Countertops can now be made from a number of environmentally wise, beautiful materials, from pressed recycled paper, recycled glass-concrete terrazzo, traditional wooden butcher block, and linoleum.

The client may have a preference for all-natural products or for those with high recycled content; both options for countertops exist. The location and potential use of the countertop largely determines which materials will be most appropriate for the situation, as well as longest lasting. Some are better suited to abuse from cutlery or water from sinks, for example, while other types are easier to fit to a particular configuration; still others require no sealants. Selecting a material that resists stains, cutlery marks, scrubbing, or frequent use is wise, especially from an eco-perspective, as it will defer future replacement of the countertop.

When remodeling, consider refinishing or repairing the existing countertop. It might also be possible to simply cover a damaged or outdated countertop with a new surface, without removal of the existing one (confirm that there will still be adequate room to house appliances underneath the cupboards after the profile is raised). Overlayment of an existing countertop surface avoids sending the original materials to the landfill. It is also a savvy way to avoid debris, VOCs, and dust from a deconstruction that might irritate the client's allergies or sensitivities.

Before settling on a particular countertop selection, carefully consider the installation methods and materials needed for it. They vary widely, and some will introduce more VOCs or irritating odors than others. Steer away from countertops that rely heavily on adhesives or mastics for installation, and instead select products that are more environmentally benign. Some countertops will also require regular oiling or sealing with chemically formulated products, which is problematic. Others require only cleaning with a damp, soapy cloth.

CONCRETE COUNTERTOPS

Concrete, a traditional construction material with tremendous design potential, is a popular choice for countertop material. It's extremely durable and long-lasting. Concrete counters can be cast off-site, to keep indoor air quality clean, or on-site if the design is more unusual and customization is desired.

Some concrete countertops, especially precast composites (see Composite Countertops, page 318) incorporate recycled material such as fly ash that reduces the overall weight and increases the compressive strength. They might also contain recycled material of questionable composition: polypropylene, recycled carpet fibers, or plastics. Request the MSDS (see MSDS, Greening Specs, page 83) and full content disclosure from the manufacturer. Also, carefully research the use of synthetics in composites for health and environmental risks.

Aggregates and seeding can add color and texture to concrete countertops, as well as strength and scratch resistance. Recycled glass is a particularly wise aggregate choice, as it rescues a nontoxic, reusable, mineral-based material from disposal. It also comes in spectacular colors. Stones, antique hardware, seashells, and botanical imprints may also embellish the concrete. Be wary, however, of synthetic aggregates such as computer chips or plastics that may contain hazardous or toxic metals or chemicals.

The drawbacks of concrete countertops include heavy energy consumption during manufacturing and transportation, as well as the pollution of water. Concrete has a porous surface that must be sealed regularly to avoid staining.

Where Does It Come From?

- Concrete is a mixture of sand, gravel, water, and cement.
- Cement is manufactured from a combination of minerals (calcium, silicon, aluminum, iron), which are fired at high temperatures, then ground and combined with gypsum.
- Concrete may use postindustrial waste as a substitute for part of the cement or some of the aggregate.
- Aggregates may also include decorative recycled glass, stones, or other manufactured or natural materials.
- A variety of chemical admixtures may be present, although it is possible to make concrete without them.
- Natural or synthetic pigments may be added to wet concrete.
- Concrete may be left unfinished, or it may be finished with epoxy, polyurethane, or other chemical sealants.
- Concrete may be acid-stained with water-based, acidic liquids that contain metallic salts.

Installation

Inquire as to the type of cement and avoid synthetic enhancers called admixtures. Surface tints or acid stains are extremely caustic and outgas considerably when applied, putting workers and occupants at risk, so specify that colorants or tints be mineral-based and be mixed into wet concrete.

As concrete is quite porous, the countertops usually require a sealant be applied to protect the surface from stains and water damage. Specify a low-VOC, water-based, food-safe sealant or wax. A wipe-on sealant will affect air quality less than a spray-on type.

Maintenance

Regular protection with a wipe-on sealant is recommended. Advise the client as to the most eco-friendly types that are low-VOC, water-based, and food-safe.

Where Does It Go?

A concrete countertop is basically a permanent design addition to a residence, as the material is difficult to remove or deconstruct and may well outlast the house itself. Although concrete recycling exists, it primarily serves larger concrete consumers such as commercial construction and road maintenance, so smaller residential design applications of concrete may not be accepted.

Should the concrete be disposed of, the cement, lime, natural minerals, natural aggregates, and mineral colorants will eventually disintegrate in a manner similar to stone. Synthetic admixtures, aggregates, or colorants have a more uncertain future and may contaminate the environment.

Spec List

Specify:
- Concrete (and cement mix) made without admixtures
- Aggregates (or "seeding") and cement from all-natural minerals
- Aggregates from safe recycled materials
- Food-safe aggregates, sealants, colorants, or admixtures for kitchen applications
- Natural mineral pigments if color is desired
- Potable water for curing
- Precast or factory-finished slabs
- Low-VOC, water-based or water-reducible, low-solvent, no-formaldehyde stains, sealants, and finishes

Avoid:
- Aggregates or recycled ingredients that may introduce contaminants
- Chemical pigments or paints with chromium, aniline, or heavy metals

- Acid stains
- Seeding with synthetic, possibly hazardous materials such as computer chips

RESOURCES

ConcreteNetwork.com
Portland Cement Association: www.cement.org
See also Concrete, page 111.

STONE COUNTERTOPS

Solid stone, such as granite, marble, or soapstone, provides a durable surface that's literally rock-hard. A stone countertop can be cut from a solid slab, or in the form of tiles. The stone itself is 100 percent natural and won't outgas (with the possible exception of radon; see the sidebar, "Radon," Chapter 7). It is heat-resistant, sanitary, and may

This powder room features a reclaimed granite countertop and slate flooring.
Architect: Mosaic Architects.

never need replacing. If and when deconstruction occurs, the stone could potentially be reused, recycled, or simply returned to the earth.

All stones are porous and must be sealed. Solid granite is the strongest of all stone building materials and is a durable option for kitchen countertops. Soapstone and slate are other possibilities for countertops. They don't react with acids such as vinegar, wine, or lemon juice, which are problematic on granite and marble. Marble and limestone are more porous and prone to stains.

Salvaged slate tiles from rooftops have emerged as an eco-friendly choice. They are scoured thoroughly prior to installation, providing a countertop that is both natural and reclaimed.

Lava stone, a volcanic rock, is crushed, glazed, and fired much in the same way as ceramic tile, making it a stone-tile hybrid with the characteristics of both. It doesn't need sealing, is very hard, and will never outgas VOCs. The negative side to lava stone is the large amount of embodied energy inherent in the firing. The glazes, while inert after firing, may be hazardous to factory workers in the liquid stage.

Stone is ultimately a nonrenewable resource and this factor should be carefully considered when selecting it as a design element. A stone countertop is there for the long term—it isn't easily or cheaply removed or replaced. The environmental impact from mining stone is especially severe, permanently scarring ecosystems. In addition, stone is heavy to transport, and some of the most popular types are shipped from overseas.

SIMULATED/CULTURED STONE COUNTERTOPS

The terms "simulated stone" and "cultured stone" usually refer to a composite countertop made with both natural rock and a synthetic binder or cement. Typically, they contain at least 90 percent quartz or other common minerals. The ground-up minerals are then pressed and superheated with a resin to form a surface that may be more impervious to stains and water than natural stone. Composite stone countertops usually don't need to be sealed, as does natural stone. According to the manufacturers, they outgas only minimally, primarily before installation. The synthetic resins used and the energy needed for manufacturing are downsides, although some are made with cement binders.

Where Does It Come From?

- Stone is mined or quarried.
- Some stone can be reclaimed from rooftops, deconstruction or other sources.

Installation

Although the risk of significant radon exposure (enough to cause illness) from a countertop is unlikely because the amount of stone is small, radon testing may be a prudent measure for any type of stone that might emit. Have the testing done before the countertop slab is purchased.

Stone tiles or veneers, which are generally more economical than solid stone, will require more adhesive, grout, or mastic for installation; specify low- or no-VOC, additive-free products whenever possible. When the supporting structure isn't strong enough to support solid stone, stone tiles or veneers may be preferred for their lighter weight.

Request that all cutting and mechanical polishing be done outdoors or off-site to prevent dust from entering the home.

Maintenance

A drawback to stone is that if left unsealed, it will be prone to stains and scratches. Use sealants that are low-solvent, low-VOC, formaldehyde-free, water-based, and don't contain heavy metals as drying agents. Spray-on sealants may affect indoor air quality or pose hazards to the workers, so wipe-on varieties are preferred.

Where Does It Go?

Stone will eventually decompose when disposed of; or it may be reused, reclaimed for another purpose, or ground up and recycled into a different product.

Spec List

Specify:
- Reclaimed, salvaged, or recycled stone
- Stone from local or regional sources
- Radon testing of materials before installation
- Low-VOC, low-solvent, water-based, formaldehyde-free sealants and adhesives
- Wipe-on or brush-on sealants

Avoid:
- Imported stone
- Adhesives, grout, mortar, or sealants with solvents, additives, or formaldehyde
- Spray-on sealants

RESOURCES

"Consumer's Guide to Radon Reduction," EPA; 800-438-4318; www.epa.gov/radon/pubs/
   consguid.html
See also Masonry, page 124.

METAL COUNTERTOPS

Stainless steel, aluminum, zinc, and copper can be used in countertop applications. Although copper is used infrequently, stainless steel is particularly common in commercial and institutional applications because it is sanitary, long-lasting, extremely durable, and easy to clean. More and more residential design applications are following suit. Commercial stainless steel shelving and counters are easily obtained from restaurant suppliers, or used ones can be purchased from equipment auctions.

This bathroom has a countertop of recycled 1/8-inch aluminum. The space also features natural concrete flooring with integral color and radiant heat and cabinets made of raw MDF with a clear, water-based sealer.
Photo by Greg Hursley.
Architect: Eric Logan, Carney Architects.

Metal is especially hygienic, apropos for use in kitchens or baths. It is nonporous, won't outgas, and can be kept clean with simple soap and water—no sealants required.

Most types of metal can be recycled into other metal products. All types of metal, however, are nonrenewable resources, obtained through mining operations that permanently alter the geology and landscape, thereby incurring a heavy cost to the environment. Look for high recycled metal content, especially in steel and copper.

Fact Check

■ Stainless steel products today contain an average of 65 to 80 percent recycled content (Specialty Steel Industry of North America, www.ssina.com).

Where Does It Come From?

- Metal is mined from various locations around the globe.
- Metal for countertop applications is usually extracted from ore through intensive manufacturing processes.
- Metals are often combined into alloys to increase their strength, sheen, or resistance to natural oxidation.
- Various factory coatings and finishes may be applied to metal such as paint, powder coating, protective (natural or chemical) oils, metal platings, and zinc galvanizations.
- Metal can be easily recovered from recycling and fabricated into new products.

Installation

Countertops and backsplashes sometimes have chemical coatings or wax applied for protection of the finish while in transit. Request that the coating be omitted, whenever possible, to eliminate odors and potential VOCs within the home; or request removal of the coating before it is brought on-site. It may also be possible to specify that a food-grade wax or oil be used as an alternative.

Although the topic is debated among experts, it is sometimes recommended that metal not be used where there is a high incidence of electromagnetic waves, such as near microwave ovens. The risk of electromagnetic exposure to humans is controversial and largely undetermined. Consult with the electrician and the general contractor before adding a metal countertop in the kitchen.

Specify that all scrap metal from the installation be recycled.

Maintenance

Avoid commercial polishes and cleaning solutions that contain chemicals such as kerosene, naphtha, perchloroethylene, chromic acid, silver nitrate, or solvents. Simple soap and water will suffice for cleaning most metal countertops (see the sidebar, "Pretty as a Penny").

Pretty as a Penny

Concerned that a copper countertop or backsplash will turn green with age? It won't, unless it comes in contact with acids, as it does outdoors where exposed to the elements. If a bright penny sheen is desired, advise the client to cleanse at least once monthly with a rubbing of salt and lemon wedges—or ketchup!—then rinse thoroughly. If only soap and water are used, the copper will develop a caramel luster. The countertop will be beautiful either way.

Source: Copper Development Corporation, www.copper.org

Where Does It Go?

Countertop metals can be recycled continually. The value is high enough that most types are sought after by salvage operations. Disposing of metal in landfills is a last resort. Most types of metal will simply deteriorate over time and pose little risk to the environment.

Spec List

Specify:

- Salvaged metal countertops and shelving
- One hundred percent recycled material, or the highest percentage possible
- Local fabricators, to eliminate transportation
- Metal that develops a natural, pleasing patina or verdigris without the need for polishing
- No paint or finish
- Careful location of large metal design applications to avoid electromagnetic fields from microwaves
- Recycling of all scrap

Avoid:

- Pieces made with virgin metal
- Synthetic oil coatings
- Chemical polishes, treatments, or cleansers

RESOURCES

Copper Development Association: www.copper.org
Specialty Steel Industry of North America: www.ssina.com
See also Metals, page 129.

WOOD COUNTERTOPS

Wooden chopping blocks are used worldwide for food preparation, and many modern kitchens feature a section of wood built into the countertop or food preparation island. A section of wooden countertop is far less demanding on the slowly renewable supply of trees than the construction of an entire house, but similar ecological considerations apply. When the sustainability of wood for a particular application is being discussed, a reasonable rule of thumb is to consider whether the use of it will outlast the life span of the tree needed to produce it. Wood countertops will last for decades, although wear and stains may eventually warrant replacement. A slightly damaged section can be sanded to restore its appearance.

Reclaimed wood is ideal for many residential applications and is a wonderful green choice, although it may not be the safest for a kitchen or bath countertop. The porous surface might have been exposed to bacteria or toxins in its prior application as flooring or as a door. Therefore, specify reclaimed wood for a countertop only if the source can be verified as food-safe and the surface is completely free of harmful finishes.

Certain species such as maple, cherry, walnut, and mahogany are hard and tightly grained and won't damage cutlery. To ensure that the desired species is not endangered and that the forest management is sustainable, specify third-party certification of new-wood products such as approval by the FSC (see FSC, page 144). Specify locally or regionally harvested wood to limit transportation and shipping, and keeping the embodied energy lower than if it were shipped long distances.

A countertop made from a nonaromatic wood species can be left unfinished or be treated with natural oils. When specifying wood countertops formed with multiple segments (of end-grain or butcher block) to counteract possible warping; specify food-safe wood glues with no formaldehyde or VOCs. Because wood warps easily, placement directly next to a sink will dictate the need for protective sealants such as healthful oils or waxes or a permanent water-resistant finish.

See also Wood, page 139.

Sanitize for Safety

The small cuts and gouges on a wooden cutting board or other porous countertop surface can harbor bacteria. Wood and acid-resistant surfaces may be cleaned with a spritz of half-vinegar and half-water mix, followed by a mist of hydrogen peroxide. Simple soap and water isn't as effective, but might be used on countertops that would be stained or marred by vinegar or peroxide. Advise the client of these natural sanitation methods to ensure a safe, healthy countertop.

Where Does It Come From?

- Wood products come from both domestic and exotic trees.
- Reclaimed wood is culled from residential, commercial, and agricultural floors, walls, and structures. It may also be culled from rivers, lakes, streams, orchards, or from fallen trees.
- Some wood products are made from downcycled wood scraps or sawdust, with acrylics or resins added.
- Wood sealants are usually polyurethane; natural resin-oil primers are a more healthful and environmentally positive option.
- Wood finishes or stains may contain a variety of natural oils, resins or pigments; solvents; chemical compounds; petroleum distillates; metal-drying agents; formaldehyde; and sometimes water.

Installation

For all kitchen applications, specify food-grade finishes and treatments. Also specify glues, adhesives, and finishes that are formaldehyde-free, contain minimal or no solvents, and are low-odor and low-VOC.

Maintenance

Regular light oiling or waxing with food-safe, all-natural vegetable oils or beeswax will help prevent water damage and stains to the wood. To remove stubborn stains or to even out a rough surface, wood countertops may be lightly sanded.

Where Does It Go?

Wood naturally biodegrades. A used, clean section of countertop could potentially be reused in another application such as a tabletop, be recycled into mulch, or even be burned (if unfinished solid wood) in a wood stove.

Spec List

Specify Wood That Is:
- Reclaimed, if the source can be verified as safe for a countertop
- Locally or domestically harvested, FSC-certified, and a nonthreatened species
- End-grain or butcher block made with food-safe glues

Specify Finishes and Stains (either on prefinished wood or to be applied on-site) That Are:
- Food-safe (for all kitchen installations)
- Water-based
- Made of natural (sometimes called food-grade) oils, resins, pigments, and waxes
- Low-VOC
- Formaldehyde-free
- Solvent-free

Avoid:
- Reclaimed wood of uncertain origin
- Chemically tainted wood (lead, arsenic, factory chemicals)
- Uncertified wood
- Rare or threatened species
- Solvent-based finishes
- Formaldehyde and other preservatives in the wood or finish

RESOURCES

Forest Stewardship Council U.S.: www.fscus.org
SmartWood (Rainforest Alliance): www.Smartwood.org

CERAMIC TILE COUNTERTOPS

Ceramic tile is a perennial favorite for kitchen and bath applications because it is resistant to abuse from knives, staining, or acidic compounds found in foods and personal care products. Glazed tile is usually preferred for maximum stain resistance. Unglazed tile can be used, but a sealant will be required to adequately protect it.

Simple ceramic is primarily made from abundant clay, although some styles now incorporate recycled tile, stone, or glass. The glazes are inert once fired, providing a zero-VOC, sanitary, superdurable surface. (Although lead-based and heavy-metal glazes were once a concern and still are in less-developed parts of the world, all tiles made for sale in the United States will have glazes free from these hazardous metals.) The practically infinite life span of tile tips the scales slightly in favor of use, in spite of the high embodied energy it has from intensive manufacturing.

Tile remnants are available at many construction exchange sites, and it's ecologically prudent to use materials that might otherwise end up in a landfill. If there are not enough remnant tiles to complete the entire job, consider using them as accents.

Where Does It Come From?

- Traditional ceramic tile is usually made of fired clay.
- Talc, cement, or other minerals may be added.
- Synthetic or recycled materials such as fly ash or glass may also be added.
- Tile may be glazed or unglazed; glazes consist of metals, pigments, and various chemicals, along with simple silicon dioxide—sand—that become inert when fired.

Installation

Cut tile outdoors, off-site, or in an open area with a wet saw to prevent dust within the home. Recycle tile remnants through a construction exchange or similar venue.

- *Underlayment.* Specify third-party-certified (FSC) wood underlayment or that made from recycled wood or biocomposites.
- *Mortar.* The use of thickset mortar (greater than 1 inch deep) reduces the need for synthetic adhesives and mastics. Thickset mortar can be done with simple portland cement, sand, and lime. Thinset mortar, more fragile and prone to cracking, usually relies on chemical and latex additives for flexibility. If thinset is the preferred installation method for the particular tile, opt for a water-based, additive-free, low-VOC variety.
- *Adhesives/mastics.* Choose mortars, adhesives, grouts, and sealants with the least toxic, low-VOC, zero-solvent, minimal-additive ingredients possible. Specify those with no petroleum base, and no toluene, hexane, benzene, or other solvents.
- *Grout.* Whenever possible, specify simple grout made of portland cement, sand, and water. Mineral pigments may be added for color (they also hide eventual staining well). When using commercial grout blends, specify that they be additive-free, without synthetics. Specify unsanded grout when the joints between tiles are very thin.
- *Sealants.* The best way to avoid grout problems and to ensure long-term tile stability and beauty is to apply a sealant. The sealants close the grout "pores." Specify a low-VOC, water-based, wipe-on variety to minimize the negative effect on indoor air quality.

Maintenance

Glazed ceramic tile needs little more than regular soap-and-water cleaning, but grout is prone to eventual discoloration and deterioration from mold, mildew, and stains.

In moist bath and kitchen areas, ventilation through windows and via exhaust fans will slow the growth of mold. Regular resealing with a low-VOC, water-based, wipe-on sealant will also discourage mold and grout discoloration.

Advise clients to avoid toxic cleansers should the grout become discolored with mildew or dirt. Instead, recommend the use of vinegar and water; borax or baking soda and a stiff brush will aid the scrubbing process. Professional steam cleaning is also helpful. As a last resort, rather than replace the tile, grout lines between tiles can be removed, then filled in with new grout.

Where Does It Go?

Fired clay, mortar, and grout are much like rock, and will eventually break up into inert pieces at the end of the tile life cycle. The glaze will also be inert. Tile remnants are popular at construction exchanges. Used tile may be recycled with other porcelain such as toilets, which are usually crushed and added to roadbed.

Spec List

Specify:
- Tile made with unprocessed, all-natural clays or with safe recycled materials such as glass
- Factory-glazed ceramic
- Natural wood underlayment, preferably made from FSC-certified wood
- Simple mortar from cement, sand, water, and possibly lime (no additives)
- Grout with no added fungicides
- Low-VOC, water-based, wipe-on sealant
- Low-VOC, low-solvent, additive-free, mortar and grout

Avoid:
- Unregulated import tile
- VOCs, solvents, fungicides, vinyls, or latex additives in mortar, grout, or sealants

RESOURCES

National Terrazzo & Mosaic Association: www.ntma.com
Tile Council of America: www.tileusa.com
See also Ceramic Tile, page 188.

GLASS AND GLASS TILE COUNTERTOPS

Recycled glass from bottles, windshields, and other sources (see the sidebar, "Bottle-neck") provides a rich source for countertop tiles or glass backsplashes. Glass itself is manufactured from abundant sand, and the tiles or plates are simply made by melting or sintering (a melting process done at an even lower temperature) recycled glass and adding color, if desired. Glass is completely inert, emits no VOCs, won't stain, and won't absorb other VOCs and toxins because it has no "pores." It's one of the most sanitary surfaces available, appropriate for both kitchens and baths. Like ceramic tiles, glass tiles wipe clean with simple soap and water or vinegar, and need no chemical up-keep. Recycled glass can be a wonderful choice for an eco-friendly home.

Ask the manufacturer about the specific recycled glass content, as it varies considerably between products. Choose the highest percentage available.

Bottleneck

- Since the first Earth Day in 1970, Americans have thrown away 600 billion glass beverage bottles, weighing approximately 166 million tons (Container Recycling Institute, www.bottlebill.org).
- More than 13 million tons of glass are generated in the United States each year (*Environmental Building News*, September, 2001; www.buildinggreen.com).
- In New York City alone, more than 175,000 tons of glass were collected for recycling in 2002 (Columbia University, www.civil.columbia.edu).

Where Does It Come From?

- Glass is made mostly from silicon dioxide (sand).
- Glass for recycled glass tile generally comes from postconsumer waste such as bottles and windshields.
- The recycled content of glass tiles varies greatly by manufacturer and product, even between particular colors of tile.
- Small amounts of metals and chemicals may be added to glass for color and texture.

Installation

Specify certified (FSC) third-party wood, high recycled wood content or biocomposite underlayment.

Specify unsanded grout as sanded grout will scratch glass tiles. Specify low-VOC mastic and additive-free grout, whenever possible. (Outgassing may still be harmful to air quality and the environment, but it will be less problematic for a sensitive client when it is done outdoors.)

Maintenance

As with ceramic tile (see page 188), a sealant should be used to protect the grout from eventual deterioration and discoloring. Specify a low-VOC, low-solvent, wipe-on type to minimize odors and the release of VOCs in the home.

Glass needs no special upkeep, only soap-and-water cleansing. Abrasives should be avoided. Regular reapplications of sealant may be necessary to protect the grout, so advise the client as to the most eco-friendly types.

Where Does It Go?

Glass can be recycled from bottles to tiles to something else, over and over and over, but only if it doesn't end up in the trash or on the roadside. Currently, only 11 states have bottle bills that require refundable deposits on beverage containers, which motivate customers to return or recycle. The growing glass tile industry, thankfully, encourages the growth of bottle bills and curbside recycling initiatives by creating a market for the recycled glass.

Spec List

Specify:
- One hundred percent recycled glass tile or high recycled glass content
- Natural backerboard, MDF, or underlayment (FSC-certified wood, plaster, or gypsum)
- Low-VOC, water-based, wipe-on sealant
- Low-VOC, low-solvent, additive-free, mortar, mastics, and grout
- Unsanded grout

Avoid:
- VOCs, solvents, fungicides, vinyls, or latex additives in mortar, mastics, grout, sealants

See also Glass Tile, page 192.

SOLID SURFACE, COMPOSITE, AND LAMINATE COUNTERTOPS

Laminate countertops made from melamine, a crystalline substance made from a synthetic resin (see the sidebar, "Melamine," under Cabinetry, page 326), were all the rage at one time. They were easy to install and easy to clean, and they could be peeled up and replaced when they wore out. Then along came composite, solid-surface, and acrylic countertops that could be cut to fit the specifications of the kitchen or bath, were practically impervious to abuse, and were far more durable than laminates. Both laminates and composites, unfortunately, are manufactured primarily from synthetics and chemicals. The countertops are energy-intensive to make, contain toxic substances, and don't biodegrade.

Solid or laminate composite countertops have come a long way in becoming more eco-friendly. Manufacturers have devised ways to incorporate a host of relatively eco-friendly ingredients into long-lasting, cut-to-fit surfaces. Hemp, recycled paper, sustainable-forest paper products, soy resins, and agricultural wastes (called biocomposites) are now found in the composition of these new materials. Some composites also feature mineral content such as fly ash, quartz, or sand. They feature the necessary water resistance for use in baths and kitchens, and most of the companies that make these greener products strive to incorporate binders that are low- or zero-VOC.

Distinct from those with a plant fiber or pulp base are composite countertops, whose primary ingredients are minerals or concrete. Recycled materials often figure into the composition, as well (see Concrete Countertops, page 305, and Cultured Stone Countertops, page 308). Precast concrete countertops (see Concrete Countertops, page 305) frequently contain postindustrial fly ash or recycled glass as a means of strengthening the surface and reducing the weight. Some precast concrete types may include ingredients such as plastics, carpet fibers, and other synthetics, which are all generally undesirable in a green home.

Composites with high recycled plastic/acrylic content are making an appearance on the market, as well. If the client has a preference for keeping recyclable materials such as plastic out of the landfill, this might be an option. However, it's important that a home be both environmentally responsible and healthy. The material content of many recycled plastic composites is difficult to ascertain, and the potential for outgassing or ill health from such a countertop is undetermined, at best.

Each composite, laminate, or solid surface countertop, whether bio-based or mineral-based, is quite distinct in its composition. Check with the supplier or manufacturer for details, and inquire specifically as to use of formaldehyde, synthetics, and VOC-producing compounds, as well as potential odors that could be a problem for sensitive clients. In addition, performance characteristics such as scratch, stain, and water resistance will vary for each particular brand, making some less appropriate for use in a kitchen or bath.

The environmental benefits and drawbacks to these composite and laminate surfaces have not been fully established. Some are more green and feature natural, renewable, or recyclable materials, and some are less so because they are made from nonrenewable resources or synthetics. Before committing to a composite or laminate countertop material, carefully consider the origin, use, installation, maintenance, and eventual disposal or recycling potential.

Where Does It Come From?

- Composite or solid-surface countertops may be made from any variety of natural or manufactured components, including (but not limited to) hemp, recycled paper, sustainable-forest paper products, soy resins, wood pulp, agricultural wastes (biocomposites), quartz, other minerals, concrete, fly ash, and polymers or plastics.
- The resin binder may be natural or synthetic.
- The countertop may be manufactured through heating, pressing, rolling, or other processes.

Installation

Because of the variability of the materials, each countertop selection should be evaluated carefully for the installation materials and processes that will be required. Inquire as to the types of adhesives or glues required, and all finishes or sealants that are recommended, and specify the most eco-friendly materials (low-VOC, low-solvent, water-based, and formaldehyde-free).

All cutting should be done off-site or outside to eliminate residential exposure to VOCs or dust. (The environment and air quality will still be affected by the outgassing of VOCs, but the process will be less problematic for a sensitive client when it is done outdoors.)

Maintenance

Maintenance will depend on the specific surface. Inquire as to the most benign methods and materials, then supply the client with a complete list of recommendations.

Some composite or solid surface countertops can be lightly sanded to restore a new appearance.

Where Does It Go?

The composition of solid surface countertops varies greatly and may be so complex that it's difficult to determine how well they will break down. Reuse of a countertop is unlikely because each is cut to spec, but may be possible if it can be successfully removed, then recut or refinished. The higher percentage of natural materials it contains, the more likely it can be recycled or disposed of safely. Synthetic content will make biodegrading slower or impossible.

Spec List

Specify:
- A high percentage of all-natural materials in the countertop material
- A high percentage of safe recycled materials
- Bio-based binders (such as soy)
- Low-VOC, formaldehyde-free binders, resins, adhesives, and finishes

Avoid:
- Synthetic ingredients or binders
- Formaldehyde, VOCs, solvents, or odorous adhesives, finishes, or binders
- Melamine

LINOLEUM COUNTERTOPS

"Linoleum" is both a brand name and a widely used term that is not brand-specific. It can be successfully used on countertop applications such as furniture tops and utility surfaces where there is not constant exposure to water, as excessive moisture can stain it or cause the surface to deteriorate. Although naturally antimicrobial and easy to maintain, linoleum can be scratched or gouged easily with cutlery, so kitchen installations need to be carefully evaluated for suitability.

This kitchen features Marmoleum countertops with a wheatsheet substrate.
Photo by Ron Pollard Photography.
Designer: Brandy Lemae.

Natural linoleum (not to be confused with vinyl) is made from linseed oil, tall oil (from pine resin), sawdust or wood flour, cork, and limestone. It usually has a burlap backing, sometimes with a preapplied adhesive. Linoleum outgasses little, if any, and the VOCs emitted are part of a naturally occurring process. Linoleum has been shown to possess natural antimicrobial properties that discourage the growth of bacteria. Small marks or indentations in the countertop may easily be patched with a matching linoleum compound (available from the manufacturer), or sections can be replaced. Finally, linoleum will successfully biodegrade when no longer usable.

Where Does It Come From?

- Linoleum is mostly made from linseed oil, pine resin, sawdust or wood flour, cork, small amounts of pigment, and limestone.
- Linoleum usually has a burlap-type backing made of jute or, sometimes, hemp.

- The finish, if there is one, is usually ultrathin acrylic.
- Linoleum adhesives are chemical compounds; some are low-VOC, water-based, and formaldehyde free.

Installation

Specify FSC- or third-party-certified wood underlayment or a biocomposite. A low-VOC, water-based type is best.

A small amount of adhesive is necessary for installation. Specify low-VOC types whenever possible. Plan for airing-out time and good ventilation, both during and after installation.

Maintenance

No chemical cleansers or finishes are necessary; simple soap and water will suffice. Patch kits, made from simple nontoxic glue and ground-up linoleum solids, can be purchased to repair small holes or gouges. Very light sanding will also restore the countertop.

Where Does It Go?

Linoleum, with the exception of the thin acrylic coating and adhesive, is fully biodegradable.

Spec List

> *Specify:*
- Linoleum made from linseed oil and other natural materials
- Low-VOC, water-based, formaldehyde-free adhesives

> *Avoid:*
- Using linoleum where it is exposed to constant moisture, standing water, or cutlery
- Linoleum blends that contain synthetics

See also Linoleum Flooring, page 214.

Cabinetry

Wood is the main component for residential finish cabinetry. Solid wood is the overall preference for the doors and drawer fronts because of its beautiful grain, but less-expensive particleboard and MDF are commonly used to make drawer boxes, bodies, and frames because the components are less visible. Bamboo, agricultural biocomposites, metal, and particleboard are also used for faces and frames, along with glass shelves and doors. Many homes feature a combination of materials for the cabinetry throughout.

This bathroom features cabinetry made from solid woods with no particleboard material. The space also benefits from daylighting; and the walls are finished with no paint tinted gypsum plaster. Sanger Residence, Bruce Millard Architect. Photo by Rebecca Hollan, All Star Photo.

Wood, by far the most popular choice for cabinetry applications, is a resource that is natural, durable, biodegradable, and renewable—albeit slowly. It's a good option for casework in an earth-friendly residence (see Wood, page 139). Fortunately, the use of forest products is under the keen scrutiny of environmentalists, as large stands of old-growth trees and wide expanses of rain forest continue to disappear. Booming construction and the desire for cleared land are the driving forces behind the losses worldwide, as is the demand for specialty or rare woods for finish carpentry and furnishings. The ecosystems are uprooted, the soil eroded, and the natural balance of life is severely disturbed when a stand of forest is cut down and destroyed. The long-term prognosis is also grim: species are lost, greenhouse gases increase, and global warming increases.

To counteract these harmful forestry practices, it is important to specify wood for casework that has been grown and cut with minimal environmental impact. Third-party certification of the chain of custody, where eco-standards are followed and documented through every step of forestry, milling, and distribution, is the surest way to maintain healthy forests for the future. The FSC sets the standard for third-party certification, and is accepted worldwide (see FSC, page 144).

Avoid selection of wood species that are endangered (see Wood Species List, page 147) or that come from unknown or uncertified sources. In particular, avoid tropical woods unless they have been certified as sustainable through the FSC or another third-party organization with equally reliable standards. Encourage the client to select from locally available or domestic wood species in order to reduce the long-distance transportation and the energy consumed for it.

If the client has sensitivities or allergies, consider whether the tree species has an inherent odor. Although much of the cabinetry can be finished or sealed, some odor may still be present in the home after installation.

Instead of purchasing all-new cabinetry, reclaimed or salvaged cabinets are excellent alternatives for a green home. Or, if remodeling, consider whether a simple change in the existing cabinet faces might be enough to customize or update the look. New drawer pulls and handles or a coat of eco-friendly paint on the boxes or faces will change the look without replacing the existing casework. It's economical, and natural resources are conserved.

Specifying reclaimed wood that can be crafted into cabinetry is another eco-minded choice. Scout for local sources of reclaimed wood and for local cabinetmakers to minimize the embodied energy added with transportation. Verify the reclaimed wood's source—kitchen applications, especially, should be free of peeling paint, chemically treated wood, or wood that may have been exposed to contaminants from a previous "life" in an industrial setting. These contaminants or toxins could come in contact with food, cutlery, or dishes.

Many reclaimed wood operations (sometimes called RWOs) are small local businesses that may not participate in a third-party certification program but recover and sell the wood locally, know the source well, and may have deconstructed the materials themselves. These sources are generally reliable if they adhere to strict internal environmental policies. SmartWood, a program of the Rainforest Alliance, provides a certification program for Rediscovered Wood Operations that sell reclaimed wood products. SmartWood certification is recognized by the FSC, and companies that voluntarily comply will follow guidelines for the selection of wood species, chain of custody, and operational practices.

Solid wood is only one option for cabinets. The boxes, frames, and shelving are often made with less expensive wood-based sheet goods such as particleboard, engineered wood products, fiberboard, MDF, or plywood. Sheet goods are often manufactured from mill by-products, wood chips, and other waste materials. These products are economical, and may be considered eco-friendly because they replace the need for wide planks of solid wood from old-growth trees.

Specify FSC or third-party certification of all engineered wood products. This ensures that the wood content was sustainably grown and not culled from endangered tropical rain forests or poorly managed tree farms. Look for sheet goods that are made from a high percentage of recycled wood.

Unfortunately, the drawback to using sheet goods is that standard cores and veneers usually contain formaldehyde in the binders or solvent-based finishes that outgas. Methylenediphenyl isocyanate (MDI) is a slightly greener binder that outgasses less, but it may still pose a risk to factory workers. Find a custom cabinetmaker who will work within specifications for all formaldehyde-free and low-VOC adhesives, binders, and finishes.

This kitchen features locally made,
unfinished cabinetry.
Photo by David O. Marlow.
Designer: Associates III,
www.associates3.com.

Biocomposite boards are another alternative for cabinetry (see Biocomposites, page 157). They are a first-class substitute for wood-based sheet goods because they are made from quickly renewable agricultural by-products, and some types are durable and attractive enough to be used for cabinet faces. In addition, biocomposite boards were developed to meet the need for renewable wood substitutes, so many manufacturers are ecologically minded and avoid the use of unhealthy chemicals in their products.

Melamine

Melamine-coated particleboard—often just called "melamine"—is a conventional option when purchasing stock cabinetry, especially for baths and closets. Melamine is a crystalline substance that is used as a resinous laminating agent for wood, countertops, paper, and textiles, and in leather tanning. It was once popular for making dishes (as in vintage Melmac). Most varieties of melamine are inert and insoluble once hardened. The shiny surface is easily wiped clean, and it's an inexpensive way to boost the appearance of particleboard.

There is concern that the manufacturing process, which is reliant on a chemical reaction with formaldehyde, is harmful to workers and to the environment. At the very least, it is an irritant to skin, eyes, and the throat. At its worst, it may cause kidney damage and is suspected of other health hazards. Melamine is neither biodegradable nor recyclable. The verdict? Although few formalized studies have established the risks from melamine to humans and to the earth, it's best to steer away from melamine in an eco-minded home.

Low-VOC, formaldehyde-free binders are common, as are low-toxic borate preservatives or pest repellants. It is difficult, however, for a designer or consumer to determine what farming standards were followed, as organic farming practices for biocomposite suppliers are not yet required.

Bamboo is another material to emerge as an eco-friendly alternative to wood. It regenerates more quickly than trees, has comparable hardness to many tree species, and is easily manufactured into sheet goods and cabinet faces and frames. Bamboo growers have been slower to adopt third-party certification standards, however, so it is difficult to verify the sustainability of the plantations or working conditions. When specifying bamboo, look for companies that set high environmental standards for themselves and can verify the working conditions of their sources.

Less common alternatives to traditional wooden cabinetry include metal or glass cabinetry and shelving (see Metals, page 129). Although metal is exceedingly durable, the environmental cost of mining, extraction of the ore, and long-distance transportation is very high. Metal cabinets and shelves, however, can easily be salvaged from commercial settings such as restaurants or vintage-era homes. Salvaging the shelves eliminates additional mining and reuses a valuable natural resource.

Glass shelving and glass for cabinet doors can be manufactured from recycled glass, or made new from common sand (see Glass Tile, page 192). Both glass and metal are inert and can be perpetually recycled or reused. The materials are ideal in homes where clients have allergies or chemical sensitivities. Cabinet hardware is made primarily from metal, (usually steel or brass), and is almost always purchased separately from the cabinets themselves. Salvaged hardware is particularly eco-friendly, as is metal or steel hardware that features high recycled content. Glass, wood, or ceramic pulls and knobs are other green options.

When researching and specifying cabinetry, inquire as to the types of glues, adhesives, paints, stains, and finishes that are used. This is particularly important if the client is sensitive to chemicals or odors. Request low-VOC adhesives or water-based wood glues ("white" or "yellow" glues) whenever possible. To seal particleboard or seams that might outgas, specify a water-based, low-VOC finish be applied before installation.

Most cabinets are finished as part of the assembly at the factory, which avoids introducing VOCs and odors into the home (although they will still outgas and affect the environment). It is possible, however, to order unfinished cabinets that can be left as they are or finished on-site. Unfinished cabinets are not ideal if they'll be exposed to high humidity, water, or stains (in a kitchen or bath, or in a very humid climate).

On-site finishing allows for more say in the exact type of finish, paint, or stain that is used. When finishing on-site, specify low-VOC, water-based products, or those made with natural oils or waxes.

Where Does It Come From?

- Solid wood cabinetry comes from trees.
- Some wood products are made from recycled wood scraps or sawdust, with acrylics or resins added.
- Sheet-good binders may incorporate low-VOC glues, outgassing solvents, formaldehyde, soy-based products, or natural or synthetic resins.
- Reclaimed wood is culled from residential, commercial, and agricultural floors, walls, and structures. Cabinets can be made from reclaimed wood, or complete units can be salvaged.
- Wood finishes or stains may contain a variety of natural oils, resins, or pigments; solvents; chemical compounds; petroleum distillates; metal drying agents; formaldehyde; or water.
- Biocomposite boards are made from a variety of agricultural by-products from wheat, rice, barley, or oat straw; sunflower hulls; bluegrass or rye grass stubble; cornhusks and sorghum stalks; hemp; soybean plants; and bagasse (sugar cane pulp).
- Biocomposites may contain residual pesticides or chemicals from crops, although the amount of such or frequency of use is unknown.
- Bamboo is technically a grass, grown for several years before harvest.
- Metal cabinetry can be made from all-new or recycled metal.
- Glass shelves and cabinet fronts are made from common sand or recycled glass.
- Hardware is usually made from steel, brass, or another metal, but it may also include components of glass, ceramic, or wood.

This bathroom has locally manufactured, reclaimed wood cabinetry. The space also features locally sourced wall sconces, an antique rug, and locally sourced mirrors wrapped with vegetable-dyed natural leather.
Photo by David O. Marlow.
Designer: Associates III,
www.associates3.com.

Installation

Cabinetry is bulky to ship. To reduce the embodied energy, employ a local cabinet-maker. When ordering stock or custom pieces, request that they be shipped in cardboard, kraft paper, or barrier cloth, instead of plastics or bulky, nonrecyclable (and possibly hazardous) foam. Specify that all shipping materials have recycled content and that they be recycled.

If the cabinets must be preassembled or finished on-site, specify that it be done outside. Request that the installer or contractor do all cutting outdoors, as well, to keep particulates and dust out of the living spaces.

If finishing the cabinets on-site, there is a higher risk of outgassing, odors, and irritation to the client. Factory-finished pieces, on the other hand, have had longer time to outgas prior to installation. Allow as much time as possible, before installation, for outgassing of the finish, paint, or adhesives (VOCs will still affect the environment but will not pose a direct risk to the occupants).

Weigh the finishing options carefully with the client. Whatever the final decision—unfinished, factory-finished, or finished on-site—specify the least toxic, lowest-VOC finish, paint, or stain available, preferably water-based or made with natural oils and extracts. Avoid finishes that contain chemical solvents, formaldehyde, or metallic drying agents.

Request that no finish or oils be applied to the hardware as a protective coating, or specify that natural waxes or oils be used instead. Specify that any oily residue on the metal from stock parts be removed with warm soapy water before installation.

Maintenance

Most casework requires little maintenance other than occasional dusting and cleaning with a damp cloth. Natural oil or wax finishes on wood or biocomposites require regular reapplications.

Where Does It Go?

Cabinets may be salvaged and reused, if in good condition. It is possible to downcycle wood cabinetry into another wood-based product. Wood or biocomposite boards will decompose easily (with the possible exception of the finishes, binders, and adhesives) back into soil. Binders, resins, stains, and finishes used within or on the cabinets will break down much more slowly. Metal and glass components can usually be recycled. Still-usable cabinet hardware such as pulls, hinges, and knobs should be taken to a construction exchange or salvage yard.

Spec List

Specify:
- Locally or domestically harvested, third-party-certified (FSC-certified), non-threatened wood species
- Salvaged cabinetry or reuse/renovation of existing cabinetry
- Glass shelving or cabinet door accents that are made from recycled glass
- Biocomposite boards or particleboard/plywood that is third-party certified, or particleboard that contains a high percentage of recycled wood
- Metal that has a high percentage of recycled material
- Hardware that is salvaged or that contains a high percentage of recycled material
- No oil finish on hardware, or its removal before installation
- Formaldehyde-free, low-VOC, water-based binders, sealants, adhesives, glues, and stains
- A minimum of shipping and handling, with recycled-content, all-recyclable paper, cloth, and cardboard

Specify Finishes and Stains That Are:
- Water-based
- Made of natural (sometimes called food-grade) oils, resins, pigments, and waxes
- Low-VOC
- Formaldehyde-free

- Free of metallic drying agents
- Solvent-free

  Avoid:
- Reclaimed wood of uncertain origin in kitchen applications or where the use of it might be unsafe
- Uncertified wood
- Rare or threatened tree species
- Solvent-based finishes
- Melamine
- Formaldehyde and other preservatives in the wood product or finish
- Metal-based drying agents in the finish
- Engineered wood, unless certified
- Formaldehyde in the binder or finish
- Preservatives or pesticides (other than borate)
- Foam, "peanuts," or plastic in the shipping materials

RESOURCES

Forest Stewardship Council U.S.: www.FSCUS.org
SmartWood (Rainforest Alliance): www.Smartwood.org

Textiles

Textiles serve many purposes in residential design, some purely utilitarian, some wonderfully aesthetic. They protect surfaces from wear, provide softness to the touch, filter light, and wrap us in warmth. To the client, however, the greatest function textiles may serve is to add beauty to the home through the use of color, texture and pattern. Residential fabrics in all their manifestations—bedding, upholstery, rugs, window treatments, accessories, and even art—bring a deep sense of personalization and comfort to the home.

The definition of textile technically includes every type of cloth, from natural knits and wovens to synthetics spun from petroleum or fiberglass filaments. When designing a home to tread softly on the earth and be healthful to the occupant, emphasize natural materials. Fibers derived from plants and animals come from renewable resources, and they can be harvested annually, or at least regularly enough to keep replenishing the supply. And when a natural fiber has worn out or needs to be discarded, it will biodegrade.

The majority of synthetic fibers are derived from petroleum, a nonrenewable resource that is then liquefied and extruded into a filament or yarn. A chemical dye is usually introduced when the liquid is blended, as most synthetic fabrics do not accept dyes well once they are made. Ultimately, the finished products won't easily biodegrade, and synthetic residential textiles are not often recycled.

This living space features all natural fabrics for the sofas, wool carpet, and a lamp made from sea branches. Photo courtesy of Stefano Dorata Architetto, www.stefanodorata.com.

Newer synthetics have been introduced that are made from renewable materials such as soy or perpetually recyclable polyester. Some of these are biodegradable or can be easily recycled or downcycled; check with the manufacturer or supplier for specifics. The manufacturing of any synthetic fabric, however, requires a heftier amount of energy than that which is spun from natural fibers or handmade.

To go fully green in the selection of residential textiles requires a commitment to more than just the basic fiber type. It is easy to find cloth made from natural materials, such as cotton, silk, hemp, flax or wool, but it's more challenging to find fibers that haven't been dyed with synthetic colorants, treated with chemicals to enhance fabric performance, or farmed or produced with the use of pesticides. Textiles made from raw materials that are organically grown or raised with sustainable methods make up only a small fraction of the market. Organic cotton, one example of an all-natural fiber that's rising in popularity, makes up only about .03 percent of the cotton supply (Organic

Textile Terminology

The word "textile" is derived from the Latin *textilis*, meaning "woven fabric." Today, the term has come to apply to any fabrics, threads, or yarns that are woven, knitted, felted, or braided together.

Textiles through Time

Prehistory	Human beings weave grasses and skins to make clothing and durable coverings for rooftops.
5000 BCE	Flax (linen), possibly the oldest spun fiber, was used to make burial shrouds for the Egyptians.
5000 to 3000 BCE	Cotton and wool are spun into fibers and used for clothing.
1725 BCE	Silk-spinning becomes an "industry" in China.
1793	Eli Whitney invents the cotton gin, which is more efficient than human labor for picking and separating cotton.
1884	The power loom is invented and mechanizes weaving.
1910	Rayon, the first manufactured fiber, is introduced and mass-produced.
Twentieth century	Acetate, polyester, polypropylene, nylon, and other manufactured fibers are introduced.
2004	The Organic Trade Association (OTA) establishes standards for the processing and certification of textile fibers.

Trade Association, www.ota.com). It will take some scouting to find all-organic textile sources.

Most textiles are mass-produced in factories, which are not immune to the problems common to other large industries: wastewater pollution, hazardous by-products, questionable working conditions, and air quality issues. In addition, any number of harsh or hazardous chemicals might be introduced to the textiles through the washing, dyeing, weaving, and finishing stages; but the specifics won't be revealed on the labels. To avoid these pitfalls, look for artisans or companies with strict environmental policies, and for products that feature natural dyes, fibers, and fabric treatments.

PLANT AND ANIMAL FIBERS (INCLUDING LEATHER)

Cotton, linen, hemp, ramie, jute, coir, silk, and wool are all common examples of textiles that are made from natural plant and animal fibers, and there are many more. Fundamentally, natural fibers are always preferable when weighing the choices for ecological characteristics They come from renewable sources that are replenished in a matter of months or years, far less time than the usual life span of the fabric. They offer breathability rarely found in synthetics, and they will biodegrade easily.

However, not all fiber farming, harvesting, or acquisition methods are alike. Some respect the earth and its inhabitants more than others. Traditional cotton crops, for example, are notoriously heavy on pesticide and fertilizer use (see "The Truth About Cotton," page 334), and the majority of animal farm operations rely on chemical pest control methods. Although it is unlikely that pesticide residual will directly harm the client after the extensive washing and processing done to fibers and fabrics in mills, the chemicals are fundamentally bad for the environment and extremely toxic to our water, air, and soil.

Organic or sustainable farming, on the other hand, uses natural methods for enriching soil and preventing pest damage and disease. Instead of relying on chemicals, strategies are employed that use natural controls such as beneficial insects, compost as a fertilizer, and crop rotation to maintain soil productivity. Sustainable agriculture may also focus on providing the animals with an open range for grazing, natural foods, and respectful and humane treatment. While initially more expensive for the farmer, and thus the consumer, the long-term yields from sustainable agriculture include less erosion, better soil, healthier ecosystems, and a quality product that harms neither the earth nor the consumer.

There is no universal certifying agency for organic fibers, although many third-party groups and growers' associations provide acceptable criteria. The Organic Trade Association (OTA) has established certification standards for the processing of textile fibers that cover postharvest handling, wet processing (including bleaching, dyeing, printing), fabrication, product assembly, storage and transportation, pest management, and labeling of finished products. If the fiber source is also a food source, such as cotton (grown for cottonseed oil), the growers may follow federal guidelines for organic food production. Wool and cotton are commonly certified through the OTA. Look for natural-fiber textiles from companies that subscribe to a certification process or follow eco-friendly farming practices.

Artisans are often excellent sources for all-natural textiles, as many eschew high-tech methods in favor of weaving or spinning by hand, dyeing with local plants, or even raising their own crops or animals. By selecting a local artisan's textiles, the energy consumed through shipping will be reduced, as well. Cooperatives are excellent resources for locating artisans; consult with local indigenous tribes, the county extension office, or artist guilds.

If the textile comes from abroad, it is worth the effort to check into whether fair trade standards are practiced. Reasonable pay and good working conditions may not seem, at first glance, to have an impact on the environment, but indirectly, they almost always do (see Fair Trade, page 379). Companies that value workers and their families will also value health and environmental well-being, and are unlikely to utilize highly toxic chemicals or strip the ecosystem for the sake of a profit. Fair trade most often focuses on maximizing the assets that a region already possesses, both human and environmental. Specify fair-trade or cooperative-made textiles if purchasing them from a developing region.

Next to its origin, the suitability of a fiber to a particular application or environment is probably the most important factor to consider. If it deteriorates when subjected to domestic rigors, washed in water, or exposed to sunlight, then it may not be the best choice for the home. Textiles should be durable enough for the intended purpose and need little upkeep. They should also be easy to wash or clean, as chemical dry cleaning and stain repellents negate many of the green attributes of natural fabrics.

Consider the following natural fibers when specifying textiles. Although this list is not comprehensive, and infinite combinations and blends exist, these are some of the most popular eco-friendly choices.

Cotton

Cotton is known for its cool temperature against the skin and its capability to absorb—20 times or more its own weight in water. The cotton fiber is harvested from the cottonseed pod. Cotton usually has a white or cream color but can be grown with other natural color variations such as rust, tan, grey, and even a bluish hue. It readily accepts dye and stands up to very hot water and sanitization, making it an ideal fiber for use in homes where the clients have allergies or health issues. Conventional cotton fabric, however, is typically farmed using large amounts of chemical pesticides and fertilizers (see the sidebar). Specify organic cotton, and look for unbleached or naturally dyed fibers. Avoid wrinkle-resistance or sizing treatments, and flame retardants.

The Truth about Cotton

- Cotton farming uses more than 25 percent of all the pesticides in the world.
- Seven times more chemical fertilizer than pesticides is used to grow cotton.
- The cotton for one T-shirt has been grown with a third of a pound of chemicals.
- The EPA has declared 7 of the top 15 pesticides used by cotton growers as potential or known carcinogens.
- Cotton is also a food crop. U.S. residents eat and drink more cotton, usually in the form of cottonseed oil (found in such foods as coffee creamer, salad dressings, and candy bars), than that which they wear or sleep on.

Sources: Organic Trade Association, www.ota.com; and Organic Consumer Association, www.organicconsumers.org

Wool

Wool is a favorite for warmth and durability, and will literally last for centuries with proper care. Various species of animal produce distinct types of wool: sheep, goat, vicuna, alpaca, llama, angora, and camel. Wool is usually acquired from the shearing of live animals, which for some species is beneficial. Some animals are bred for their different coat coloration that produce subtle, natural hues.

Wool absorbs approximately 30 times its weight in moisture before actually feeling wet; conversely, the natural lanolin and oils present in wool help it to shed water. Some people dislike wool because the curly fibers cause them to itch, although a true allergy to wool is very rare. Certain species, such as merino, are less troublesome for those with such sensitivities.

The particular "scales" of the wool fiber strands enable them to stick together when abraded, producing a dense felt that is popular for making rugs, blankets, and clothing.

Whenever possible, specify organic wool that is sustainably farmed. Also specify no dyes, or that natural dyeing processes be used.

Silk

Silk is derived from the natural protein fibers from the cocoon of the silkworm, which are then spun into filaments. Silk is very durable—a strand of steel will break before a strand of silk of the same diameter. It is incredibly lustrous and accepts dye well; it is warm in the winter and cool in the summer, is moisture-absorbent, and will not shrink. Bright sunlight or high heat will damage silk, however.

Organic methods of cultivating silk are becoming more common, where cocoons are harvested after the butterfly has left, rather than harvesting by boiling the cocoons to remove the larvae.

The issue of child labor has arisen in some Asian countries where silk is produced. Look for silk producers that prohibit child labor, as well as those that promote sustainable, organic production.

Linen

Linen is probably the oldest textile in the world. It is a fiber taken from the stalk of the flax plant, and it obtains its luster from the natural waxes present. Although it has poor elasticity (the fabric can actually fray along creases), the fiber itself is several times stronger than cotton. It can also be sanitized in hot water. The natural color is a light tan or cream, and linen readily accepts dye.

Hemp

Hemp (sometimes called mountain grass) is a controversial fiber, if only because it comes from the species from which marijuana is acquired. The plant can't be cultivated for any purpose in the United States. However, hemp textiles are made from the stems, not the narcotic flowers, seeds, or leaves. The fabric is similar to linen in feel. It wrinkles easily and will break if excessively creased.

Ramie, Jute, Coir, and Sisal

Ramie comes from a plant in the nettle family. It is similar to linen and is often used in cotton blends to increase the strength of the fabric—though it may be prone to shrinkage or become rough when washed. Most ramie fibers are grown in Asia.

Jute, coir, and sisal are similar fibers. They are very durable, but quite rough in texture, hence most often used for rope, twine, rugs, and backings. Both jute and sisal are acquired from the stalks of plants, whereas coir is made from coconut husks.

Leather and Skins

Leather and skins, although not traditionally categorized as textiles, are used for many of the same purposes: upholstery, accessories, and rugs. Leather breathes, is soft and pliable, and is very durable.

In many cultures, the use of animal skins for shelter, clothing, and ornament is considered fundamental—even sacred—as no part is wasted in the continuum of life and death. However, some persons object to the use of animal products for ethical reasons, others, because of their faith. Therefore, consult with the client when contemplating the use of animal products.

That said, the primary criterion for incorporating leather or skins into a green home focuses on whether the processing is natural or chemical. Modern tanning of leather relies on toxic chromium and chemical baths, and an enormous amount of water for rinsing and processing those chemicals. These baths are a health risk for workers. The chemicals may also impart an odor to the home. Opt instead for leather or skins from companies that feature vegetable-based tanning processes that rely on natural tannins from rhubarb, tree bark, tare, and valonea. These same companies feature natural vegetable and mineral dyes.

Leather or skins are often obtained as a secondary product of the meat industry. Tanneries with a focus on sustainable, natural methods may acquire their materials from organic ranches that provide a pesticide-free, all-natural environment for the animals. Inquire as to the source. Conversely, if seeking a natural tannery, check with an organic ranch.

BIO-BASED SYNTHETICS

Rayon was the first synthetic textile. It is produced through the chemical treatment of wood pulp (cellulose), which is liquefied and then extruded as a filament. It's not exactly an all-natural fiber, but the incorporation of renewable materials has its merits. In recent years, in the drive to lessen our dependence on nonrenewable resources such as petroleum, manufacturers have been developing other bio-based synthetic textiles that are derived from sustainable sources such as corn, soybeans, sugar beets, rice, or wood pulp. Some of these textiles are designed to improve particular characteristics that are difficult to find in all-natural materials, such as for surgical applications or institutional settings.

The development of new textile fibers is a commendable effort, especially if the raw material is renewable and the final product biodegrades or can be recycled. However, the intensive manufacturing process required adds considerable embodied energy over that of a plant or animal fiber that is simply spun or woven. For most residential applications, the benefits of bio-based synthetics may be negligible.

SYNTHETICS

The big names in synthetic fabrics and fibers include, but are not limited to: acetate, acrylic, nylon, and polyester. The vast majority are derived from chemicals or petroleum. In a few cases, synthetics have characteristics that are difficult to duplicate in nature, such as the elasticity of nylon. In general, they are less breathable and don't absorb moisture well (either an asset or a drawback, depending on the application). Most synthetics are dyed with artificial colorants, then treated with more chemical finishes. Limit the use of these conventional synthetic textiles.

There has been a concerted effort among textile manufacturers to develop synthetics that act like natural materials in that they are not harmful to the consumers and they biodegrade or can be recycled indefinitely. These new synthetics may even improve on natural materials, with longer life cycles, greater durability, or a specialized application such as for medical use. Some are made from consumer and commercial waste, further diverting materials from the landfill. Others are hybrids that are made from natural materials in a synthetic process. A few manufacturers accept their synthetic textiles back for recycling into new fibers or fabric, therefore maintaining a closed-loop system.

The vast majority of these new synthetics have been developed for commercial use, but a few have entered the residential market. While natural materials are still the top choice for most applications in green residential design, there will be more options in the future for more environmentally friendly synthetic textiles.

RECYCLED TEXTILES

Before the era of industrialization, fabric scraps were seldom wasted because the making of any textile required vast amounts of personal energy spent preparing the fibers, spinning, knitting, and weaving. One of the best examples of this frugality is the patchwork quilt. Following this idea, the most innovative eco-strategy of all might be to use what the client already has. Antique or vintage quilts, tea towels, and other linens

These pillows are made from reused French linen tablecloths.
Heiberg Cummings Design, Southampton Design Project, www.Hcd3.com.

that have been relegated to a drawer might be ready for a new life as pillowcases, window coverings, tablecloths, or slipcovers.

Everyone, from the large manufacturers to individual artisans, in a nod to growing environmental concerns, is coming up with resourceful ways to use waste textiles. Scraps from the mill floors, yarn ends, and even recycled denim jeans are finding their way into new fabrics or other products such as insulation. Sometimes the processes require little additional energy, such as when rags are handsewn into patchworks or handwoven into rugs. Others are more energy-intensive methods performed in factories, such as turning the fibers into pulp, or respinning them, then weaving or pressing them into new textiles. In an effort to reclaim materials that might otherwise be landfilled, mills now recycle polyester, carpet fibers, or other synthetics into new textiles. Some synthetics or natural-fiber textiles may be continually recycled, and a few manufacturers will accept back their own textiles at the end of the life cycle.

If the client is interested in recycled materials, these options may be appealing. Check with the manufacturer or artisan for details on the content and processing for specific recycled textiles.

DYES

The natural dyes from plants, animals, and minerals are preferred for coloring textiles that will be in an eco-friendly home. Berries, bark, insects, spices, and many common plants can be used to tint the dye bath, and simple vinegar or pickling alum is often used to set the dye. Natural dyes are unlikely to be a problem for sensitive individuals, but if chronic allergies are an issue, it may be advisable to specify no dye.

The entire spectrum of color is available from natural dyes, although they are generally a bit more muted than the brightest chemical dyes. Naturally dyed textiles will require more gentle washing (cold water, little agitation, mild soap) to retain the vivid hues.

Chlorine bleach is frequently used to whiten cotton and other fibers, but it is highly caustic and toxic. In addition, bleach removes some of the natural finish present in cotton, making the texture slightly rougher. Recommend no chlorine bleach.

Chemical dyes and colorants are frequently used on both natural fibers and synthetics, especially those that are commercially made. The textile label is not required to list the type of dyes used, but those who specialize in natural textiles frequently supply this information. Request information on the dyes to avoid all synthetic substances, or specify no dye.

FABRIC TREATMENTS

Textile mills employ the use of hundreds of different chemicals for stiffening, softening, sheen, wrinkle-proofing, stain and water resistance, and colorfastness. The treatments of potential interest to the consumer—special stain resistors, for example—are listed on the labels, but there's no requirement to do so. Some of these chemical agents are under scrutiny for health hazards (see page 356, "PBDEs"), and others may be issues for those who are chemically sensitive. To avoid chemical treatments altogether, seek out specialty textile producers such as artisans or small mills that make all-natural fabrics.

Some fibers inherently possess resistance to water and stains. Wool, for example, contains lanolin, an oily substance that is so effective at waterproofing that it's used in furniture polish and hand creams. The best method for preventing textile damage and ensuring longevity is careful selection of the most appropriate fabric for the intended purpose.

A few specialty retailers and distributors that cater to environmentally friendly interiors offer prewashed textile choices that have been cleansed of all finishes and fabric treatments. The companies that offer this washing process, in some cases, may provide it for textiles other than those they have manufactured. If the client has chemical sensitivities, this service may be especially valuable.

TEXTILE LABELING

Although not all textile products are required by law to carry labels, many companies provide them voluntarily. They may be attached to the product, on the end of a bolt, or on a separate tag, depending on the item. The content of the label is strictly governed by the Textile Fiber Products Identification Act of 1960, which prohibits misrepresentation of the content. When purchasing off-the-shelf textiles or those from a standard retailer, the labels can be helpful in determining whether a product possesses eco-friendly qualities.

What the labels must include:

- Generic fiber name (wool, cotton, etc.)
- Percentage, by weight, of each kind of fiber
- The manufacturer, by name or registered number (The Federal Trade Commission has a list; www.ftc.gov/bcp/conline/pubs/buspubs/thread.htm.)
- Where the textile was made or assembled

What they typically don't include:

- How the fabric was made (woven, braided, etc.)
- Dye content
- Finishes or fabric treatments

Wool and cotton are governed under separate labeling acts that require more specific information. Wool labels tell whether the fibers are virgin (new) or recycled, and the species of animal (merino, vicuna). If the fiber content is 100 percent wool or 100 percent cotton, the textile label will display a special mark.

Care labels, which are optional on nonclothing and nonfabric (leather or fur) items, indicate the best possible cleaning and pressing methods according to the manufacturer. The manufacturer always recommends the most gentle cleaning technique that is least likely to change the quality of the textile in any way, but it is often possible to clean the textile using another method. Avoid textiles that are labeled "Dry Clean Only" unless it's reasonably certain they may be washed instead. Wool, silk, and even cotton, for example, carry "Dry Clean Only" labels, and with careful precautions or the use of a test swatch, are often washable.

Where Does It Come From?

- Textiles may come from all-natural plant or animal fibers; from recycled fabrics and yarns; from petroleum-based or chemical synthetics, extruded fibers; or from bio-based synthetics.
- Bio-synthetic fabrics are made from renewable, natural products such as paper or wood pulp, soy, corn, or bamboo.
- Plant-based fibers such as cotton, jute, hemp, and ramie may be organically grown, or may be grown with conventional farming methods.
- Animal products such as wool and leather may come from sustainably managed or "humane" ranches, or may come from conventional ranch facilities.
- Dyes are derived from natural sources such as plants and minerals, and are also made from chemicals.
- Most common fabric treatments are chemically based, but there are all-natural options made from plants and minerals.
- Leather may be tanned with chromium and chemicals or, less commonly, with natural bark and vegetable agents.

Maintenance

The best "maintenance" for textiles is in careful selection of materials that are most appropriate to the setting and intended use. If the client has children or animals and the textile will be used daily or will be subjected to regular washing or sunlight, then delicate fabrics with special care requirements would not be eco-friendly choices. A poor choice of fiber may wear out too soon, the color may fade, or the textile may need special chemical cleaning methods to restore its appearance.

Simple soap and water, dusting, or vacuuming are the preferred cleaning methods for residential textiles. Borax or borate, a mineral found in nature, can be added to the wash cycle as a whitening agent. For deodorizing, baking soda is still the champion, either washed in water or sprinkled on the textile (such as a rug) and vacuumed. Natural stain removal "tricks" may even work better than commercial, eco-unfriendly solvents. Visit the Internet for healthy cleaning tips, or give the client a book on the subject for future reference. The county extension office is another valuable source for helpful hints on textile care.

Fabrics that need dry cleaning are less desirable simply because they require transportation to a dry cleaner; special equipment is needed; and conventional dry cleaning methods use chemicals and solvents. There has been a recent movement toward healthier dry cleaning methods, where carbon dioxide (CO_2)—the "fizzy" gas in soda pop—is being successfully used. Employ businesses that rely on CO_2 methods if dry cleaning is absolutely necessary.

Where Does It Go?

Natural plant-fiber textiles can be shredded for compost. A few types of synthetic fabrics can be recycled, downcycled, or reprocessed into new textiles or other polymers. Most synthetics, however, end up in landfills and biodegrade slowly, if at all.

> **Textile Maintenance Tips**
>
> There are dozens of commercial detergents, stain removers, bleaches, and fabric softeners on the shelves, mostly made from a variety of chemical compounds that aren't safe for the environment or for human health. Traditional, natural, nontoxic methods are best for keeping textiles clean.
>
> - Use water temperature and proper care as recommended on the label; use cold water if no label is present or no instructions are listed.
> - Purchase laundry soap that is biodegradable.
> - If the client is sensitive to odors, avoid scented soaps.
> - Avoid chlorine bleach.
> - To boost cleaning power, add baking soda or borax to the wash water.
> - To brighten their appearance, hang all-cotton whites in direct sunlight to dry.
> - Avoid hanging darker colors or brights in direct sunlight.
> - If using the dryer, choose a medium temperature setting instead of a hotter one, to reduce wear on the fabrics and to keep them softer. A low dryer temperature also conserves energy.
> - Hang or fold textiles immediately when they are dry to avoid the need for ironing, which is hard on the fabrics.

Although leather is by nature resilient to deterioration from the elements, it will eventually decompose. Tannery chemicals and synthetic fabric treatments, usually considered hazardous waste in quantity, pose serious risks to water and soil when landfilled.

Spec List

Specify:

- Natural plant- or animal-based fibers
- Fibers that are organically grown or sustainably farmed/obtained
- Textiles that are minimally processed, without added chemicals or dyes
- Textiles without dyes
- Textiles with natural dyes from plant, animal, or mineral sources
- Textiles that may be cleaned with natural or benign methods such as dusting, soap and water, or vacuuming
- Natural stain and water repellants (tightest weave, lanolin in wool, etc.)
- Biosynthetic fabrics, preferably recyclable or biodegradable, made from a high percentage of renewable, natural products such as paper or wood pulp, soy, corn, or bamboo

- Vegetable tanning and dyeing processes for leather that rely on natural elements such as tare (vetch seed), rhubarb, valonea (oak tree acorn "beard" in Turkey or Greece), and tree bark
- Locally tanned leather with minimal chemical processing or dyes
- Locally made textiles by artisans, especially those who use nonmechanized methods
- Recycled-content textiles
- Reuse of textiles

Avoid:

- Synthetic fibers made from petroleum products or chemicals
- Fibers from farms or suppliers that use pesticides or biocides
- Chlorine bleach
- Chemical deodorizers, detergents, or dry cleaning agents
- Fireproofing treatments
- Chemical dyes
- Synthetic waterproofing/stainproofing treatments
- Leather tanned with chromium
- Chemically dyed or treated leather

RESOURCES

Hemp Industries Association:www.thehia.org
International Federation of Organic Agriculture Movements: www.ifoam.org
Organic Trade Association: www.ota.com
Sustainable Cotton Association:www.sustainablecotton.org

Case Pieces

Strive to make every case piece eco-friendly. To do so usually requires ordering specialty or custom-made furniture to detailed green specifications, as big-box retailers or large furniture manufacturers generally don't have items that meet these standards. Look for all-natural materials, those made with recycled components, and those finished with nontoxic, low-VOC substances (see Stains, Finishes, and Adhesives, page 248).

Whether restoring an antique or purchasing new furnishings, evaluate each component for its effect on the earth and home. If new furniture will be ordered, select a company with established environmental guidelines that uses all-natural materials or third-party certified or those with a high percentage of recycled or salvaged materials. Look for furniture manufacturers who: keep a "clean" manufacturing floor, free from toxins and VOCs; ship the pieces with a minimum of packaging, made from recycled content and recyclable or reusable materials; and have an eco-friendly waste management program for scraps.

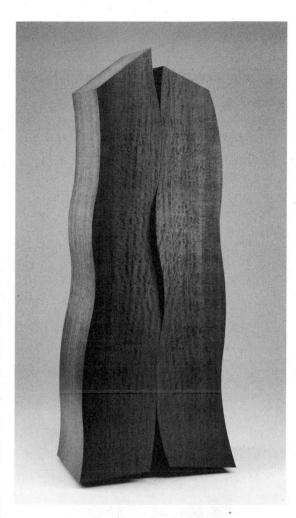

Fitted as a humidor, this armoire is certified by the Forest Stewardship Council (FSC) for being crafted primarily of certified wood that was harvested in a sustainable manner from a well-managed forest.
Photo by John Glos Designer: John Wiggers.

RECYCLED/SALVAGED CASE PIECES

Before purchasing new furnishings, consider what the client already owns or has access to. One of the most practical ways to have eco-friendly furnishings is to start with salvaged frames and case goods. Residential furnishings are major contributors to landfills—so much so that many landfills charge fees for disposal of large items such as chairs, sofas, desks, and dressers. Yet a high percentage of what is tossed is still perfectly usable or could be restored with elbow grease. Ask the client if there are pieces that might be reupholstered, antiques that could be refinished, or furnishings that need only touch-ups or repairs to be revitalized. In addition to being environmentally thrifty, the client might appreciate the TLC given to a worn-out but cherished furnishing.

Flexibility Is Eco-Friendly

Modular case pieces are eco-smart choices because they are versatile. As children grow up, as design tastes change, or if the client moves to a new home, the components can be put together in new configurations or rearranged. No new furniture need be purchased and no more resources need to be consumed.

Request modular case pieces made from certified solid wood or recycled metal such as steel. Many modular components are made from particleboard; if this is the client's preference, be sure to specify formaldehyde-free, low-VOC binders and finishes, and request certified wood or biocomposite wood substitutes.

This bench is made of felled, torched fir.
© 2006 Johngranen.com.
Designer: John Wells.

Freecycling

"Think globally, recycle locally." That's the mantra of a loosely organized, nonprofit, Web-based initiative called Freecycle that diverts millions of items from landfills around the globe by putting them into the hands of those who can use them. The idea is simple: Announce still-usable items you have to give away through the Freecycle Web site. Those seeking such items scout the listings, then respond and arrange for pickup. Even items that others have set out to be picked up by the trash collectors can be listed.

There are millions of Freecycle participants worldwide, in thousands of communities (it's organized by region or city); "membership" is free. It's a great place to scout for furniture, or to give away the bunk bed that the kids outgrew. And ultimately, by extending the life span of items and diverting them from the landfills, this grassroots effort is helping save the environment.

For more information, or to find a Freecycle online group, visit www.freecycle.org .

The older the furniture, the more likely it was made from solid wood and steel, iron, or brass components—materials that may last for many more decades. Case pieces constructed after 1960 were frequently made with cheaper plywood, particleboard, or aluminum, and may not be salvageable if damaged. Sometimes, however, a component of the old furnishing can be adapted for a new use. For instance, if the tabletop is damaged but the legs are still good, brainstorm with a furniture restorer for reuse ideas.

Also take into account whether the piece can be renovated without the use of harsh chemicals, especially if the client is sensitive to odors or chemicals. Conventional furniture restoration relies on toxic solvents to strip the finish or paint. Consult with a restoration specialist to determine whether minor touch-ups, a new coat of zero-VOC paint, or a thorough cleaning and conditioning with all-natural oils or waxes might suffice.

There are a few new furniture stripping products on the market that are derived from soy or natural resins, rather than petrochemicals. Although these certainly are an improvement, as they rely on a renewable resource and are usually lower in VOC emissions, they potentially pose health risks and should be used with caution.

Another advantage to using older furnishings is that the longer the life span of the piece, the more sustainable the resources become. A century-old rocker, for example, may have survived longer than the tree from which it was made. It may cost a bit more to restore a piece of such furniture, but it saves our natural resources.

WOOD CASE PIECES AND WOOD SUBSTITUTES

The majority of furnishings feature wood as the main component of the frame. Solid wood has a beautiful grain and is very durable. It's natural, recyclable or biodegradable, and basically renewable if the furnishing outlasts the tree from which it was made. On the other hand, cheaply made pieces that don't last and are quickly disposed of only contribute to the problem of deforestation and ecosystem loss. Selecting and specifying wood case pieces that will last through several generations is a fundamental ecological principle.

Kiln-dried wood is highly desirable for furniture that must bear weight because the process strengthens the frame and keeps it from warping or splitting. By thoroughly eliminating all but a small percentage of moisture through kiln drying, the wood becomes less vulnerable to changes in humidity and temperature. The method does in-

This loveseat is made from storm-felled hornbeam and wood dye.
Charcoal Love Gulliver's Chair, Field, Monika Zanolin, 2006
Designer: Julienne Dolphin-Wilding.

crease the embodied energy, but the improved longevity makes it worthwhile. Most quality furniture makers use kiln-dried wood.

Whenever possible, specify third-party-certified wood (such as through the FSC) to ensure environmentally friendly forestry, milling, and distribution practices. Some furniture makers now offer this option. Also specify wood species that are not endangered (see Wood Species List, page 147), avoiding those that come from unknown or uncertified sources. Local or domestic wood sources should be favored over tropical species and those that are shipped long distances, in order to lower the embodied energy.

Turning reclaimed or salvaged wood into new furnishings is another worthy approach. SmartWood, a program of the Rainforest Alliance, provides a certification program for rediscovered wood operations (RWOs) that sell reclaimed wood products, as well as for new wood. Many RWOs still do not carry this certification, however. Whenever specifying wood for interior use, inquire as to the source. Avoid reclaimed wood that has been treated for outdoor use, or that may have been exposed to contaminants from industry or agriculture.

Particleboard, MDF, and other engineered, wood-based sheet goods are commonly used in less expensive furnishings. The eco-advantage to engineered wood is that it avoids using wide planks of solid wood from older-growth trees, and uses "scrap" instead. Look for engineered wood and sheet goods that are manufactured with a high percent of the content from mill by-products, wood chips, and other "waste" materials. Specify FSC or third-party certification to ensure that the wood content was sustainably grown.

Unfortunately, sheet goods often contain formaldehyde in the binders or solvent-based finishes, so they outgas harmful emissions. Specify formaldehyde-free and low-VOC adhesives, binders, and finishes in all engineered wood products.

See also Wood, page 139.

OTHER CASE PIECE MATERIALS

Biocomposites (see Biocomposites, page 157) are sheet goods made from continually renewable agricultural by-products such as wheat, sunflowers, soybeans, or rice. They are enjoying increased popularity as a wood substitute in furniture case pieces, and each type of biocomposite has a distinctive textural grain or look. Binders are necessary to hold the fibers together, so specify that they be low-VOC, formaldehyde-free, and solvent-free. Also specify low-VOC, formaldehyde-free finishes and stains.

Bamboo is a grass that regenerates quickly and has the hardness of wood, and is another alternative to wood. It is often used as a veneer over a wood core. Sometimes, solid bamboo is used as furniture legs or in decorative pieces. Some manufacturers of bamboo case pieces rely on urea formaldehyde binders, so specify formaldehyde-free. Also specify water based or low-VOC finishes.

Third-party certification of bamboo plantations or products is still uncommon, so look for companies that set high environmental standards for themselves.

Metal frames, legs, tabletops, and even chair seats are popular because they are extremely sturdy, need little upkeep, and can support a great deal of weight. The disadvantages to using newly mined and fabricated metal include the high embodied energy from the mining and smelting, and the depletion of nonrenewable resources (see

This clerestory end table is made from found chestnut, with a steel top.
© 2006 Johngranen.com.
Designer: John Wells.

Metals, page 129). On the other hand, metal is perpetually recyclable, so most metal components can be recycled. Look for new metal furniture that has been fabricated from a high percentage of recycled steel, aluminum, or other metal.

Because metal furnishings and frames are so durable, they are often available for salvage. If the metal is in good condition, simple cleaning may restore the piece so that it is usable. Consider reuse of the client's existing metal case pieces, or salvage from a second-hand source.

If the metal won't rust or corrode, specify it be left unfinished. Request that any synthetic oil protectant used on the metal be removed before installation in the home (soap and warm water usually suffices), or specify no oil or natural oils instead. Synthetic oils may also aggravate chemical sensitivities.

Factory-finished metal is better than metal that must be painted or finished on-site, especially when client chemical sensitivities are an issue, as paint or finishes for metal are solvent-based and emit VOCs. Manufacturers can control the conditions for application, and the piece will be able to outgas before it is in the home. Avoid plating, which is environmentally hazardous and dangerous to factory workers. Powder coatings outgas very little after the initial drying, and are virtually inert when dry, making them the best paint choice for metal in a green home.

Recycled Plastic—To Use or Not to Use?

Recycled plastic is showing up in a variety of home furnishings. Outdoor furniture, children's play sets, folding tables and chairs, and bathroom accessories often incorporate plastic because it is waterproof, stainproof, and impervious to abuse. Plus, plastic recycling saves the environment. Or does it?

At its best, plastic is easy to clean, can be molded into any shape, and is sanitary—hence its indispensability in hospitals and health care settings. At its worst, plastic manufacturing uses nonrenewable petroleum and a variety of chemical ingredients, many of which are toxic to humans. PVC, probably the most notorious example, is known to outgas considerably, giving off a distinct smell characteristic to soft plastics and vinyl. It is now considered a health risk to workers and consumers alike. And it doesn't biodegrade.

Recycling of plastic is, fundamentally, a good idea. Americans generate more than 26 million tons of plastic waste every year (EPA, www.epa.gov), much of it from food and beverage containers and retail packaging (e.g., "clamshells" and polystyrene foam). The plastic recycling process takes plastic objects of the same type (the numbers on the bottom indicate this), melts them down, and reforms them into new objects such as decking and plastic "lumber," picnic tables and toddler-sized chairs. The question is, is this the best use?

Although some plastic in the home is practically inevitable in modern society, we strongly recommend that natural materials be the first choice. In particular, avoid plastics where they might cause the most harm through accidental ingestion or constant exposure to them, especially in children's furnishings and kitchens.

Sources: Healthy Building Network, www.healthybuilding.net; Greenpeace, http://archive.greenpeace.org/toxics/pvcdatabase; Grassroots Recycling Network, http://www.grrn.org/pvc/; Healthcare Without Harm, http://www.noharm.org/us/pvcDehp/issue)

Where Does It Come From?

- Solid wood case pieces and furnishings come from trees.
- Some wood products are made from recycled wood scraps or sawdust with acrylics or resins added.
- Reclaimed wood is culled from residential, commercial, and agricultural floors, walls, and structures and can be made into beautiful furniture.
- Biocomposite boards are made from a variety of crops, residues, and grains that may include: wheat, rice, barley, or oat straw; sunflower hulls; bluegrass or rye grass stubble; cornhusks and sorghum stalks; hemp; soybean plants; and bagasse (sugar cane pulp).
- Biocomposites may contain residual pesticides or chemicals from crops, although the amount or frequency of such is unknown.
- Bamboo is technically a grass, grown for several years before harvest.
- Sheet-good binders may include low-VOC glues, outgassing solvents, formaldehyde, soy-based products, and natural or synthetic resins.
- Metal is mined from various locations around the world, smelted at high temperatures, then fabricated into furnishings. Some metal is recycled from used metal products.
- Finishes, paints, or stains may contain natural oils, resins or pigments; solvents; chemical compounds; petroleum distillates; metal drying agents; formaldehyde; and sometimes water.
- Plastics are made from petroleum by-products.

Installation

When ordering, request that all case pieces be shipped in cardboard, kraft paper, or barrier cloth, instead of plastics or bulky, nonrecyclable (and possibly hazardous) synthetic foam "peanuts" or pieces. Specify that all shipping materials be made with recycled content, and that they be recycled after use.

If the case pieces will be factory assembled and finished, specify the use of low-VOC adhesives or water-based wood glues ("white" or "yellow" glues) whenever possible. Factory-finished pieces will be able to outgas prior to installation, which is helpful for those with chemical sensitivities—although the outgassing still negatively affects the environment.

If finishing the furniture on-site, there is a higher risk of outgassing, odors, and irritation to the client. Specify the least toxic, lowest-VOC finish, paint, or stain available, preferably water-based or made with natural oils and extracts. Avoid finishes that contain solvents, formaldehyde, or metals as drying agents. Allow as much time as possible for outgassing of the finish, paint, or adhesives and for them to cure before bringing the case piece into the home.

Maintenance

Most case pieces require little maintenance other than occasional dusting and cleaning with a damp cloth. Natural oil or wax finishes on wood require regular reapplications.

Using old wood and found objects, this library tabletop and bottom shelf were constructed from curly birch; the legs were made with maple. The landscape in the center was handpainted by the artist.
Furniture Design and Construction by Barney Bellinger (Sampson Bog Studio).

Where Does It Go?

Furniture may be salvaged for a similar or different use, if in good condition. Wood or biocomposite boards will decompose easily (with the possible exception of the finishes, binders, and adhesives) back into soil, or they may be downcycled into other wood or pulp products. Binders, resins, stains, and finishes will break down much more slowly—if at all.

Spec List

Specify:

- Locally or domestically harvested, third-party-certified, nonthreatened wood species
- Reclaimed wood, preferably certified by a third party
- Salvaged furnishings or reuse/renovation of existing case pieces
- Biocomposite boards or particleboard/plywood that is third-party certified, or particleboard that contains a high percentage of recycled wood
- No oil finish on hardware, or removal of it before installation
- Formaldehyde-free, low-VOC, water-based binders, sealants, adhesives, glues, and stains

Specify Finishes and Stains (either on prefinished wood or to be applied on-site) That Are:

- Water-based
- Made of natural (sometimes called food-grade) oils, resins, pigments, and waxes
- Low-VOC
- Formaldehyde-free
- Free of metallic drying agents
- Solvent-free

Avoid:

- Reclaimed wood of uncertain origin where the use might be unsafe (especially in children's rooms)
- Uncertified wood
- Rare or threatened species
- Solvent-based finishes
- Formaldehyde in the binder or finish
- Plastics

RESOURCES

Forest Stewardship Council U.S.: www.FSCUS.org

Upholstery

Soft goods, such as the cushions on the sofa or the upholstery on a chair, help to make homes comfortable and provide warmth. Upholstery adds softness and personality, color and texture to furnishings.

This living space features all-natural fibers, including wool rugs and linen upholstery fabric on the furniture. The space also features fluorescent lighting, low-VOC paints, and radiant floor heating.
Used by Permission of
My House Magazine.
Photo by Mikel Covey.
Designer: Gail Madison Goodhue.

When researching, specifying and purchasing upholstery, be certain to consider all of the components—batting, backing, webbing, fabric and trim, dye, and fabric treatments—for their green characteristics. Specify each element to minimize the environmental impact and maximize home health. It's best to work with a custom upholsterer or local artisan, as most large furniture distributors offer limited eco-friendly options. In recent years a handful of specialty furniture makers with environmental concerns have emerged: seek them out.

The upholstery, pillows, and batting have a profound effect on the health of the client and the indoor environment. Soft goods, because of their porous nature, collect airborne particulates such as dust, mold, allergens, and environmental toxins, and are therefore called "sinks." Unlike a countertop, plumbing fixture, or wall, upholstered goods can't be wiped clean. Essentially, small particles can "sink" into the fabric and filling, to potentially be rereleased into the atmosphere of the home.

At its most benign, a "sink" may collect dust, pet hair, or mold, contributing to allergic reactions. At its worst, soft goods function as a holding point for toxins: chemicals from the pavement carried in on shoes and clothing, VOCs released from drying paint or adhesives, or fabric stainproofing that flakes away. The particulates settle until disturbed, residing in the foam in a sofa or the down of a pillow for weeks, years, or even decades. There are unestablished risks from constant or repeated exposure through the rerelease of toxins from soft goods.

The conditions in the furniture-making facility can contribute significantly to the sink phenomenon. Cigarette smoke, fumes from paint or finishes, or odors can contaminate the piece before it ever reaches the client's home. Know the manufacturer, and request clean, odor-free conditions and excellent ventilation for all upholstered pieces, especially if the client is chemically sensitive. When in doubt, allow time for outgassing in a well-ventilated, protected environment, or have the upholstery cleaned in the most benign manner possible before use. (The outgassing will still affect the environment, but the health of the home will be improved.)

While salvaged furnishings are a sound environmental choice because the items are diverted from the landfill, the pieces should always be thoroughly cleaned before reuse. The battings and fabrics, especially if vintage or antique, may harbor dust mites, mold, or toxins such as cigarette smoke or cleaning solutions. Unless the piece is in superb condition, reupholstery of all salvaged items is advised to eliminate any chemical irritants or allergens, especially if the client has sensitivities.

UPHOLSTERY FABRICS AND TRIMS

All-natural textiles have the least environmental impact overall and the highest degree of health benefits for the client. Plant and animal fibers come from rapidly renewable resources and they also biodegrade easily enough that they can be used as compost. Leather and skins, if they have been prepared with eco-friendly methods, are very durable choices that also biodegrade. (Note: Some individuals are opposed to the use of animal products.)

Other ecologically minded options are synthetic fibers that are derived from all-natural materials and can be easily recycled or are biodegradable: cloth made from recycled fibers, especially natural sources like cotton or wool; and reclaimed, recycled, or salvaged textiles put to new uses in the home.

This study features several locally manufactured items, including upholstery and throw pillows, a naturally shed antler chandelier, and reclaimed wood cabinetry. The space also features antique rugs, an antique Victorian lamp, a reclaimed wood mantle, and reclaimed wood floors.
Photo by David O. Marlow.
Designer: Associates III, www.associates3.com.

Synthetic upholstery, especially petroleum-based fabrics, should be avoided, as should chemical dyes, stain resistors, and waterproofing and other chemical treatments. Most synthetic fabrics can't be recycled and require energy-intensive manufacturing methods to produce them. Common chemical textile treatments should be avoided, as well, as they pose health risks for factory workers or consumers. Even those with no supposed risks may create problems for a client with chemical sensitivities.

BATTINGS, FILLERS, AND FOAM

There are just a few basic options when it comes to selecting the battings, foam, or fillers. Traditionally, cotton, wool, sisal, straw, hair, rags, moss, feathers, and fur were commonly used as stuffings, and many are still available today. The modern versions are usually thoroughly cleaned and sanitized to elemenate mold and insects.

Wool is available in a loose form (stuffing), in felted sheets, and in thicker pads. Wool is naturally flame retardant and antimicrobial. It absorbs water and does not dry quickly, so avoid using wool in very humid environments. Look for wool that is obtained from sustainable, organic, and humane resources.

Cotton batting comes in sheets and in loose form. It compresses easily so it is often combined with other materials for "support." It also absorbs moisture, so avoid using cotton in very humid environments unless the upholstery can be easily removed for thorough drying. Because traditional cotton farming relies heavily on pesticides and fertilizers, specify organically grown cotton.

Grasses and plant fibers such as straw, jute, hemp, or sisal are rougher to the touch and are usually surrounded with a softer batting or cloth encapsulation. They provide durable, breathable loft. Some are water-repellent and, therefore, are ideal for use in baths or outdoor furniture. Sisal and similar plant fibers are often precoated in (synthetic) latex foam or "rubberized" for use in upholstery, so specify all-natural fibers without coatings.

Natural down is still prized for pillows and upholstery, often applied around a firmer core as the final layer of batting. It is very soft and easily "fluffed" to regain loft. Allergies are usually reactions to the dust and dander, not the down itself, and are lessened if the product is thoroughly sanitized by the manufacturer before use and then regularly washed at home. Down soaks up water and doesn't dry quickly, so avoid use in moist or humid locations.

Animal hair is only occasionally used today by artisans and specialty upholsterers as stuffing, but it is frequently found in antiques. It lasts indefinitely, but must be thoroughly washed and sanitized, and may be attractive to pests.

All-natural latex foam is derived from rubber trees, but it should not be confused with synthetic latex that is derived from chemical processes. The term "latex" is used for both and for blends of the two. All-natural latex foam is durable, waterproof, and resilient. Consult with the manufacturer to ensure the foam is 100 percent naturally derived.

Most big-name furniture makers today rely on synthetic paddings because of their predictable, durable results. These foams and battings are made by blowing gases into petroleum-based polymers. The end product is long-lasting—so much so that it won't biodegrade and can't usually be recycled. In addition, synthetic foams are suspected of releasing some of their chemicals over time as VOCs or, worse, as hazardous particulate or molecules that collect in the environment and human tissue (see the sidebar, "PBDEs," page 356). Avoid synthetic foam and battings, and the chemical compounds that are associated with them, including chlorofluorocarbons (CFCs), polystyrene, and formaldehyde.

As with textiles, specify no bleaches, no synthetic dyes, and no chemical treatments to the batting or filler.

WEBBINGS, BACKINGS, AND BARRIER CLOTHS

As with upholstery and batting, all webbings, barrier cloths, backings, and functional fabrics should be made from all-natural plant or animal textiles. Jute, natural (rubber) latex, organic cotton, and wool are durable materials for these utilitarian purposes. Avoid the use of synthetics such as plastic, nylon, polyester, synthetic latex, and acrylic.

Where Does It Come From?

- Upholstery, webbings, backings, and barrier cloths may come from all-natural plant or animal fibers; from recycled fabrics and yarns; from petroleum or chemical synthetic, extruded fibers; synthetic or natural rubber latex; or from bio-based synthetics.

PBDEs

Controversy has erupted over polybrominated diphenyl ethers (PBDEs), a group of flame retardants. PBDEs are frequently used in home textiles to slow the spread of fire, should it start. The substances are most commonly found in foam cushions and upholstery treatments, but they also appear in plastic casings for electronics. They are no longer used in children's sleepwear and have been phased out of mattresses sold in the United States.

Studies have indicated that PBDEs build up in the food chain, soil, and air; they don't break down easily in the environment. They've been discovered in human breast milk, as they tend to collect in fat, and may be transferred to infants. PBDEs have been linked to slowed brain development and thyroid problems. How the chemical enters humans and animals is still unknown, but it is most likely through dust, airborne particulates, and possibly food.

Even more frightening is that persistent traces have been found in remote and sparsely populated places like the Arctic Circle. It's no longer just a problem in industrialized areas, but one that threatens the whole planet.

The sole U.S. producer of two types of PBDEs has agreed to discontinue production, but the chemical still has widespread use throughout the world. The most reliable way to avoid PBDEs is to select textiles from companies that have strict policies against its use.

Source: Washington State Department of Ecology, www.ecy.wa.gov

- Plant-based fibers such as cotton, jute, hemp, and ramie may be organically grown, or may be grown with traditional farming methods.
- Animal products such as wool and leather may come from sustainably managed or humane ranches, or may come from traditional ranch facilities.

Installation

Whenever possible, test wash a sample, then wash or air out the fabrics that are not labeled as "all-natural" before use in upholstery. This will help rid the fabric of chemical treatments, dust, particulates, VOCs, and odors.

Maintenance

Because an upholstered piece can become a "sink" where toxins, mold, dust, and allergens accumulate, regular dusting, vacuuming, or laundering is recommended. Rotating the cushions, slipcovers, and pillows will avoid soiling in the places where the use is highest.

When possible, specify fabrics that can be laundered or spot-cleaned with simple soap and water. Recommend natural spot-cleaning methods and avoidance of solvent-based treatments. If dry cleaning is recommended by the textile maker, look for local dry cleaners that employ carbon dioxide in an environmentally safe process.

Where Does It Go?

Natural textiles and upholstery will decompose; the plant-based types can be shredded for compost. Some synthetic fabrics can be recycled or reprocessed into new textiles or other polymers. Most synthetics break down slowly, if at all, after disposal.

Spec List

Specify:

- Natural plant- or animal-based fibers
- Fibers that are organically grown, sustainably farmed, or obtained using humane methods
- Textiles that are minimally processed, without added chemicals or dyes
- Textiles with natural dyes from plant, animal, or mineral sources
- Textiles that may be cleaned with natural or benign methods such as dusting, soap and water, or vacuuming
- Natural stain and water repellants (tightest weave, lanolin in wool, etc.)
- Bio-synthetic fabrics made from a high percentage of renewable, natural products such as paper or wood pulp, soy, corn, or bamboo
- Vegetable tanning and dyeing processes that rely on natural elements such as tare, rhubarb, valonea, and tree bark
- Locally tanned leather with minimal chemical processing or dyes
- Locally made textiles by artisans who use natural/hand methods
- Battings, fillers and foams from plant fibers that are all natural, organically grown, sustainably farmed, or obtained using humane methods

Avoid:

- Leather tanned with chromium
- Chemically dyed or treated leather
- Synthetic fibers made from petroleum products or chemicals
- Fibers from farms or suppliers that use pesticides or biocides
- Chlorine bleach
- Chemical deodorizers, detergents, or dry cleaning agents
- Fireproofing treatments
- Chemical dyes
- Waterproofing/stainproofing treatments
- Synthetic, petroleum based foams or padding
- Chemical treatments to batting or fillers

RESOURCES

International Federation of Organic Agriculture Movements: www.ifoam.org
Organic Trade Association: www.ota.com
Sustainable Cotton Association: www.sustainablecotton.org
See also Textiles, page 330.

Lighting

Hardwired light fixtures are specified during the design phase in preparation for the construction and/or remodeling stage (see Chapter 15). Freestanding floor and table lamps are specified as furnishings to highlight finishes, furnishings, and art; provide optimal lighting for tasks such as reading, entertaining, or crafts; and set the mood in a

This lamp was handmade from naturally shaped stones cut only at the base to provide stability. Zen stone lamp bases feature living lichen, which covers the stone, adding color, texture, and life to the rock.
Photo courtesy of Zen Stone Lighting & Furnishings.

room. Accomplishing these tasks with maximum energy efficiency is the goal for the environmentally sensitive design team.

Chapter 15 covers most of the basic principles of lighting design that are eco-friendly and minimize energy usage. When selecting lighting, take into consideration the natural light in a room and the desired placement of the fixture in relationship to furnishings and windows. Try various lightbulbs with different wattages and color renderings, using a light fixture similar to the one that might be purchased for that precise location. Then specify the bulb desired that will have the lowest electricity usage.

Choosing more efficient bulbs is one of the simplest yet most effective ways to reduce energy consumption by lighting. An incandescent bulb will only last 750 to 2000 hours, compared with a compact fluorescent (CFL) that has a life span of 20,000 hours. Plus, CFLs only give off approximately 30 percent of their energy as heat, while incandescents give off up to 90 percent—raising the surrounding air temperature. CFLs are initially more expensive, but pay for themselves in the utility bill dollars saved.

It may seem backward to specify the bulb before the fixture, but some fixtures, especially collectibles, can't accommodate the newer, highly efficient bulbs that are desirable in an energy-efficient home. This factor may dictate the selection of a different lamp or shade altogether, or influence the decision to have a lamp rewired or reconfigured to accommodate a particular high-efficiency bulb. (For more information on bulbs, see page 295).

Controls such as motion detectors, light sensors, and timers are often used to improve safety by turning lights on automatically in dark rooms. When the human factor is unreliable, such as with small children who can't reach the switches, controls can actually improve energy savings by shutting off lights automatically when a room is empty or when the natural light is sufficient. Controls may actually increase energy use, however, by turning lights on when they aren't needed, so consider all such applications carefully.

Lamp bases and fixtures can be made from practically anything—coconut shells, recycled aluminum cans, pottery, bicycle parts—as long as the material is safe to use near electrical wiring and the heat generated by lightbulbs. Shades may also be made from a large variety of materials, as long as adequate light filtration is present. When specifying materials for the light fixture itself, the greenest choice will always be the most easily renewable, longest-lasting, natural material. Next on the list might be recycled or salvaged materials, to keep them from landfills.

Avoid potential health hazards, especially materials that might outgas, disintegrate, or emit odors when affected by the warmth of a lightbulb. Plastics, oils, and synthetic fabrics are all undesirable. If the client has allergies or chemical sensitivities, these are especially important considerations.

Unstable paints and finishes are not intended for use on light fixtures. Metal light fixtures that have been factory-finished with a powder coat are acceptable. Wood and other porous surfaces should be left unfinished, or have a heat-tolerant, water-based, low-VOC finish, preferably applied at the factory.

Textiles, skins, and papers may be used as shades if they have not been chemically treated and don't emit VOCs. Dyes—even those made with all-natural substances—may be affected by the bright light and heat, so it may be preferable to avoid the use of dyes for the shades. Also avoid fire retardants that may contain PBDEs (see PBDEs, page 356) and opt instead for cool-temperature bulbs (CFLs) and an appropriate distance between the shade and bulb.

Bulbs and light fixtures are fragile, requiring the use of special packaging and shipping materials that may present environmental dilemmas. Request that all boxes and packaging be made from recyclable paper, cardboard, or similar material. Avoid "peanuts," plastic "clamshells," plastic bags, and other synthetics; not only are they difficult to recycle, they can taint the contents with outgassed odors and chemicals.

Where Does It Come From?

- Most electricity for residential lighting is generated by the burning of fossil fuels at power plants. Smaller portions are created through nuclear fission and renewable wind, water (hydroelectric), and solar sources.
- Residential light fixtures rely on metal and glass for integral components; the decorative parts may be made from any material that is not flammable or won't melt when in close contact with wiring and lightbulbs.
- Lamp shades are most often constructed from materials that filter light, such as textiles, paper, or skins, but may be made from a wide variety of materials.

Maintenance

Provide a list of preferred bulb types and wattages for the client once the fixture selections are complete. This will aid in future bulb replacements and will maximize energy efficiency in the long run.

Lamp shades and light fixtures should be dusted or lightly vacuumed.

Where Does It Go?

Once "spent," electricity from nonrenewable sources can never be recovered. There are, however, recycling options for bulbs:

- There may be a local program for recycling fluorescent bulbs. Consult with the municipality or waste management district to see if they are collected at hazardous waste or recycling sites.
- Mail-in boxes are another method for recycling bulbs. The consumer must purchase a bulb-collection box that has prepaid postage, then send it off to the recycling facility when full. These programs are currently oriented toward businesses, but may become more available to individual consumers.

Light fixtures should be disassembled and the components recycled, if possible. Natural paper or fiber shades (without finishes or chemical treatments) may be composted or mulched.

Spec List

Specify:
- Bulbs with the lowest energy use that still meet the client's needs
- Controls such as dimmers, occupancy sensors, and timers, if they will reduce lighting use

- ENERGY STAR fixtures
- Recyclable shipping and packing materials for bulb and light fixture purchases

  Avoid:

- Incandescent bulbs (Use only when all other options are not adequate or adaptable to current fixtures.)
- Light pollution, by overlighting a location or misdirecting light
- Landfill disposal of fluorescent bulbs (Encourage the homeowner to recycle.)
- Packing materials for bulbs and fixtures that are made of nonrecyclable materials and synthetics such as plastic or foam

RESOURCES

Bulb Recycling: www.lamprecycle.org
ENERGY STAR: www.energystar.gov
Earth911: www.earth911.org
See also Electrical, page 293.

Mattresses and Bedding

We spend approximately a third of our lives asleep. And most of us, at least in the Western world, sleep on manufactured mattresses and pillows. Once upon a time, people slept on simple mats or frames, or mattresses stuffed with straw, feathers, or moss. The sleep systems were certainly earth-friendly, and the materials easily biodegraded. But mold, insects, rodents, and general discomfort kept us searching for a better place to sleep.

Today, mass-produced mattresses are made with steel springs, polyurethane foam, polyester encasings, typically with box springs and a second base below. But in trying to assure ourselves a good night's rest, we have, by ridding mattresses and pillows of natural materials and replacing them with petroleum-derived fibers, vinyl, flame retardants, and other synthetics, disturbed something much more important than our sleep. These modern-day mattresses are also made from nonrenewable materials that bulk up landfills with nonbiodegradable materials. And we haven't been all that successful in solving the initial problem, for many individuals suffer from a host of allergies and chemical sensitivities, some of which are aggravated by the eight hours per night spent lying on a not-so-natural bed. Even some all-natural materials may be allergens or irritants for particular clients.

Test swatches of bedding and mattress materials are helpful in determining the environmentally safe options that are also the most comfortable. Replacing the mattress, frame, and bedding may be one of the most significant and positive changes in the "greening" of a home. Take care to specify materials that are not only eco-friendly, but that promote health and a sense of well-being for the client.

BED FRAMES

If the client wishes to purchase a new, all-natural sleep system, begin with the frame. Select a wood frame with finishes that are low-VOC, water-based, and formaldehyde-free. Also specify third-party-certified or FSC-certified wood be used.

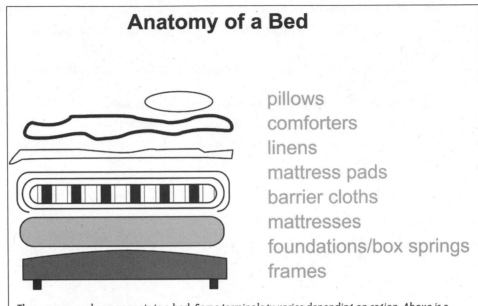

Anatomy of a Bed

pillows
comforters
linens
mattress pads
barrier cloths
mattresses
foundations/box springs
frames

There are several components to a bed. Some terminology varies depending on region. Above is a diagram of all the possible components of a sleep system. The bed starts with a frame that can be made of wood or metal and is the support for the box spring or foundation. The foundation can be a box with wood slats or a box with spring support. The mattress goes either on a foundation or on a platform bed frame. The barrier cloth is of tightly woven cotton that zips around the whole mattress and protects against dust mites. The mattress pad is like a fitted sheet, which is made with layers of cotton to protect the pad from spills and body oils. The linens are the sheets and blankets on the bed. A comforter, also called a duvet, can be filled with wool, polyester, or down. Pillows can be made with wool fill, cotton fill, down fill, or rubber fill. © www.suitesleep.com. Used with permission.

A metal frame is slightly less eco-friendly because the resources are nonrenewable. Look for a steel frame that has been made with high recycled material content, if possible. Avoid metal platings (see Metals, page 129) on the frame and decorative headboard and footboard, as they create toxic hazards for factory workers. Look instead for alloys that are rustproof, or for powder-coated, factory-applied finishes that don't outgas.

Adaptability is an eco-friendly principle, as one piece of furniture with multiple functions conserves natural resources that would be otherwise used to manufacture another piece. Fold-up beds also conserve valuable floor space, convenient for a smaller residence.

MATTRESSES

There are several different materials that are commonly used in natural sleep systems for fillers, casings, and frames and/or springs (optional). When purchasing a mattress or having one custom-made to specifications, look for these materials:

- *Latex.* All-natural latex made from rubber trees is an eco-friendly and healthful choice. It is resistant to mold, bacteria, dust mites, and other allergens, and comes in different levels of firmness to accommodate the client's preference.

Some natural latex beds have interchangeable "plates" of rubber that allow for the creation of variable degrees of firmness. Natural latex should not be confused with synthetic latex, although both are called simply "latex" on labels and are often blended. The definition of "100 percent natural latex" is not strictly defined by labeling laws, so it may include synthetic content. Request specific content information from the manufacturer, and specify all-natural rubber latex without synthetic content.

- *Wool.* Tufted wool is another popular choice for eco-friendly, healthy sleep. It breathes and allows moisture exchange, making it comfortable in all temperatures. Wool mattresses are usually only a few inches thick, so a natural latex layer added underneath may be more comfortable than wool alone. Wool also provides an excellent encasement or barrier cloth for wool-filled or latex mattresses. Look for wool that comes from sustainably managed ranches that use no pesticides, or that which is certified through the Organic Trade Association. Avoid wool that has been chemically treated or bleached.

- *Cotton.* Cotton is rarely used as the primary mattress core because it will flatten and lose its loft, but is occasionally used for filler in pillows. Cotton is, however, commonly used in the mattress encasement or barrier cloth, and is the number-one choice for pillow ticking. It breathes and is particularly comfortable in warmer climates. Cotton is also easy to spot-clean or launder with soap and water. Specify cotton that is organically grown, unbleached, and undyed, without any chemical treatments. Cotton fiber may be certified through the Organic Trade Association, as with wool.

Mattresses are best if they come with zippered or removable covers that can be aired, laundered, or taken to earth-friendly dry cleaners. This will ensure the mattress's cleanliness and reduce the amount of allergens and irritants.

Steel springs are optional, either within the mattress (called innersprings) or underneath (called box springs). Visit showrooms with your client to try out several mattress types, including those with and without springs, before making a purchase. A few manufacturers offer mail-order swatches of their mattress materials, specifically in the interest of those consumers who might have allergies or sensitivities.

In the event that the client does not wish to replace their existing mattress, a wool mattress topper is an excellent addition. It puts a layer of natural, healthy materials between the person and the conventional mattress. A topper is easy to wash or air regularly, making it ideal for anyone with allergies, whether used on top of a conventional or all-natural mattress.

FILLERS (FOR PILLOWS, COMFORTERS, BATTINGS, AND MATTRESS PADS)

In addition to wool, cotton, and latex, pillows, comforters, and mattress pads may include a number of other filler materials. Look for 100 percent natural fillers that are unbleached and not chemically treated. Specify organic, sustainably farmed materials, and request third-party certification of organic fiber content, whenever available.

- *Buckwheat, spelt, millet, and other grains.* These feel similar to a soft bag of sand, and hold contours easily for support of the neck and spine. Look for organically

Fact Check

ALLERGIC RESPONSES—HEALING EFFECTS

- Allergies—to all manner of things—are the 6th leading cause of chronic disease in the United States, costing the health care system $18 billion annually.

- *Latex*—Relatively unknown before 1990, allergies to latex are becoming increasingly common for reasons that are unclear. It is now estimated that up to 6% of people may be allergic to latex.

100% pure, natural latex is inherently hypoallergenic, anti-microbial and dust mite resistant. Although rare, an individual may have a true latex allergy that can cause an anaphylactic response. This is usually developed through repeated exposure and sensitization to products such as surgical gloves.

A good source of information is MedlinePlus, www.nlm.nih.gov/medlineplus. A booklet on Latex allergy is available from 1-800-7ASTHMA.

- *Wool*—For most people with allergies, wool offers major benefits as it resists mold and mildew. Wool "itch" is not usually a true allergy, but a reaction to the particular fiber shape and length, or from contact with lanolin.

Wool is usually tolerable for allergy sufferers, merino wool reportedly the least scratchy. Wool also helps to reduce dust mites, the biggest source of airborne allergies in the United States, as dust mites do not like wool.

- *Healing*—Synthetic materials do not provide a connection to the healing properties of nature. Studies conducted at both the Polytechnic Institute of Wales, and the Hohenstein Institute in Germany have shown that "sleeping with untreated natural fibers actually slows the heart rate and helps regulate body temperature."

Sources: American Lung Association, www.lungusa.org; American Academy of Allergy Asthma & Immunology, www.aaaai.org; Green Home Environmental Store, http://www.greenhome.com/info/articles/sleep_well/91/; National Institute of Allergy and Infectious Diseases National Institutes of Health www.niaid.nih.gov.

grown, naturally cleaned and sifted grain that has not been fumigated. Some grain pillows may be heated in the microwave for therapeutic use.

- *Down and feathers.* Down was, and still is for many, the most coveted material for pillows. Goose down is loftier and softer than feathers, and is sometimes combined with synthetic fillers or less desirable duck down. Specify 100 percent goose down, from sustainably managed or organic farms, that has been collected after the animals molt naturally. Chemical washings and treatments may exacerbate sensitivities, so specify down that has been cleansed with turbid water (a process that agitates the dirt free from the fibers).

- *Kapok.* Kapok is taken from the pods of the ceiba tree, found in the rain forests of Java. It was so commonly used in lifejackets before World War II that soldiers called the preservers "kapoks." Although the long-distance importation of kapok reduces its desirability as an eco-friendly material, it may be a viable, all-natural option for those with allergies or ethical objections to wool or down.
- *Milkweed or syriaca.* The fluffy stuff from milkweed pods is being cultivated for use in bedding and other natural products. Syriaca, the scientific name for milkweed, is reputed to be allergy-free. It is usually mixed with wool or down.

This bedroom features organic bedding, low-VOC paint, and local artistry.
Photo courtesy of Cheryl Terrace, Vital Design, Ltd., vitaldesignltd.com.

Many environmentally conscientious pillow and bedding makers go one step further to cater to those with allergies, by providing samples to potential customers. Request samples of pillows and bedding, whenever possible, so the client can test the products before committing to purchase them.

Because the mattress and pillows are in such close contact with human airways and skin, it is advisable to avoid synthetics because they can be hazardous to health. They are also bad for the environment, as most are made from nonrenewable resources and won't biodegrade. The use of synthetics is widely accepted by mattress and bedding manufacturers, unfortunately, so avoid the following materials in particular:

- *Polystyrene foam and foam beads.* Polystyrene contains the chemical component styrene, which has been linked with nervous system disorders. In addition, the small foam beads are a choking hazard for children. Several states are adopting laws that prohibit the use in children's clothing, toys, and other items, and also require the beads to be double-bagged within pillows and other products as a preventative measure.

- *Memory foam.* This popular mattress and pillow material is also called viscoelastic polyurethane or urethane foam. It is manufactured from derivatives of petroleum and as such, won't biodegrade. It is supposedly inert and won't outgas VOCs, but is often made with other chemicals or treatments that give off odors and may be especially problematic for chemically sensitive individuals.

- *PBDE.* Synthetic pillow foam is a flammable material because of its open cell structure and chemical makeup, and it is often treated with the fire retardant PBDE (polybrominated diphenyl ether; see sidebar, "PBDEs," page 356). The substance has been implicated in a number of serious health issues, and California is leading the way in phasing out the use in U.S. mattresses. Avoid the use of fire retardants altogether.

Law Labels

If the client prefers to purchase bedding from conventional retailers, the content of the mattress or pillows should be prominently displayed on a "law label" or large affixed tag. Many states subscribe to this system, which requires large tags be affixed to the mattresses and pillows, as well as items such as car seats, stuffed toys, sofas, sleeping bags, and beanbag chairs. Developed by the Association of Bedding and Furniture Law Officials (www.ABFLO.org) and the International Sleep Products Association (www.SleepProducts.org), the tags specify the filler content. They list, as examples: "All New Material" or "Secondhand," "80 Percent Goose Down" or "Polyurethane Foam Filler," and so on. Unfortunately, some states have opted out of this system, although most manufacturers apply the labels to all products to ensure compliance in the states that do require them.

■ *Polylactide acid (PLA).* This is a biosynthetic fiber that is engineered from corn, and there are many similar compounds in development. It eventually biodegrades and is made from a renewable resource—both ecological positives—and it's being used in everything from disposable plates to bedding. PLA holds promise as a replacement for petroleum-based synthetics, which don't biodegrade. The environmental attributes of these bio-based synthetics for sleep products are hard to justify, however, when so many other natural, renewable materials are already available.

SHEETS, PILLOWCASES, AND OTHER BEDDING

For selection of sheets, pillowcases, and other bedding items, follow the general guidelines for selecting earth-friendly textiles (see Textiles, page 330). Optimally, all bedding should be washable, especially if the client has allergies. As with any textile, avoid fabric treatments, stain repellents, waterproofing compounds, fire retardants, or any other chemicals and specify natural dyes if color is desired.

This bedroom features a bed constructed of reclaimed Douglas fir with environmentally friendly cotton linens. Interior design, Tracy Fox. Photography: Helga Sigvaldadottir.

Cotton is the most popular and affordable fiber for sheets, pillowcases, and comforters. Pillow ticking (encasings) is almost always made of cotton, as it can be tightly woven with a high thread count to enclose the battings. Certified organic cotton is no longer difficult to obtain, so specify it for all cotton bedding.

Silk, wool, linen, or other natural fibers (see Textiles, page 330) may be preferred by the client. If allergies are an issue, a double pillowcase with a high thread count will provide a barrier against dust and other particulates.

Where Does It Come From?

- Frames are usually made from metal or wood.
- Mattresses may be filled with wool, natural (rubber) latex, synthetic latex, synthetic fibers, or a blend.
- Mattress casings and barrier cloths are commonly made from wool, synthetics, or cotton.
- Mattresses may also feature innersprings or box springs made from steel.
- Pillows may be filled with wool, cotton, synthetic battings, latex, or sometimes grains, kapok, milkweed/syriaca, down, or feathers.
- Sheets, pillowcases, and bedding are made from a wide variety of textiles, including (but not limited to) cotton, wool, linen, silk, hemp, synthetics, and bio-based synthetics.

Maintenance

Mattresses should be designed so that they can be flipped and rotated regularly to ensure good ventilation and to redistribute fillers for maximum support and comfort. Advise the client to spot-clean with soap and water or natural cleansers when necessary. Avoid solvent-based cleaning solutions. Launder mattress covers and air out toppers.

Follow manufacturer directions carefully for cleaning pillows that contain down, grains, or specialty fibers. Specify that all sheets, pillowcases, and bedding be washable. If the client has health concerns or allergies, unbleached and undyed bedding should be specified because it can be washed in hot water. Encourage the use of eco-friendly, biodegradable laundry products. Air-dry pillows, quilts, and similar items that contain batting, then fluff by hand to avoid clumping.

Where Does It Go?

Mattresses are a bane to landfills, taking up large amounts of space with materials that slowly—or never—disintegrate or biodegrade. Conventional mattresses can't be sanitized easily, and eventually lose their loft, so reuse is not a healthful option. Disposal of any mattress, made with synthetic materials or all-natural, should not be done too hastily. Consult with the local waste management authority to determine if there are restrictions for large item disposal. At least one or two bed manufacturers accept mattresses and frames for recycling, and salvage yards will also accept the steel frames.

Other bedding such as sheets and pillows will last for many years if carefully maintained. All-natural bedding may be reused as rags, or even composted.

Spec List

Specify:

- Bed frames made from natural materials such as wood or metal, with nontoxic, low-VOC finishes
- Mattresses made from all-natural materials such as (natural rubber) latex, wool, and cotton
- Mattress toppers for clients with allergies or sensitivities, made from all-natural materials
- Pillows made with all-natural wool, cotton, latex, down, grains, kapok, or milkweed/syriaca
- Bedding made from all-natural cotton, wool, silk, linen, hemp, or other textiles
- No stain or water repellents, fabric treatments, sizing, or fire retardants applied to any bedding
- No chemical bleaching
- All-natural dyes or no dyes

Avoid:

- Natural latex if the client has a true latex allergy
- Synthetic latex
- Synthetic fabrics and fillers
- Foam, especially memory foam and polystyrene beads or pieces
- Fire retardants, especially PBDE
- Chlorine or chemical bleaches
- Synthetic dyes
- Fabric treatments such as stain and water repellents

RESOURCES

Association of Bedding and Furniture Law Officials: www.ABFLO.org
International Federation of Organic Agriculture Movements: www.ifoam.org
International Sleep Products Association: www.SleepProducts.org
Organic Trade Association: www.ota.com
Sustainable Cotton Association: www.sustainablecotton.org

Area Rugs

Area rugs may be as small as a breadbox or as large as a room. The fibers that support a rug may be much more delicate in their composition, made from cotton rags, chenille, or even paper. The client will have a wider selection of styles and fibers to choose from that fit eco-friendly specifications with an area rug than with wall-to-wall carpet.

Small rugs are easily laundered at home with detergent and water, and larger ones can be taken to an eco-friendly cleaner—a distinct advantage over large expanses of carpet that must be cleaned in place. This is of particular value to a client with allergies or sensitivities.

In addition, many rugs have lower embodied energy. While most carpet is manufactured on broadlooms in factories, many types of rugs are woven on small hand looms, often from local specialty fibers obtained from indigenous sheep or native grasses. Rug makers and weavers sometimes do their own dyeing, as well. All-natural colorants can usually be specified when working with an artisan.

Rugmark: Putting an End to Child Labor

There is a particular hazard associated with area rug making that has been exposed in recent decades: child labor. In many countries, children are employed as rug weavers through forced labor or because their families were victims of debt bondage. While it may not directly affect the environment as does clear-cutting forests or strip mining, the negative, long-term ills associated with unfair labor practices negatively affect human health and welfare on a broad scale.

To put an end to these practices, several trade unions, religious and human rights organizations, and consumer groups have formed Rugmark. The nonprofit organization monitors rug making in factories, oversees product labeling, and even helps run schools for children who were formerly employed in the industry. Several countries, including the prominent rug exporters of India, Pakistan, and Nepal, participate in and promote the Rugmark standards.

Look for the Rugmark label on all imported rugs—and avoid those without it.

Almost anything that can be made into a textile (see Textiles, page 330) can be woven, knotted, or knit into a rug. Natural fibers are the obvious choice. Area rugs are made from a wide variety of plant and animal fibers, another distinct advantage over wall-to-wall carpet, which is usually made from synthetics. The possibilities for rugs include, but are not limited to: wool, cotton, silk, jute, hemp, coir, sisal, and seagrass. Select the fiber or blend that best fits the intended purpose and that will last the longest.

Whenever possible, choose fibers that are organically grown or farmed according to sustainable methods. Wool and cotton growers may subscribe to third-party certification, but it is uncommon for most other fiber producers to do so. Look for manufacturers that have strict standards for environmentally friendly production practices, waste management and recycling, and worker safety programs. Or purchase from local artisans who take pride in working with all-natural materials, and thus eliminate the energy that would be wasted with long-distance transportation.

Specify all-natural dyes, or none at all. Avoid chlorine bleaching and chemical colorants.

Felted Wool

Wool has a unique property: If it is abraded (rubbed and agitated) when wet, and detergent is used in the water, the fibers will cling together. The final product, a densely matted, soft, thick wool, is said to have been "felted." The process can be used to create beautiful, durable rugs and paddings.

When specifying felted wool, request that only mild soap or detergent be used in the process, no chemicals.

Avoid synthetic materials such as polyester, olefin, nylon, acrylic, or acetate, as they are mostly petroleum-based and are unlikely to be recyclable. Some synthetic rug fibers outgas or carry odors that can be irritating, as well.

Avoid stain repellants, waterproofers, and other chemical treatments; they may not be listed on the label, so request details from the manufacturer. If working with a local artisan or specialty rug maker, request that only natural dyes be used. Specify no dye if the client suffers from sensitivities or allergies that might be triggered by it.

Area rugs are made from a wide variety of recycled materials, as well. Old denim jeans, T-shirts, and other clothing items or fabrics, even paper, can be torn into rags and woven, braided, or sewn into rugs. Such materials are thrifty and ecologically smart because no new materials or natural resources are used. The drawback is that the content of the fabrics will be highly variable and unknown, so it might not be a good option if the client is sensitive to synthetics or dyes.

RUG PADS

The padding underneath a rug, whether part of the rug itself or a separate layer, provides more than just comfort and safety. It protects the floor from abrasion by dust particles trapped underneath the rug or rough backings. It also extends the life of the rug.

There are two basic types of rug pads: those that cushion, and those that also grip the floor to prevent slipping. Cushioning pads can be made from all-natural wool. Synthetic pads are the most common type available, but not desirable in a green room. The gripping pads are usually made from latex; specify all-natural rubber latex. (The term "latex" is used for both the natural type and synthetic, so make precise inquiries when purchasing the pad.) Never use pads made from PVC, (see PVC, page 224), also called vinyl, which carries a distinct odor and outgasses harmful substances.

Where Does It Come From?

- Rugs may be made from all-natural fibers such as wool, silk, jute, coir, sisal, seagrass, and cotton or from artificial fibers such as nylon, olefin, and acrylic.

- Rug pads may be made from PVC or vinyls, synthetic or natural latex, recycled carpet fibers, wool, jute, camel hair, or mohair.

Maintenance

Regular vacuuming of both sides of the rug will extend the life of the fibers and prevent particles underneath from scratching the floor. If the fiber content allows, small rugs should be laundered regularly with mild detergent and water. Larger rugs may be cleaned by a service that uses only water, or dry cleaners that use carbon dioxide processes. Advise the client to avoid solvent-based stain treatments, chemical dry cleaners, and stain repellents.

Where Does It Go?

Wool, cotton, jute, coir, sisal, seagrass, cotton, paper, and silk rugs, along with natural backings and pads, will biodegrade easily. Rugs made from recycled clothing or rags may be problematic if they contain a high percentage of synthetics. Synthetic-fiber rugs might possibly be recycled, and a few rug manufacturers accept products back at the end of their life cycles (see Carpet, page 221), but the effort is primarily directed at commercial wall-to-wall carpet. Otherwise, synthetic fibers simply add to landfill waste and environmental problems.

Spec List

Specify:
- One hundred percent natural-fiber carpets (wool, cotton, silk, jute, coir, sisal, seagrass, paper)
- All-natural dyes, or no dye at all
- Recycled-content "rag" rugs
- Locally made or artisan-produced rugs
- Rugmark certification on every rug that is imported
- Rug pads made from all-natural rubber latex, wool, or other natural materials.

Avoid:
- Manufactured fibers such as nylon, polyester, olefin, and acetate
- Stain repellents, waterproofers, or other chemical treatments
- Synthetic dyes
- Synthetic rug pads, especially those made with PVC-vinyl

RESOURCES

Carpet and Rug Institute: www.carpet-rug .org
RUGMARK Foundation: www.rugmmark.org

Window Treatments

When specifying window treatments for an eco-friendly home, consult with the client first to determine whether the purpose of the treatment is functional, decorative, or

This sitting room features handwoven window coverings, locally manufactured upholstery and throw pillows, and an antique occasional table.
Photo by David O. Marlow.
Designer: Associates III,
www.associates3.com.

even necessary. Usually, window treatments serve a variety of purposes. They regulate sunlight through the opening and keep weather extremes at bay—both important for energy conservation—in addition to framing the view of the outdoors providing privacy and enhancing the room's ambience.

Although the location of windows is critical when designing for new construction, in order to maximize solar gain or minimize heat loss (see Windows, page 165), it isn't usually practical to change the orientation of the windows once the house is built. When a home is located in a climate with temperature fluctuations, appropriate

Fact Check

- The average household uses 42 percent of its annual energy on heating and cooling.
- A third of all heat loss occurs through windows and doors.

Source: Energy Information Administration, www.eia.doe.gov.

window coverings boost energy efficiency by keeping the house warmer in winter and blocking hot sun in the summer. They may also prevent drafts. Insulating, reflective, or blackout window treatments may make a noticeable difference in the comfort level and the utility bills, as well as the overall consumption of nonrenewable fuel for heating and air conditioning.

It is rare that no additional window insulation or regulation of light is needed in a home. If the windows are both the centerpiece of a room and highly efficient, the client may wish for window treatments only to highlight the view or improve the ambience.

DRAPERIES AND WINDOW TEXTILES

Focus on textiles and materials that will be long-lasting, need little maintenance, and won't deplete the environment. Organically grown cotton, hemp, flax (linen), ramie, wool or silk from sustainably managed operations are ideal choices for window coverings. They might also be made from a variety of grasses, bamboo, or wood. Look for products that have been certified as sustainable or organic.

The client may request that no dyes be added; or if color is desired, specify that all dyes be natural, not chemical. Then specify low-impact finishes and no additional fabric treatments such as stain repellents or flame retardants (see Textiles, page 330).

Avoid specialty coatings on textiles that contain vinyl, plastic, synthetic rubber, or other manufactured polymers. If stain resistance is the goal, look for tight weaves or fabrics that are washable. Synthetic waterproofing treatments may actually encourage condensation on the window or fabric, defeating the intended purpose. For moisture control, specify highly breathable textiles with natural resistance to mold, such as wool.

SHUTTERS

Shutters on the inside of a window provide a high degree of control over light and privacy, and to a lesser degree, temperature, if they cover the full window and are snug-fitting. Wood shutters may be ordered unfinished and left as is, or finished at the site with low-VOC, low-odor paint, all-natural waxes, or oils. The wood is long-lasting and the shutters can eventually be salvaged and reused or repurposed, or they will decompose naturally over time. Specify FSC-certified or third-party-certified wood (see Wood, page 144).

Factory-finished wood shutters are another option that may be a good choice if the client has sensitivities, as they will have time to outgas off-site. (The outgassing will still affect the environment and air quality, however.) Specify low-VOC, formaldehyde-free finishes.

Wood shutters are often the most expensive, but are a far better choice than outgassing and potentially hazardous vinyl (see PVC, page 224). Vinyl and polymer shutters are sometimes called "satinwood," "faux wood," or "composite," so request specific composition details from the manufacturer whenever the description is ambiguous. With the possible exception of shutters that are manufactured from a certified recycled wood product, these composite types are basically plastics made from petroleum and other chemicals. They are not acceptable in a green home, and may be irritants to those who are chemically sensitive.

BLINDS

Blinds, made from a variety of materials, are primarily intended to block out sunlight and provide privacy. Conventional venetian blinds are usually made from PVC-vinyl or metal. PVC-vinyl outgasses and poses significant health risks for workers and consumers (see PVC, page 224). Metal blinds can be troublesome because they may be statically charged and collect dust, which is especially irksome for those with allergies. Moreover, blinds made of metal are particularly energy-inefficient because they conduct heat, cold, and moisture.

Bamboo, wood, and natural textiles are terrific choices for all types of blinds. Look for unfinished slats or those with low-VOC, no-odor finishes. Natural materials that are certified by the FSC or another third party are not commonly used in the making of blinds; however, the search is worth the extra effort if they can be found.

INSULATING, REFLECTIVE, AND BLACKOUT WINDOW TREATMENTS

In hot climates or where little shade exists, consider using a textile or backing that is reflective. The most environmentally benign and healthy options would include natural textiles that are light-colored or possess a reflective sheen. Less eco-friendly are reflective synthetics, such as Mylar, that are used as backings or liners. While they keep the heat and sun out of the house, they are manufactured from petroleum and other chemicals, negating some of the energy benefits overall. In addition, they are not at all breathable and will trap moisture.

Reflective textiles can be sandwiched between insulating layers in blinds or heavy draperies, but may not be necessary if the fabrics and fit are carefully designed. Batting or heavy textiles are particularly effective in home temperature regulation, especially if the window treatment seals to the frame with the help of magnets, weights, or fasteners. Natural cotton, wool felt, and suede are more breathable and trap less moisture than synthetic backings, while still providing a barrier to drafts, light, and harsh weather.

Other offerings that decrease the energy deficit are usually made with synthetic textiles—the environmental pros and cons should be evaluated with the client and weighed against the need for comfort and privacy. If home comfort is a serious issue and window replacement is not an option, synthetics may aid in lowering utility bills and improving the temperature within. Cellular or honeycomb shades trap air between the cells, controlling heat loss in the winter and solar gain in the summer. Triple-cell types offer the greatest barrier for heat and light, but double- and single- cell varieties are also available. Solar screens, another specialty window textile, allow for maximum visibility from the inside, but diffuse harsh sunlight. Most solar screens are made with PVC, PVC-free alternatives are available, so specify those.

CONTROLS

Perhaps the most environmentally sound way to regulate light and darkness, privacy, and heating or cooling is to employ the use of manual controls. Window treatments should be adjustable so that they can be opened or closed easily or maneuvered for subtle changes in light. This can be achieved through a multiple-layer system of sheer curtains, shades, and heavy draperies, or by mechanical pulleys, levers, drawstrings, or sashes. The client can still have eco-friendly, all-natural window coverings while achieving maximum energy efficiency and lower utility bills.

Consider the total impact of the manufacturing needed to make these specialty controls, built-in window shades, and electrical systems, along with the shipping and the electricity needed to run them. Then ask whether reliance on "human power" to pull a curtain shut or open a blind makes more sense.

HARDWARE

Consider the ease with which window treatments can be removed for cleaning before specifying the hardware for them. Some rods, rings, blind mechanisms, and drawstrings are problematic—or impossible—to detach and reattach.

Hardware for window treatments is usually made of metal (see Metals, page 129), but may incorporate glass, ceramic, bamboo, wood, or other materials in the structure or decorative accents. Whenever possible, specify all-natural materials (such as wood or bamboo) or a high percentage of recycled content (as in metal or glass).

Local fabricators or metalworkers may be able to custom-make hardware to specifications and incorporate recycled steel from a minimill or other recycled metals. Specialty artisans might also make finials from salvaged items, recycled glass, or hand-thrown pottery.

Avoid finishes that emit VOCs, or platings on metal. Specify low-toxic, durable finishes such as powder-coating on steel or natural beeswax on wood.

Where Does It Come From?

- Window treatments and hardware are made from a wide range of materials, including (but not limited to): wood, bamboo, grasses and reeds, natural textiles, synthetic textiles, metal, and vinyl.

Maintenance

If made from textiles, the porous nature of the window covering may collect allergens, dust, and possible toxins and become a "sink" for them. Ideally, the textiles should be easy to dust or vacuum, wipe clean, or launder with soap and water.

Reflective and specialty textiles are not usually washable; if part of a thermal system or blind, they may eventually inhibit the laundering of the other layers.

If the textiles require dry cleaning, they should be compatible with carbon dioxide methods that are easy on the environment; advise the client as to local eco-friendly dry cleaning outlets.

Where Does It Go?

Window treatments are rarely recycled into other materials, but usable components may be offered for reuse at thrift stores or similar outlets. All-natural textiles, bamboo, and wood are biodegradable, and might possibly be composted or shredded if the finishes are natural as well. Synthetic window treatment, however, will contribute to landfills indefinitely.

Spec List

Specify:
- Window treatments that minimize heating and cooling needs
- Window treatments that can be manually opened, closed, or adjusted as the needs for privacy, lighting, and comfort change
- All-natural materials and textiles such as wool, cotton, wood, bamboo, and grasses, preferably from sustainable or organic enterprises
- Window treatments that can be easily cleaned or laundered
- No dye or natural dyes on all textiles
- Inert, low-VOC metal finishes such as powder coating
- No finish or low-VOC, all-natural finishes on wood, bamboo, and reeds

Avoid:
- Synthetic materials
- Metal blinds
- PVC-vinyl
- Electronic controls, unless the window treatment is difficult to reach or too large to open manually
- Textiles finishes such as stain repellents, waterproofings, or sizing
- Finishes on rods or blinds that emit VOCs or odors

RESOURCES

Energy Efficiency and Renewable Energy, (U.S Department of Energy).
Window Treatments and Coverings: www.eere.energy.gov/consumer/your_home/windows_doors_skylights/index.cfm/mytopic=13500

Accessories and Art

Accessories and art are the special touches a client chooses that individualize a home. They are statements of taste. Because art and accessories are so very personal, it is difficult to impose eco specifications on them. Yet it's important to guide the client in making wise decisions about what to keep and what to purchase so that the client's life is enriched and the environment is not unduly harmed.

Artworks are, by definition, things chosen essentially for their beauty. Traditionally, we think of art as an oil painting on the wall or a piece of sculpture that graces the entryway. But the category of art could include a blanket, a hand-thrown pottery urn, a particularly cherished photograph, or even a collage of vintage license plates. The value of art and accessories is in the eye of the beholder.

This wall sculpture was handmade from natural sticks and twigs.
Photo courtesy of artist David Ward.

If these design elements are so influenced by personal taste, how then can we as designers guide a client to make wise decisions about the accessories and art in an environmentally friendly home? The answer lies in values and guidelines, not strict specifications. By focusing on what is most important to the client, and by choosing to eliminate frivolous or environmentally harmful purchases, the designer can help enhance the life of the client while improving the living space and tending the earth.

NEW ACCESSORIES AND ART

Ideally, an accessory or new work of art should be made from all-natural materials such as wood, clay, bone, rock, or another readily available resource. It's best if the resource is renewable, but if not, evaluate whether it might be recycled or reused at the end of its useful life. The piece should not emit VOCs or odors or otherwise be harmful to the occupants. Locally or domestically made objects lower the embodied energy by reducing on the shipping. These are the basics, be it a countertop or a work of art, for a green home.

Trading Fairly

The International Fair Trade Association (IFAT), a global network of fair trade organizations, is a fine resource for locating vendors and products. Simply visit the organization's Web site or look for its logo to ensure the following criteria are met.

IFAT Key Principles of Fair Trade

- *Creating opportunities for economically disadvantaged producers.* Fair Trade is a strategy for poverty alleviation and sustainable development. Its purpose is to create opportunities for producers who have been economically disadvantaged or marginalized by the conventional trading system.
- *Transparency and accountability.* Fair Trade involves transparent management and commercial relations to deal fairly and respectfully with trading partners.
- *Capacity building.* Fair Trade is a means to develop producers' independence. Fair Trade relationships provide continuity, during which producers and their marketing organizations can improve their management skills and their access to new markets.
- *Payment of a fair price.* A fair price in the regional or local context is one that has been agreed through dialogue and participation. It covers not only the costs of production but enables production that is socially just and environmentally sound. It provides fair pay to the producers and takes into account the principle of equal pay for equal work by women and men. Fair Traders ensure prompt payment to their partners and, whenever possible, help producers with access to preharvest or preproduction financing.
- *Gender equity.* Fair Trade means that women's work is properly valued and rewarded. Women are always paid for their contribution to the production process and are empowered in their organizations.
- *Working conditions.* Fair Trade means a safe and healthy working environment for producers. The participation of children (if any) does not adversely affect their well-being, security, educational requirements, and need for play, and conforms to the U.N. Convention on the Rights of the Child as well as the law and norms in the local context.
- *The environment.* Fair Trade actively encourages better environmental practices and the application of responsible methods of production.

Source: IFAT, www.ifat.org

FAIR
TRADE
ORGANIZATION
IFAT • THE INTERNATIONAL
FAIR TRADE ASSOCIATION

Frequently, foreign-made objects are desirable for their unique beauty and for the cultural messages they convey. Exercise caution when selecting them. Sometimes in the quest to offer the best price, companies in developing countries neglect or even enslave workers and subject them to miniscule wages and poor living and working conditions. The environment will eventually suffer when high output at the lowest cost is the ultimate goal, and resources will be stripped without concern for regrowth or renewability.

One way to counteract these alarming trends is to support fair trade (see the sidebar, "Trading Fairly," page 377). The fair trade movement, in essence, ensures decent working conditions and adequate pay for artisans and workers, especially in underdeveloped areas. These principles are especially important when considering the purchase of art or accessories, since many of these interior design elements are made abroad and where working conditions are difficult to determine.

Consider whether materials are eco-friendly and safe, whether they will conservatively consume natural resources (such as electricity or water), whether they will have a long life span, and whether they will ultimately improve the client's home and lifestyle. Honor the component of fair trade into any purchase of items from abroad.

As an example, think through the request to research and procure a work of art or an accessory. Rather than selecting the piece that simply matches the décor, perhaps there could be a brief discussion about its value. Is it needed? Will it be used every day, or is it just for appearance? Will it still be beautiful and usable in five years? Ten? Are the materials all-natural? Is it made from components that can be recycled, or from materials that are fundamentally healthy? Where was it made? Were the workers treated fairly?

With artwork, it is possible to ask: Where does it come from and where will it go? Many artists are devoted to the well-being of the earth and choose mediums that are all-natural and least toxic, or they work with salvaged materials. Since the goal is to enhance the living environment within the guidelines of eco-friendliness, approach the client with examples of artists (and their artwork) who are in touch with the earth.

Finally, consult with the client to ensure that all accessories and art that are purchased will be of value in the long run. Avoid fashions and trends that quickly become outdated, and instead focus on the elements that the client has always found most beautiful and interesting. What inspires the client? What draws the eye or stimulates the mind? Are there materials, colors, or textures that bring the client to a deeper appreciation of the earth?

A values-driven approach will align selections with the client's core. Determining what's most important to an individual ensures satisfactory results that will last for many years, serving the environment and the client.

EXISTING ACCESSORIES AND ART

A client's possessions may or may not have been acquired with ecological sensibilities in mind. When evaluating a client's existing accessories and artwork, the environmental double mantra "Where does it come from and where does it go?" is not the only criteria. Value and function play integral roles. Does the piece have a function or purpose in the home? Does it have lasting value? If the client can answer yes to either of these questions, then the accessory or art has a place. There's no need to ponder dis-

This kitchen features recycled glass tableware resting upon solid cherry shelving. Also featured here are unfinished honed-slate countertops.
Photo by Laurie E. Dickson.
Architect: Baker Laporte & Associates.

posal if the aforementioned antiques, collectibles, useful accessories, or precious artwork if they are being used or enjoyed. Ultimately, it is environmentally friendly to appreciate what we already have.

If, on the other hand, the client has items that are no longer useful or appreciated—especially if they are taking up valuable storage space, or needing continual maintenance or cleaning that usurps time and resources—discuss where they might be donated, sold, or disposed of.

Thankfully, there is always a better place for an item than a too-full attic, basement, garage, or closet. Charitable organizations, thrift stores, garage sales, and even online auctions are all splendid places to find homes for still-usable household items. It is a sound ecological principle to find uses for unused things and homes for items where they will be appreciated. If the objects in question are beyond repair, encourage the client to disassemble all the parts, then recycle as many components as possible.

> *Have nothing in your houses that you do not know to be useful, or believe to be beautiful.*
> —WILLIAM MORRIS, 1882

Where Does It Come From?

- Art and accessories can be made from virtually any material.
- Ideally, a green home should focus on art and accessories that are natural, healthy, environmentally sustaining, and biodegradable-or, at the very least, so valuable and beautiful that they will never be thrown away.
- Articles purchased from abroad should have been made under the umbrella of fair trade guidelines.

Installation and Maintenance

Assist in finding ways to best display possessions such as collectibles, heirlooms, and art that will conserve and preserve them. Protect paintings, antiques, textiles, delicate collections, and similar items to last indefinitely. This will provide years of satisfaction to the client and even to future generations and, ultimately, prevent waste.

These pillows were made from used, reclaimed flour sacks.
Photo courtesy of Heiberg Cummings Design, www.Hcd3.com.

Choose proper framing, display, and conservation techniques appropriate to the unique needs of a piece or collection. For old photos, framed art, and other two-dimensional objects, specify protective frames and matting that are acid-free (often called "conservation grade" or "museum grade"). If the piece is especially fragile or valuable, it is also advisable to specify that all components that touch it be dye-free; even natural dyes or colorants that come in contact with paper can cause deterioration over time. Some frames and mattings may contain recycled paper or wood. If the criteria for preservation can be met, then use of these recycled-content materials is a bonus for the environment.

For some two-dimensional art and three-dimensional collections, antiques, or sculptural pieces, it may be beneficial to conserve them under glass. This prevents dust and grime from harming them. Specify UV-protective glass to minimize fading from sunshine and artificial light.

Textiles and paper usually require very specific methods of conservation. If the art or accessory needs care that is beyond the scope of interior design, consult with an art or history museum to learn of specialists who might be of assistance.

Where Does It Go?

Consider: Where will this accessory or piece of art be in a few years, a decade, or even a century? Items that have short life spans—a trend that will soon be outdated, components that will wear out, or collections that will be outgrown—are not fundamentally wise choices for the environment. Select items that will be of value in the long term.

This bedroom features several antiques, including a wooden bowl, spurs, and rug. The rug is naturally dyed wool; the design is based on a traditional Navajo design. The bed frame was manufactured by a local artisan.
Photo by David O. Marlow.
Designer: Associates III,
www.associates3.com.

Whenever possible, specify all-natural materials that biodegrade or that can be recycled, especially for accessories with shorter life cycles.

Spec List

For Existing Accessories and Art

Specify:

- Accessories that are regularly appreciated and used.
- Collectibles, heirlooms, memorabilia, and art that are appreciated or cherished

Avoid

- Accessories that are never used
- Accessories or art that are not appreciated or cherished (i.e., they are in storage and will continue to be) or that might be better appreciated by someone else
- Items that take up valuable space in the home that is needed for another purpose
- Objects that require maintenance or cleaning beyond their value to the client

For New Accessories and Art

Specify:

- All-natural materials
- Recycled materials
- Materials that are safe, not harmful, within the home
- Materials that won't harm the environment
- Accessories that are long-lasting and durable
- Art and accessories that will still be valuable to the client many years from now

Avoid:

- Manufactured, synthetic, or chemically derived materials
- Materials that outgas VOCs, emit odors, or are unsafe for use within a home
- Materials that harm the environment, either through manufacturing or upon disposal
- Trends, fashions, and impulses

CHAPTER 17

green business development

Photo courtesy of Mithun Architects.
Architect: Mithun.

Business is the only mechanism on the planet today powerful enough to produce the changes necessary to reverse global environmental and social degradation.
—PAUL HAWKEN

An effective marketing effort incorporates relationship building, networking, speaking, writing articles, and sharing successful projects, along with focusing on specific target markets and value bonding with clients. It is no different as you move into the realm of marketing sustainable design services.

The commitment to green design, both individually and as a firm, provides even greater potential to serve clients and establishes you as a leading-edge interior designer. Consider this: Who doesn't want a healthy environment in which to live and work while contributing to the well-being of the planet and its future generations? Hold this thought while greening your marketing efforts.

The following survey results, compiled by Jerry Yudelson, Interface Engineering, illustrate the most effective marketing methods and reflect the desire of building design professionals to let successful projects be their preferred marketing approach, while also reinforcing the positive effect of networking, speaking, and writing articles.

Most Effective Methods for Marketing Sustainable Design Services
Successful projects, with LEED certification goal
Networking or speaking
Direct selling to interested prospects
Successful projects, without LEED certification goal
Public relations
Writing articles
All others

What Can Be Done to More Effectively Promote Sustainable Design?
Case studies of successful projects
More independent cost information, in conventional formats
More training
More project experience
More successful local projects (ours or others)
Greater life-cycle analysis (LCA) of products
Better marketing materials

Relationship Building

Your internal team is the key to seeking success on the road to sustainability. This is a journey, not a destination. By building a strong company commitment to responsible design and business practices, you become a truly sustainable firm. Garner support and buy-in from your internal team—making a major commitment to sustainability at all levels of your business.

Nurture and support your team, and encourage them to learn all that they can about sustainable principles and practices, as they are among your greatest environmental advocates. Take time for training, complementing standard continuing education with a consistent in-house sustainable program. Provide the resources to attend green conferences and promote green certifications such as LEED Accreditation and Green Advantage. Encourage your environmental champions to be actively involved in sharing their knowledge with both the internal and external teams. If your team feels confident and understands that building green adds value to their projects, they will enthusiastically embrace helpful tools in moving forward.

With clients, architects, and contractors, reinforce these principles and strategies, so that your passion for, and expertise in, sustainable design become the key identifiable characteristics of the firm. Seek out like-minded team players who share a sustainable vision. The prospect of professionals coming together with aligned vision opens doors to work on projects that are innovative and exciting. This is the basis of relationship building.

Center your initial efforts on past, current, and potential project team members. As you begin to solicit work, identify those who are also caring of the environment. Together, you can seek out collaborative opportunities and engage well-trained and knowledgeable people for your project teams.

Designers who already embrace close working relationships with clients, architects, contractors, and other project professionals will have a greater ratio of success in greening their projects. Being an integral member of the team will ensure that your designs will get built within established budgets, time, and resource constraints, utilizing appropriate technology and meeting sustainable project goals.

Positioned as thoughtful environmental leaders within the industry, our clients will regard us, in our role as their interior design consultants, as trusted business professionals. We can tangibly demonstrate the ways that home environments impact health and quality of life, providing their basic needs. We complete projects thoroughly from start to finish, including preparation of construction documents for bidding and permitting, as well as supervision of the construction and installation of the work. With the architect, contractors, and manufacturers, we are the clients' advocate through thick and thin. We are proficient at working with different players, serving our clients—who may or may not have the time or inclination to deal with the project details and nuances. We provide a valuable service.

As your company's culture matures, and each person within the firm becomes more fully engaged in embodying sustainable values, external branding will strike a valuable balance. Through gained expertise and a growing passion, and by creating a composed and credible presence, clients will want to connect with you—forging deeper and more productive relationships.

Networking

What is "networking" all about? The Merriam-Webster dictionary defines it is an extended group of people with similar interests or concerns who interact and remain in informal contact for mutual assistance or support.

Begin sharing and exhibiting your commitment and passion for the welfare of people and for the environment. Network with others by joining organizations with aligned values. ASID, IIDA, AIA, USGBC, and ADPSR are examples of professional organizations within the building industry that incorporate sustainability within their core values.

Our role as environmental stewards within the building industry has become paramount to a growing number of organizations, where ecological accountability is one of the primary tenets of their mission.

The American Society of Interior Designers (ASID) Sustainable Design Council, composed of professional members, oversees the ASID sustainable design strategic initiative. They also provide a Sustainable Design Information Center on their Web site with access to general information on sustainability and green design. You will also find multiple links to resources available online.

The International Interior Design Association (IIDA) established the Foundation's Sustainable Design Education (SDE) Fund to offer IIDA members and the interior design community an opportunity to apply for financial support to further their knowledge and to increase environmental awareness about the importance and effect of sustainable design in everyday life. The SDE Fund offers financial assistance for activities including but not limited to:

- Tuition reimbursement to IIDA members who pass the LEED Accredited Professional Exam
- Financial assistance to attend conferences, seminars, and exhibitions (Green-Build, Environ Design, etc.) whose primary focus and intent is devoted to sustainable design issues and providing learning opportunities to further one's knowledge about sustainable design

The American Institute of Architects Committee on the Environment (AIA-COTE) works to advance, disseminate, and advocate to the architectural profession, the building industry, and the public, design practices that integrate built and natural systems and enhance both the design quality and environmental performance of the built environment. The U.S. Green Building Council (USGBC) is the nation's foremost coalition of leaders from across the building industry that is working to promote buildings that are environmentally responsible, profitable, and healthy places to live and work, producing a new generation of buildings that deliver high performance inside and out. Through its LEED products and resources, the GreenBuild annual conference and expo, policy guidance, and educational and marketing tools that support the adoption of sustainable building, USGBC forges strategic alliances with key industry and research organizations and federal, state, and local government agencies to transform the built environment.

Architects/Designers/Planners for Social Responsibility (ADPSR) work for peace, environmental protection, ecological building, social justice, and the development of healthy communities. Its members believe that design practitioners have a significant role to play in the well-being of our communities.

The goals of ADPSR's programs are to:

- Raise professional and public awareness of critical social and environmental issues.
- Further responsive design and planning.
- Honor persons and organizations whose work exemplifies social responsibility.

Many of the building industry organizations and design associations recognize the importance of educating design professionals in the theory and practice of sustainable design. There is an ongoing commitment to promoting informed environmental responsibility throughout the industry. We are living in a world with limited natural resources, which are being squandered needlessly. By committing to being environmentally responsible, and making every reasonable effort to view their practices through an environmental filter, credible organizations are dedicated to leading the way in making a positive difference.

In addition, there are countless citizen organizations, among them the National Resources Defense Council (NRDC), the Sierra Club, and Friends of the Earth, that provide knowledge, resources, inspiration, and relevant information focusing on environmental issues.

Get to know other professionals in your area with a similar vision and passion for green design. Contact manufacturers and encourage them to share information on their environmentally friendly products with you on a regular basis. Align yourself with similarly focused architects and contractors; exchange experiences over brown bag lunches; and invite them to join in a green training program. This is an effective way to rally potential project players up front before a project comes onboard, to promote early alliances. Work together toward creating the opportunities to design ecologically oriented architecture and interiors that celebrate the vernacular of your region.

Target Markets

Aligning yourself with like-minded professionals is exhilarating, and provides a solid launching pad as you begin to define the specific target markets and strategies for attracting clients. With your commitment to sustainability, critical thinking skills, foundation of knowledge, research strategies, and technological savvy all in hand, this is an exciting time to market yourself and to meet the sustainable needs of your future clients.

You have gained confidence that your design solutions will contribute to a sustainable future. By incorporating designs that reduce waste and by using products that are environmentally friendly, your work will begin to show the results and benefits of ecologically appropriate design solutions. See yourself as an expert educated and trained to safeguard the health and welfare of people and the planet in the life-supporting environments you design. As you take on the responsibility and significance of green design leadership and embrace the societal need for safer materials, transformation begins. Your design solutions will contribute to a sustainable future!

As interior designers, we bring to fruition the human interface with buildings, demonstrating a vital role in creating quality indoor environments. Building on your qualifications, project experience, and evident passion for the work, carve out your area of specialization and capitalize on the importance of your role within the building industry.

Increased market competition necessitates the need for differentiation and innovation, and demands a specific and strategic course of action from each of us. There is no particular competitive response to the green building market that rings true for every firm; the marketing efforts must instead focus on the intention of your mission, your specific and special capabilities, and the culture of your firm.

Market Differentiation

Green design services will encourage potential clients to think about the broader environment and can bring back those who are aligned with your message. Emphasize that green does not necessarily cost more, and can often save money in the long run. Marketing green provides unique opportunities by distinguishing your company from others and can move it into a new arena of expertise.

Create a distinction in the psyche of the buyer, by building on your unique qualities and, thereby, differentiating yourself from others. Encourage potential clients to think of you as the leading-edge firm in your area, specializing in green design. This may initially limit your market, but will sharply delineate you to buyers seeking that essential quality when searching for an interior designer for their projects.

Another means of positioning yourself is to focus on healthy, sustainable design solutions. You will find that if you mention the health benefits to potential clients, they will almost always express interest in hearing more. Who does not want a healthy, eco-friendly home for their family and future generations, which saves energy and uses resources responsibly? This approach encourages discussion about what the client wants and needs, and reframes his or her thinking regarding return on investment.

Innovation Benefits

Innovation is a key component to any thriving design practice. Clients hire you for your originality in design and services, so clearly identify and communicate your strengths in this area in your marketing tools and messaging. Green concepts—such as energy efficiency, improved indoor air quality, environmentally preferable products, higher durability and lower maintenance materials, and resource conservation—while easy to describe, do not necessarily address all of your clients' needs. Assemble a story intertwining these concepts with the core values and needs of your target market.

What can you give to your clients to provide a positive experience throughout the process? Design is an unfolding journey keeping in mind that, ultimately, the intention is to reflect the clients' wishes. Creating a home is one of the most deeply satisfying experiences, and this passage taps into those meaningful emotions. A bonding process that links together everyone involved leads to discovery and provides lasting memories. By slowly unveiling itself, a story materializes and unfolds.

Your greatest resource for building a sustaining business practice is success with your past clients. They hold the key to your future—they spread the word about you and return with new projects. The value of your creativity is timeless, in particular when the heart of a home is one that also integrates environmentally responsible solutions.

Strategic Action Plan

Differentiate yourself with focus and clarity, outlining your distinct characteristics. Knowing which markets to compete in, which to stay away from, and which clients you want simplifies your course of action.

Sharing your fresh brand, consider the following strategies to grow your firm as it embraces sustainability as a core value and as this passion permeates every level of the design process:

- Create specialized marketing materials.
- Craft a new division.
- Hire outside experts.
- Be the green expert in your region.
- Target regional versus national clients, or vice versa.
- Define ideal client types and projects.
- Seek out clients who value sustainability.
- Commit to improving IAQ on all projects.
- Develop a cost-competitive approach.
- Consider giving a discount to truly green clients.

Be cost-competitive; that is, for the same cost, incorporate sustainable solutions as part of your design procedures so that the client need not pay more in design fees. Keeping operational costs low will give a firm pricing flexibility. Given the tight budgets of many projects, the ability to compete on price is a valuable asset. A firm that is good at managing the process of integrated design is able to design a green home at the same fee as a conventional project. Lowering costs might be even more advantageous than branding as a means of competing in the marketplace, although it does take commitment and great discipline to manage a project within tight budgets.

Outline the techniques necessary to successfully complete green projects without additional design fees. Take time to attend training sessions and seminars, and acquire new information, as you stay current with design trends. Consider absorbing the extra time that it may take to become a knowledgeable green designer; it will be worth the investment. Despite the up-front costs and learning curve, it will benefit you and your firm in the long term.

Key areas that clients generally respond to:

- *Energy cost savings.* Clients want to save energy, save money, save resources.
- *Health of the planet.* Clients want to do their part to restore the health of the planet.
- *Healthier environment.* Clients want better quality of light, improved ventilation, and healthier indoor air quality to support quality of life and rejuvenation for themselves and their families.
- *Increased property values.* Clients are interested in a green home that brings higher property values.

Outreach

Sharing your expertise is an effective and valuable method of nurturing a strong sustainability presence in the marketplace. Activities such as speaking, lecturing, networking, writing articles, and gaining publicity and awards for successful projects enhance the visibility of the firm, reaffirming and highlighting your green message.

We have found that the green building community brings together a diverse group of professionals who are a passionate and inclusive bunch, willing to give of their time and to share openly. Connecting with open-minded individuals will help to realize the benefits of sharing successes and supporting one another through the challenges related to eco-friendly design.

By encouraging the training of project professionals, you get them on board and they become responsive to the need for sustainable solutions. Get to know and recommend green experts in related fields of sustainable design, such as mechanical, electrical, and lighting consultants. Offer to share knowledge and experiences with contractors and subcontractors. Discuss how to improve health conditions on the site through low-emitting products. Encourage environmentally friendly practices in the field.

Trusted experts are needed to widely and openly share their knowledge with others and transform our market. We observe daily how word of mouth and photos in publications proliferate style. Similar to the fashion and design industry, the tipping point for environmentally responsible green buildings will occur more swiftly through the combined actions of well-respected individuals within the industry. Such individuals, who have the ability to influence and inspire through compelling and successful stories, will assist in spreading the vision of a sustaining building industry.

Establish yourself as a credible resource within the interior design community, and beyond. Strive to energetically communicate your knowledge, practices, and values with others. Boldly question processes, methods, and products, moving toward sustainable solutions. Encourage the application of environmental principles and practices on all projects, using guiding tools such as LEED for Homes, a trademarked Green Building Rating System developed by the U.S. Green Building Council, or comparable home-building programs that support the adoption of sustainable buildings.

Embrace the promotion of responsible design within the building industry. Inspire and engage others in green design conversations, creating a lasting image for your firm. By modeling and educating the external team on sustaining practices and materials, you can become the sought-after expert in your area.

Sharing Successful Projects

As you take responsibility for your influence and the choices that you make in the marketplace, and do the work well, your good intentions will be rewarded by successfully accomplishing the green project goals and exceeding clients' expectations.

As part of your approach, consider developing internal tools that measure how sustainability is attained on projects. Refer to Chapter 5 for several checklists helpful in developing your own metrics toward quantifying the success of green projects.

Sharing success stories about your projects is one of the best vehicles to promote and celebrate your firm's commitment to sustainability. Stories capture people's attention—what worked, what didn't work—and by spreading this information, your credibility grows within the industry and with potential and current clients. Every time the story of a project is published or showcased, the industry becomes aware of the latest green developments, and your resume of expertise grows, demonstrating to clients that you can be trusted with their next project.

Openly share information about successful projects with your peers. Provide case study information by presenting the results at design conferences and submitting articles to trade magazines. Consider submitting projects for sustainable competitions now being offered by most design organizations and eco-magazines. Your efforts will further influence market transformation and provide additional credibility for your firm.

Cost Considerations

One of the first areas of resistance to greening a project from clients is often cost related: their perception is that green products cost more and, therefore, their homes will be more expensive. Having information that shows them clearly that this is not the case is invaluable.

Although some costs may be higher for more energy-efficient HVAC and appliances, energy- and water-conserving construction, and healthier nontoxic and environmentally friendly building materials, studies in the commercial sector are available to prove that an integrated design approach can minimize any increases—and often there are none.

Find out whether the project is in an area where local or state agencies are giving significant tax rebates and credits for going green. These incentives encourage

The Value of Energy Savings

A tangible starting position is focusing your client on energy savings. Sharing cost studies with clients confirms the need for a sustainable design approach and for solutions connecting back to the values that motivate. The Sustainable Building Task Force, a group of more than 40 California state government agencies, issued a report in October 2003 entitled "The Costs and Financial Benefits of Green Buildings." The report indicated that green buildings use an average of 30 percent less purchased energy than conventional buildings. The Department of Energy has estimated that homeowners can cut their utility costs by as much as 50 percent. These are just two examples that may assist in rousing your client's interest.

development and construction of smarter, more sustainable homes and communities, help conserve undeveloped land, reduce air and water pollution, improve public health, reduce traffic congestion, ensure more efficient water usage, and reduce energy bills and transportation costs.

Remind the client that green building and environmental benefits will add value to their home in the long run. Green or energy-efficient homes generally command a higher selling price, a tangible return on investment. Incorporating green features into a home, such as long-lasting materials, energy savings, and lower maintenance and costs of operation also saves money year by year, over the lifetime of the home.

Concerns about health and well-being are still the best areas where you can connect with clients. Communicate how their family will benefit from a healthier home through improved ventilation and indoor air quality, as well as less toxic finishes and materials. Remind them: Good health is priceless.

Commitment to Green

- Save money and resources by saving energy.
- Be energy-independent.
- Use home as a net energy exporter (producing more energy than the home demands).
- Build to last with low maintenance.
- Save money and resources by using fewer building materials.
- Help to drive the market for green building.
- Create healthy living environments for your family.
- Reduce your personal impact on the community and planet.
- Be a good neighbor.
- Become more self-sufficient.
- Live in harmony with your beliefs.
- Set an example for others.
- Use local materials and labor to support local economy.

Source: Angela Dean, AIA, LEED AP, author of *Green by Design* (Salt Lake City, UT: Gibbs Smith, 2003)

Value Bonding

What motivates and interests your client? Interior designers have a professional responsibility to educate clients about the need to build responsibly. Meet the needs of your clients by understanding their personal values and principles. Knowing that sustainable design fundamentally makes better buildings, improving their performance, saving money, and improving health are basic objectives. Better still is the idea of bonding with your clients over mutual values. What are the reasons that your client wants a green home? They might include one or more or all of the following:

- Meeting family's needs and desires.
- Embracing or exemplifying environmental stewardship and responsibility.
- Creating ambience and feeling of home.
- Doing the right thing.
- Being energy-efficient.
- Saving water and energy.
- Having healthy indoor air quality.
- Using recycled, salvaged, renewable, and sustainable materials.
- Protecting natural resources.
- Ensuring a healthy home for the family.
- Showing concern for global warming.
- Desiring a green building certification.
- Saving on operating costs.
- Enhancing quality of life.
- Accessing outdoor activities.
- Addressing health issues or chemical sensitivities.
- Protecting natural habitats.
- Using less energy; saving money.

Homeowners generally agree that designing a green or sustainable home is a benefit to their families and to the environment. In a survey conducted in 2002 by *Professional Builder Magazine,* consumers were asked the following questions regarding their search for a new home. Their responses indicate that most were aware of green building features, that they would add value to their homes, and, most importantly, were willing to pay *more* for them.

What are the most important environmental issues in a new home?

- 78 percent: Saving energy
- 56 percent: Using recycled content materials
- 38 percent: Improving IAQ
- 36 percent: Saving old-growth forests
- 33 percent: Slowing global warming

In addition:

- 42 percent are looking for a healthier home.
- 52 percent think ENERGY STAR certification should be standard in a new home.
- 46 percent knew sustainable harvested wood is available and said they wanted it in their home.

How much more would they be willing to pay for green features in a home?

- 32 percent said $2,500.
- 36 percent said $5,000.
- 20 percent said $10,000.

There is a growing segment of Americans that demographers are calling the "Cultural Creatives." This emerging segment of the population is educated, affluent, and ready to act on their social, environmental, and spiritual values. They care deeply about ecology, about saving the planet, about relationships, and about peace and social justice. They seek authenticity, are self-actualized, genuinely mindful of spirituality and self-expression. Also significant is that at least 60 percent of Cultural Creatives are women.

The Cultural Creatives market is larger and stronger than many realize, comprising a quarter of the population of the United States and Europe. That's a lot of people interested in integrating core values into their purchasing and investment decisions. Thus, businesses incorporating social and environmental relevance into their values are uniquely positioned to cater to this sector. The majority of Cultural Creatives are not looking for absolutes; they are seeking sound alternatives that resonate with them and demonstrate their values.

Ranging in age from 18 to 70, the Cultural Creatives are cross-generational; they are mainstream, grounded, and reasonable individuals, who are embracing a political alignment, balanced between liberal and conservative—they don't see themselves as political extremists. And they cover all income levels, from working class to very affluent, and embrace all ethnic groups.

There is vast market potential for companies integrating sustainable design into their practices. The Cultural Creatives are eager to learn about environmental sustaining options, including services and products; they are concerned for the whole planet. It will, literally, pay to align your firm with this sector of the marketplace that values a lifestyle of health and sustainability: in 2000, it was documented to be worth $230 billion in the United States and $540 billion worldwide. Food for thought!

A marketing approach that inspires by incorporating social and environmental equality offers benefits of "doing good" by tapping into the intuition of humankind. Seek out clients like the Cultural Creatives through value bonding, individuals who are reframing their life and values, and walking their talk in demonstrable ways. At any given time, one in four Americans is shifting his or her lifestyle and mind in fundamental ways—it's worth paying attention to these people! They are practical individuals who are inner-directed and socially concerned, looking for alternatives so that they can integrate their core values into every purchasing decision they make.

By embracing the tenets of sustainability you will be aligning yourself with countless others whose values define their work and lifestyle. As you come to fully appreciate how effective you can be as a driving force of change in the marketplace, you can begin to effectively analyze and formulate more innovative ways of marketing your sustainable design services in the twenty-first century.

RESOURCES

The Insider's Guide to Marketing Green Buildings, Jerry Yudelson, www.yudelson.net, (Green Building Marketing, February 2005)

"Selling Green Design to Clients Who Don't Ask For It," Jason F. McLennan and Peter Rumsey, *Environmental Design + Construction,* June 2003

"Selling Green: Show Them the Money," Penny Bonda, *Interior Design,* July 2005

CHAPTER 18

sustaining life

*This truth window offers insight
into the strawbale wall.
Photo by Doug Graybeal.
Architect: Doug Graybeal.*

*We might peer into the future at the generations yet unborn and ask ourselves if
we're really trustworthy custodians of their heritage. Do we have the right to tell
them that they can never see a whale?*

—DAVID R. BROWER

ntuitively, we are passionate about our beautiful blue planet, knowing that there is only one Earth that sustains all life. We can see that there is a gap between our values and the condition of the world, and that inspires us to action. The journey to narrow this gap between our values and the state of the environment begins to close as we become more involved in questioning the way we live and the way we work.

As we conclude this adventure of writing our first book, we come full circle to the question we asked as we set out: Why be sustainable? Without doubt, the health of our planet is important to each and every one of us, and how we respond to the challenge ahead will differ from one person to the next.

Questioning the Status Quo

The only real voyage of discovery exists, not in seeing new landscapes, but in having new eyes.

—MARCEL PROUST

How does change begin? Does it come from a longing and a willingness to attempt to make sense of something that is not making sense—from a deep desire to create, to look at a situation from a new, fresh perspective? We are continually inspired by extraordinary individuals who ask penetrating questions and cause real change. They reframe issues and provide fresh viewpoints, and their brilliance is that they challenge the assumptions of conventional thinking.

What was Rachael Carson saying?

Keep pollution out of your backyard? No. She was saying that we were beginning to see the death of nature. Carson's *Silent Spring,* which, in 1962, exposed the hazards of the pesticide DDT, eloquently questioned humanity's faith in technological progress and helped set the stage for the environmental movement.

What are Paul Hawken, Amory Lovins, and Hunter Lovins saying?

Bring an end to human economic activity because it is exceeding the planet's limits? No. Rather, in their groundbreaking book, *Natural Capitalism: Creating the Next Industrial Revolution* (Back Bay Books: New York, 2000), they are reframing the ways of doing business. This is the first book to explore the lucrative opportunities for businesses to transform themselves in an era of approaching environmental limits. Although we have been pushing those environmental limits back with clever new technologies, living systems are still undeniably in decline. These seemingly mutually exclusive trends need not be in conflict—in fact, there are opportunities and fortunes to be made in reconciling them.

In their revolutionary blueprint for a new economy, these three leading business visionaries explain how the world is on the verge of a new industrial revolution—one that promises to transform our fundamental notions about commerce and its role in shaping our future. *Natural Capitalism* describes a future in which business and environmental interests increasingly overlap, and in which businesses can better satisfy their customers' needs, increase profits, and help solve environmental problems, all at the same time.

"Natural capital" refers to the natural resources and ecosystem services that make possible all economic activity, indeed all life. These services are of immense economic value; some are literally priceless, as they have no known substitutes. Yet current business practices typically fail to take into account the value of these assets—which is rising with their scarcity. As a result, natural capital is being degraded and liquidated by the wasteful use of such resources as energy, materials, water, fiber, and topsoil.

Source: Modified excerpt from www.natcap.org.

What are William McDonough and Michael Braungart saying?

Stop the accepted ways of the industrial world and the building industry? No. They are saying that we can transform industry with Cradle-to-Cradle Design, MBDC's paradigm that models human industry on natural processes, creating safe and healthy prosperity. *Time Magazine* called it "a unified philosophy that—in demonstrable and practical ways—is changing the design of the world."

Instead of designing cradle-to-grave products, dumped in landfills at the end of their "life," MBDC transforms industry by creating products for cradle-to-cradle cycles, whose materials are perpetually circulated in closed loops. Maintaining materials in closed loops maximizes material value without damaging ecosystems.

Source: Modified excerpt from www.mbdc.com/c2c_home.htm.

What is Ray Anderson saying?

Stop striving for financial prosperity? No. The soft-spoken CEO of Interface, Inc., an Atlanta-based commercial carpet company, shares his personal realization that businesses need to embrace principles of sustainability. Upon reading Paul Hawken's book, *The Ecology of Commerce* (Collins, 1994), Anderson said he felt "the spear in his chest." In an extraordinary moment of corporate leadership and responsibility, he decided to turn his near $1 billion company around and become zero-waste and energy-efficient (and then energy self-sufficient) and improve the working conditions for all of his 7,000 employees in 40 cities worldwide.

In his book, *Mid-Course Correction* (Peregrinzilla Press, Atlanta, 1999), Anderson shares his efforts, at times frustrating, to apply these principles within a billion-dollar company. But, today, Interface has become one of the leaders in the industry by demonstrating that the principles of sustainability and financial success can coexist within a business, and can lead to a new prosperity that includes environmental stewardship and social equity.

Modified excerpt from http://sustainable.state.fl.us/fdi/fscc/news/world/9904/midcc.htm.

What is Al Gore saying?

Change our politics to stop global warming? No. "An Inconvenient Truth" by Al Gore gives voice to a crisis that impacts us all: global warming.

Scientists agree that global warming is increasing, and as a result, the Earth is literally heating up. Carbon dioxide and other gases that warm the surface of the planet naturally trap solar heat in the atmosphere. But instead of protecting life on this planet as normal, the increase in temperature caused primarily by human activities and fossil fuel use is causing temperatures to rise at an unprecedented and detrimental rate.

We are beginning to realize that our lives and actions directly affect global warming—this is not a natural occurrence. Al Gore asks us to look around and see the signs: glacier icecaps are melting, plants and animals are being forced from their habitat, and the number of severe storms and droughts is increasing.

What will the future hold if we continue to allow this warming trend to continue?

- Deaths from global warming will double in just 26 years—to 300,000 people a year.
- Global sea levels could rise by more than 20 feet with the loss of shelf ice in Greenland and Antarctica, devastating coastal areas worldwide.
- Heat waves will be more frequent and more intense.
- Droughts and wildfires will occur more often.
- The Arctic Ocean could be ice free in summer by 2050.
- More than a million species worldwide could be driven to extinction by 2050. (www.climatecrisis.net, www.an-inconvenient-truth.com)

Global warming is a moral issue and we have a responsibility to act, and to reverse these catastrophic events. There are many practical and worthwhile actions we can all take and our choices today will influence whether or not there is life for the next generation. Our collective action, at the smallest level, can make a difference and there is no doubt together we can solve this problem.

What will you now be saying?

Begin by questioning the unspoken assumptions in your practice. Question your own business practices and procedures, and then begin to question others throughout the interior design industry. Questioning has a remarkable potential for opening up creativity in our lives. It gives us courage as we venture into unfamiliar territory. Ask vital questions that are critical to blowing wide open your reality. Expand your mind, which will lead to new ways of thinking, which will lead to environmental stewardship.

- Is it really okay to allow destruction of the environment? No!
- Is it really okay to pollute our waters with toxic chemicals? No!
- Is it really okay to allow pollution that is killing our forests and lakes with acid rain? No!
- Is it really okay to use pesticides that poison the land and the crops that we and our children eat? No!

As we reframe major concepts, two things begin to happen. The content of the questions change our viewpoint, and we grow comfortable with the process of questioning the unspoken assumptions of the old culture. This creates and encourages a passionate new direction.

In a paper entitled, "Places to Intervene in a System," Dr. Donella (Dana) Meadows, the founder of the Sustainability Institute and a professor at Dartmouth College, concluded that the most effective, and most difficult, place to intervene in a system is to challenge the mind-set behind the system in the first place—the paradigms, the perceptions of reality, the mental model of how things are that underlie the system.

It is time for a paradigm shift, based on an accurate view of reality. The life support systems of the earth are clearly in decline. Many different species are disappearing at a rate unknown in the last 65 million years. Paul Hawken calls it "the death of birth." This also includes our own species.

Each time we make a choice, it affects the planet, either positively or negatively. With every positive action we take, we change the world. Our responsibility is to question, respond, and take action. Gather reliable information on how to apply sustainable design principles and practices, and model change by respectfully, yet tenaciously, questioning the status quo.

Purposeful Living

Designers literally set the stage for creating memorable and inspirational environments, connecting with clients on an emotional level through our art, the art of design. We cultivate the spirit of a home, through an intricate language that speaks of texture, color, scale, layer, tone, and style. Today, we play a key role in incorporating a holistic approach to solving environmental problems and creating sustainable homes for our clients. Intention brings forth a relationship with core values, and results in a deeper respect for nature, reconnecting us with all that is life-affirming.

Through design and personal growth, intertwined with environmental advocacy, we become more deeply engaged in community and global concerns. As we become more involved in ecological issues and in our own personal growth, we are better able to achieve balance in our lives. This reframing process is a defining step. It compels us to question the status quo—the old opinions and beliefs that have been dictating how we work and live. A new perspective and a new take on reality pave the way to redefining our moral concerns. And by paying close attention, we gain clarity in unsuspecting ways—ways that anchor our thinking. At first this may feel somewhat overwhelming: we realize there is so much to tackle and so many other areas we still have to deal with. This is a normal part of the process. As we learn to affirm our values and find new solutions to old problems, we become optimistic about the future. As we redefine the meaning of success we begin to lead more passionate, purposeful lives; we accept responsibility for and become accountable to the environment and society at large, ultimately creating a better future for everyone on the planet. What could be more personally fulfilling?

- Be part of the solution.
- Walk the talk.
- Adopt environmental principles and practices.
- Develop your own personal vision and action plan.

In sum, to quote Nike's marketing tagline: "Just Do It!" Integrate sustainable design into your projects. Move forward with energy-saving concepts, sustainable materials, and healthy alternatives for both your client and your planet. Embrace sustainability through your passion for design, and have the determination to stay committed. Invigorate your spirit, the work, the clients and the project team; bring synergistic sustainable solutions to all projects. The reward will be a profound connection to a sense of place.

Connection to a sustaining world inspires ingenious designs, so be courageous, spirited, and persistent in your practice. Enjoy and embrace the journey. Offer environmentally responsible designs that showcase your integrity—designs that are so beautiful that they bring out the best in people.

Inspirational Mentors

Over the last decade we have had the good fortune to experience many of our environmental mentors. From William to Janine, Ray to Hunter, Paul to Paula, Daniel to Julia, David to Penny, Michael to Steve, these insightful teachers have inspired us to think and act. Filled with intense commitment and enthusiastic intention, we can, likewise, aspire to be responsible citizens of planet Earth.

With these motivational leaders and world-renowned environmental entrepreneurs as our guides, we can truly transform the practice of residential interior design. By seeking out advisors and mentors who inspire us; by reading, engaging in conversations with role models; attending seminars and conferences, and then reading more, we can integrate the language and spirit of sustainable design into our beings.

As you know by now, we regard Ray Anderson, the chairman and founder of Interface, Inc., and former co-chair of the President's Council on Sustainable Development, as an inspiring role model. He addressed the 21st Century Policy Project, along with other interested parties involved in forming a new consensus for the future of solid waste management in California. We are highlighting parts of Ray's speech here because we wholeheartedly believe in his passionate and powerful message. He inspires us, once again, to action:

> I am often asked to make the business case for sustainability, and here it is in my opinion. First, to provide the framework: The economy is the wholly owned subsidiary of the environment. Without a healthy parent the child is doomed. Therefore, the first case for sustainability in a pure business sense is survival. If we don't get there, if we don't move there rapidly, our descendants will see markets, as well as society, disintegrate. We must do better than that by them.
>
> The second case is that it is really possible to do well by doing good, and we're seeing it in our business every day. I believe that is the paradigm for success in the next industrial revolution. In the twenty-first century, the companies that do well and do good will be recognized as successful. And it will not be possible to do well without doing it responsibly.
>
> The third case, I believe, is that there are new and noble fortunes to be made in bringing the technologies and the products of those technologies to market in the next industrial revolution. I think entrepreneurs everywhere should thank Rachel Carson for starting it all in 1962 with that wonderful book,

Taking Action: David Suzuki

David Suzuki, one of our favorites, is leading the sustainable way in Canada through the David Suzuki Foundation, a science-based environmental organization, working to protect the balance of nature and quality of life. To put Canada on a direct path to sustainability by the year 2030, the foundation has developed an action plan called Sustainability within a Generation: A New Vision for Canada. Written by a leading environmental thinker, David Boyd, the report clearly outlines the solutions to Canada's environmental challenges.

Sustainability is neither a lofty ideal nor an academic concept, but an urgent imperative for humanity. Sustainability means living within Earth's limits. In a sustainable future, no Canadian would think twice about drinking a glass of tap water. Food would be free from pesticide residues, antibiotics, and growth hormones. Air, water, and soil would be uncontaminated by toxic substances. In a sustainable future, it would be safe to swim in every Canadian river and lake and safe to eat fish wherever they were caught. Clean, renewable energy would be generated by harnessing the sun, wind, water, and heat of the Earth.

A sustainable future would mean a global climate undisturbed by human pollution. Canadians would no longer fear sunburn or cancer caused by damage to the ozone layer. No one would worry about nature's extraordinary diversity diminishing at human hands. Endangered ecosystems and species would recover and thrive. Canadians would be confident that future generations would enjoy the same spectacular natural heritage and quality of life that we enjoy today.

Source: The David Suzuki Foundation, www.davidsuzuki.org/WOL/Sustainability, 2005.

Silent Spring. In the next industrial revolution, the technophobes—the people who hate technology and say it's the problem—and the technophiles—the people who say it is the solution—will be reconciled, and [the resultant] technologies [will be] sustainable technologies. Technology and labor, so at odds throughout the whole industrial revolution, will be reconciled in the next industrial revolution.

The interest of business, the interest of nature, so at odds in the first industrial revolution will be reconciled—thesis, antithesis, synthesis, the Hegelian process of history again, but leading us toward a sustainable earth. I think one more important characteristic of the next industrial revolution is the ascendancy of women in business, in government, in education, in all of our institutions. It is coming just in the nick of time. Women bring that right-brain nurturing instinct to the table, and any man who has been in a meeting where there was a woman present knows it's a better meeting, with a better outcome, because of a woman's presence.

* * *

A few days later, totally out of the blue, came a message from one of the people in that audience. It was one of the most encouraging moments of my life because it told me that at least one person in that audience really "got it." It was an original poem composed after that Tuesday morning meeting and sent to me by e-mail from Glenn Thomas:

Tomorrow's child,
without a name,
an unseen face
and knowing not your time or place.

Tomorrow's child though yet unborn,
I met you first last Tuesday morn.
A wise friend introduced us two,
and through his shining point of view,
I saw a day that you would see,
a day for you,
but not for me.

Knowing you has changed my thinking,
for I never had an inkling
that perhaps the things I do
might someday, somehow,
threaten you.

Tomorrow's child,
my daughter, son,
I'm afraid I've just begun
to think of you
and of your good,
though always having known I should.

Begin I will,
to weigh the cost of what I squander,
what is lost
if ever I forget,
that you will someday come and live here too.

"Tomorrow's Child" speaks to us across the generations with a message so simple yet so profound, reminding us that we are all part of the web of life, every last one of us. During our brief visit here, on this beautiful blue planet, we have a really simple but profound choice to make—to help that web of life or to hurt it—and it's your call how you live your life.

Keynote address by Ray Anderson, reprinted with permission; www.ciwmb.ca.gov/2000Plus/Events/SummitJan99/keytext.htm.

In Conclusion

It is time: we must begin to think beyond ourselves. We must consider, not just our own species (and living environment), but all species and all ecosystems, taking into consideration the impact of our brief time on this planet we call Earth. Maintaining the health and the diversity of nature (which includes the entire world of living things and the outdoors) is crucial to sustaining the web of life.

By keeping ourselves open to questions that we should care about, and seeking answers to those questions, we will continue to move forward to a more purposeful life. And don't forget to share your questions, share your answers, share your knowledge, share your experiences, share your hopes and dreams, and share your spirit. Set your goals, engage your peers in the respectful exchange of ideas, and make things happen. Doing so is vital to sustaining life on our planet.

Decide to be a positive force in transforming the market, to be a catalyst for change. By promoting change within the residential interior design industry, you will be doing your part in contributing to a healthy planet and the well-being of our children's children—for all the generations to come.

Get motivated. Get informed. Reach out with courage and commitment. Grab hold of this purposeful journey of responsibility, education, accountability, power of choice and passion. Help to create a better world.

If not you, who?

Whatever you can do, or dream you can, begin it. Boldness has genius, power and magic in it.

—GOETHE

RESOURCES

Web Sites

American Institute of Architects Committee on the Environment (AIA COTE): www.aia.org/cote.
The Committee on the Environment works to advance, disseminate, and advocate—to the profession, the building industry, the academy, and the public—design practices that integrate built and natural systems and enhance both the design quality and environmental performance of the built environment.

American Society of Interior Designer (ASID): www.asid.org.
ASID is a community of people—designers, industry representatives, educators and students—committed to interior design. Through education, knowledge sharing, advocacy, community building and outreach, the Society strives to advance the interior design profession and, in the process, to demonstrate and celebrate the power of design to positively change people's lives. Its more than 38,000 members engage in a variety of professional programs and activities through a network of 48 chapters throughout the United States and Canada. They have a well developed Sustainable Design Information Center on their website at http://www.asid.org/resource/Sustainable+Design+Information+Center.htm

Architects / Designers / Planners for Social Responsibility (ADPSR): www.adpsr.org.
Established in 1981, Architects / Designers / Planners for Social Responsibility works for peace, environmental protection, ecological building, social justice, and the development of healthy communities. They believe that design practitioners have a significant role to play in the well-being of our communities.

Architecture Research Institute: www.architect.org/institute/programs/sustainable.
Provides a comparative list of differences between conventional and sustainable design processes. Also includes a list of sustainable resources and of architects who practice ecological design.

Associates III: www.associates3.com (the authors).
An interior design firm in Denver, Colorado, that embodies Earth-sustaining principles. Associates III practices exceptional green design that encompasses green principles and practices that are beautiful, practical, lasting, creative, and life-enhancing. In the Green Links zone of the site is an extensive list of online resources.

ASTM International: www.astm.org.
One of the largest voluntary standards development organizations in the world, ASTM is a valuable source for technical standards for materials, products, systems, and services that are globally accepted and utilized.

Building Concerns: www.buildingconcerns.com.
Directories (organized by geographic region) of organizations, businesses, and professionals working in the field of sustainable design, building, and development.

BuildingGreen: www.buildinggreen.com.
A subscription-based online resource for environmentally sensitive design and construction. Building Green Suite offers a range of information, from articles and product listings to project case studies.

Build It Green: http://builditgreen.org.
Professional nonprofit organization whose focus is to transform the building industry so that buildings are remodeled and built using green practices and products. This Web site offers a diverse list of references and links for sustainable building.

Built Green: www.builtgreen.org.
Located in Denver, Colorado, Built Green is one of the largest green building programs in the nation. It is a voluntary program, which encourages homebuilders to use technologies, products, and practices that will lessen the negative impacts of building on natural and indoor environments. On its "Other Related Sites" Web page is a list of various Web sites that address many sustainable building options and questions.

Carpet America Recovery Effort (CARE): www.carpetrecovery.org.
CARE, a voluntary initiative of the carpet industry and the government to prevent carpet from burdening landfills, focuses on developing carpet reclamation and recycling methods.

Carpet and Rug Institute (CRI): www.carpet-rug.org.
The national trade association representing the carpet and rug industry. Headquartered in Dalton, Georgia, the institute's membership consists of manufacturers representing over 90 percent of all carpet produced in the United States, and suppliers of raw materials and services to the industry. The CRI Green Label Plus logo displayed on carpet and adhesive samples informs customers that the product type has been tested and certified by an independent laboratory and has met stringent criteria for low emissions.

Centre for Design: www.cfd.rmit.edu.au.
An Australian company that seeks to research and document options that support environmentally friendly design. Information, publications, and case studies detail sustainable products, buildings, and materials, as well as life-cycle assessment.

Cornell Cooperative Extension: www.cce.cornell.edu/schuyler/recycle/businesses.htm.
A source of helpful information on recycling for businesses; also contains a reference list for further recycling research.

e-build: www.ebuild.com.
An online directory of more than 300,000 building supplies, listed by category. A helpful overall guide for construction, but not necessarily for sustainable construction.

Ecological Building Network: www.ecobuildnetwork.org/general.htm.
An international association of builders, engineers, architects, academics, and developers committed to promoting intelligent building methods and materials for a sustainable future. Contains an extensive list of resources for building green.

Ecology Action: www.ecoact.org.
The Green Building Program area of this site provides a Green Building Materials Guide, which explains in detail many of the pros and cons of a variety of sustainable building materials.

Efficient Lighting Fixtures for the Home: www.elflist.com.
This site, sponsored by Seattle City Light & Puget Sound Energy, offers articles and lighting design tips that help in creating efficient and healthy interior lighting plans. Also here are resources for additional lighting research.

ENERGY STAR: www.energystar.gov.
A partnership program between industry and the U.S. government (through the EPA) that labels and promotes energy-efficient products. The program began in 1992, and now the blue-star logo appears on those appliances that excel in energy efficiency. ENERGY STAR qualifies computers, heating and cooling equipment, major home appliances, lighting, home electronics, and office equipment, and even new homes built with the most energy-efficient appliances and equipment.

Environmental Home Center: www.environmentalhomecenter.com.
An online store offering a large variety of home and building products that protect health, use energy and other resources sparingly, and are very well made.

Environmental Protection Agency (EPA): www.epa.gov.
Web site detailing current events in energy news. Also provides sections dedicated to more specific environmental issues, such as mold, waste, and recycling.

Forest Stewardship Council (FSC): www.fscus.org.
An international nonprofit organization founded in 1993 to support environmentally appropriate, socially beneficial, and economically viable management of the world's forests. FSC administers a forestry certification program to assure that businesses supply trees and wood from a forest managed in an ecologically sustainable manner. Products bearing the FSC logo guarantee that the wood is from a certified well-managed forest, available across the world from a variety of mills, manufacturers, and distributors.

Global Green USA: www.globalgreen.org.
An American affiliate of Green Cross International, Global Green USA works with governments, industry, and individuals to create a global shift toward a sustainable and secure future.

Green Blue Institute: www.greenblue.org.
A non-profit institute inspiring transformation in the design of human industry and raising awareness on sustainable issues.

Green Building Pages: www.greenbuildingpages.com.
A sustainable building materials database and design tool for the environmentally and socially responsible designer, builder, and client.

Green Clips Newsletter: www.greenclips.com.
Summarizing news on sustainable building design and related government and business issues, this newsletter is published every two weeks and delivered via email.

Greener Choices:
www.eco-labels.org/greenconsumers/home.cfm.
The green version of *Consumer Reports,* providing information on a variety of household products and identifying which choices are most environmentally sustainable.

Greenguard Environmental Institute (GEI):
www.greenguard.org.
An industry-independent, nonprofit organization that oversees the GREENGUARD Certification Program. As an ANSI-Accredited Standards Developer, GEI establishes acceptable indoor air standards for indoor products, environments, and buildings. GEI's mission is to improve public health and quality of life through programs that improve indoor air.

Green Home Guide: www.greenhomeguide.com/index.php.
Offers unbiased views from professionals on a variety of home-related materials and products.

GreenTreks: www.greentreks.org.
Offers entertaining programming about ordinary people doing extraordinary things for the environment. Educational links and resources listed here, as well.

Green Sage: www.greensage.com.
Promotes sustainable building materials and furnishings, for the trade and for residential consumers. Provides a helpful list of professionals that can be contacted for further support in green construction and design projects.

Green Seal: www.greenseal.org.
An eco-labeling group that works at certifying products, through a rigorous scientific process, that are ecologically responsible. Product evaluations are conducted using a life-cycle approach to ensure that all significant environmental impacts of a product are considered, from raw materials extraction through manufacturing to use and disposal. Green Seal works with manufacturers, industry sectors, purchasing groups, and governments at all levels to "green" the production and purchasing chain.

HOK Sustainable Design: www.hoksustainabledesign.com.
A design firm committed to sustainability practices and principles. Its Web site offers resources that include case studies and green design checklists, as well as a list detailing the firm's "Ten Keys to Sustainable Design" process.

InformeDesign: www.informedesign.umn.edu.
A research and communication tool developed by the University of Minnesota and sponsored by the Association of Interior Design (ASID), which offers extensive research on a number of products, including many building products.

Institute for Global Communications: www.igc.org.
A source of news and informational articles on a wide variety of topics, including sustainability issues around the globe.

Institute for Market Transformation to Sustainability (MTS): www.mts.sustainableproducts.com.
This organization creates standards to gauge the success of manufacturers in addressing three key areas of sustainable practices: environmental, social, and economic. The standards page of the Web site details many well-known product standards to look for in choosing products for projects.

Interface Sustainability: www.interfacesustainability.com.
A leader in the commercial interiors market, offering floor coverings and fabrics. The company is committed to the goal of sustainability and doing business in ways that minimize the impact on the environment. The Web site offers insight into the philosophy that is leading Interface in its vision to cause less of a negative impact from its manufacturing processes and to have an overall positive influence on the many facets of running the business.

Interior Design Magazine: www.interiordesign.net.
A publication dedicated to the field of interior design. On the Web site is an area called the "Green Zone," which has links to articles and information on manufacturers that produce sustainable interiors products.

Interiors & Sources Magazine: www.isdesignet.com.
Industry trade publication and Web site that offers articles and news on cutting-edge sustainability and interior design issues; also provides helpful information on products and associations.

International Council for Local Environmental Initiatives:
www.iclei.org.
An association of local governments and national and regional local government organizations that have made a commitment to sustainable development. Its focus is on programs and strategic planning that address local sustainability while protecting the global common good.

International Fair Trade Association (IFAT): www.ifat.org.
IFAT is the International Fair Trade Association, the global network of Fair Trade Organizations. IFAT's mission is to improve the livelihoods and well being of disadvantaged producers by linking and promoting Fair Trade Organizations, and speaking out for greater justice in world trade.

International Interior Design Association (IIDA):
www.iida.org
The International Interior Design Association (IIDA) is a professional networking and educational association of more

than 10,000 members in eight specialty forums, nine (9) Regions, and more than thirty (30) chapters around the world. IIDA is committed to enhancing the quality of life through excellence in interior design and advancing interior design through knowledge. IIDA advocates for interior design excellence; provides superior industry information; nurtures a global interior design community; maintains educational standards; and responds to trends in business and design.

Massachusetts Sustainable Design Roundtable Links to Research Studies and Web Sites: www.mass.gov/envir/Sustainable/initiatives/initiativesroundtablewgresearch.htm.
An extensive list of online resources for sustainable design research and application.

McDonough Braungart Design Chemistry (MBDC): www.mbdc.com.
A product and process design firm dedicated to transforming the design of products, processes, and services worldwide. Founded by William McDonough and Michael Braungart, MBDC offers innovative support to businesses interested in implementing sustainable practices. The group supports the new design paradigm called Cradle-to-Cradle Design, and assists with the implementation of eco-effective design principles.

National Park Service Sustainability News: www.nature.nps.gov/SustainabilityNews.
This online publication includes a searchable database of articles related to many aspects of sustainability.

National Resources Defense Council: www.nrdc.org.
A comprehensive Web site dealing with a multitude of environmental and social issues, locally and globally. Articles on environmental impacts are provided, as well as links to related sites and resources. NRDC's mission is to safeguard the Earth, its people, its plants and animals, and the natural systems on which all life depends.

Natural Capitalism: www.naturalcapitalism.org.
Natural Capitalism: Creating the Next Industrial Revolution by Paul Hawken, Amory Lovins, and L. Hunter Lovins (Boston, MA: Back Bay Books, 2000) is the first book to explore the lucrative opportunities for businesses in an era of approaching environmental limits.

Natural Step: www.naturalstep.org.
An international agency that focuses its research on sustainable resource use and solution implementation worldwide. Its U.S. office, located in Oregon, can be accessed via www.ortns.org. This Web site offers sustainable building resources as well as guidelines for sustainable building processes.

Not So Big House: www.notsobighouse.com.
This rich Web site, of the same name of the book by Sarah Susanka, is full of inspiration on creating homes that are scaled to a size that serves the inhabitants as well as the planet. Many resources are listed here, along with the opportunity to purchase sustainable-sized house plans.

Oikos Green Building Source: www.oikos.com.
Articles and products with a focus on sustainability are featured on this site. Oikos is also an independent bookseller offering sustainable book choices online.

Rainforest Alliance Network (RAN): www.ran.org.
The Rainforest Alliance protects ecosystems and the people and wildlife that depend on them by transforming land-use practices, business practices, and consumer behavior. Companies, cooperatives, and landowners that participate in their programs meet rigorous standards that conserve biodiversity and provide sustainable livelihoods. Based in New York City, with offices worldwide, RAN works with people whose livelihoods depend on the land, helping them transform the way they grow food, harvest wood, and host travelers. RAN has helped convince dozens of corporations, including Home Depot, Citigroup, Boise Cascade, and Goldman Sachs, to change their practices.

Rocky Mountain Institute: www.rmi.org.
As described on its Web site, "Rocky Mountain Institute is an entrepreneurial nonprofit organization that fosters the efficient and restorative use of resources to make the world secure, just, prosperous, and life-sustaining. We do this by inspiring business, civil society, and government to design integrative solutions that create true wealth." This wonderful organization promotes research and conversation on many of the environmental issues of concern to the planet, and offers positive information that can assist people in making more environmentally responsible choices.

Scientific Certification Systems (SCS): www.scscertified.com.
The nation's first third-party certifier for testing pesticide residues in fresh produce, established in 1984. In the past 18 years, the company has evolved to become a certifier of multiple facets of the food industry and of the environmentally sound management of forests, marine habitats, and a wide variety of manufacturing-related businesses.

Slash the Trash/Wabash County Solid Waste Management District: www.slashthetrash.com/grbld.htm#div9.
Overview of a program initiated in Wabash County, IN, to reduce construction waste and diminish the waste that enters the landfill. The program supports green building measures as well.

**Society for Responsible Design:
www.green.net.au/srd/index. html.**
A nonprofit group that works toward a sustainable future through environmentally and socially responsible design practices. It promotes and disseminates material, providing a forum for the exchange of information on responsible design.

Steel Recycling Institute: www.recycle-steel.org.
Lists places to recycle steel, offers articles on steel construction recycling, and provides a locator to find a steel recycling facility close to you.

Sustainability Institute: http://sustainer.org.
Offers workshops, classes, and coaching in sustainability procedures, using systems thinking and organizational learning tools to help people put the principles of sustainability into practice.

**Sustainable Architecture, Building and Culture:
www.sustainableabc.com.**
Helpful Web site listing sustainable products, events, and services under various categories, including additional sustainable design research.

Sustainable Builder: www.greenbuilder.com.
This comprehensive site focuses on all aspects of the field of sustainable building, including where to locate resources and professional contacts. The Sourcebook section was developed to foster the implementation of environmentally responsible practices in homebuilding.

Sustainable Design Resource Guide: www.aiasdrg.org.
Developed by the Denver chapter of the American Institute of Architects Committee on the Environment, and the Colorado Chapter of Architects, Designers, and Planners for Social Responsibility, with the intention of assisting people in finding suitable materials and available products that help sustain the Earth and human health. The guide is divided into 16 divisions to make researching easy.

**Sustainable Development Web Sites:
www.library.gatech.edu/architect/CRP6233.htm#web.**
Designed by students of Georgia Tech, this site is a wealth of information listing Web sites under several categories that are useful for gathering information on sustainable building and design.

Treehugger: www.treehugger.com.
A Web-based magazine that provides the latest news, reviews, and information about green products and other environmentally responsible topics.

U.S. Department of Energy: www.eere.energy.gov.
Offers information, including articles and links, on many energy-related topics, in particular on creating energy-efficient buildings.

U.S. General Services Administration (GSA): www.gsa.gov.
GSA's mission is to help other agencies better serve the public by meeting their needs for products and services. This site simplifies citizen access to government information and services. The building page details laws that apply to many types of building use.

U.S. Green Building Council (USGBC): www.usgbc.org.
The mission of the USGBC is to be the nation's foremost coalition of leaders from across the building industry who are working to promote buildings that are environmentally responsible, profitable, and healthy places to live and work. The Web site details the LEED program, which is a revolutionary program aimed at helping companies create sustainable structures.

Recommended Reading

BOOKS

Biomimicry: Innovation Inspired by Nature, Janine Benyus (London, UK: Harper Perennial, 2002)

Cradle to Cradle: Remaking the Way We Make Things, William McDonough and Michael Braungart (New York, NY: North Point Press, 2002)

Designing the Good Home, Dennis Wedlick (New York, NY: Collins Design, 2003)

Eco, Elizabeth Wilhide (New York, NY: Rizzoli, 2003)

EcoHome: A Healthy Home from A to Z, A. Krueger (New York, NY: Avon Books, 1992)

Eco Interiors, Grazyna Pilatowicz (Hoboken, NJ: Wiley & Sons, 1994)

Ecological Design, Sim Van Der Ryn and Stuart Cowan (Washington, D.C.: Island Press, 1995)

The Ecology of Commerce, Paul Hawken

Every Breath You Take, BP Loughridge (New York, NY: Collins Design, 1994)

Good Green Homes, Jennifer Roberts (Layton, UT: Gibbs Smith, 2003)

The Good House Book, Clarke Snell (Asheville, NC: Lark Books, 2004)

Healing Environments, Carol Venolia (Berkeley, CA: Celestial Arts, 1988)

Healthy by Design, David Rousseau and James Wasley (Vancouver, BC: Hartley & Marks Publishers, 1999)

The Healthy Home, Linda Mason Hunter New York, NY: Backprint.com, 2000)

The Healthy Home Kit, Ingrid Ritchie & Stephen J. Martin (Chicago, IL: Dearborn Financial Publishing, 1994)

Healthy House Building: A Design & Construction Guide, John Bower (Bloomington, IN: Healthy House Institute, 1993)

Homes That Heal, Athena Thompson (Gabriola, BC: New Society Publishers, 2004)

The Household Environment and Chronic Illness: Guidelines for Constructing & Maintaining a Less Polluted Residence, Guy O. Pfeiffer and Casimer M. Nikel (Springfield, IL: Charles C. Thomas Pub Ltd, 1980)

Indoor Air Quality and Human Health, Isaac Turiel (Palo Alto, CA: Stanford University Press, 1985)

Ishmael, Daniel Quinn (Rebound by Sagebrush, 1999)

Mid-Course Correction, Ray C. Anderson (Atlanta, GA: Peregrinzilla Press, 1999)

Natural Capitalism, Paul Hawken, Amory Lovins, and L. Hunter Lovins (Boston, MA: Back Bay Books, 2000)

The Natural House Book, David Pearson (New York: Simon & Schuster Inc., 1989)

The Natural Step Story, Karl-Henrik Robert (Gabriola, BC: New Society Publishers, 2002)

The Non-Toxic Home & Office, Debra Lynn Dadd (New York: NY: Tarcher/Putnum Books, 1992)

The Not So Big House, Sarah Susanka (Newton, CT: Taunton, 2001)

Places for the Soul, Christopher Day (Burlington, MA: Architectural Press, 2003)

Prescriptions for a Healthy House, Paula Baker Laporte (Gabriola, BC: New Society Publishers, 2001)

A Primer on Sustainable Building, Dianna Lopez Barnett & William D. Browning (Snowmass, CO: Rocky Mountain Institute, 1995)

Silent Spring, Rachael Carson (New York, NY: Mariner Books, 2002)

Starting Points for a Healthy Habitat, Carl E. Grimes (Denver, CO: GMC Media, 1999)

Your Health & the Indoor Environment, Randall Earl Dunford (Dallas, TX: NuDawn Publishing, 1994)

Your Home, Your Health & Your Well-Being, David Rousseau (Berkeley, CA: Ten Speed Press, 1988)

Your Natural Home, Janet Marinelli & Paul Bierman-Lytle (London, UK: Little Brown & Co., 1995)

MAGAZINES

Dwell	www.dwell.com
Ecological Home	www.ecologicalhomeideas.com
Eco-Structure	www.eco-structure.com
ED&C	www.EDCmag.com
The E Magazine	www.emagazine.com
Environmental Building News	www.buildinggreen.com.
Green @ Work	www.greenatworkmag.com
GreenSource	www.greensourcemag.com
Interiors & Sources	www.interiorsandsources.com
The LOHAS Journal	www.lohas.com
Metropolis	www.metropolismag.com
Natural Home & Garden	www.naturalhomeandgarden.com
Plenty	www.plentymagazine.com
Sustainable Industries Journal	www.sijournal.com
Ultimate Home Design	www.UltimateHomeDesign.com
Worthwhile	www.worthwhilemag.com
Yes Magazine	www.yesmagazine.org

GLOSSARY

Acetone. A chemically derived solvent, usually found in masonry, caulking, wallcoverings, strippers, adhesives, polyurethane, stains, and sealers.

Admixtures or additives (concrete). Minor ingredients mixed with concrete to impart particular properties such as color, decreased drying time, or improved workability.

Air-exchange rate. (1) The number of times that the outdoor air replaces the volume of air in a building per unit of time, typically expressed as air changes per hour. (2) The rate at which the ventilation system replaces the air within a room or building.

Air pollution. Airborne contaminants that adversely affect the environment or human health.

Allergen. Any substance capable of producing an allergic response. Some common allergens are proteins contained in pollens, grains, fungi, nuts, and seeds.

Anaphylactic. A severe and sometimes life-threatening immune system reaction to an antigen that a person has been previously exposed to. The reaction may include itchy skin, edema, collapsed blood vessels, fainting, and difficulty in breathing.

Aromatic hydrocarbons. A large family of chemicals, characterized by the elements of hydrogen and carbon in ring-shaped molecules. Many aromatic hydrocarbons (e.g., toluene and xylene) evaporate readily and have strong odors. Many (e.g., benzene) are toxic or carcinogenic. All contaminate air and groundwater.

Barrier cloth. A special synthetic or cotton fabric that does not allow dust to penetrate. It has a very high thread count (300 per inch or greater) and is tightly woven.

Benzene. A carbon and hydrogen compound made from petroleum and coal, with a ring-shaped molecule. Benzene is one of the most common building blocks for synthetic chemicals, found in synthetic fibers and plastics. Highly toxic and carcinogenic, it is listed as a hazardous air pollutant under the 1990 Clean Air Act.

BHA or BHT. Butylated hydroxyl anisole (BHA) is a preservative, listed as a carcinogen by state of California. BHT (butylated hydroxy toluene) serves as an ultraviolet inhibitor and an antioxidant. It was used through the years as a preservative in polypropylene yarn systems, carpet adhesives, some latex formulations, various backings and back coatings, and many other consumer products. Many rebond carpet padding products may contain BHT and has been attributed to numerous carpet yellowing complaints. BHT is considered nontoxic and is even contained in many food items.

Biocide. An additive that will prevent growth of bacteria or fungi. Biocides are used in paints, floor coverings, and sometimes in fabrics. They are often toxic materials, safe only in very low concentrations.

Biodegradable. Able to decompose through the normal action of bacteria and fungi, without harmful effects to the environment. Typical examples of biodegradable materials are paper and wood products, natural fibers, and starches.

Biological. Of, relating to, caused by, or affecting life or living organisms.

Blackwater. Wastewater that is unfit for reuse because of sanitary concerns, such as that from toilets. See also *graywater.*

Borax. A low-toxicity mineral with insecticidal, fungicidal, and herbicidal properties. It does not evaporate or volatilize into the air or pose the considerable health concerns associated with synthetic pesticides. Boric acid and borate salts are the refined forms of borax commonly used in structural pest control; these have been refined with low-grade acids and allowed to crystallize to form borates.

Building-related illness (BRI). Serious and diagnosable health condition, usually of the respiratory system, that can be attributed to specific air quality problems within a building.

Cadmium. A soft, easily molded heavy metal, used in pigments and as heat stabilizers in the vinyl-making process. Cadmium is quite toxic, causing permanent kidney and liver damage, and accumulates in the environment.

Candela (candle power). A unit of luminous intensity equal to 1/60 of the luminous intensity per square centimeter of a blackbody radiating to the temperature of solidification of platinum (2046°K). Also called *candle*.

Carcinogen. Any naturally occurring or synthetic substance known to increase the risk of cancer.

Cementitious. Any material based on cement or cementlike products, i.e., inorganic, noncombustible, and hard-setting.

Certified wood. Wood that has been certified through a third party and supplied from sources that comply with sustainable forestry practices that protect trees, wildlife, habitat, streams, and soil.

Chain of custody. The path that a raw material follows, through harvesting, manufacturers, and retailers, to consumers. Verification of chain of custody is a key component to most eco-certifications.

Chemical sensitivity. A loosely defined condition experienced by some people who are affected by very small concentrations of chemicals in air, water, and food that would not have apparent effects on most people. Symptoms may be similar to minor allergies, although they may also include moderate-to-severe pains, muscle weakness, dizziness, confusion, and even seizures.

Chemical sensitization. Health problems caused to some people when they are exposed to chemicals, often characterized as dizziness, eye and throat irritation, chest tightness, and nasal congestion. Reactions may occur even to trace amounts of the chemicals when an individual has chemical sensitization.

Chlorofluorocarbons (CFCs). A group of volatile gases manufactured from hydrocarbons such as methane, chlorine, fluorine, or bromine that can deplete or destroy the ozone layer of the Earth's stratosphere when released. These gases have been discontinued from use in refrigerants, solvents, and blowing agents in the making of foam. Most are being phased out by an international ozone treaty.

Chromated copper arsenate (CCA). A chemical wood preservative containing chromium, copper, and arsenic, used in pressure-treated wood to protect it from rotting due to insects and microbial agents. The EPA has classified CCA as a restricted-use product, for use only by certified pesticide applicators. CCA has been used to treat lumber since the 1940s; after the 1970s, the majority of the wood used in outdoor residential settings was CCA-treated wood. However, pressure-treated wood containing CCA is no longer being produced for use in most residential settings, particularly decking or playsets.

Clean Air Act of 1972. Groundbreaking legislation administered by the EPA that mandates specific measures to protect the air quality and respiratory health of U.S. inhabitants.

Closed loop recycling. Reclaiming or reusing wastewater for non-potable purposes in an enclosed process.

Compact fluorescent lightbulb (CFL). A fluorescent lightbulb designed for use in fixtures that take standard-size incandescent bulbs. CFLs are many times more energy-efficient than incandescent bulbs.

Construction Specifications Institute (CSI). A national professional association that provides format standards for the organization and presentation of specification documents (specs).

Construction waste management plan (CWMP). A plan that diverts construction and demolition debris from landfills through conscientious plans to recycle, salvage, and reuse. Optimally, this type of plan also eliminates packaging materials and is carefully monitored or audited by the contractor on a construction site.

Cradle To Cradle. A concept introduced by architect William McDonough and chemist Michael Braungart that describes a product that, at the end of its useful life, will decompose entirely with no negative environmental impact or otherwise be used again when recycled into a new product.

Cradle To Cradle Design Protocol. A scientifically based, peer-reviewed process used to assess and optimize materials used in products and production processes, to maximize health, safety, effectiveness, and high-quality reutilization over many product life cycles.

Cradle To Grave. Introduced by architect William McDonough, a term that describes a product that is used for a period of time and then discarded.

Curing. The process and time period for a finish to achieve its final state of hardness, color, etc. A chemical reaction is usually involved.

Daylighting. Natural daylight introduced into interior spaces and controlled specifically to reduce levels of electric lighting, to minimize glare, and to optimize lighting quality. Daylighting reduces the need for artificial light during the day. Common strategies for daylighting include proper orientation of windows and use of skylights, clerestory windows, and reflective surfaces.

Deciduous. Deciduous means "temporary" or "tending to fall off." Deciduous trees lose all of their foliage for part of the year. In some cases, the foliage loss coincides with the incidence of winter in temperate or polar climates, while others lose their leaves during the dry season in climates with seasonal variation in rainfall. The converse of deciduous is evergreen.

Design for disassembly. Designing so that a product may be dismantled for easier maintenance, repair, recovery, and reuse of components and materials.

Dichloromethane. A solvent found in paint remover, adhesives, paints, and aerosols. May cause cancer and heart attacks, and is a known water pollutant.

Diethylhexyl phthalate (DEHP). A known carcinogen found in plasticizers, used to keep vinyl flexible in products such as wall and floor coverings, furniture, upholstery, and shower curtains. DEHP is a colorless liquid with almost no odor.

Dioxin. A highly toxic chemical found in PVC products. Low levels cause cancer and endocrine disruption.

Downcycling. The practice of recycling a material in such a way that much of its inherent value is lost (for example, paper or wood).

Ecologically sustainable forestry. Dictates the management of a productive forest that supports a healthy ecosystem. See also *sustainable yield forestry*.

Embodied energy. The sum of the energy used to grow, extract, and manufacture a product, including the amount of energy needed to transport it to the job site and complete the installation. For example, as a comparison aluminum embodies 4 times as much energy as steel, and about 12 times as much as wood.

ENERGY STAR rating. A label developed by the EPA and the U.S. Department of Energy to identify appliances and products that exceed established energy-efficiency standards. This label helps consumers identify products that will save energy and money. ENERGY STAR-labeled equipment and appliances often exceed the efficiency levels of other new products.

Environmentally friendly. Refers to the degree to which a product may harm the environment, including the biosphere, soil, water and air.

Environmental tobacco smoke (ETS). Tobacco smoke producing airborne, cancer-causing particles that are exhaled by smokers and inhaled by all.

Ethylene glycol. A synthetic solvent often used in water- and oil-based paints, lacquers, and stains. It is a nasal irritant and a neurotoxin, highly toxic when ingested or inhaled, and may cause damage to blood and bone marrow. It is also the main ingredient in automotive antifreeze. Ethylene glycol is listed as a hazardous pollutant under the 1990 Clean Air Act.

Fair trade. A system that allows workers and artisans to receive a fair wage for their products, at least the minimum wage established for their country. Since the minimum wage is often not enough for basic survival, whenever feasible, workers are paid a living wage, which enables them to cover basic needs, including food, shelter, education, and health care for their families. Fair trade does not necessarily cost the consumer more, as middle agents are often bypassed, cutting costs and returning a greater percentage of the retail price to the producers.

Feldspar. A natural silica mineral used in glassmaking and ceramic glazes.

Fiberboards. Construction panels made from compressed fibers including wood, paper, straw, or other plant fibers. Three common types of fiberboards are high-, medium-, and low-density. *High-density* (low toxicity) is highly compressed fiber, usually made with no added adhesive; it may also be "tempered" to provide an even harder surface. It is commonly used for furniture backs, interior doors, industrial flooring, and pegboard. *Medium-density* (MDF) is moderately compressed fiber held together with glue or binder, and commonly used for cabinet and furniture frames, carpet underlayment, and as a core for decorative laminate paneling. Toxicity depends upon adhesive. *Low-density* (low toxicity) is slightly compressed fiber, usually with no added adhesive, and is commonly used for installation sheathing, acoustic panels, and tack boards.

Fire or flame retardant. A substance added to a flammable material to reduce its flammability. Fire retardants, used in fabrics, carpet, bedding, upholstery, and foamed plastics, only slow the spread of fire; they do not make flammable materials fireproof. Some, such as phosphates and chlorinated compounds, are irritating or hazardous.

Fly ash. A by-product of coal-fired electric generating plants. It is the finely divided residue resulting from the combustion of ground or powdered coal, which is then transported from the firebox through the boiler by flue gases. Fly ash improves the performance and quality of concrete, improving workability, reducing water demand, reducing segregation and bleeding, and lowering heat of hydration. Fly ash increases strength, reduces permeability, reduces corrosion of reinforcing steel, increases sulphate resistance, and reduces alkali-aggregate reaction. Fly ash reaches its maximum strength more slowly than concrete made with only portland cement. Two classifications of fly ash are produced: Class C and Class F. Class C fly ash is preferable and is the main type offered for residential concrete applications from ready-mix suppliers.

Forest Stewardship Council (FSC). An international nonprofit organization, founded in 1993, that supports environmentally appropriate, socially beneficial, and economically viable management of the world's forests. The FSC administers a third-party, chain-of-custody forestry certification program to assure that businesses supply trees and wood from forests managed in an ecologically sustainable manner.

Formaldehyde. Pungent and irritating, formaldehyde is a colorless gas compound used to bind together and preserve building materials and household products. It does such a good job as a resin and binding agent, as well as being very inexpensive to produce, which contributes to its wide usage (approximately 6 billion pounds are produced each year). It is found virtually everywhere, indoors and out, and can be naturally occurring or manufactured. It can irritate eyes, mucous membranes, and the upper respiratory system, and can be inhaled or absorbed by the skin. Its use should be avoided whenever possible, as even at low levels, formaldehyde can cause serious health problems. Symptoms of low-level exposure include: runny nose, sore throat, cough, dermatitis, sleeping difficulties, headache, fatigue, breathing difficulties, sinus irritation, chest pain, frequent nausea, bronchitis, and decreased lung capacity. Signs of acute exposure include: abdominal pain, anxiety, coma, convulsions, diarrhea, and respiratory problems such as bronchitis, pneumonia or pulmonary edema. In 2004, the World Health Organization (WHO) upgraded formaldehyde from a probable carcinogen to a known one after evidence was shown that formaldehyde caused nasopharyngeal cancer.

Fossil fuels. Fuels such as coal, oil, and natural gas, which are extracted from beneath the earth's surface, often with significant environmental and political cost. These fuels are finite resources and are nonrenewable.

Fungi (molds, mildew, mushrooms). Plantlike organisms that do not require light for growth and survival because they do not produce chlorophyll. A few fungi are safe and edible, such as some species of mushrooms, while most produce allergenic spores and odors.

Fungicide. Any substance added to inhibit the growth of fungus and consequent spoilage of a material. Paints, stucco, floor coverings, treated wood, and outdoor fabrics are commonly treated with fungicides. Many fungicides are compounds with hazardous metals or chlorine. Safer fungicides include those with boron or that are sulfate-based. See also *biocide*.

Genetically modified organisms (GMOs). Plants and animals that have had their genetic make-up altered to exhibit traits that are not naturally theirs. In general, genes are taken (copied) from one organism that shows a desired trait and transferred into the genetic code of another organism.

Glycols. A family of alcohols used as solvents in many paints, coatings, and the like. Some glycols are very safe while others are toxic. Examples of glycols are ethylene glycol and propylene glycol.

Graywater. Wastewater coming from sinks, showers. and laundry that can be collected and treated for some reuse, such as that from sinks. See also *blackwater*.

Grout. A cementitious material used to fill the joints between tiles. May contain acrylic or epoxy additives for greater durability.

Hazardous waste. By-products with physical, chemical, or infectious characteristics that pose hazards to the environment and human health, especially when improperly handled.

Heavy metals. The elemental series of metals, which includes mercury, lead, cadmium, thallium, cobalt, nickel, and aluminum. Most are very toxic and persistent in the environment.

Hexane (n-hexane). A solvent derived from petroleum, used in adhesives and paints. Hexane is moderately hazardous in low concentrations, causing symptoms of nerve toxicity such as numbness, trembling, or disorientation.

High-efficiency particulate arrestance (HEPA). A HEPA filter removes at least 99.97 percent of contaminants from air that are 0.3 microns (.3 one-thousandths of a millimeter) in size or larger. Manufacturers of HEPA filters often advertise how many times per hour air would be cleaned, per square foot or per room; the greater the rate, the better.

High-performance green building. A building whose design includes features that conserve water and energy; use space, materials, and resources more efficiently; minimize construction waste; and have healthy indoor environments.

Hydrogenated chlorofluorocarbons (HCFCs or HFCs). Substitute refrigerants and solvents that do not have as much potential to destroy atmospheric ozone, if released, as CFCs. Most are less efficient as refrigerants than CFCs and some are quite toxic. HCFCs are slated to be banned along with CFCs by 2030. See also *chlorofluorocarbons*.

Indoor air quality (IAQ). Indoor pollution sources that release gases or particles into the air are the primary cause of indoor air quality problems in homes. Inadequate ventilation can increase indoor pollutant levels by failing to allow in enough outdoor air to dilute emissions from indoor sources, and to carry indoor air pollutants out of the home. High temperature and humidity levels can also increase concentrations of some pollutants. The supply and introduction of adequate air for ventilation and control of airborne contaminants, acceptable temperatures, and relative humidity.

Indoor environmental quality (IEQ). Refers to the quality of the air and environment inside buildings, based on pollutant concentrations and conditions that can affect the health, comfort, and performance of occupants. These include temperature, relative humidity, light, sound, and other factors. Improving IEQ involves designing, constructing, commissioning, operating, and maintaining buildings in ways that reduce pollution sources and remove indoor pollutants, while ensuring that fresh air is continually supplied and properly circulated.

Inorganic compound. Any compound that does not contain carbon atoms in its structure. Minerals, metals, ceramics, and water are examples of inorganic compounds. Most tend to be very stable and persistent because they oxidize slowly or not at all. See also *organic compound*.

Integrated design team. Refers to all individuals involved in a project from very early in the design process, including the design professionals (architects, engineers, landscape architects, and interior designers), the owner's representatives (investors, developers, building users, facility managers, and maintenance personnel), and the general contractor and subcontractors.

Kiln-dried. A method of drying wood in an oven after sawing. Kiln-drying results in 10 percent or less moisture content, which makes the wood more dimensionally stable and better able to resist fungus in storage.

Lacquer. A glossy liquid finish for woods or metals, traditionally prepared from plant resins. Nitrocellulose lacquer, made from wood or cotton fiber treated with acid and dissolved in butyl acetate (lacquer thinner), is a more typical formulation today. Lacquer also refers to many types of hard, high-gloss industrial finishes, such as acrylic auto finishes.

Laminate. A thin layer of material (veneer) bonded to another surface. Wood and plastics are both commonly laminated.

Latex. A substance that remains flexible at room temperature. Natural latex is derived from rubber trees, a naturally occurring, sticky resin from rubber tree sap used for rubber products, carpet backing, and paints. It is associated with a rare yet severe allergic response in some people. Synthetic latex is often called simply "latex," but is usually derived from petrochemicals, for example styrene butadiene. See also *styrene butadiene rubber*.

Leadership in Energy and Environmental Design (LEED). USGBC's Green Building Rating System for green building design, a voluntary, consensus-based national standard for developing high-performance, sustainable buildings. LEED standards were created to define green building by establishing common standards of measurement, promote integrated whole-building design practices, recognize environmental leadership within the building industry, stimulate green competition, and raise consumer awareness of green building benefits.

Life-cycle analysis (LCA). A process or framework to evaluate the environmental burdens associated with a product, process, or activity by identifying, quantifying, and assessing its energy and material usage and environmental releases, to identify opportunities for environmental improvements. Extraction and processing of raw materials, manufacturing, transportation and distribution, use/reuse/maintenance, recycling, and final disposal are all considered.

Life-cycle cost. Total cost of a product or material, including the initial cost of materials extraction, transportation, manufacturing, maintenance, and operations and end use. This approach can often be used to justify more expensive and energy-efficient systems that save money over the life of the product.

Linseed oil. Nontoxic oil from the seed of the flax plant, used in paints, varnishes, linoleum, and synthetic resins.

Low-toxic. A lower degree to which a product is poisonous to people or other living organisms.

Lumen (lm). A unit of measurement of the rate at which a lamp produces light. A lamp's light output rating expresses the total amount of light emitted in all directions per unit time.

Material safety data sheets (MSDS). An MSDS is a legal requirement for all potentially hazardous products. The data sheet indicates the risks from using and disposing of the product and recommends safe practices. It identifies hazardous chemicals and health and physical hazards, including exposure limits and precautions for workers who may come into contact with these chemicals. Review product MSDS when specifying materials and require their submittal during the shop drawing phase.

Methylene diphenyl isocyanate (MDI). The other type of binder used in structural engineered wood products today is polymeric diphenyl methylene diisocyanate (PMDI—sometimes referred to as MDI). This is a polyurethane-type binder that is totally waterproof and contains no formaldehyde. Designers involved with green building like PMDI binders because there are no formaldehyde emissions. This binder is used in Medite medium-density fiberboard and all of the straw particleboard products, but among structural engineered wood products, only OSB and TimberStrand LSL are available made with PMDI binder.

Medium-density fiberboard (MDF). A manufactured board that is made with very small particles of wood held together with a binder. (*See* fiberboards).

Melamine. A polymer used for plastics and paints made from formaldehyde, ammonia, and urea. Similar to urea formaldehyde resin. Melamine is nontoxic once heated and cured.

Metamorphic. Relating to a change of physical form, structure, or substance especially by supernatural means or a striking alteration in appearance, character, or circumstances.

Mica. A naturally occurring silica mineral used as a filler in paints, gypsum fillers, and as electrical insulation. Low toxicity, but the dust is hazardous.

Mitigation. To make something less severe or painful and cause it to become less harsh or hostile.

Mortar. A cement-based mixture used to lay stone or ceramic tiles, or for use as a grout for these materials.

Multiple chemical sensitivity (MCS). A term coined to identify people considered to be sensitive to a number of chemicals at very low concentrations. There are numerous views about the existence, potential causes, and possible remedial actions regarding this phenomenon.

Naphtha. A colorless or reddish to brown colored, highly volatile, flammable liquid mixture of hydrocarbons distilled from petroleum, coal tar, and natural gas and used as fuel, as solvents, and in making various chemicals. It is used widely as a solvent for various organic substances, such as fats and rubber, and in the making of varnish. Used as a cleaning fluid because of its dissolving property, it can also be found in certain laundry soaps. Considered to be an irritant of the skin, eyes, and mucous membranes and a central nervous system depressant.

Nasopharyngeal cancer. Develops in the nasopharynx, an area in the back of the nose toward the base of the skull. Considered an oral cancer, it is not often treated by surgery and has differing risk factors than most oral cancers.

Natural. A substance or material taken from nature as directly as possible, with minimal intervention of processing or chemical synthesis.

Natural capitalism. Natural resources and ecological systems that provide vital life-support services to our planet. *Natural Capitalism,* the book (see Resources, "Recommended Reading"), describes a future in which business and environmental interests increasingly overlap, and in which businesses can better satisfy their customers' needs, increase profits, and help solve environmental problems, all at the same time.

Nonrenewable. A finite resource that does not replenish itself, e.g., stone.

Organically grown. Products grown with minimal use of synthetic fertilizers or pesticides. Various state and industry definitions are used to determine which products can be sold as "organically grown."

Organic compound. Any chemical compound based on the carbon atom. Organic compounds are the basis of all living things; they are also the foundation of modern polymer chemistry. Several million are known and their characteristics vary widely.

Oriented strand board (OSB). A manufactured wood product that contains a binder. OSB is usually made with fast-growing farmed trees instead of old-growth trees.

Outgas. The release of gases or vapors from solid materials. It is a form of evaporation, or a slow chemical change, which will produce indoor air pollution for prolonged periods after installation of a material. Sometimes referred to as off-gas.

Ozone layer. The protective layer of atmosphere, 15 miles above the Earth, that absorbs some of the sun's ultraviolet rays, thus reducing the amount of potentially harmful radiation from reaching the Earth's surface. Ozone depletion is caused by the breakdown of certain chlorine and/or bromine-containing compounds such as CFCs or halogens.

Particulates. Particles of dust, mold, mildew, and so on small enough to become suspended in air. Very small particulates (less than .005 millimeter) can be inhaled deep into the lungs. Particulates containing plant or animal proteins are allergenic, while those containing mineral fiber (silica, asbestos) cause lung disease or cancer.

Passive solar. Solar energy is a radiant heat source that causes natural processes upon which all life depends. Some of the natural processes can be managed through building design in a manner that helps heat and cool the building. The basic natural processes that are used in passive solar energy are the thermal energy flows associated with radiation, conduction, and natural convection. When sunlight strikes a building, the building materials can reflect, transmit, or absorb the solar radiation. Additionally, the heat produced by the sun causes air movement that can be predictable in designed spaces. These basic responses to solar heat lead to design elements, material choices, and placements that can provide heating and cooling effects in a home.

Perchloroethylene (PERC). A chlorinated solvent used mostly in the dry-cleaning process. PERC is implicated in 90 percent of all groundwater contamination.

Perlite. A volcanic glass, which is expanded and used as a plaster additive and fire-resistant insulation.

Phenol formaldehyde. An adhesive resin used for exterior plywood and other wood products. It is dark brown in color and low in formaldehyde emissions.

Phenols. Hydrocarbons used to make resins and glues. They are usually very toxic and output VOCs.

Photovoltaic (PV). The capacity of photocells to generate electricity from the sun's energy.

Picocurie. A unit for measuring radioactivity, often expressed as picocuries per liter (pCi/L) of air.

Plasticizer. A chemical such as a phthalate added to a plastic or rubber to keep it soft and flexible, particularly common in vinyl upholstery and flexible floor coverings. The plasticizers outgas slowly.

Pollution prevention. Reducing the amount of energy, materials, packaging, or water in the design, manufacturing, or purchasing of products or materials in an effort to increase efficient use of resources, reduce toxicity, and eliminate waste.

Polybrominated diphenyl ether (PBDE). A flame retardant commonly used in plastics and foam, especially in consumer products such as furnishings and electronics. PBDE is similar in chemical structure to PCB (polychlorinated biphenyl) and PBB (polybrominated biphenyl), both banned in many countries for their toxicity to humans and to the environment. PDBE has been found in concentrations in human breast milk, as well as remote environmental locations, and is also strongly suspected as a hazard. Its use is under review, and some types of PDBE are already banned from use in products such as mattresses.

Polyethylene. A chemically simple, semitransparent plastic used widely as a vapor barrier sheet over insulation, for packaging film, and containers. There are both high-density (HDPE) and low-density (LDPE) varieties. It is a low-toxicity material and produces low-risk vapors when it is burned.

Polyethylene terephthalate (PET). A polyester plastic used widely in soft drink bottles.

Polyurethane. A particular type of plastic known as a *thermoset*. Polyurethane is formed by reacting a polyol (an alcohol with more than two reactive hydroxyl groups per molecule) with a diisocyanate or a polymeric isocyanate in the presence of suitable catalysts and additives. Polyurethane can be found in liquid coatings and paints, tough elastomers such as rollerblade wheels, rigid insulation, soft flexible foam, elastic fiber, or as an integral skin.

Polyvinyl butral (PVB). A resin usually used for applications that require strong binding, optical clarity, adhesion to many surfaces, toughness, and flexibility. PVB is prepared from polyvinyl alcohol by reaction with butanal. The major application is laminated safety glass for automobile windshields.

Polyvinyl chloride (PVC). A polymer derived from oil or liquid natural gas and sodium chloride. The liquid natural gas or petroleum is refined and reacted with chlorine from the salt to form vinyl chloride monomer. Vinyl chloride monomer, a known carcinogen, is polymerized to form PVC resin. It is typically very durable and chemically stable, unless plasticized to keep it soft, and is the basis of most flexible flooring, plastic upholstery, and plastic siding. As defined by the EPA, PVC is a tough, environmentally indestructible plastic that releases hydrochloric acid when burned.

Portland cement. A kind of cement made by burning limestone and clay in a kiln. It is the base for most concrete, mortar, and floor tile grouts.

Postconsumer. A material or finished product that served its intended use as a consumer item. It may be recycled and incorporated into building materials, after which it may be identified as containing postconsumer recycled content or recovered material.

Postindustrial (also called preconsumer). Refers to waste produced during the manufacturing process of virgin material and rerouted from one step in the process to the next. This does not refer to recycled material.

Pre-consumer recycled content. Containing materials generated in manufacturing, such as damaged or obsolete products, overruns and trimmings. Does not include materials commonly reused in the manufacturing process.

Propylene glycol. An oily alcohol used in paints, waxes, and sealers. Unlike ethylene glycol, it is low toxicity, and approved as a food additive.

Radon. A radioactive, colorless, odorless gas formed in the decay of uranium. The radon decay products (also called *radon daughters* or *progeny*) can be breathed into the lungs, where they continue to release radiation as they further decay. Radon passes from some soil types into buildings and is often found in basements or sublevel rooms. Concentrations build up when trapped within and can cause health hazards, and may cause cancer.

Rapidly renewable. Materials that are not depleted when used, but are typically harvested from fast-growing sources and do not require unnecessary chemical support, such as bamboo, flax, wool, and certain types of wood.

Reclaimed. Material that is recovered for reuse or another purpose, such as wood barn siding that becomes flooring. See also *salvaged*.

Recyclable. The capability of a product or material to be recovered or otherwise diverted from the solid wastestream for the purpose of recycling.

Recycled/recovered materials. Waste materials and by-products that have been recovered or diverted from solid waste, not including those materials and by-products generated from and commonly reused within an original manufacturing process.

Recycling. The process of converting waste into a reusable product: a series of activities including collection, separation, and processing, by which products or materials are recovered from the solid wastestream for use in the form of raw materials in the manufacture of new products, other than fuel for producing heat or power by combustion.

Renewable energy. Energy harvested from sources that are not depleted when used, typically causing very low environmental impact, such as solar energy, hydroelectric power, and wind power.

Resilient. Capable of withstanding shock without permanent deformation or rupture. Rubber, vinyl, and linoleum floor coverings are called resilient because they are elastic.

Resin. A sticky substance that flows from certain plants and trees, especially pine and fir. Resin is used in paints and varnish. Artificial resins, used in the manufacture of plastics and synthetic finishes, are usually petroleum-based polymers.

Resource efficiency. A practice in which the primary consideration of material use begins with the concept of "reduce, reuse, recycle, repair," stated in descending order of priority. This concept may be applied in everyday life to help promote a sustainable society. In design, begin by reducing the amount of material that is specified; find ways to reuse materials, recycle products or product waste; specify products made from recycled materials; and repair or restore products instead of replacing them.

Rugmark. A global nonprofit organization working to end illegal child labor and offer educational opportunities for children in India, Nepal, and Pakistan. The Rugmark label is an assurance that no illegal child labor was employed in the manufacture of a carpet or rug.

R-value. A unit of thermal resistance; the opposite of thermal conductance. The higher the R-value, the greater the insu-

lating quality. By knowing the resistance of a material, it is possible to predict how much heat will flow through it and to compare it with other materials. A high R-value indicates a low rate of heat transfer.

Salvaged. Material that is recovered or reclaimed for possible reuse or recycling.

Scientific Certification Systems (SCS). The nation's first third-party certifier for testing pesticide residues in fresh produce, established in 1984. In the past 18 years, the company has evolved to become a certifier of multiple facets of the food industry and of the environmentally sound management of forests, marine habitats, and a wide variety of manufacturing-related businesses.

Shellac. Purified lac (a resin from a beetle) is used for making varnishes and leather polishes. Shellac is dissolved in methyl alcohol, and can be thinned with safer ethyl alcohol. Low toxicity.

Sick Building Syndrome (SBS). The occurrence of health complaints such as nasal congestion, headache, irritated eyes, lethargy, and tiredness, which are difficult to medically diagnose but are present in individuals when they are within a building and disappear or diminish once they leave the building. The cause of SBS is suspected to be poor air quality and conditions within the building, and related to the construction and mechanical systems of the building.

Silicone. Organic compounds of silicon used for caulking and flexible plastics, lubricating oils, and sealers. A very low-toxicity material.

Sink. In buildings, surfaces that tend to capture volatile organic compounds from the air and release them later. Carpets, gypsum board, ceiling tile, draperies, and upholstery are all sinks. Also, a place in the environment where a compound or material collects, as defined by the EPA.

Sizing. A temporary, formaldehyde-based liquid treatment that seals a surface against absorption of adhesive. Sizing adds stiffness or shine, particularly to fabrics and wallpaper, providing "tooth" for the wallcovering. Fabric sizing is very irritating to some people.

Slake. To combine lime chemically with water or moist air.

SmartWood. An independent agency, accredited by the FSC, that certifies for chain-of-custody and rediscovered wood products. Through independent auditing, certification and the promotion of certified forest products, SmartWood's purpose is to improve forest management by providing economic incentives to businesses that practice responsible forestry. SmartWood is a program of the Rainforest Alliance, a global nonprofit conservation organization.

Solvents. Petroleum-based liquids that can dissolve solids and keep them in solution. Solvents may contribute to pollution through evaporation.

Styrene-butadiene rubber (SBR). A synthetic latex formed from petroleum and used for carpet backings and elastic fabrics. SBR has a characteristic pungent odor and releases several irritating gases. The earliest synthetic rubbers were styrene-butadiene copolymers, Buna S, and SBR, whose properties are closest to those of natural rubber. SBR is the most commonly used elastomer because of its low cost and good properties; it is used mainly for tires.

Suberin. A waxy, waterproof substance present in the cell walls of cork tissue in plants.

Sunspace. A well-glazed space, generally south-facing, that collects heat and supplies some of it to another space (typically adjoining). Temperatures within sunspaces are not normally controlled; they float daily and seasonally.

Sustainability. Meeting or satisfying the needs of the current generation without diminishing or compromising the ability of future generations to meet their own needs (World Congress of Architects, Chicago, June 1993).

Sustainable. An ecosystem condition in which biodiversity, renewability, and resource productivity are maintained over time.

Sustainable yield forestry. A type of forestry dictating that the same numbers of trees cut down are also planted. "Clear-cutting with 100 percent replanted" is an example of sustainable yield. It differs from ecologically sustainable forestry, which dictates the management of a productive forest that supports a healthy ecosystem.

Terpenes. Organic, aromatic substances contained in the sap of softwoods, and in linoleum. Terpenes can be highly irritating to sensitive people.

Terrazzo. Marble or granite chips embedded in a binder that may be cementitious, noncementitious (epoxy, polyester, or resin), or a combination of both. Terrazzo can be used with divider strips of brass, zinc, or plastic.

Thermal comfort. The appropriate combination of temperatures, warm or cool, combined with airflow and humidity, which allows one to be comfortable within the confines of a building. This comfort is not usually achieved by the fixed setting of thermostats but through careful design and planning.

Thickset method. Installation procedure used for uneven material, such as ungauged stone. The mortar bed is 3/4 inch

to 1-1/4 inch thick (2 to 3 cm), often using cement based mortar.

Thinset method. Installation procedure used for evenly gauged material, such as ceramic or granite tile. A mortar as thin as 3/32 inch (.24 cm) is used, often containing an acrylic adhesive.

Titanium dioxide. A white pigment used in paint, vitreous enamel, linoleum, rubber and plastics, printing ink, and paper. It has low toxicity but high covering power, brilliance, reflectivity, and resistance to light and fumes. Production creates large quantities of toxic waste.

Toluene. An aromatic component of petroleum with a strong solvent odor. Highly flammable and moderately toxic, toluene is used as a solvent for adhesives and inks. May cause lung cancer.

Toxic. Any substance that causes harm to living organisms. There is a wide range of toxicity, from very low to extremely high.

Traditional materials. Materials that have been used for several generations. Their properties and toxicity are known from experience.

Trombe wall. A masonry wall that is usually separated from the outdoors by a glass wall and is designed to absorb solar heat and release it into the interior of a building.

Tung oil. Oil obtained from the seed of the tung tree, widely used as a drying oil in paints and varnishes and as a waterproofing agent.

Ultraviolet (UV). Short-wavelength, high-energy invisible light responsible for sunburn, skin cancer, and bleaching and deterioration of many materials.

Undercushion. A padding material laid prior to laying a carpet. Foamed plastic, rubber, and felts are the most common types. All tend to capture dust and deteriorate with time.

Underlayment. A sheet material, usually wood or wood fiber, laid under resilient flooring, carpet, or tile to minimize irregularities in the subfloor or to add acoustic separation.

Urea formaldehyde. An inexpensive polymer used widely as glue for interior wood products. A source of toxic formaldehyde gas. (*See* formaldehyde.)

U-value (Btu/hr-ft2-F). Measures the energy flowing through a wall, roof, window, door, or floor per hour per each degree of temperature difference between the inside and outside air temperatures. The most technical literature describes the thermal characteristics of wall or roof systems in terms of heat flow coefficient, *U*, rather than the total thermal resistance, or R-value. See also *R-value*.

Vapor barrier. In addition to the moisture carried into building cavities by air movement, a small amount is also transferred by vapor diffusion. Because water vapor tends to move from a moist area to a dryer one, it can be forced through permeable materials such as wood and plaster. A vapor barrier is a material that resists moisture movement in materials.

Veneer. A thin sheet of high-grade wood formed by cutting a thin strip from it. The veneer is applied to thicker wood or paper to make plywood and decorative wood-surfaced panels for furniture and doors. Also, a plastic sheet, typically melamine.

Ventilation rate. The rate at which indoor air enters and leaves a building, expressed in one of two ways: the number of changes of outdoor air per unit of time (air changes per hour, or *ach*) or the rate at which a volume of outdoor air enters per unit of time (cubic feet per minute/cfm).

Volatile organic compounds (VOC). Substances that are indoor air pollutants or chemical compounds that exist as vapor or gases at normal temperatures. VOCs are carbon-based molecules typically used as solvents in products such as household cleaners, paints, inks, and dyes. Many are irritants; some are toxic. Sources of VOCs include formaldehyde (a suspected carcinogen), xylene, toluene, benzene (a known carcinogen), and acetone. Indoors, VOCs are major air pollutants; outside, VOCs react with other pollutants, producing ground-level ozone.

Waste equals food. A principle of natural systems that eliminates the concept of waste, whereby waste produced is used as the raw materials for another process (McDonough & Braungart, 1998). In this design strategy, all materials are viewed as continuously valuable, circulating in closed loops of production, use, and recycling.

Waste reduction. A process to reduce or eliminate the amount of waste generated at its source or to reduce the amount of toxicity from waste or the reuse of materials. The best way to reduce waste is not to create it in the first place.

Wastestream. The total flow of solid waste from homes, businesses, institutions, and manufacturing that is recycled, burned, or disposed of in landfills.

Wastewater. Water that has been used and contaminated. Wastewater must be purified before being used again or before being returned to the environment.

Well-managed forest. Refers to a forest that has been cared for with particular concern for conserving biological diversity and functioning ecosystems, maintaining high conservation-value forests, advancing the economic and social well-being of workers, local communities, and indigenous groups, and establishing sound and long-term management practices.

Xylene. An aromatic component of petroleum; it has a sharp solvent odor. Xylene is moderately toxic and is used as a solvent for dyes, inks, paints, and adhesives.

Zero-VOC. Having volatile organic compounds (VOC) outgassing levels that are so low as to not be measurable by standard EPA methods.

Zinc oxide. A white pigment used in paints, ointments, plastics, and rubber that resists ultraviolet light and mold growth. Low toxicity, but the dust is hazardous.

INDEX

WILEY BOOKS ON
Sustainable Design

Also from Wiley and the American Society of Interior Designers

Sustainable Commercial Interiors
by Penny Bonda, FASID, and Katie Sosnowchik

Other Wiley Books on Sustainable Design

Alternative Construction: Contemporary Natural Building Methods
by Lynne Elizabeth and Cassandra Adams

Cities People Planet: Liveable Cities for a Sustainable World
by Herbert Girardet

Ecodesign: A Manual for Ecological Design
by Ken Yeang

*Green Building Materials: A Guide to Product Selection and Specification,
    Second Edition*
by Ross Spiegel and Dru Meadows

The HOK Guidebook to Sustainable Design, Second Edition
by Sandra Mendler, AIA, William O'Dell, FAIA, and Mary Ann Lazarus, AIA

Sustainable Construction: Green Building Design and Delivery
by Charles J. Kibert

Environmental Benefits Statement

This book is printed with soy-based inks on presses with VOC levels that are lower than the printing industry standard. The paper, Rolland Enviro 100, is manufactured by Cascades Fine Paper Group and is made from 100 percent post-consumer, de-inked fiber, without chlorine. According to the manufacturer, the following resources were saved by using Rolland Enviro 100 for this book:

Mature trees	Waterborne waste not created	Waterflow saved (in gallons)	Atmospheric emissions eliminated	Energy not consumed	Natural gas saved by using biogas
225	103,500 lbs	153,000	21,470 lbs.	259 million BTU	37,170 cubic feet